Great Source

Reading Advantage

TEACHER'S EDITION
FOUNDATIONS

READING LEVEL GRADES 1–2

Laura Robb, James F. Baumann, Carol J. Fuhler, Joan Kindig

Avon Connell-Cowell, R. Craig Roney

GReat★SOURCe®

HOUGHTON MIFFLIN HARCOURT
Supplemental Publishers

Reading Advantage Team

Laura Robb has more than forty years of experience in grades 4 through 8. Robb also coaches teachers of kindergarten through grade 12 in Virginia, New York, and Michigan. She speaks at conferences all over the country and conducts staff development workshops. Robb is a coauthor of these Great Source products: *Summer Success: Reading, Reader's Handbooks* grades 3, 4–5, 6–8, and *Daybooks* and *Sourcebooks* grades 2–5. In addition, she has written three books for Scholastic, *Teaching Reading in Middle School; Teaching Reading in Social Studies, Science, and Math;* and *Teaching Reading: A Complete Resource for Grades 4 and Up.*

James F. Baumann is a teacher and university professor. He has taught students in several school districts, and he has been a professor of reading education at three universities. His research and writing have examined how to provide students both rich, literate learning environments and effective instruction in reading skills and strategies. Baumann is also a coauthor of *Summer Success: Reading* (Great Source, 2001).

Carol J. Fuhler is currently an Associate Professor at Iowa State University. Dr. Fuhler is coauthor of *Teaching Reading: A Balanced Approach for Today's Classrooms* and contributed a chapter to *Young Adult Literature in the Classroom: Reading It, Teaching It, Loving It.*

Joan Kindig is an Associate Professor at James Madison University, where she teaches both Reading and Word Study courses. Dr. Kindig is also a frequent presenter at workshops and conferences.

Avon Connell-Cowell is a mentor for the New York City Department of Education. Dr. Connell-Cowell's area of interest is effective teaching practices in urban education.

R. Craig Roney is a Professor of Teacher Education at Wayne State University in Detroit, specializing in Children's Literature and Storytelling. He has also written numerous publications on these topics including *The Story Performance Handbook* (Lawrence Erlbaum Publishers, 2001), a research-based "how-to" text on reading aloud, mediated storytelling, and storytelling.

Editorial: Ruth Rothstein, Lea Lorber Martin, Sue Paro

Design/Production: Bill Smith Studio

Printed in the United States of America

International Standard Book Number: 978-0-669-01417-4

4 5 6 7 8 9 10 - 1420 - 15 14
4500462672

Contents

Great Source Reading Advantage
Starts with Reading

The components in Reading Advantage were designed to help students

- ▶ develop essential reading comprehension skills, including decoding multiple-syllable words, comprehending complex syntax, and understanding context clues;
- ▶ strengthen reading fluency and gain experience reading a wide range of nonfiction genres including interviews, news articles, and photo-essays;

- ▶ build reading strategies, background knowledge, and vocabulary;
- ▶ transition from guided reading to independent reading;
- ▶ become proficient, confident readers who enjoy reading.

For the STUDENT

Reading, Reading, Reading

(6 copies of 4 different magazines)

Magazines At the heart of the program are high-interest magazines based on themes that offer original selections (primarily nonfiction) written below grade level.

Paperback Books (12 titles) for independent reading practice.

eZines CD-ROMs reinforce the skills and strategies taught in the program through additional theme-based magazine articles offering text highlighting, real voice audio, embedded strategy activities, and end-of-article comprehension quizzes and reports.

Activities

Student Journal copymaster that supports students as they read each selection and provides practice in comprehension and vocabulary (also available as consumable Student Journals).

For whole classroom instruction, purchase extra copies of Theme Magazines, Paperback Books, and Student Journals separately!

Teacher's Edition with point-of-use instruction wrapped around full-color theme magazine facsimiles; detailed lesson plans that follow the before, during, and after reading process; and comprehension, writing, vocabulary, and phonics/word study instruction.

Word Study Manual that serves as a teacher resource for expanded, in-depth word-building lessons, word sorts, and activities that target compound words, homophones, homographs, long and short vowels, multiple-syllable words, and word parts.

Assessment with instructions for determining students' reading level, mid- and end-of-magazine tests to track student progress, and checklists and observation notes for ongoing assessment.

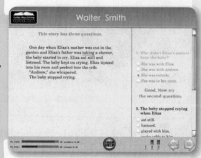

Also Available!
Gates-MacGinitie Reading Tests® allow teachers to assess the reading level of individual students.

Seven levels to help your struggling readers!

Great Source

Reading Advantage

Laura Robb

James F. Baumann • Carol J. Fuhler • Joan Kindig

Each kit contains the items shown for student and teacher

Great Source Reading Advantage

Features the Reading Process

Reading Advantage is infused with the **Reading Process** to model for students that there are actions they can take **BEFORE** they read, **DURING** their reading, and **AFTER** they read to make themselves better readers.

BEFORE

- Activate prior knowledge
- Preview the selection and vocabulary
- Set a purpose for reading
- Make predictions

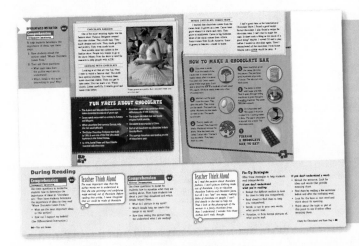

DURING

- Check and adjust predictions
- Monitor understanding of a text
- Apply comprehension strategies

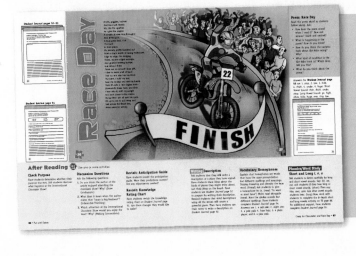

AFTER

- Respond to and discuss the selection
- Return to the purpose
- Write in response to reading
- Learn and apply skills and strategies

Annotated Lesson

Every lesson in *Reading Advantage* is set up to model the reading process:
BEFORE READING
DURING READING
AFTER READING
Each lesson is designed to last for three or four sessions when the reading period is about forty minutes long.

Magazine Pages

The magazine pages, shown as facsimiles throughout the Teacher's Edition, were designed to look sophisticated and, therefore, appeal to students. The text, however, was constructed to be clear, provide abundant context for vocabulary, and increase gradually in difficulty across the magazines within a level.

BEFORE READING

The first part of each lesson prepares students to read through discussion, writing, and/or graphic organizers. The lesson always suggests activities for building background, previewing the selection and vocabulary, and making predictions and setting a purpose. The more support a student needs for reading, the more substantive the introduction should be. Choose the part or parts that your students need to support their reading.

LESSON **11**
Crazy for Chocolate! *and* Race Day
Fun and Games, pages 22–27

SUMMARY
This **newspaper article** describes the sights, smells, and tastes that greet visitors to the annual International Chocolate Show. The **poem** "Race Day" is about the excitement of a dirt-bike race.

COMPREHENSION STRATEGIES
Determining Importance
Monitor Understanding

WRITING
Description

VOCABULARY
Homophones

PHONICS/WORD STUDY
Short and Long *i, o, u*

Lesson Vocabulary
mannequins   pods
astrologer   kneading
nibble

MATERIALS
Fun and Games, pp. 22–27
Student Journal, pp. 51–55
Word Study Manual, p. 45

What would get yo_ of bed on a cold, ra_ Saturday morning?_ cup of hot chocolat_ How about a fountai_ of chocolate? Think I'm dreaming? I saw it at the International Chocolate Show.

International Chocolate S
PRES

CRAZY FOR CHOCOLATE

22

Before Reading WHOLE CLASS Use one or more activities.

Anticipation Guide
Create an anticipation guide for students. (See TE page 214 for an anticipation guide BLM.) Ask studen_ to place a check in the AGREE or DISAGREE box before each statement. The discussion of anticipation guide statements can be a powerful motivat_ because once students have reacted to the statements, they have a stake in seeing if they are "right." Have students read the article to check _ eir choices. Revisit the guide later.

82 • Fun and Games

Anticipation Guide		
AGREE	DISAGREE	
		1. Artists have used food coloring a_ white chocolate t_ make paintings.
		2. The largest chocolate bar ever made weighed over 5,000 pounds.
		3. Cacao beans, from which chocolate is made, grow mostly in the United States.

Vocabulary Preview
Write the vocabulary words on the board or on chart paper and read th_ aloud to clarify pronunciations. Ask students to share what they know about a particular word or words. T_ have students begin the knowledge rating chart on *Student Journal* page_ Use the vocabulary word *nibble* to m_ del a response for the page. Student_ will revisit the chart after they hav_ _inished reading the selection. (See _ifferentiated Instruction.)

Build Background Use knowledge about students' abilities to select or adapt lesson plan suggestions or strategies as appropriate to accommodate students' needs and your instructional style.

Graphic Organizers
Graphic organizers are used throughout the program. Blackline masters (BLMs) of most organizers are in the Appendix of this Teacher's Edition.

My Day at the International Chocolate Show

By Jenny Velasquez

Every year thousands of chocolate lovers come to New York City. The International Chocolate Show is a attraction. It is a place to learn new chocolate recipes. There are fantastic items made of chocolate to see. And, of course, there is lots of chocolate to eat. I was there to write this report.

The International Chocolate Show is in a big industrial building. Mannequins wearing chocolate fashions greet you. They look beautiful—and delicious. But no eating the clothes!

The main room has hundreds of tables. Each table has something to do with chocolate. Some are piled high with chocolate candies. Others have chocolate cakes and cookies. You'll find chocolate-making machines. You can see chocolate molds.

You can consult a chocolate expert. You can also buy books about chocolate. An astrologer will even read the swirls in the bottom of your hot-chocolate cup. What is your chocolate fortune today?

You can sample chocolate from all over the world. Each kind is different. You will probably want to try everything.

CHOCOLATE TASTES

I ate white chocolate. I ate dark chocolate. I ate milk chocolate. I ate strawberries dipped in chocolate. I ate things covered with chocolate. There were fortune cookies, peanuts, potato chips. I even tried chocolate-covered hot peppers. Wow! And I ate chocolate dusted with gold.

After all that tasting, I needed a break. Luckily, there was more to do than eat.

CHOCOLATE ART

I walked the Chocolate Art Walk. Music from the Andes Mountains was playing. That's one of the places where cocoa comes from.

I went to the Chocolate Art Gallery. There, I saw chocolate statues and sculptures. There were even paintings created in chocolate.

Artists use food coloring and white chocolate for these paintings.

23

Differentiated Instruction

Students who need deeper instruction in and/or a different approach to a strategy or skill will benefit from instruction that provides more support, or scaffolding. Use the ideas in tutorials with individual students or with a small group of students who need the support for the same skill or strategy.

English Language Learners

Students who are acquiring English as a second language will benefit from a variety of techniques and tools embedded in *Reading Advantage*. In the magazines, text provides rich context to help define unfamiliar words, illustrations and photographs provide visual support, and plays offer a natural way to practice oral fluency. In the Teacher's Edition, background concepts, oral discussion, graphic organizers, and the Differentiated Instruction feature all work together to help students build confidence in using the English language.

Preview the Selection

Have students look through the selection. Ask:

• What information do you learn from the introductory note?

• Do you think the selection is fiction or nonfiction? How can you tell?

• Why do you think the author includes section headings? (to signal changes in topic)

Teacher Think Aloud

I know from the title and the introductory note that this will be a nonfiction article about a chocolate show. I've never heard of a chocolate show. As I scan the photographs in this selection, it's unclear how a painting or a ballerina costume relate to chocolate, so I'll read to find out.

Make Predictions/ Set Purpose

Students should use the information they gathered in previewing the selection to make predictions about what they will learn. If students have trouble generating a purpose for reading, suggest that they read to learn what happens at the International Chocolate Show.

Crazy for Chocolate! *and Race Day* • **83**

Teacher Think Aloud The Teacher Think Aloud makes the thinking of a good reader public knowledge for all students.

Comprehension
DETERMINING IMPORTANCE

To help students determine the importance of ideas, use these steps:

1. Have students reread the section called "Where Chocolate Comes From."

2. Then ask these questions:
   - What main idea does the author want you to understand?
   - Which detail is the most interesting to you? Why?

CHOCOLATE FASHION

One of the most amazing sights was the fashion show. Famous designers created chocolate clothes. They made hats. They made dresses and suits. They made gowns and jewelry. They even made boots.

Real models wear the clothes in the fashion show. People buy tickets to go to the show. Money from the show is used for research to help people with AIDS.

COOKING WITH CHOCOLATE

Looking at all that art was fun. Next I went to watch a famous chef. The chefs have special kitchens. You watch them make chocolate dishes. Then you get to taste some. You can learn a lot. Watch closely. Listen carefully. It smells good and tastes even better.

These gowns are pretty. But I wouldn't w[ear] on a hot day!

FUN FACTS ABOUT CHOCOLATE

- The Aztecs and Mayans discovered how to make chocolate thousands of years ago.
- Cacao seeds were used as money by Aztecs and Mayans.
- When chocolate first came to Europe, only the rich could afford it.
- The Baker Chocolate Company was built in 1780. It was one of the first chocolate factories in the United States.
- In 1875, Daniel Peter and Henri Nestle invented milk chocolate.
- Chocolate makers use more than three million pounds of milk every day.
- The largest chocolate bar ever made weighed 5,026 pounds.
- Chocolate is not popular in China.
- Half of all Americans say chocolate is the[ir] favorite flavor.
- The average American eats twelve poun[ds] of chocolate a year.

24

DURING READING

Instruction is provided for strategies that students will learn to apply while they are reading. If students print the prompts on a bookmark or card, they will have a handy reminder for all their reading. While students are reading independently, meet with small groups or do "walk-by" conferences. In a walk-by conference, stop briefly beside a student and ask a couple of questions to assess how the student is doing. "Tell me about what you just read," "What does that word mean? How do you know?" and "Read aloud the paragraph you just finished reading" are prompts that allow you to do a quick check on a student's comprehension of text.

During Reading

Comprehension
DETERMINING IMPORTANCE SMALL GROUP

Use these questions to model for students how to determine the importance of ideas in "Chocolate Art." Then have students determine the importance of ideas as they read "Where Chocolate Comes From."

- What are the most important ideas in this section?
- How can I support my beliefs?

(See Differentiated Instruction.)

Teacher Think Aloud
The most important idea that the author wants me to understand is that she saw paintings and sculptures made entirely out of chocolate. Before reading this article, I never imagined that art could be made of chocolate.

Comprehension
MONITOR UNDERSTANDING

Use these questions to model for students how to visualize what the[y are] reading about. Then have students [talk] about a part they visualized and w[hat] details helped them.

- What do I picture in my mind?
- Which details help me create thi[s] image in my mind?
- How does seeing this picture he[lp] me understand what I am readi[ng?]

Each comprehension strategy features a **Teacher Think Aloud** that models the strategy.

x

I learned that chocolate comes from the
cao bean. It grows on a tree. Cacao trees
w where it is warm and rainy. They
w in rainforests. Cacao is big business.
st of the cacao comes from Africa.
e comes from South America. Some
rown in Mexico—closer to home.

I had a great time at the International
Chocolate Show. I found a good recipe
for hot chocolate. I also found a recipe for
chocolate cake. I can't wait to make the
cake. Is there such a thing as too much of a
good thing? Maybe. I vowed I'd wait a year
before I looked at chocolate again. Then I
remembered all the chocolate I took home.
Maybe just a nibble would be okay. ◆

OW TO MAKE A CHOCOLATE BAR

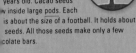

Chocolate is made
from the seeds of the
ao tree. A cacao tree
es seeds after it is about
years old. Cacao seeds
w inside large pods. Each
is about the size of a football. It holds about
seeds. All those seeds make only a few
colate bars.

Workers cut the pods
from the trees. They
n the pods. They scoop
the seeds. The seeds are
e. Workers put the seeds
nats to dry. The seeds
brown.

The dry seeds are
roasted. They have thin
lls. Machines remove the
lls. Now the seeds are
ed "cacao nibs." Farmers
the shells. They feed
m to cows.

4 Giant machines grind
the cacao nibs into
tiny pieces. The machines
grind hundreds of pounds
of cacao. The nibs turn into
thick paste.

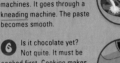

5 The paste is mixed
with sugar and milk.
Then it goes through rolling
machines. It goes through a
kneading machine. The paste
becomes smooth.

6 Is it chocolate yet?
Not quite. It must be
cooked first. Cooking makes
it shiny. The warm chocolate
is poured into a mold. The
chocolate cools.

7

FINALLY,
A CHOCOLATE
BAR TO EAT!

25

Fix-Up Strategies

Offer these strategies to help students
read independently.

**If you don't understand
what you're reading:**

- Reread the difficult section to look
  for clues to help you comprehend.
- Read ahead to find clues to help
  you comprehend.
- Retell, or say in your own words,
  what you've read.
- Visualize, or form mental pictures of,
  what you've read.

If you don't understand a word:

- Reread the sentence. Look for
  ideas and words that provide
  meaning clues.
- Find clues by reading a few sentences
  before and after the confusing word.
- Look for the base or root word and
  think about its meaning.
- Think about the topic or plot at
  this point to see if either offers
  meaning clues.

Crazy for Chocolate! *and* Race Day • **85**

Fix-Up Strategies Each
lesson includes fix-up strategy
reminders to help students
become independent problem
solvers.

Writing: Description Planning Page

Choose an interesting place that you have visited and remember well. Make a sketch of the place. Add labels to the sketch and jot down notes about the location.

Name of place:

Sketch of place

Notes about place:

Building Vocabulary: Homophones

The phrases in the box all contain pairs of homophones. Read each riddle. Then write the answer from the box.

| a peer pair | here hair | a plain plane |
| a tall tale | a pale pail | eight ate |

1. What do you call an event where you can buy cheap boat items?

2. What did a group of hungry mice do?

3. What is a light-colored bucket called?

4. What is fur on a rabbit?

5. What do you call a not-so-fancy aircraft?

6. What are a couple of curvy fruits called?

Think of a pair of homophones and write your own riddle and answer.

Student Journal

Student Journal Reduced facsimiles are placed near the point of use to help you quickly identify which pages are used in the lesson.

Race Day

Boots, goggles, helmet
And blue suit. Ready.
My 250 Pro sparkles
As I give the engine
A couple of easy kick-throughs—
And at the gun,
A truly good kick. I hit
The track
In third place.
It's already pretty bombed out
From a day's worth of racing motocross.
Edge to edge, I'm dodging
Holes, square-edged whoops,
And gnarled braking bumps.
Just when I think
There are no smooth lines left,
I dare to work a bit of track
That no one else has touched—
The bank. I hold my line,
Save my energy and rest my hands.
Then it's into a 180-degree turn—
Downshift, brake hard, and slide.
I lean into it, shift my weight
And inch closer to the leader.
By lap five I am all over his cycle.
It's up to me to pull away and
Sail across the finish line,
Arms raised in victory.

26

AFTER READING

The After Reading section provides a variety of response ideas that include discussion, instruction, vocabulary, writing, and phonics/word study. Select the activity or activities most appropriate for your students.

After Reading 🔵 Use one or more activities.

Check Purpose

Have students determine whether their purpose was met. Did students discover what happens at the International Chocolate Show?

Discussion Questions

Ask the following questions.

1. Do you think the author of the article enjoyed attending the chocolate show? Why? (Draw Conclusions)

2. What does it mean when the author states that "cacao is big business"? (Inferential Thinking)

3. Which attraction at the International Chocolate Show would you enjoy the most? Why? (Making Connections)

Revisit: Anticipation Guide

Have students revisit the anticipation guide. Were their predictions correct? Are any adjustments needed?

Revisit: Knowledge Rating Chart

Have students revisit the knowledge rating chart on *Student Journal* page . Are there changes they would to make?

Discussion Questions Strategy- and skill-based questions allow students to review their reading and teachers to check comprehension. By discussing the questions together, students learn from each other. The technique called Think-Pair-Share is sometimes recommended for discussion. In it, students think through a question, talk about it with a partner, and then share with the whole group. This technique takes the pressure off students, especially English Language Learners, because it allows them time to think and provides the verbal support of a partner.

Poem: Race Day

Read the poem aloud as students follow along. Ask:

- How does the poem sound when I read it? Slow and serious? Quick and excited?
- What is happening in the poem? How do you know?
- How do you think the narrator feels about dirt-bike racing? Why?
- What kind of condition is the dirt-bike track in? Which lines tell you this?
- What do you think about the poem?

Answers for **Student Journal page 55** are 1. *stop*, 2. *low*, 3. *hide*, 4. *thick*, 5. *under*, 6. *huge*; Short Vowel Sound: *thin, thick, under, stop*; Long Vowel Sound: *go, high, show, hide, huge, over, tiny, low.*

Writing | Description

Tell students that they will write a description of a place they have visited. Have students share ideas about the kinds of places they might write about. List their ideas on the board. Have students use *Student Journal* page 52 to prepare for writing their description. Remind students that vivid descriptions using all the senses will create a powerful piece. Then have students use their notes to write a description on *Student Journal* page 53.

Vocabulary Homophones

Explain that homophones are words that have the same pronunciation but different spellings and meanings. Display *kneading* and identify the base word. (*knead*) Ask students to give a homophone for it. (*need*; "to want or must have") Write *need* alongside *knead*. Note the similar sounds but different spellings. Have students complete *Student Journal* page 54. Answers are 1. a sail sale; 2. eight ate; 3. a pale pail; 4. hare hair; 5. a plain plane; and 6. a pear pair.

Phonics/Word Study

Short and Long *i, o, u*

Tell students to listen carefully for long and short vowel sounds. Say: *kit, cot, cut.* Ask students if they hear long or short vowel sounds. (short) Then say: *kite, coat, cute.* Ask what vowel sounds students hear. (long) Now, work with students to complete the in-depth short and long vowels activity on TE page 88. For additional support, have students complete *Student Journal* page 55.

Focus on... Two pages at the end of every lesson provide a choice of activities.

Phonics/Word Study lesson (with references to *Word Study Manual*)

Phonics/Word Study

Review: Short and Long *i, o, u*

▶ Here's an opportunity to revisit and review the three vowels. Provide students with the Short *i, o, u* versus Long *i, o, u* Sort sheet and have them sort for both speed and accuracy as they practice the vowels they have studied thus far. (See *Word Study Manual* page 45.)

▶ Because it's important for students to hear the difference between the two vowels, and not just see the difference, have students work in pairs. One student can read the word aloud while the other determines the placement. When pairs are finished, have both students read each column to see if all the words have the same sound. Then have students switch roles.

▶ When confronted with a word with two or more syllables, students should choose a syllable to sort.

▶ Once both partners have taken turns reading the words aloud and sorting them, have students time themselves to see how fast they can do the sort. Being able to sort both quickly and accurately means the student has mastered these vowel sounds.

Short *i, o, u* versus Long *i, o, u* Sort					
Short *i*	Long *i*	Short *o*	Long *o*	Short *u*	Long *u*
milk	pile	hot	show	cup	suits
will	high	bottom	gold	consult	use
dip	find	chocolate	go	sculpture	shoot
chips	white	lot	close	discuss	cool
tickets	China	not	ago	public	school
discover	five		only	us	room

For more information on word sorts and spelling stages, see pages 5–31 in the *Word Study Manual*.

Focus on . . .

Use one or more activities in this section to focus on a particular area of need in your students.

Comprehension STRATEGY SUPPORT

To help those students who need more practice using the strategies covered in this lesson, work one-on-one or in small groups to apply the strategy prompts below. Apply the prompts to a *Reading Advantage* paperback classroom library book, or a new or familiar selection the magazine. Always model your own thinking first.

Determining Importance

• What is the most important idea in the paragraph? How can I prove it?
• Which details are unimportant? Why?
• What does the author want me to understand?
• Why is this information important (or not important) to me?

Monitor Understanding

• Do I understand what I'm reading? If not, what part confusing to me?
• What fix-up strategies can I use to solve the problem (See During Reading for fix-up strategies.)
• Why did a character say (do, think, ask) that?
• What images do I visualize from the text? What part can't I visualize?
• Why did the author include (or not include) those details?

Writing Advertisement

Have students write an advertisement for a new kind of chocolate bar. Tell them to create a name for their chocolate bar, list the main ingredients, and write a slogan for it.

Introducing the NEW (name of bar)

It is filled with (list main ingredients)

Slogan

Comprehension, reteaching of strategies

Writing, in response to the selection

Fluency: Pacing

After students have read the selection at least once, use the "Chocolate Tastes" section on page 23 to model reading smoothly and at an even pace. Then have pairs of students take turns reading aloud "Chocolate Art" and "Chocolate Fashion," on pages 23 and 24.

As you listen to partners read, use these prompts to guide them.

◆ Review the text to avoid starts and stops.

◆ Read at an even, natural pace—not too quickly or too slowly.

◆ Use the punctuation, such as commas and periods, to help guide your pauses and expression.

When students read aloud, do they—

✓ demonstrate a smooth pace, not too fast or too slow?

✓ incorporate well-timed pauses between words and phrases?

✓ reflect an awareness and understanding of punctuation?

English Language Learners

To support students as they visualize, extend the fourth fix-up strategy on TE page 85.

1. Remind students that active readers visualize, or make mental pictures in their minds, as they read.

2. Read and discuss "Chocolate Tastes" on page 23 of the selection. Have students use details from the text to draw a picture of the chocolate treats.

3. Have partners describe their drawings and tell what words from the text helped them, such as *dipped*, *covered*, or *dusted*.

Independent Activity Options

While you work with individuals or small groups, others can work independently on one or more of the following options.

▷ Foundations paperback books, see TE pages 195–200

▷ Foundations *eZines*

▷ Repeat word sorts for this lesson

▷ *Student Journal* pages for this lesson

Assessment

Strategy Assessment

To help you and your students assess their use of comprehension strategies, ask the following questions. Students can complete a written response or provide verbal answers in a one-on-one reading conference.

1. **Determining Importance** Which details are the most important in this selection? How can you support your answer? (Answers will vary. Students may think that the most important details are the descriptions of the chocolate art and clothes. The surprising and interesting information may make students want to go to the Chocolate Show just to see the exhibits.)

2. **Monitor Understanding** What did you have trouble visualizing in this selection? How were you able to "see" these images in your mind? (Answers will vary. Students may say that they couldn't picture what a chocolate painting would look like, just by reading the text, but that the photograph on page 23 helped them.)

For ongoing informal assessment, use the checklists on pages 61–64 of *Foundations Assessment*.

Word Study Assessment

Use these steps to help you and your students assess their understanding of short and long *i*, *o*, and *u* sounds.

1. Display a chart like the one below, but include only the headings and the words in the first column.

2. Have students read the words and sort them into the correct column. The answers are shown.

Word	Short *i*	Short *o*	Short *u*	Long *i*	Long *o*	Long *u*
cup	thicket	hot	cup	flight	slow	suit
suit	milk	bottle	dungeon	white	behold	room
slow						
flight						
thicket						
hot						
behold						
room						
dungeon						
milk						
white						
bottle						

Assessment, ongoing assessment, helps you and your students assess what they have learned in the lesson with questions about the strategies and word study. A reference to the formal assessment appears in time for the Mid-Magazine and Magazine Tests.

Fluency suggestions focus on reading aloud with expression, pacing, and phrasing

ELL boxes target ways to accomodate English Language Learners

Independent Activity Options help teachers manage individuals and small groups

Great Source Reading Advantage
Is Supported by Research

No Child Left Behind has placed a national spotlight on the critical issue of reading proficiency. Educators across the nation face the challenge of helping their students read at or above grade level by the end of the third grade; however, many students continue to struggle with reading through high school. In fact, according to the National Center for Education Statistics (2003) **only 33% of eighth graders and 36% of twelfth graders are reading at or above the proficient level.**

Teachers want to help these students improve their reading and writing ability; however, the task is daunting because of a lack of appropriate instructional materials to address the specific issues with which these students struggle.

Reading Advantage, designed by **Laura Robb** with a team of nationally known university educators and master classroom teachers, including **James F. Baumann**, **Carol J. Fuhler**, and **Joan S. Kindig**, can help this adolescent population improve their reading and writing skills. The seven kits address the needs of at-risk adolescents who are reading between the middle of first grade and eighth grade reading level.

The program focuses on critical areas where students need the most support: comprehension, word study and phonics, vocabulary and fluency building, and assessment, and includes enough reading materials to support each student's progress.

Great Source Reading Advantage

Matches the Level to Your Classroom Needs!

Program Level	Grade Level	Lexile Measure	Guided Reading Level	DRA
Foundations Motion Fun and Games Survival Arts	1-2	350L-470L	J-L	18-24
Level A Mystery Space Odyssey Water Cities	2-3	500L-630L	M-P	28-38
Level B Flight Underground Heroism Music	3-4	630L-700L	M-Q	28-38
Level C Emotions Racers & Racing Boundaries Ecology	4-5	730L-780L	M-Q	28-40
Level D Travel the World Revolution Mountains Changes	5-6	820L-920L	N-R	30-40
Level E Communications Relationships Discoveries Money	6-7	940L-990L	T-W	44-50
Level F Adaptation Justice Sports Disasters	7-8	1030L-1100L	T-W	44-50

Lexile® is a registered trademark of MetaMetrics, Inc.

Guided Reading Levels are from *Guiding Readers and Writers, Grades 3-6* by Irene Fountas and Gay Su Pinnell (Portsmouth: Heinemann, 2001).

Developmental Reading Assessment® is a registered trademark of Pearson Education, Inc. DRA is a trademark of Pearson Education, Inc.

Great Source Reading Advantage
Offers Differentiated Instruction

Not all students in your class need the same instruction at the same time. Therefore, using the whole-class model is not always the most effective way to teach reading. Use a pattern of whole-class, small-group, and individual instruction to address the needs of all students.

	WHOLE CLASS	SMALL GROUP	INDEPENDENT
Purpose	Build community knowledge	Address students who have similar needs	Target individual needs and promote independent work
Instructional Activities	▶ Introduce theme ▶ Before-reading activities ▶ Lesson wrap-up	▶ During-reading strategy instruction and modeling ▶ Discussion questions ▶ After-reading skills & strategy instruction	▶ After-reading skills & strategy instruction ▶ Enrichment ▶ Assessment ▶ *Reading Advantage* paperback collection

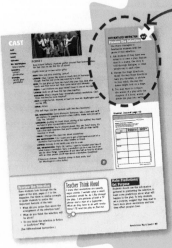

Differentiated Instruction Students who need deeper instruction in and/or a different approach to a strategy or skill will benefit from instruction that provides more support, or scaffolding.

More to Read!
Keep the *Reading Advantage* paperback books and the *eZines* CD-ROM available for students who have finished their assigned work. See the Teacher's Edition appendix for applying the reading strategies to the paperback books.

Great Source Reading Advantage
Is Easy to Manage

How can you address the needs of your students while still maintaining order in the classroom? Routines and schedules are key.

Establishing Routines

Students can work independently if they know

▶ what to expect each day;

▶ how to use the material;

▶ what they can do to solve most problems on their own;

▶ how to respect their classmates.

The following charts will help your students to work productively and independently and will foster an atmosphere of respect.

Post guidelines, procedures, and schedules on a bulletin board or a wall. Have students in the independent groups take turns being the group leader to help keep the rest of the group on task.

Behavior Guidelines During Teacher-led Group Work

▶ Come prepared.

▶ Be a good listener.

▶ Respect ideas of others.

▶ Use details from the magazine article to support your position.

▶ Participate in the discussion.

▶ Talk quietly so others can work independently.

"I-Need-Help" Procedure Chart for Independent Work Times

If you need help, try the four steps below. (If you need to speak, use a quiet voice.)

1. Think for a moment. Try to solve the problem yourself.

2. Ask a group member for support.

3. If that person can't help, ask another student from your group.

4. If none of the steps work, put your name on the "Needs Help" clipboard. Work on something you can do until the teacher helps you.

Class Gathering

Use this time to present an overview of the day's learning events. Explain which groups you will meet with and go over the directions for the independent work other groups will do. Writing the class schedule on the board as a reference and time-management guide for you and your students lets everyone know what the plan is.

Strategic Think Aloud or Minilesson

Present instruction that will benefit the whole class. Use this whole-class time to introduce a new theme, teach a new comprehension strategy, or to do the Before Reading activities. Support for all these teaching ideas is in the *Reading Advantage* Teacher's Edition.

Read Aloud

Why read aloud to older students? Research shows that reading aloud to students on a daily basis develops their listening capacity, builds their background knowledge, develops their vocabulary, and enlarges their knowledge of literary language and syntax by attuning their ears to the language of different genres.

What can you read aloud? Use articles from the *Reading Advantage* magazines or choose short selections such as poems, short stories and folk tales, or fascinating passages from nonfiction texts.

Small-Grouping Instruction

The following chart shows how two or three groups rotate through the major learning events related to *Reading Advantage*. Vary the rotation according to the number of groups you have (no more than 3 groups are recommended) and the length of time you have to spend on *Reading Advantage*.

TWO GROUPS

	Teacher-led Group	Student Journal Word Study Independent Reading
Time 1	Group 1	Group 2
Time 2	Group 2	Group 1

THREE GROUPS

	Teacher-led Group	Student Journal Independent Reading	Word Study Independent Reading
Time 1	Group 1	Group 2	Group 3
Time 2	Group 2	Group 3	Group 2
Time 3	Group 3	Group 1	Group 1

WRAP-UP Bring the class back together to give any instructions, such as homework or preparation necessary for the next class.

Establishing Schedules

Write the class schedule on the board as a reference and time-management guide. This technique enables your students to take responsibility for what they should be doing. A daily session could follow these schedules:

	WHOLE CLASS		**SMALL GROUP / INDEPENDENT**		**WHOLE CLASS**	
30 minutes	Class Gathering	3 min	Small-Group Instruction Independent Work (1)	20 min	Wrap-up	2 min
	Strategic think-aloud or minilesson	5 min				
55 minutes	Teacher Read Aloud	5 min	Strategic think-aloud or minilesson	5 min	Wrap-up	2 min
	Class Gathering	3 min	Small-Group Instruction Independent Work (2-3)	40-45 min		
90 minutes	Teacher Read Aloud	5-10 min	Small-Group Instruction Independent Work (2-3)	65 min	Wrap-up and homework	5 min
	Class Gathering	5 min				
	Strategic think-aloud or minilesson	5-10 min				

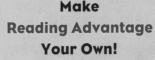

**Make
Reading Advantage
Your Own!**

Use these schedules as a guide and tailor them to your schedule and teaching style.

If you use *Reading Advantage* as a supplement in your 90-minute block, for example, follow one of the shorter schedules and leave the remaining time for your other reading and language arts activities.

Great Source Reading Advantage
Comprehension

To become skillful readers, students must develop the reading strategies necessary to understand and learn from text. *Reading Advantage* provides for instruction in five high-utility reading strategies:

 STRATEGY 1 Monitor Understanding

The ability to determine whether comprehension is occurring and to take corrective (fix-up) action when comprehension becomes difficult

 STRATEGY 2 Making Connections

The ability to activate prior knowledge, predict, self-question, and make connections to personal experiences and other texts

 STRATEGY 3 Determining Importance

The ability to evaluate and determine the importance of ideas, and support one's beliefs with evidence

 STRATEGY 4 Understanding Text Structure

The ability to recognize and understand the organization an author uses to write a narrative or expository selection, which includes knowledge of text features and genre

 STRATEGY 5 Inferential Thinking

The ability to infer and synthesize ideas that are not directly stated in the text

These strategies are integrated into *Reading Advantage* lessons to provide students "point-of-use" strategy instruction and application using suitable texts. If you wish to extend these point-of-use instructional suggestions, there are references to the more robust Model Lessons that follow on pages xxiv–xxxiii.

Each Model Lesson provides a definition of the strategy, supporting research, and a three-part teaching sequence:

Explain:	Information to help you provide students with a verbal explanation of the strategy and how to employ it
Model:	Examples for how to demonstrate to students the application of the strategy
Practice:	Guidance for how to provide students practice in the strategy to promote its independent use

We encourage you to refer to and use the Model Lessons flexibly, drawing from them as needed when you determine that students would benefit from more extensive instruction in the strategies incorporated into *Reading Advantage*.

REFERENCES

Alvermann, D. E., & Hagood, M. C. (2000). Critical media literacy: Research, theory, and practice in "new times." *Journal of Educational Research, 93,* 193–206.

Anderson, R. C., & Pearson, P. D. (1984). A schema-theoretic view of basic processes in reading comprehension. In P. D. Pearson (Ed.), *Handbook of reading research* (pp. 225–292). New York: Longman.

Armbruster, B. B., Anderson, T. H., & Ostertag, J. (1987). Does text structure/summarization instruction facilitate learning from expository text? *Reading Research Quarterly, 22,* 331–346.

Baker, L. (2002). Metacognition in reading comprehension. In C. C. Block and M. Pressley (Eds.), *Comprehension instruction: Research-based best practices* (pp. 77–95). New York: Guilford.

Baker, L., & Brown, A. L. (1984). Metacognitive skills and reading. In P. D. Pearson (Ed.), *Handbook of reading research* (pp. 353–394). New York: Longman.

Barron, J. B., & Sternberg, R. J. (Eds.). (1987). *Teaching thinking skills: Theory and practice.* New York: Freeman.

Brown, A. L., & Day, J. D. (1983). Macro rules for summarizing texts: The development of expertise. *Journal of Verbal Learning and Verbal Behavior, 22,* 1–14.

Commeyras, M. (1993). Promoting critical thinking through dialogical-thinking reading lessons. *The Reading Teacher, 46,* 486–494.

Duke, N. K., & Pearson, P. D. (2002). Effective practices for developing reading comprehension. In A. E. Farstrup & S. J. Samuels (Eds.), *What research has to say about reading instruction* (3rd ed., pp. 205–242). Newark, DE: International Reading Association.

Ennis, R. H. (1987). A taxonomy of critical thinking dispositions and abilities. In J. B. Baron & R. J. Sternberg (Eds.), *Teaching for thinking* (pp. 9–26). New York: Freeman.

Hahn, A. L., & Garner, R. (1984). Synthesis of research on students' ability to summarize text. *Educational Leadership, 42* (5), 52–55.

Hare, V., & Borchardt, K. M. (1984). Direct instruction of summarization skills. *Reading Research Quarterly, 20,* 62–78.

Fitzgerald, J. (1989). Research on stories: Implications for teachers. In K. D. Muth (Ed.), *Children's comprehension of text: Research into practice* (pp. 2–36). Newark, DE: International Reading Association.

Fitzgerald, J., & Spiegel, D. L. (1983). Enhancing children's reading comprehension through instruction in narrative structure. *Journal of Reading Behavior, 15,* 1–17.

Gordon, C. J. (1989). Teaching narrative text structure: A process approach to reading and writing. In K. D. Muth (Ed.).

Children's comprehension of text: Research into practice (pp. 79–102). Newark, DE: International Reading Association.

Griffin, C. C., & Tulbert, B. L. (1995). The Effect of Graphic Organizers on students' comprehension and recall of expository text: A review of the research and implications for practice. *Reading and Writing Quarterly, 11,* 73–89.

Hansen, J., & Pearson, P. D. (1983). An instructional study: Improving the inferential comprehension of good and poor fourth-grade readers. *Journal of Educational Psychology, 75,* 821–829.

Langer, J. A. (1995). *Envisioning literature: Literary understanding and literature instruction.* New York: Teacher's College Press.

Mandler, J. M., & Johnson, N. S. (1977). Remembrance of things parsed: Story structure and recall. *Cognitive Psychology, 9,* 111–151.

McGee, L. M., & Richgels, D. J. (1988). Teaching expository text structure to elementary students. *The Reading Teacher, 38,* 739–747.

Meyer, B. J. F. (1984). Organizational aspects of text: Effects on reading comprehension and applications for the classroom. In J. Flood (Ed.), *Promoting reading comprehension* (pp. 113–138). Newark, DE: International Reading Association.

National Reading Panel. (2000). *National Reading Panel: Teaching children to read: An evidence-based assessment of the scientific research literature on reading and its implications for reading instruction: Report of the subgroups* (NIH Publication No. 00-4754). Washington, DC: National Institute of Health and National Institute of Child Health and Human Development.

Nickerson, R. S. (1988). Improving thinking through instruction. In E. Z. Rothkoph (Ed.), *Review of research in education* (pp. 3–57). Washington, DC: American Educational Research Association.

Paris, S. G., Wasik, B. A., & Turner, J. C. (1991). The development of strategic readers. In R. Barr, M. L. Kamil, P. Mosenthal, & P. D. Pearson (Eds.), *Handbook of reading research, Volume II* (pp. 609–640). White Plains, NY: Longman.

Pearson, P. D., & Camperell, K. (1981). Comprehension of text structures. In J. T. Guthrie (Ed.), *Comprehension and teaching: Research reviews* (pp. 27–55). Newark, DE: International Reading Association.

RAND Reading Study Group. (2002). *Toward an R & D program in reading comprehension.* Santa Monica, CA: RAND Corporation.

Rosenshine, B., Meister, C., & Chapman, S. (1996). Teaching students to generate questions: A review of the intervention studies. *Review of Educational Research, 66* (2), 181–221.

Tierney, R. J., Sofer, A., O'Flahavan, J. F., & McGinley, W. (1989). The effects of reading and writing upon thinking critically. *Reading Research Quarterly, 24,* 134–173.

Comprehension continued
Monitor Understanding

DEFINITION: Monitoring understanding involves a reader's conscious effort to determine whether comprehension is occurring and to take corrective (fix-up) action when comprehension becomes difficult. Fix-up strategies include rereading, reading ahead, retelling, visualizing, asking questions, and using context.

RESEARCH SUPPORT

Skillful reading comprehension requires that readers reflect on whether a text is being understood and employ strategies for promoting comprehension when it is impeded (Baker & Brown, 1984; Paris, Wasik, & Turner, 1991). Research demonstrates that students can be taught to monitor their understanding and employ comprehension fix-up strategies as a means to enhance their text understanding (Baker, 2002; National Reading Panel, 2000; RAND, 2002).

MODEL LESSON

Explain: How the Strategy Helps and When to Use It

Explain to students that monitoring understanding will help them improve comprehension and learn new information. It's especially helpful with nonfiction but can be used with any challenging text. Self-monitoring is a multi-step process that happens during reading. Here's how it works:

In Step 1, the reader reads a section of text.

In Step 2, the reader asks: *Do I understand what I just read well enough to retell it?* The reader retells the section without looking at the text.

In Step 3, the reader looks back at the section of text and evaluates the retelling. If the retelling includes the most important details from the text, the reader reads on. If the retelling includes incorrect or few details, the reader chooses a fix-up strategy to try to resolve the confusion.

Five Fix-Up Strategies

- *Reread* a difficult section to see if that improves understanding. Rereading includes careful rereading of diagrams, captions, and photographic details. Rereading can also be done to connect newly read ideas with earlier text.

- *Read on* to see if the next section gives clues for comprehension.

- *Visualize* to form mental pictures of what's happening or of specific words and phrases.

- *Ask questions* to clarify confusing details. Then try another fix-up strategy to find the answer.

- *Use context clues* in the sentences before and after the difficult word and word-structure clues to help figure out meaning.

Model the Strategy

Materials *Survival*, "Racing Death: The Balto Story," pages 5–6

Step 1 Name the strategy and explain to students what it is and how it helps them.

Think Aloud Here's a good way to break down the Monitor Understanding strategy: read, pause, retell, evaluate. This process will help you confirm your understanding of a text and pinpoint areas of confusion. After reading a paragraph, section, or page of text, pause and retell in your own words what you've read. Then check the text and evaluate yourself. Ask: *Did I recall enough details to show that I understand?* If you recalled several important details, then read on. If you had trouble retelling what you read, you probably didn't understand or remember enough. Try applying a fix-up strategy to make better sense of the passage.

Now, I'll model the whole strategy. Listen as I read, pause, retell, evaluate, and apply a fix-up strategy.
Step 2 Read aloud the section called, "Taking the Lead," on pages 5–6. (Provide background for the beginning of the article, if necessary.)
Think Aloud Now I'll retell what I read, without looking at the sections.

When the serum got to the last stop, Gunnar and the dogs were there, waiting to take it to Nome. Balto was in the lead. It was hard work for the dogs to pull the sled through the snow. The dogs were scared and they had difficulties pulling the sled. The serum was almost lost on the way.

When I look back at the section, I see that I left out several details. I'll try rereading as a fix-up strategy. Here's my second retelling. Notice how I add more details and provide more context.

Gunnar and his team of dogs were waiting in Bluff, the last stop before Nome. Balto and another dog, Fox, were in the lead. They had a difficult task of guiding the dogs and staying on the trail. When the deep snow practically covered the dogs, some of the dogs panicked. But Balto stayed calm and the other dogs followed his lead. Then a strong wind flipped the sled and the dogs. When Gunnar righted the sled, the serum was gone. He dug through the deep snow with his bare, frostbitten hands until he found it, and the team continued on.

Step 3 Discuss how to choose a fix-up strategy.
Think Aloud It can be hard to figure out which fix-up strategy to choose when you're confused about your reading. Ask yourself these questions to help you make the choice: *Do I need to slow down and reread? Do I need to connect ideas from this last section to text that came before? Am I having trouble visualizing images? What ideas are most unclear? Did a specific word confuse me?*

Guided Practice

1. Set aside time when you can observe students as they self-monitor, evaluate, and, if necessary, apply a fix-up strategy.

2. Circulate and listen to students think aloud as they monitor their understanding. Support students who have difficulty by first modeling the entire process, then sharing the process, and finally having them complete the process on their own.

Independent Practice

1. Assign a section of text for students to monitor understanding on their own.

2. Give each student a piece of paper, have them write their retelling, evaluate it, and note the fix-up strategy they plan to apply.

Following Up
Continue to encourage students to self-monitor their reading, especially when they need new or challenging texts.

Making Connections

DEFINITION: When readers make connections to a text, they link their life experiences and prior knowledge to the information, characters, themes, and topics in the text. Connections can be to a reader's own experience, to other texts, or to the larger world.

RESEARCH SUPPORT

Reading comprehension is a meaning-construction process (Duke & Pearson, 2002) that involves interactions among the reader, text, reading task, and social context (RAND, 2002). When readers engage with text actively, they use their prior knowledge (Anderson & Pearson, 1984) and their ability to predict (Hansen & Pearson, 1983), self-question (Rosenshine, Meister, & Chapman, 1996), and make connections to personal experiences and other texts (Langer, 1995) to comprehend and appreciate what they read.

MODEL LESSON

Explain: How the Strategy Helps and When to Use It

Explain to students that when they make connections, they compare the information in a text to their own experiences, to other texts, and to issues in the larger world. The more connections they make to a text, the better they will understand and remember it. Making connections will also help students learn new information and better understand the experiences of the characters or people in a text. If a reader can't make a connection, the text will be harder to understand. In those cases, provide any necessary background and encourage students to read on and re-evaluate at the end of each section, page, or chapter. If students discover that their prior experience doesn't match what is in the text, discuss possible reasons for the mismatch.

Readers begin making connections before reading, as they preview the text to access prior knowledge. The process should then continue during and after reading. Encourage students to make connections with all texts.

Model the Strategy

Materials *Motion*, "Motion of Myself," page 32

Step 1 Name the strategy and explain to students what it is and how it helps them.

Think Aloud When you make connections with a text, it strengthens your comprehension in two important ways: It makes the text more interesting, which helps you stick with it, and it helps you remember what you read. The connections you make can be to your own experience; to other texts, movies, or TV shows you know; and to issues in your community or in the world.

Step 2 Explain that posing questions is a good way to make connections to a text. Display these questions so students can refer to them as they read:

• What do I connect to in the text?

• What makes me feel these connections?

Provide sticky notes to students and have them jot their connections on them. Students can place the sticky note next to the passage with which they connect.

Step 3 Have students read the poem on page 32. Show them how the questions help you connect with it.

Think Aloud I can definitely connect with the feelings of this poem. Like the poet, I, too, enjoy being still. Many mornings when I wake up, I lie in bed, enjoying the quiet and calm before the start of the day. I really connected with the part about looking at the cars and imagining the lives of the people who own them. I like to look at houses and imagine who lives inside and what their lives are like. I especially connect with the part about not enjoying constant company. Some of my favorite moments are when I can sit quietly by myself, gazing at the view.

Step 4 Point out that the more specific the connections, the deeper the understanding.

Step 5 Organize students into partners. Have partners discuss their connections to the poem, explaining why they feel them. Then have pairs share their thoughts with the class.

Step 6 After reading, post these questions to encourage students to self-reflect.

- Which connections made the reading more meaningful?
- How did these connections help me move beyond myself to thinking about other people, other texts, and larger issues that affect the community or the world?

Step 7 Have students share their insights with the class.

Guided Practice

1. Provide sticky notes for students so that they can respond to the questions in Step 2 as they read.

2. Point out that you want students to begin making connections before reading, as they preview the text and begin to access what they know.

3. Have students share their connections with a partner or small group. Circulate and listen so that you can identify students who need more guidance.

4. Support students who need your expertise to make connections and reflect on them.

Independent Practice

1. Continue to offer students opportunities to practice making connections.

2. Confer with students you supported during guided practice to make sure they can work productively on their own.

Following Up

Periodically review this strategy and point out that making connections is a part of inferential thinking, another important comprehension strategy.

Determining Importance

DEFINITION: Determining importance involves making decisions about what is important in a text. To determine the importance of ideas in a text, a reader must have a purpose for reading. Purposes can differ among readers and situations. By reflecting on important information in a text, a reader can infer big ideas and build new understandings.

RESEARCH SUPPORT

Students are presented with large amounts of information in texts, so it is essential for them to be able to identify and remember the important ideas in selections they read. Important ideas in expository texts are the main ideas, which are supported by major details. A number of studies document that students can be taught to look for and identify main ideas and major details in expository text, enabling them to comprehend and recall important information (e.g., Armbruster, Anderson, & Ostertag, 1987; Sjostrom & Hare, 1984; Taylor & Beach, 1984). Important information in narrative texts consists of central story ideas, often represented in a story map. There is considerable research demonstrating that students can be taught to identify the key ideas in stories and that this enhances their understanding of and memory for narrative texts (Fitzgerald & Spiegel, 1983; Idol & Croll, 1987; Singer & Donlan, 1982).

MODEL LESSON

Explain: How the Strategy Helps and When to Use It

Explain to students that finding important ideas in a text is an important skill for students. When students identify what's important, they will better comprehend and remember what they read. An awareness of important ideas will also help students create and infer new understandings. Determining importance is dependent on a purpose for reading. Students can set purposes before reading a passage, a chapter, an article, or an entire book.

Point out that students should begin setting purposes and determining importance during a selection preview. Then, they should use their purposes as support for selecting important ideas both during and after reading.

Model the Strategy

Materials *Fun and Games*, "Crazy for Chocolate!," pages 22–25

Lesson 1: Determining Important Details

Step 1 Name the strategy and explain to students what it is and how it helps them.

Think Aloud Nonfiction often has a lot of information, and fiction can be complex and detailed. It can be tough to sort out what is important in both kinds of texts. A helpful way to figure out the important details is to use the purposes for reading that you set before you started reading. I will show you how I set purposes. Be on the lookout that my purposes might change as I read and gather more information.

Step 2 Show students how you preview pages 22–25 and then set purposes for reading. Explain that to preview, you'll first read the title and the headings. Then, you'll study the photographs and green-shaded sidebars.

Think Aloud After previewing, I set these purposes for reading. I would like to discover

- what a chocolate show is
- what visitors can see and do at the show
- how chocolate is made

Step 3 Have students read pages 22–25 and show them how you figure out important ideas. Be sure to point out any changes in importance that occurred.

Think Aloud My purposes for reading helped me find the important information in the article. I discovered that the International Chocolate Show is held in New York City every year, and that thousands of chocolate lovers attend in order to see, taste, and learn about all kinds of chocolate. Visitors can sample chocolate from around the world, view art made from chocolate, and watch chefs create chocolate treats. There is even a fashion show of chocolate clothes!

An important fact I learned is that chocolate is made from seeds that come from the cacao tree. The shells of the seeds are removed, and the inside parts, called "cacao nibs" are ground into a paste to which milk and sugar are added to make the chocolate.

Step 4 Have students comment on your think-aloud and add details that they believe relate to your purposes.

Lesson 2: Finding Big Ideas

Step 1 Explain that you will now show students how you reflect on your purposes for reading and important details to determine (or infer) a big idea.

Think Aloud Now that I've read and thought about the article, I can combine my prior knowledge with new information I've learned to create a big idea. According to the article, the average American eats twelve pounds of chocolate a year. I know that Europeans make and eat lots of chocolate, too. I now know that you need cacao seeds to make chocolate, and that cacao trees grow in rainforests. I know that many rainforests have been destroyed over the past several decades. I wonder how the diminishing rainforests will affect the chocolate industry. This question is a big idea.

Step 2 Organize students into partners. Have pairs discuss and suggest other big ideas.

Guided Practice

1. Organize students into partners.

2. Have all pairs preview the same article and write their purposes for reading in a journal or notebook.

3. Have pairs discuss the selection, pinpoint important ideas, and jot them in their journals or notebooks.

4. Ask partners to share and discuss the important ideas they identified.

5. Have pairs use their purposes and important ideas to figure out a big idea. Pairs can share their big ideas with the class. Tell students that when they find big ideas, they are inferring.

6. Support pairs who need more practice with setting purposes and determining important ideas.

Independent Practice

1. Continue to give students practice with setting purposes and determining importance.

2. Confer with individuals to determine who needs more support with finding big ideas.

Following Up

Review this strategy throughout the year. Finding big ideas helps students comprehend, remember, and infer new meaning.

Understanding Text Structure

DEFINITION: Text structure involves the organization an author uses to write a selection. There are text structures for narrative and expository texts, and readers' knowledge and recognition of various text structures can enhance their text comprehension, recall, and learning.

RESEARCH SUPPORT

There are common patterns or structures for narrative (Fitzgerald, 1989; Mandler & Johnson, 1977) and expository texts (Duke & Pearson, 2002; Meyer, 1984; Pearson & Camperell, 1981). Research demonstrates that students can be taught to recognize and use narrative (Fitzgerald & Spiegel, 1983; Gordon, 1989) and expository (Armbruster, Anderson, & Ostertag, 1987; McGee & Richgels, 1988) text structures to enhance their comprehension, and there is evidence that the use of graphic representations of text structures can enhance students' understanding (Duke & Pearson, 2002; Griffin & Tulbert, 1995).

MODEL LESSON

Explain: How the Strategy Helps and When to Use It

Explain to students that all selections are organized into one or more text structures. Before beginning to write, an author chooses how to organize the information. When students can identify and understand the text structures, their comprehension and recall improve. When reading fiction, students can use the **narrative structure** of **setting, characters, plot,** and **outcome** to better understand the story and remember the text. When reading nonfiction, students can identify the structures of **sequence, cause-effect, problem-solution, question-answer, compare-contrast**, and **description** to improve their understanding of the author's purpose and to identify details and big ideas. It's important to note that informational text often contains more than one structure.

Point out that skilled readers tune into text structure before reading, as they preview a text. Being aware of the text structure before reading will help students anticipate and predict what they will read. During reading, students can use text structure to comprehend, predict, and remember. After reading, students can discuss material in terms of text structure.

Model the Strategy

Materials *Arts*, "Picture This," pages 22–27; "Meet the Author: An Interview with Jaqcueline Woodson," pages 28–31

Lesson 1: Understanding Text Structure
Before Reading

Step 1 Name the strategy and explain to students what it is and how it helps them.

Think Aloud 1 Today, we'll preview a text to determine if it's narrative or informational. Look at pages 22–27; there are no section headings, there's dialogue between characters, and the illustrations look like those you'd see in a fiction story. These are all clues that the text is narrative. To preview a narrative text, read the first page and look at the illustrations. We meet Miss Miro, the art teacher, and Ronnie, a student who hangs around her classroom. This looks like a narrative text.

Think Aloud 2 Today, we'll preview pages 28–31 to determine if this text is narrative or informational. If it's informational, we'll try to see what kind of structure the author uses. I know this is informational because it's about a real-life author. There are photographs, sidebars, and an interview. These are all features of nonfiction.

Step 2 Organize students into pairs. Have pairs preview a text to decide whether the text is narrative or informational. Encourage students to give you the clues that led them to their conclusion.

Step 3 Have students read the texts. Then identify and discuss the structure(s).

Step 4 Remind students to use their knowledge of text structure as they read.

Lesson 2: Using Text Structure After Reading

Step 1 Organize students into pairs. Have them read "Picture This."

Step 2 After reading the story, have pairs complete a graphic organizer showing the structure of the story. (See TE page 212 for a plot organizer.)

Step 3 Show students how you use the setting and plot to understand the actions of Miss Miro and Ronnie.

Think Aloud Every day during third period, Ronnie stands outside Miss Miro's art class, listening to the lesson she's teaching. Several times, Miss Miro invites Ronnie to join the class, but he refuses. Then Miss Miro gives Ronnie a detention.

Step 4 Ask pairs to use setting and plot to explain other actions in the story.

Step 5 After reading "An Interview with Jacqueline Woodson," show how you use the question-answer structure to figure out a big idea. Explain that the first question and answer about what Woodson wanted to be when she grew up leads you to understand that published writers don't always plan on becoming a writer.

Step 6 Have pairs use another question and answer to find a big idea.

Guided Practice

1. Provide guided practice before and after reading with other narrative and informational texts from the magazines.

2. Ask students to preview to figure out structure and then use structure to deepen meaning and recall.

3. Support students who need your expertise to help identify text structure to improve comprehension and recall.

Independent Practice

1. Provide students with opportunities to practice using text structure.

2. Confer with students you helped during guided practice to make sure that they are learning to identify and use text structure.

Following Up

Continue to review this strategy throughout the year. Remind students to use this strategy when they read textbooks in their other classes.

Inferential Thinking

DEFINITION: Inferential thinking is the process of creating personal meaning from text. An inference is created when a reader combines prior knowledge with details from a text to create new, unstated meaning.

RESEARCH SUPPORT

Writers rely on readers' ability to use their prior knowledge and their ability to make inferences to fill in information that is not explicit in text. This is a challenging task for many readers (Graesser, Singer, Trabasso, 1994; RAND, 2002). Fortunately, there exist a number of studies that demonstrate that students can be taught to make inferences about the texts they read by relying on prior knowledge and by making text-based and schema-based inferences (Dewitz, Carr, & Patberg, 1987; Hansen, 1981; Hansen & Pearson, 1983; McGee & Johnson, 2003).

MODEL LESSON

Explain: How the Strategy Helps and When to Use It

Explain to students that writers purposely do not include all the details in a text. Writers expect readers to combine their prior knowledge with the information in the text to create new, unstated meanings. When readers infer meaning, they deepen their comprehension by becoming more involved or connected with the text and create new understandings. Students can use this strategy with fiction, poetry, biography, and informational texts. Point out that inferential thinking starts before reading, when students make logical predictions, and continues during and after reading.

Model the Strategy

Materials *Motion,* "Crazy Cars," pages 7–10; "When Nothing Can Stop You," pages 17–21

Lesson 1: Biography/Profile

Step 1 Name the strategy and explain to students what it is and how it helps them. Display these questions to guide students' inferring:

- What does the text tell me?
- What do I already know about the topic?
- What new meaning can I infer?

Think Aloud Today, I'll show you how to make inferences from the profile on artist Chuck Close. First, I'll notice what the text says. Then I'll combine it with my prior knowledge to create an inference. I'll use the three questions to guide me.

Step 2 Read aloud "A Terrible Blow" on page 18 and "Fighting Back" on page 19, and show students how you make an inference.

Think Aloud First, here's what the text tells me: When Chuck Close was forty-eight, he had a stroke and was paralyzed. Despite being unable to move his body, he figured out a way to continue painting portraits. Here's my prior knowledge: Some people who suffer a stroke are never able to walk or use their arms again, and some have difficulty speaking. I know that a stroke can destroy parts of the brain that control these functions. Now, here's my inference, or new meaning: I infer that creating art is so important to Chuck Close that he couldn't bear the thought of not being able to paint, so he pushed himself and his body to create a new way to paint.

Step 3 Organize students into partners.

Step 4 Have students read page 20 and have them infer new ideas about Chuck Close.

Lesson 2: Informational Text

Step 1 Have students read the section "Green Cars" on page 8 of "Crazy Cars."

Step 2 Show students how you use the three questions to infer. (See Step 1 in Lesson 1: Biography/Profile.)

Think Aloud Here's a fact from page 8: Some people have made cars that run on used cooking oil. The oil is usually free. Here's my prior knowledge: I know that this process was invented by college students. I also know that gasoline prices keep rising. Now, here's my inference, or new meaning: As young people begin their careers, they may be motivated to discover and create less expensive, non-polluting, alternative fuels for cars.

Step 3 Have students find facts in the remainder of the article and use the three questions to help them infer new, unstated meanings.

Guided Practice

1. Organize students into partners.

2. Use parts of fiction and nonfiction selections from the magazines. Have pairs read or reread the same selection.

3. Have pairs use what they know to explore implied meanings. Then have partners share their findings with classmates.

4. Circulate and listen to pairs working together. Identify students who can work on their own, and those who need your support.

5. Help pairs who need extra practice and guidance until they grasp making inferences.

Independent Practice

1. Continue to give all students practice with making inferences. Use fiction and nonfiction texts. Make sure students use the three questions to guide their inferring.

2. Confer with students in brief one-on-one meetings. Ask them to show you how they make inferences using part of an article from one of the magazines. Or have them write inferences they have made about a fictional character, person, or information.

Following Up

1. Keep reviewing inferential thinking with students even though they're learning another strategy.

2. Support students who need your expertise by modeling how you infer from a magazine passage. Then listen to students infer.

Teacher Talk

Word Study

You remember the adage: *I hear and I forget;*
I see and I remember; I do and I understand.
This is why active learning is so important!

Why bother with Word Study?

Word Study promotes word knowledge and word fluency by
having students take an active role in examining words and exploring patterns.
Each word study activity has students engage in the following activities:

▶ **study** a group of words to find common features

▶ **sort** the words into categories

▶ **discuss** and explain the relationship between the words

How do I do Word Study?

The *Word Study Manual* has everything you need to know about Word Study. Use
it as a resource to create your own free-standing word-study program or use it
as a support for the Phonics/Word Study lessons right in the *Reading Advantage*
Teacher's Edition. You can do Word Study with the whole class, but you might find
it more manageable to do the activities with a single small group. This will also
reduce the number of card sets that you will need for sorting.

Sorting words is an important—and the most engaging—part of word study.
Try these steps to familiarize yourself with word sort.

▶ First of all, read through Chapter 5, "What Is Sorting?" in the *Word Study*
  Manual to build background for yourself.

▶ Try a practice sort with your students.

  • Prepare a set of about a dozen index cards for every two or three students
    by writing an animal name on each one (e.g., hippo, giraffe, deer, manatee,
    buffalo, whale).

  • Hand out the cards to pairs or triads of students. Read aloud each animal
    name to be sure that everyone knows the words.

  • Ask students to sort the cards into categories. Suggested categories for the
    animals above include these: number of syllables, double letters, land animals,
    water animals.

  • There are no right answers, but students must have a reason for each category!
    Ask them to share their categories and reasons with the class. Listening to
    students explain how they sorted the words gives you a window into their way
    of thinking about words.

Here's how to go about doing a Phonics/Word Study lesson in *Reading Advantage*.

Preparation

▶ Read through the activity.

▶ Open to the page in the *Word Study Manual* that has the words for the word sort. The page number will be in the Teacher's Edition lesson.

▶ There are three choices for sorting the words:

- Students sort word cards.
- Students write the words in categories on paper.
- You and/or students work with a cut-apart transparency on an overhead projector.

If students will sort word cards, prepare a set of word cards for each pair or triad of students. Make a photocopy of the page from the *Word Study Manual* and cut apart the word cards.

If students will write the words on paper, make sure they have paper and pencil.

If you have an overhead projector, photocopy the page from the *Word Study Manual* onto a transparency and cut apart the word cards.

Word Study

Long *e* Vowel Sort from Level B

ee	ie
agreed	chief
speech	brief
cheer	shriek

eCe	Oddball
these	friend
theme	rein
scene	seize

Sorting the Words

▶ Explain the categories for the day. For example, the activity might focus on different spellings of the long *e* sound (modeled on this page), or words with prefixes or suffixes.

▶ Read aloud each word to be sorted.

▶ Model how to sort the words by placing the first few words into the appropriate columns, explaining your thinking as you work: The word *chief* has *ie*, so I will place it in the *ie* category. The word *friend* also has *ie*, but the sound is different, so I will place it in the Oddball category.

▶ Have students continue to sort the words.

▶ Help students move misplaced words to the correct category.

Follow-up

▶ Discuss the sort and what students learned.

▶ Have students sort the words again, trying to increase their *personal* speed (this is not a competition!) and accuracy.

▶ If students keep a Word Study Notebook, they can record their sorts and add words that fit the patterns. (See *Word Study Manual*, page 13.)

Planning a Reading Advantage Lesson

You open the *Reading Advantage* box. You lift out the Teacher's Edition and flip through the pages. Then you think, "Now what do I do?" What you want to do is to **skim through the lesson**, thinking about your students, and decide which activities will benefit them. **Then make a plan** to do those activities.

STEP 1 Skim through the lesson

Look over the lesson to get a sense of the instructional opportunities available. Think about your students' needs as you skim the activity headings: Do your students need work in comprehension? Vocabulary? Make a note of the areas on which you will concentrate.

STEP 2 Choose how to introduce the magazine selection

Each lesson begins with a variety of activities to prepare students to read. (See Before Reading.) You know your students best and can decide whether they need a lot of support up front or just a little. Is this a topic or genre new to students? Then they might benefit from some extra pre-reading instruction. If students are comfortable with the topic and genre, then complete only Preview the Selection and Make Predictions/ Set Purpose.

STEP 3 Decide how students will read the selection

Choose any one or more of these ways to have students read the selection.

▶ Read all or part of the selection aloud.
▶ Have students read with a partner or in small groups.
▶ Have students read independently.

While students are reading in a small group, with a partner, or on their own, use the questions in During Reading to monitor students' comprehension in brief one-on-one conferences.

STEP 4 Select after-reading activities for the whole group

The activities in After Reading are a follow-up to the reading selection. They work well in a whole-group setting.

STEP 5 — Prepare the Phonics/Word Study activity

Check the Phonics/Word Study activity for any preparation that needs to be done before class, such as creating word cards and using resources from the *Word Study Manual*.

STEP 6 — Select follow-up instruction

Look over the activities listed under Focus On. Choose one or more activities that suit your students' needs.

STEP 7 — Assign a time frame

How long are your class periods? That will determine how much you can do in a single day. You may want to break up a lesson into two or three parts if you have short periods. To fill in around the edges, make the paperback books (see Teacher's Edition appendix) and *eZines* available to your students to use independently.

STEP 8 — Keep your students moving

Use the Assessment questions at the end of each lesson to check whether students have understood the main concepts in each lesson. Use the more formal mid-magazine and end-of-magazine tests to monitor students' progress through a level. If students do well on the mid-magazine test, consider moving them up a level or accelerating the remainder of a level by using some of the magazine selections as independent reading (without the instruction).

Planning a **Reading Advantage** Lesson continued

Plan Your Lesson • 3-Day Plan

Here's one way to plan a *Reading Advantage* lesson! This plan is for Lesson 3 in Level C, but it serves as a model for all *Reading Advantage* lessons.

	Activity	Page Numbers	Time
Before Reading	K-W-L chart Vocabulary Preview Preview the Selection Make Predictions/Set Purpose	TE 20-21 SJ 8	Day 1 **20** minutes
During Reading	Read aloud Independent reading Comprehension: Making Connections	TE 22	Day 1 **20** minutes
After Reading	Discussion Questions Revisit the K-W-L chart Writing: Evaluate Masks	TE 24 SJ 9	Day 2 **40** minutes
Phonics/ Word Study	Plural endings -s, -es	TE 26 WSM 36	Day 3 **20** minutes
Additional Instruction	**2 groups:** ▶ Article: Say It with Emoticons (read on their own) ▶ Comprehension: Understanding Text Structure (teacher-led group)	TE 26	Day 3 **20** minutes
When students finish their work	Paperback books eZines CD-ROM		

TE = Teacher's Edition   SJ = Student Journal   WSM = Word Study Manual

Great Source Reading Advantage
Assessment

Reading Advantage includes assessment options to help you place students in the program, check students' progress, and plan tailored instruction:

Place students in the right level

Use the *Reading Advantage* **Placement Test** to make sure that your students are reading text that is on their instructional level. When text is neither too hard nor too easy, students can attend to learning strategies and skills that will help them make progress in their reading ability. You have a choice of administering a Group Reading Inventory or an Individual Reading Inventory. Both have reading passages followed by multiple-choice questions and are available in each kit as well as online at http://www.greatsource.com.

Monitor students' progress informally

Each lesson ends with an opportunity for you to check your students' understanding of the featured comprehension strategy and word study skill for the lesson.

Assess students' progress formally

With each *Reading Advantage* kit, you will receive an Assessment book. Inside, you will find formal assessments for testing students' progress within a level. The **Mid-Magazine Tests** and **Magazine Tests** have reading passages followed by multiple-choice and extended-answer questions. The reading level and selection vocabulary in the passages match those in the magazine.

Observe students informally

At the back of the Assessment book you will find an **Interest Survey**, a **Reading Survey,** and four **Observational Checklists**. The purpose of the surveys is to help you learn about students' interests and feelings toward reading so that you can help them choose books they will enjoy. The main purpose of the Observational Checklists is to help you monitor students' progress during the year. The information you collect will enable you to make instructional decisions based on your observations and interactions with students.

Measure students' achievement

The *Gates-MacGinitie Reading Tests*® (*GMRT*®) are nationally recognized and respected for providing accurate assessment based on current research in reading. GMRT results have been directly correlated to *Reading Advantage* levels, so you can make the most of your *Reading Advantage* instruction by placing new students into the proper level, organizing instructional groups, targeting individual needs, and evaluating the effectiveness of *Reading Advantage*. GMRT is available online or in print.

Great Source Reading Advantage
Professional Development

Research is very clear that teacher expertise is one of the most important factors influencing student achievement. High quality professional development that is research-based, aligned with adult learning theory, and structured to promote the transfer of learning to classroom instruction is one of the most effective ways to enhance teacher expertise and student achievement.

Districts that partner with Great Source to create a sustained professional development plan for *Reading Advantage* benefit in many ways:

▶ **The professional development workshops** are based on a proven, research-based delivery model that will impact teacher instruction.

▶ **Trainers are experts in the field of reading**, bringing years of experience to their work. They have used the *Reading Advantage* program and provide many suggestions for classroom use.

▶ **Interactive and hands-on activities, trainer modeling, simulations, role playing, discussions, and practice teaching** prepare teachers for working with their students.

▶ **The workshop** insures teachers will implement *Reading Advantage* appropriately.

▶ **Well-trained teachers result in greater student achievement.**

Great Source Reading Advantage
Scope and Sequence

The instructional lessons in *Reading Advantage* are set up in three parts: Before Reading, During Reading, and After Reading. Below is an outline of the skills and strategies that are taught throughout the program and where in the lesson they appear. All skills and strategies are addressed at each level.

Leveling, Strategies, and Skills	Foundations	A	B	C	D	E	F
Reading Level							
Grade 1 Reading Level	•						
Grade 2 Reading Level	•	•					
Grade 3 Reading Level		•	•				
Grade 4 Reading Level			•	•			
Grade 5 Reading Level				•	•		
Grade 6 Reading Level					•	•	
Grade 7 Reading Level						•	•
Grade 8 Reading Level							•
Before Reading							
Build Background Concepts	•	•	•	•	•	•	•
Vocabulary							
Context	•	•	•	•	•	•	•
Association	•	•	•	•	•	•	•
Categories	•	•	•	•	•	•	•
Word Meanings	•	•	•	•	•	•	•
Preview/Make Predictions							
Text Features (boldface, italics, headings, subheadings, captions, sidebars, graphics)	•	•	•	•	•	•	•
Text Structure (fiction, nonfiction)	•	•	•	•	•	•	•
Genre	•	•	•	•	•	•	•
Set Purpose	•	•	•	•	•	•	•
During Reading							
Comprehension Strategies							
Monitor Understanding (read on, reread, retell, visualize, ask questions, context, word structure)	•	•	•	•	•	•	•
Making Connections (use prior knowledge, make predictions, make connections, compare to other texts)	•	•	•	•	•	•	•
After Reading							
Comprehension Strategies							
Monitor Understanding (read on, reread, retell, visualize, ask questions, context, word structure/breaking apart long words)	•	•	•	•	•	•	•
Making Connections (use prior knowledge, make predictions, make connections, compare to other texts)	•	•	•	•	•	•	•
Determining Importance (ideas and details)	•	•	•	•	•	•	•
Understanding Text Structure (narrative [story elements], expository [description, sequence, cause/effect, compare/contrast information, problem/solution, question/answer]; text features; genre)	•	•	•	•	•	•	•
Inferential Thinking (make inferences, draw conclusions, identify themes)	•	•	•	•	•	•	•
Phonics/Word Study							
Vowels (long, ambiguous [e.g., *oo, ew, ou*])	•	•	•	•	•	•	•
Consonants (digraphs, blends, doubled)	•	•	•	•	•	•	•
Prefixes, Suffixes, Roots, Compound Words, Syllables	•	•	•	•	•	•	•
Vocabulary							
Synonyms/Antonyms, Homophones, Acronyms/Initialisms, Multiple-meaning Words, Idioms, Context, Denotation/Connotation, Classification, Association, Dictionary Skills	•	•	•	•	•	•	•
Writing	•	•	•	•	•	•	•
Ongoing Assessment	•	•	•	•	•	•	•

Integration with other Great Source Products

Great Source offers a variety of products that enable you to group students for instruction and reach every reader in your class.

What if my *Reading Advantage* students want more reading?

▶ The *Reading & Writing Sourcebooks* are an ideal supplement because they use a strategic approach and provide scaffolded reading and writing activities. Students in Level A of *Reading Advantage* can use Sourcebook grade 4, students in Level B can use Sourcebook grade 5, and students in Levels C and D will be comfortable using Sourcebook grade 6.

▶ Using the *Summer Success: Reading* program ensures a consistent instructional approach in summer school. Used alone, the magazines are perfect for additional independent reading.

▶ *Leveled Libraries* are ideal for independent reading and include nonfiction and fiction collections.

How can I meet the needs of English Language Learners?

▶ *Access*, a program for ELL students, provides materials and instructional guidelines to help students learn the content information their classmates are learning.

▶ *Leveled Libraries* in English and Spanish help students practice basic reading skills.

How can I extend reading and writing for my students?

▶ *Reader's Handbook* puts information about the reading process and reading strategies right into the students' hands.

▶ *Daybooks of Critical Reading and Writing* promote fine literature and improve students' critical reading and writing skills.

▶ *Lessons in Literacy* is a teacher resource that puts reading and writing skills and strategy lessons at your fingertips.

▶ *Science Daybooks* (Life, Earth, and Physical) help middle school students learn and review concepts in physical, life, and earth science.

▶ The *Write Source* program supports students' writing with student-friendly information on writing process, traits of effective writing, forms of writing, writing across the curriculum, and conventions.

Great Source

Reading Advantage

TEACHER'S EDITION
FOUNDATIONS

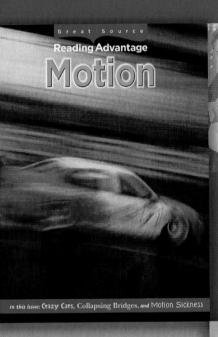

Great Source
Reading Advantage
Motion

In this issue: **Crazy Cars**, Collapsing Bridges, and Motion Sickness

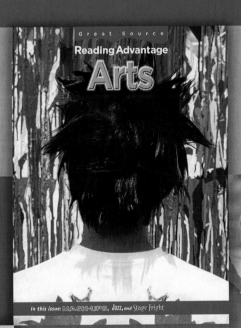

Great Source
Reading Advantage
Arts

In this issue: **MASH-UPS**, Jazz, and Stage Fright

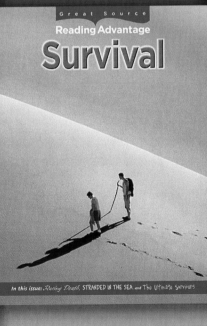

Great Source
Reading Advantage
Survival

In this issue: Racing Death, **STRANDED IN THE SEA**, and The Ultimate Survivors

Great Source
Reading Advantage
Fun and Games

In this issue: Stuck on Top of a Ferris Wheel, **DESIGNING COMPUTER GAMES**, and Chocolate Art

Foundations, Magazine 1

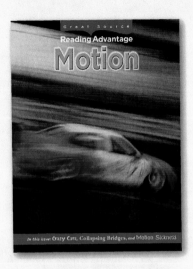

Motion

Magazine Summary

Motion magazine contains plays, poems, articles, and a story. Students will consider motion in many forms—as ideas and messages that move through communication, as forms of transportation, and as ingenious apparatus that provide movement to the disabled. Students will also read about the science behind motion pictures and motion sickness.

Content-Area Connection: social science, science
Lexile Measure: 350L

Motion Lesson Planner

LESSON	BEFORE READING	DURING READING	AFTER READING
LESSON 1 **Tell a Friend** (play) page 6	Game Vocabulary Preview Preview the Selection Make Predictions/ Set Purpose	Monitor Understanding	Check Purpose Discussion Questions Writing: short dialogues Vocabulary: word meaning Phonics/Word Study: short *a* and short *i*
LESSON 2 **Crazy Cars** (guidebook) page 13	T-Chart Vocabulary Preview Preview the Selection Make Predictions/ Set Purpose	Making Connections	Check Purpose Discussion Questions Writing: descriptive paragraph Vocabulary: multiple meanings Phonics/Word Study: short *e* and short *o*
LESSON 3 **Tacoma's Bridge Is Falling Down** (radio play) page 19	List Vocabulary Preview Preview the Selection Make Predictions/ Set Purpose	Inferential Thinking Understanding Text Structure	Check Purpose Discussion Questions Writing: news article Vocabulary: illustrated mini-glossary Phonics/Word Study: short *u* and short *a*

Overview

Preview the Magazine

Give students time to preview the magazine. Have them look at the front and back covers, selection titles, photographs, illustrations, captions, and sidebars. Start a group discussion about *motion*. Work together to come up with a definition of the word. Then discuss associations you have with the word *motion*, for example, *When I think of motion, I think of running a race*. Write the denotation, or dictionary meaning, of *motion* in the center and record students' connotations in the surrounding ovals.

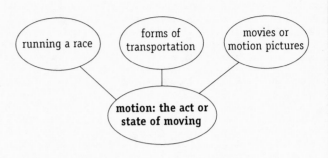

PHONICS/ WORD STUDY	FOCUS ON	ASSESSMENT	HIGHER-ORDER THINKING QUESTIONS
Short *a* and Short *i*	Writing: advice letter Fluency: punctuation English Language Learners Independent Activity Options	Monitor Understanding Short *a* and Short *i*	Sofia calls Tayo from her cell phone. Tayo answers. Why is it not obvious to the girls that there is an immediate communication problem? Use details and information from the play to support your answer. What does Lane learn about Georgia as she does research on the Internet? Use details and information from the play to support your answer.
Short *e* and Short *o*	Writing: double-entry journal Fluency: pacing English Language Learners Independent Activity Options	Making Connections Short *e* and Short *o*	Which would you prefer, an art car, a racecar, or a green car? Why would you choose this car? How does your choice fit your personality? Use details and information from the article to support your answer. Review the car timeline. Why were these cars designed and for what purpose did they serve? Use details and information from the article to support your response.
Short *u* and Short *a*	Writing: acrostic poem Fluency: expression English Language Learners Independent Activity Options	Inferential Thinking Understanding Text Structure Short *u* and Short *a*	What does Clark Eldridge imply when he says, "They should have used my design. They wanted to save money. That roadway deck is too light. And those cables aren't spaced out right." Use details and information from the radio play to support your answer. Why did the Tay Railway Bridge, the Niagra-Clifton Bridge, the Quebec City Bridge, and the Tacoma Narrow Bridge collapse? What was it that scientist and bridge engineers did not know? Use details and information from the article to support your answer.

Motion Lesson Planner

LESSON	BEFORE READING	DURING READING	AFTER READING
LESSON 4 **When Nothing Can Stop You** *and* **Sea Legs** (profiles and poem) page 27	Association Web Vocabulary Preview Preview the Selection Make Predictions/ Set Purpose	Inferential Thinking Determining Importance	Check Purpose Discussion Questions Writing: letter Vocabulary: prefixes *im-*, *dis-* Phonics/Word Study: sorting across the short vowels (*a, e, i, o, u*)
LESSON 5 **The Other Side of Flying** (story) page 36	Chart Vocabulary Preview Preview the Selection Make Predictions/ Set Purpose	Monitor Understanding	Check Purpose Discussion Questions Writing: character sketch Vocabulary: antonyms Phonics/Word Study: short and long *a*
LESSON 6 **Ask the Science Wizard** *and* **Motion of Myself** (question-answer and poem) page 43	Anticipation Guide Vocabulary Preview Preview the Selection Make Predictions/ Set Purpose	Understanding Text Structure Making Connections	Check Purpose Discussion Questions Writing: explanatory paragraph Vocabulary: word web Phonics/Word Study: short and long *e*

PHONICS/WORD STUDY	FOCUS ON	ASSESSMENT	HIGHER-ORDER THINKING QUESTIONS
Sorting across the Short Vowels (*a, e, i, o, u*)	Writing: personal timeline Fluency: pacing English Language Learners Independent Activity Options	Inferential Thinking Determining Importance Sorting across the Short Vowels (*a, e, i, o, u*)	What artistic techniques do Chuck Close and Christy Brown use? Use details and information from the biography to support your answer. In the poem, "Sea Legs," how are "standing on Earth" and "standing on the ocean" symbolic? Use details and information from the poem to support your answer.
Short and Long *a*	Writing: story map Fluency: expression English Language Learners Independent Activity Options	Monitor Understanding Short and Long *a*	What is the "other side of flying" that Maverick learns when he boards the plane for flight camp? What else will Maverick learn as he begins to train at flight camp? Use details and information from the story to support your answer. What is the meaning of the following quotation from the passage? "Just when you think your life is getting boring, the winds of change come along." Use details and information from the story to support your answer.
Short and Long *e*	Writing: explanation Fluency: expression English Language Learners Independent Activity Options	Understanding Text Structure Making Connections Short and Long *e*	Explain how movies are tricks we play on ourselves. Use details and information from the Science Wizard to support your response. What is the tone of the poem, "Motion of Myself"? Use details and information from the poem to support your answer.

Tell a Friend

Remember the game of telephone?
Sometimes you can play it without even realizing it.

Characters:

Sofia—a high-school student

Tayo—Sofia's best friend

Charlie—Tayo's friend

Sam—Charlie's friend

Julie—Sam's friend

Lane—Julie's brother, also a high-school student

Marcus—Lane's friend

2

LESSON 1
Tell a Friend
Motion, pages 2–6

SUMMARY
In this **play**, a series of miscommunications among friends leads to some unexpected misunderstandings.

COMPREHENSION STRATEGIES
Monitor Understanding

WRITING
Short Dialogues

VOCABULARY
Word Meaning

PHONICS/WORD STUDY
Short *a* and Short *i*

Lesson Vocabulary
personally	definitely
options	chemicals
remains	volunteer

MATERIALS
Motion, pp. 2–6
Student Journal, pp. 1–5
Word Study Manual, p. 35

Before Reading Use one or more activities.

Play a Game ▶

Discuss miscommunication and how often it occurs in daily life. Then give each student a small piece of paper on which to write a short message. Students can create their own logical shorthand or use abbreviations to convey a piece of information. Have each student give his or her message to a partner to see if the partner can read and understand it. Discuss the results as a group.

> C U L8R
> (See you later.)

> Y G T B K M
> (You've got to be kidding me.)

Vocabulary Preview

Have students complete the first column of the predictions chart on *Student Journal* page 1. Ask them to predict how the words might be used. Use the vocabulary word *personally* to model a response for the page. Students will complete the chart after they have finished reading. (See Differentiated Instruction.)

(As different characters talk, the setting will vary. The scene begins with Sofia on her cell phone. She is in her bedroom calling Tayo. Tayo is sitting on her bed in the room she shares with her sister.)

Sofia: Hey, Tayo.

Tayo: What's up?

Sofia: Nothing much. I have the most awesome summer planned.

Tayo: A summer plant? What's so awesome about that?

Sofia: I'm going to visit my Aunt Dinah in Florida.

Tayo: Well, if you like that kind of thing . . . I mean, personally, I'm not that fond of plants. I guess your aunt's a gardener.

Sofia: She sent me a booklet about it. We can go to the beach. I love beaches.

Tayo: You're breaking up.

Sofia: I said I love beaches.

Tayo: I'm not that crazy about them. I like plums better. Uh, oh. Got to go. Charlie's trying to get me.

(Charlie is standing on a street corner, leaning up against a building. There's a lot of traffic noise.)

Charlie: What took you so long? Who were you talking to?

Tayo: Sofia. She's going to be working this summer with plants. It's some kind of thing with her Aunt Dinah, and peaches. It sounds as if they'll be working in her aunt's garden every day.

Charlie: Her Aunt Dinah—snore, snore!

Tayo: They didn't say anything about dinosaurs. Maybe they'll see some in a museum.

Charlie: Whatever!

Tayo: So are you coming over tonight?

Charlie: Got to go to the library and check with my man, Sam.

(Charlie is at a computer in the library. He is talking to Sam, who is standing next to him.)

Charlie: I've got to call Tayo back. Have to let her know what we're doing.

Sam: I thought you just talked to her. What was that about?

Charlie: She was telling me what Sofia's doing this summer. It sounds so weird. She's going to work someplace with giant ants and dinosaurs.

Sam: Maybe she can get me a job. I need one. Then I could buy my own computer instead of using the library's.

Charlie: There was something about peaches, too. I don't remember what it was.

Sam: I'm going to e-mail Julie. She's friendly with Sofia. Maybe she can find out where this job is.

(Sam moves Charlie away from the computer and sits down.

The setting moves to Julie's house. She is on the computer at a desk. Her brother Lane is next to her in his wheelchair.)

Julie: Oh, an e-mail from Sam.

Lane: *(clutching his heart)* Be still my heart.

 3

DIFFERENTIATED INSTRUCTION
Vocabulary Preview

Work with students to read, pronounce, and establish the meaning of the word *options*.

What are the word parts?	op	tions
Where have you seen these word parts before?	mop stop optical	station information
What's a synonym for this word?	choices	
When might you use this word?	There are lots of flavor *options* at the ice cream shop.	

Student Journal page 1

Building Vocabulary: Predictions

How do you predict these words will be used in "Tell a Friend"? Write your answers in the second column. Next, read the play. Then, clarify your answers in the third column.

Word	My prediction for how the word will be used	How the word is actually used
personally		
options		
remains		
definitely		
chemical		
volunteer		

Preview the Selection

Have students look through the selection. Ask:

- What information does the introductory note on page 2 give you?
- What form of writing is this selection? How do you know?
- From the illustrations, what predictions can you make about the play?

Teacher Think Aloud

I can tell that this is a play because I see a cast of characters, and lines for each speaker. I predict that the telephone is going to be an important part of this play. Just about every illustration shows someone talking on a phone.

Make Predictions/ Set Purpose

Students should use the information they gathered in previewing the selection to make predictions about what they will learn. If students have trouble generating a purpose for reading, suggest that they read to discover what happens when words in a telephone conversation are misunderstood.

Comprehension
MONITOR UNDERSTANDING

To help students understand how to resolve confusion when reading, share these strategies:

1. If you feel confused, try retelling what you have read.

2. If you can't retell it, reread the difficult part. You may have missed something the first time.

3. If that doesn't help, try reading ahead to see if there are clues to help you understand.

4. If the story has illustrations, look at those for clues.

Julie: Don't be so childish. Sam wants me to find out where Sofia is working this summer. It's some place with peaches and ants and dinosaurs. *(turns to Lane)* I feel a little weird about asking Sofia. I'm not that friendly with her.

Lane: No problem. I'll check it out on the Internet. See, I'll type in "peaches" here. Now I'll look at the options. Hmmm . . . "Peaches" seems to mean Georgia. I guess that's where she's going.

Julie: Okay. I'll let Sam know.

Lane: Just as soon as I look at *my* e-mail.

Julie: Hey, I was on there first.

Lane: But I did you a favor. Besides, remember what Mom said.

Julie: *(leaving room)* I know. We have to share. Call me when you're done.

Lane: *(answers his cell phone as he types)* Hey, Marcus.

Marcus: What are you up to?

(We see Lane in Julie's room. At the other end of the stage, we see Marcus at his computer in his room. As they talk, they type on their computers.)

Lane: *(talking as he is typing)* Trying to check out something for my sister. Her friends want to grow peaches and search for dinosaur remains this summer. They're going someplace with giant ants, too.

Marcus: Where's that?

Lane: Georgia.

Marcus: There are two Georgias. One is in the United States and one is in Russia.

4

During Reading

Comprehension
MONITOR UNDERSTANDING

Use these questions to model how to monitor understanding by asking questions. Then have students ask their own questions and try to resolve any confusion.

- What is going on here?

- Why did that character say that?

- What fix-up strategy can I use to resolve my confusion?

(See Differentiated Instruction.)

Teacher Think Aloud

I was confused at the beginning of the play. Why did Tayo say "a summer plant?" I decided to keep reading for clues to help me understand. When I read that Tayo said to Sofia, "You're breaking up," it all became clear. There was a bad cell phone connection, and the word planned *sounded like* plant *to Tayo.*

Fix-Up Strategies

Offer these strategies to help students read independently.

If you don't understand what you're reading:

- Reread the difficult section to look for clues to help you comprehend.

- Read ahead to find clues to help you comprehend.

- Retell, or say in your own words, what you've read.

- Visualize, or form mental pictures of, what you've read.

Lane: Would they have peaches and dinosaurs and giant ants in Russia?

Marcus: <u>Definitely</u>. There are a lot of experiments going on there. I read they're doing experiments all over to find a cure for sick people.

Lane: Experiments with giant ants and peaches?

Marcus: Could be. They treat things with <u>chemicals</u>, then they get people to eat them.

Lane: Why would anyone do that?

Marcus: For the money, I guess.

Lane: Cool. It's just like that movie.

Marcus: Which one?

Lane: You know . . . I can't remember the name, but . . . oops, here comes Julie. Have to go.

(Julie enters and stands over Lane.)

Julie: Can I get on now, please? I have to e-mail Sam. He's waiting.

Lane: Okay. Oh, tell him not to bother about that job. It's in Russia.

Julie: I thought it was in Georgia.

Lane: There are two Georgias. One is in the United States and one is in Russia. Marcus told me that the job is probably in Russia. I don't think Sam would like it. It's an experiment to feed people chemical ants and peaches. I don't know how the dinosaurs got in there.

Julie: Really? That can't be true.

Lane: It is true! I saw it in a movie. It's an experiment that helps doctors learn more about how to cure sick people.

5

DIFFERENTIATED INSTRUCTION

Writing
Short Dialogues

To help students create short dialogues, share these two-line miscommunications.

Ana: I'm going to take my dog to the pet shop after school.

Jed: You're going to tape your dog to the pet shop? I don't think your dog will like that.

Sam: I like to lie on the beach.

Mai: Why would you want to lie on a peach? That would be messy.

Discuss possible illustrations for each line in the dialogues.

Student Journal pages 2–3

Name _____ Date _____

Writing: Short Dialogues Planning Page
List words or phrases below that could be misunderstood. Add some notes about possible sentences in which the words could be misheard.

1. take/tape
   I'm going to tape my dog to the pet shop.
2. beach/peach
3. _____
4. _____
5. _____
6. _____
7. _____
8. _____
9. _____
10. _____

After Reading *Use one or more activities.*

Check Purpose

Have students determine whether their purpose was met. Did students discover what happened when words in a telephone conversation were misunderstood?

Discussion Questions

Continue the group discussion with the following questions.

1. How could the miscommunications in the play have been avoided? (Cause-Effect)

2. What kinds of miscommunications have you experienced? (Making Connections)

3. Do you think the situation in this play could happen in real life? Why or why not? (Making Connections)

Revisit: Predictions Chart

Have students return to the predictions chart on *Student Journal* page 1 to complete the third column, in which they should show how the vocabulary words are actually used in the play.

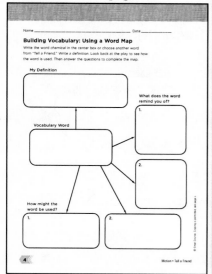

Possible answers for **Student Journal page 5** include Short *a* Words: *plants, than, back, track, happy, chat, format;* Short *i* Words: *didn't, still, sister, is, in, sick, this.*

Julie: I'll check it out. *(She calls Sam.)*

(Sam and Charlie are still at the library. Sam's cell phone rings. He takes the call outside. Then he comes back in, visibly shaken.)

Sam: That was Julie. She found out that Sofia's going to Russia this summer to volunteer for a dangerous experiment. She might not come back.

Charlie: Whoa! What do you mean?

Sam: Just what I said. Julie couldn't tell me any more than that. But Lane looked it up. He found out it's true.

Charlie: I'd better call Tayo. I don't think she knows this. Sofia's her best friend. Maybe she can talk her out of it.

(Tayo's phone rings. She is in her bedroom.)

Tayo: What? She didn't tell me that. What kind of experiment? Oh, really? I feel terrible. I sort of blew her off when you called. I'd better call her back.

(Both girls are in their bedrooms on their cell phones.)

Tayo: Hi, Sofia. I'm so happy to talk to you.

Sofia: Are you all right, Tayo? You sound a little strange.

Tayo: Of course I'm all right. It's you I'm worried about.

Sofia: What about me?

Tayo: Your summer plans, of course.

Sofia: What about them? It'll be fun.

Tayo: I think you're the bravest person I've ever known. I can't believe you're doing this.

Sofia: What's so brave about going to the beach?

Tayo: You don't have to pretend with me, Sofia. Aren't I your best friend?

Sofia: Of course.

Tayo: I want you to call me every day while you're there. I'll do the same for you. Do you think you can use your cell?

Sofia: In Florida? I think so.

Tayo: I'm getting off now. I'm going to throw a big party for you before you leave.

Sofia: Really? That's cool. Thanks, Tayo.

(They both hang up. Then Tayo realizes what Sofia said.)

Tayo: *(in questioning tone)* Florida? Why did she say *Florida?* ◆

6

Writing Short Dialogues

Have students brainstorm words or phrases that could be misheard for other words or phrases. Write the list on the board and brainstorm some two-line dialogues. Have students use *Student Journal* page 2 to create their own list of words. Then students should choose two word pairs and use *Student Journal* page 3 to write two short dialogues in which two characters mishear each other and express confusion. (See Differentiated Instruction.)

Vocabulary Word Map

Point out the word *chemicals* on page 5. Ask a volunteer to read the sentence in which the word appears. Then ask:

• What does the word mean in this context? What clues tell you that?

• When might you use the word *chemicals*?

• What are some other words that begin with a hard *ch* sound as in *chemicals*? (*chemistry, chemist*)

Have students complete the word map activity on *Student Journal* page 4.

Phonics/Word Study

Short *a* and Short *i*

Display and read aloud the following sentence: *The flea bit the cat.* Ask: *Which word in the sentence has a short a sound?* (*cat*) *Short i sound?* (*bit*) Together, list other words with short *a* and short *i* sounds that students know. Now, work with students to complete the in-depth short vowel activity on TE page 11. For additional support, have students complete *Student Journal* page 5.

Short *a* and Short *i*

Short vowels can be difficult to hear, but their visual spelling patterns are relatively easy. Conversely, the sounds that long vowels make are clear and obvious, but the spelling patterns can be problematic.

▶ Place the following words on the board as headings: *back* and *sit*. Read aloud the words. Ask: *What two short vowels do you hear? How are they different in the way they sound?* Segment each word so that students can find and concentrate on the vowel. First, say the whole word. Then, say the vowel and what comes after it, followed by the vowel alone. This helps students hear the vowel clearly.

back	*ack*	*a*
sit	*it*	*i*

▶ Provide students with copies of the Short Vowel Patterns Sort One: Short *a* and Short *i* sheet and have them begin sorting by the three headings shown. (See *Word Study Manual* page 35.) Model the correct placement for the first few words. Then have students work in pairs. One student can read the word aloud while the other sorts it. When they are finished, have both students read each column to see if all the words have the same sound. Then have students switch roles.

▶ When confronted with a word with two or more syllables, students should identify the syllable with the short *a* or *i* vowel sound and concentrate only on that syllable.

▶ Note: Discuss with students that there are slight variations in the short *a* sound.

▶ Discuss the sort, students' observations, and why the words *was, ring, first,* and *party* ended up in the Oddball column. *Was* looks like it should have a short *a* sound, but it sounds like a short *u* (*wuz*). In *ring*, the short *i* is absorbed into the *-ing* sound. Both *first* and *party* have an *r* following the vowel, and that always makes the vowel lose its pure sound.

Short Vowel Patterns Sort One: Short *a* and Short *i*		
Short *a*	**Short *i***	**Oddball**
back	sit	was
lap	flip	ring
plant	which	first
traffic	strip	party
stand	begin	what
planet	with	wants
ants	sister	talk
crash	visit	
	still	

For more information on word sorts and spelling stages, see pages 5–31 in the *Word Study Manual*.

Focus on . . .

Use one or more activities in this section to focus on a particular area of need in your students.

Comprehension · STRATEGY SUPPORT

To help those students who need more practice using the strategies covered in this lesson, work one-on-one or in small groups to apply the strategy prompts below. Apply the prompts to a *Reading Advantage* paperback, a classroom library book, or a new or familiar selection in the magazine. Always model your own thinking first.

Monitor Understanding

• Do I understand what I'm reading? If not, what part is confusing to me?

• What fix-up strategies can I use to solve the problem? (See During Reading for fix-up strategies.)

• Why did a character say (do, think, ask) that?

• What images do I visualize from the text? What parts can't I visualize?

• Why did the author include (or not include) those details?

Writing Advice Letter

Have students select a character from the play to write a friendly letter to. The letter should give the character advice on how to avoid miscommunication while using the phone, cell or otherwise. Encourage students to talk over their ideas as a group or with a partner before they begin to write. Next, have each student jot down a list of ideas to include in the letter. Be sure students include the date, a salutation, a body, and a closing signature.

Ideas for Advice Letter

1. Speak slowly.
2. If you get an unexpected reaction, find out why.
3.

Fluency: Punctuation

Tell students that one way to develop reading fluency is to pay attention to punctuation, using punctuation marks as clues for when to pause (comma or period) or when to change one's voice (rising voice at a question mark; louder or emphatic voice at an exclamation point). To model how to rely on punctuation, read aloud the beginning of the play and stop to think aloud about how you recognized and used punctuation marks.

After students have read the selection at least once, have them form groups to reread the play aloud, practicing using punctuation to promote fluency.

As you listen to groups read, use these prompts to guide them.

▶ Preview what you will read. Notice the different punctuation marks and what they signal to you.

▶ Read with expression. Put yourself in the place of the character. How would he or she sound?

When students read aloud, do they—

✓ demonstrate appropriate meaning and usage of punctuation marks?

✓ incorporate appropriate timing, stress, and intonation?

✓ exhibit well-timed pauses between words and phrases?

English Language Learners

Support students as they make connections in the second discussion question on TE page 9.

1. Explain that active readers make connections to what they read. List some miscommunications from the play.

2. Model using the language of making connections with this sentence frame: *Based on my experiences, the miscommunications remind me of . . .*

3. Have students use the sentence frame to make personal connections with the play.

Independent Activity Options

While you work with individuals or small groups, others can work independently on one or more of the following options.

▶ Foundations paperback books, see TE pages 195–200

▶ Foundations *eZines*

▶ Repeat word sorts for this lesson

▶ *Student Journal* pages for this lesson

Assessment

Strategy Assessment

To help you and your students assess their use of comprehension strategies, ask the following questions. Students can complete a written response or provide verbal answers in a one-on-one reading conference.

- **Monitor Understanding** What questions did you have as you read the story? What fix-up strategies did you use to try to resolve your confusion? (Answers will vary. You might further ask students whether the strategies they tried were successful. If not, suggest other strategies students can try in the future.)

For ongoing informal assessment, use the checklists on pages 61–64 of *Foundations Assessment*.

Word Study Assessment

Use these steps to help you and your students assess their understanding of short *a* and short *i* vowel sounds.

1. Display the following words: *grip, lack, brand, will, mash, it, whistle, map, nip,* and *grant*.

2. Have students say each word and tell whether it has a short *a* or short *i* sound. The answers are shown.

Short *a*	Short *i*
lack	grip
brand	will
mash	it
map	whistle
grant	nip

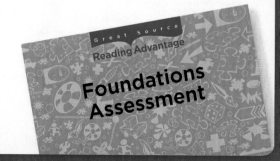

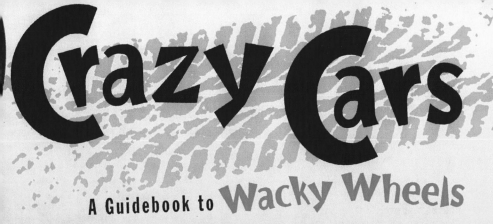

Crazy Cars
A Guidebook to Wacky Wheels

What would your dream car be like? Check out these cars. Some are fun to look at. Some are built for speed. Others are built to save the planet. For their owners, they're more than a set of wheels.

Art Cars

They've got wheels. But they don't look like cars. They're "Art Cars." They're cars that look like works of art. You could call them crazy cars.

Artists use these cars as their canvases. What do the cars look like? Just about everything! There's a giant telephone car. A grass car is covered with real grass. There are guitar cars and shark cars.

What if you pulled up in the Lizard King car? What would your friends say? It's covered with 4,000 toys. That's a lot of glue!

One artist has even made a camera van. It has thousands of cameras. It takes pictures as it drives.

To see more, go to Houston, Texas. Every April, car artists meet for Art Car Weekend. You can also see the cars on the Internet at www.artcars.com.

This car is named Manta.

7

SUMMARY
This **guidebook** tells about some atypical cars—art cars, racecars, and "green," or environmentally friendly, cars.

COMPREHENSION STRATEGIES
Making Connections

WRITING
Descriptive Paragraph

VOCABULARY
Multiple Meanings

PHONICS/WORD STUDY
Short *e* and Short *o*

Lesson Vocabulary
canvases	hybrid
flats	solar power
sleek	

MATERIALS
Motion, pp. 7–10
Student Journal, pp. 6–10
Word Study Manual, p. 36

Before Reading
 Use one or more activities.

Make a T-Chart

Create a T-chart to help students compare and contrast ordinary cars and so-called crazy cars. List students' ideas. Revisit the chart later on.

Ordinary Cars	Crazy Cars
• use gas	• talking cars
• two- or four-doors	• Batmobile
• SUVs	• stunt cars
• compacts	• flying cars
• convertibles	

Vocabulary Preview

Have students begin the word map on *Student Journal* page 6. They will come back to the page after reading. (See Differentiated Instruction.)

Preview the Selection

Have students look through the selection. Ask:

* What three categories of cars will you read about? How do you know?

* Why do you think some information is presented in a timeline?

Make Predictions/Set Purpose

Students should use the information they gathered in previewing the selection to make predictions about what they will learn. If students have trouble generating a purpose for reading, suggest that they read to learn about unusual cars in the past, present, and future.

DIFFERENTIATED INSTRUCTION
Vocabulary Preview

Work with students to read, pronounce, and establish meaning for the adjectives *sleek*, *sleeker*, and *sleekest*.

What is the base word? What are the endings?	*sleek* *sleeker* *sleekest*
What is a synonym for the base word?	*neat, trim*
How might the words be used?	June's new car was *sleek*. She thought it was *sleeker* than Dad's minivan. But Lena's sports car was the *sleekest* of all.

Student Journal page 6

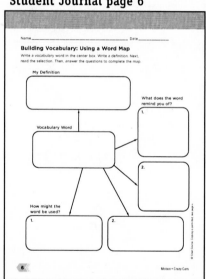

Racecars

For some people, driving 65 mph is slow. To them, it is a crawl. They want to put their pedals to the metal. They want speed! Racecar drivers try to set new records. Some cars have gone over 600 miles per hour. That's faster than jets.

You can't go 600 mph on the highway. It's not possible. It's not safe. For that, go to Utah. You can test your speed on a huge open plain. Bonneville Salt Flats covers 30,000 acres. It looks like another planet. The ground is covered with salt. The salt makes a good surface for racing.

Racecars are sleek. Some look like alien rocket ships. They're low to the ground. That way, the wind doesn't slow them down.

The first record was set there in 1914. A racer reached 142 mph. New records keep being set. In 1970, a car named "Blue Flame" reached 622 mph.

Then, in 1997, something amazing happened. People had thought it was impossible. Andy Green raced a car 763 mph! How fast is that? Andy Green went faster than the speed of sound. Racers everywhere were stunned.

Green Cars

Can french fries save the earth? Can egg rolls point the way? Maybe old ones can. Or, at least, maybe their grease can. That's what some drivers think. They've made cars that run on used cooking oil. The oil often comes from fast-food places. What's the best part? The oil is usually free.

Reinventing the Wheel

The wheel was first made well over 5,000 years ago. Ever since then, people have been inventing different ways to use it. Some crazy ideas have cropped up.

Here's a timeline of some crazy car inventions.

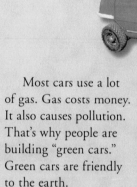

Most cars use a lot of gas. Gas costs money. It also causes pollution. That's why people are building "green cars." Green cars are friendly to the earth.

During Reading

Comprehension
MAKING CONNECTIONS

Use these questions to model how to make connections with the text. Then have students share connections they have made.

- What does this selection remind me of?
- What do I already know about this topic?
- How does my experience help me understand this selection?

Teacher Think Aloud

This article reminds me of how I have always thought that most American cars are boring to look at. Car ads try to make each one seem different and exciting, but cars all seem similar to me. I've seen pictures of European cars, and they look more interesting. It may be because I don't see them very often, or because their designs really do seem more clever.

Fix-Up Strategies

Offer these strategies to help students read independently.

If you don't understand what you're reading:

- Reread the difficult section to look for clues to help you comprehend.
- Read ahead to find clues to help you comprehend.
- Retell, or say in your own words, what you've read.
- Visualize, or form mental pictures of, what you've read.

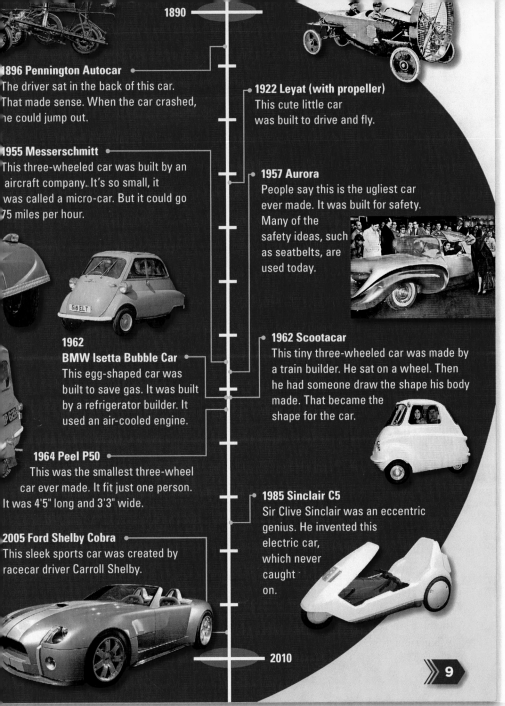

1890

1896 Pennington Autocar
The driver sat in the back of this car. That made sense. When the car crashed, he could jump out.

1955 Messerschmitt
This three-wheeled car was built by an aircraft company. It's so small, it was called a micro-car. But it could go 75 miles per hour.

1962 BMW Isetta Bubble Car
This egg-shaped car was built to save gas. It was built by a refrigerator builder. It used an air-cooled engine.

1964 Peel P50
This was the smallest three-wheel car ever made. It fit just one person. It was 4'5" long and 3'3" wide.

2005 Ford Shelby Cobra
This sleek sports car was created by racecar driver Carroll Shelby.

1922 Leyat (with propeller)
This cute little car was built to drive and fly.

1957 Aurora
People say this is the ugliest car ever made. It was built for safety. Many of the safety ideas, such as seatbelts, are used today.

1962 Scootacar
This tiny three-wheeled car was made by a train builder. He sat on a wheel. Then he had someone draw the shape his body made. That became the shape for the car.

1985 Sinclair C5
Sir Clive Sinclair was an eccentric genius. He invented this electric car, which never caught on.

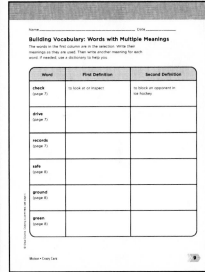

2010

9

After Reading
WHOLE CLASS Use one or more activities.

Check Purpose
Have students determine whether their purpose was met. Did they learn about unusual cars in the past, present, and future?

Discussion Questions
Continue the group discussion with the following questions.

1. What do art cars, racecars, and "green" cars have in common? How are they different from one another? (Compare-Contrast)

2. What type of person might like to drive a racecar? Explain your choice. (Inferential Thinking)

3. What kind of car would you like to drive? Why? (Making Connections)

Revisit: T-Chart
Have students look back at the T-chart from Before Reading. Are there any ideas on the chart they want to correct or change? Add responses or modifications to the chart.

Revisit: Word Map
Have students complete the word map on *Student Journal* page 6. Are there any changes they would like to make to their definition?

Vocabulary
Multiple Meanings

To help students with multiple meanings, use the following activity:

1. Tell students that many words in English have more than just one meaning. Ask students to give a meaning for *ring* when it is used as a noun. (a piece of jewelry) Ask volunteers to suggest a different meaning for the noun *ring*. (a circle, the sound a bell makes, an area where boxers compete)

2. Display the words *bowl*, *bank*, and *date*. Have students give two different meanings for each.

3. Ask other students to use each of the words in oral sentences that convey the different meanings.

Student Journal page 10

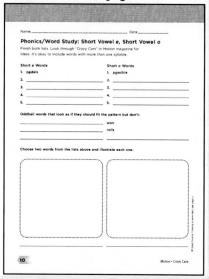

Name _____ Date _____

Phonics/Word Study: Short Vowel *e*, Short Vowel *o*

Finish both lists. Look through "Crazy Cars" in Motion magazine for ideas. It's okay to include words with more than one syllable.

Short *e* Words
1. pedals
2. ____
3. ____
4. ____
5. ____

Short *o* Words
1. possible
2. ____
3. ____
4. ____
5. ____

Oddball words that look as if they should fit the pattern but don't:
____ won
____ rolls

Choose two words from the lists above and illustrate each one.

10   Motion • Crazy Cars

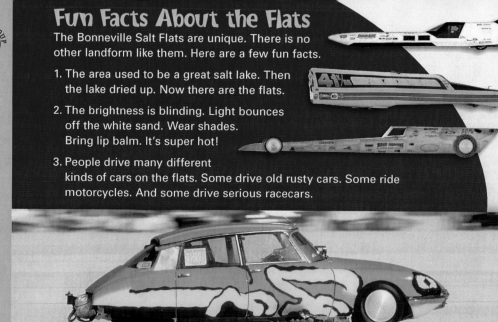

Fun Facts About the Flats

The Bonneville Salt Flats are unique. There is no other landform like them. Here are a few fun facts.

1. The area used to be a great salt lake. Then the lake dried up. Now there are the flats.

2. The brightness is blinding. Light bounces off the white sand. Wear shades. Bring lip balm. It's super hot!

3. People drive many different kinds of cars on the flats. Some drive old rusty cars. Some ride motorcycles. And some drive serious racecars.

There are many kinds of green cars. Some use just electricity. Others run on cow manure. Really! Some even run on chicken manure. People used to think these cars were crazy. But gas prices are very high. Also, people worry about the greenhouse effect. They worry about global warming. Now they are taking another look at green cars.

Hybrid cars are hitting the roads in large numbers. What are hybrids? These cars are a combination. They run on electricity. They also use some gas. They don't use much gas, though. Some hybrids can get over 60 miles to a gallon of gas. That's almost three times what many regular cars get. Right now, hybrid cars are more expensive to buy than regular cars. However, their owners feel that they save in the long run. And they know they are helping the earth.

All of this is good. But is it good enough? People are still trying to invent "greener" cars. What are other green ideas? The sun can create solar power. Imagine cars that can run on the energy from the sun. What about cars that can run on air or water? Some people have formed the Green Car Club. This club helps people who want to drive "green." Every year, they hold a race. They want to show that green cars are good. Some are even fast. Green and fast. That's a good combination. ◆

10

Writing
Descriptive Paragraph

Discuss with students some ideas for an art car of their own. How would they want it to look? Ask students to use *Student Journal* page 7 to draw and label their own art car. On *Student Journal* page 8, students should then use their labeled sketch to write a description of their car.

Vocabulary Multiple Meanings

Have students find the word *Flats* on page 8 and read the sentence in which it appears. Ask what the word means. (large, level stretches of land, used especially for races) Ask students if they can think of other meanings for the word. (Possibilities include "tires that have become deflated," "musical notes that are lowered a half step," or "shoes with low heels." Have students complete the multiple-meanings chart on *Student Journal* page 9. (See Differentiated Instruction.)

Phonics/Word Study
Short *e* and Short *o*

Write the words *stop, jet,* and *head* on the board and read them aloud. Ask students to tell how many different short vowel sounds they hear. (two: short *o* and short *e*) Ask students to name other short *o* and short *e* words they know. Now, work with students to complete the in-depth short vowel activity on TE page 17. For additional support, have students complete *Student Journal* page 10.

Phonics/Word Study

Short *e* and Short *o*

▶ Display the following words: *check, crop,* and *bread.* Read them aloud. Ask: *How many short vowel sounds do you hear?* (Students should hear two.)

▶ Explain that there is a short *o* in the word *crop,* and that the short *e* is represented in two ways: *ch<u>e</u>ck* and *br<u>ea</u>d.* Segment each word so that students can find and concentrate on the vowel. First, say the whole word. Then, say the vowel and what comes after it, followed by the vowel alone. This helps students hear the vowel clearly.

check	eck	e
crop	op	o
bread	ead	ea

▶ Most short *e* words will have the single *e,* but there are some words that have the short *ea* pattern. (*head, dead, lead, read, tread*)

▶ Provide students with copies of the Short Vowel Patterns Sort Two: Short *e* and Short *o* sheet and have them begin sorting by the four headings shown. (See *Word Study Manual* page 36.) Be sure to model the correct placement for the first few words. Then have students work in pairs. One student can read the word aloud while the other determines the placement. When they are finished, have both students read each column to see if all the words have the same sound. Then have students switch roles.

▶ Because the short *e* and short *ea* in this sort cannot be distinguished by sound, students will have to use visual clues to separate the words.

▶ When confronted with a word with two or more syllables, students should identify the syllable with the short *e* or *o* vowel sound and concentrate only on that syllable.

▶ As a group, discuss the sort, students' observations, and the oddballs. *Gone* is an example of a word that sounds like short *o* but has the long *o* spelling. The first syllable in *person* has the short *e,* but it is tainted by the *r* influence.

Short Vowel Patterns Sort Two: Short *e* and Short *o*			
Short *e* (e)	**Short *o***	**Short *e* (ea)**	**Oddball**
check	lot	bread	gone
planet	possible	dead	person
telephone	not	dread	from
Internet	on	read	
pedal	stop	head	
jet	bebop	tread	
French	chop	lead	
effect	shop		
egg	crop		
best			

For more information on word sorts and spelling stages, see pages 5–31 in the *Word Study Manual.*

Focus on . . .

Use one or more activities in this section to focus on a particular area of need in your students.

Comprehension STRATEGY SUPPORT INDEPENDENT

To help those students who need more practice using the strategies covered in this lesson, work one-on-one or in small groups to apply the strategy prompts below. Apply the prompts to a *Reading Advantage* paperback, a classroom library book, or a new or familiar selection in the magazine. Always model your own thinking first.

Making Connections

• What does this story (article, passage) remind me of?

• What do I already know about this topic?

• Where have I heard about this topic before?

• What do I have in common with the characters, people, or situations in the text?

• What other books, stories, articles, movies, or TV shows does this text make me think about?

Writing **Double-entry Journal** INDEPENDENT

Have students make double-entry journal notes about "Crazy Cars" to show a personal connection to the selection. Ask students to look back through the guidebook to find phrases, passages, and ideas that were especially interesting to them. Explain to students that they should use the first column to write these interesting quotations from the selection. Then, in the second column, they should write their thoughts about the quotations. Students can interpret, disagree with, or make an association with each quotation. (See TE page 206 for a double-entry journal BLM.)

Quotation	My Thoughts
"There are guitar cars and shark cars."	I wonder if you can actually play a guitar car.

Fluency: Pacing

After students have read the selection at least once, use the "Art Cars" section on page 7 to model reading aloud smoothly and at an even pace. Then have pairs of students take turns reading aloud fluently the "Racecars" section on page 8.

As you listen to pairs read, use these prompts to guide them.

▶ Preview the text to avoid starts and stops.

▶ Read at an even pace. This will hold your partner's attention.

▶ Use the punctuation to help guide your pauses and expression.

When students read aloud, do they—

✓ demonstrate a smooth pace, not too fast or too slow?

✓ incorporate well-timed pauses between words and phrases?

✓ reflect an awareness and understanding of punctuation?

English Language Learners

To support students as they visualize, extend the fourth fix-up strategy on TE page 14.

1. Remind students that active readers visualize, or make mental pictures in their minds, as they read.

2. Read and discuss the information on page 7 of the selection. Have students use details from the text to draw a picture of one of the cars.

3. Have partners describe their drawings.

Independent Activity Options

While you work with individuals or small groups, others can work independently on one or more of the following options.

▶ Foundations paperback books, see TE pages 195–200

▶ Foundations *eZines*

▶ Repeat word sorts for this lesson

▶ *Student Journal* pages for this lesson

Assessment

Strategy Assessment

To help you and your students assess their use of comprehension strategies, ask the following questions. Students can complete a written response or provide verbal answers in a one-on-one reading conference.

- **Making Connections** Some companies are making small three-wheeled cars for people to drive in the city or around a suburb. These cars very fuel efficient and easy to park. Do you think this is a good idea? Why or why not? (Answers will vary. Students might say that such cars would be unsafe, even in slow-moving city traffic. Other students might think that small cars in the city make sense, especially for parking.)

For ongoing informal assessment, use the checklists on pages 61–64 of *Foundations Assessment*.

Word Study Assessment

Use these steps to help you and your students assess their understanding of short *e* and short *o* vowel sounds.

1. Display the following words: *met, mop, nest, plot, medal, prom, telegram, dread, drop,* and *on*.

2. Ask students to say each word and tell whether it has a short *e* or short *o* sound. The answers are shown.

Short *e*	Short *o*
met	mop
nest	plot
medal	prom
telegram	drop
dread	on

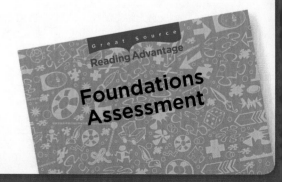

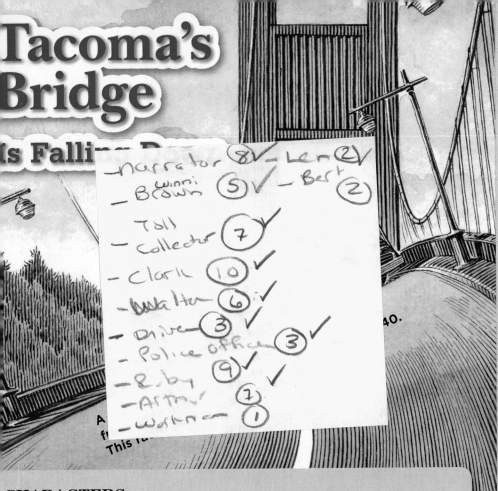

Tacoma's Bridge Is Falling Down

Tacoma's Bridge Is Falling Down
Motion, pages 11–16

SUMMARY
This **radio play** describes the fall of the Tacoma Narrows Bridge on November 7, 1940.

COMPREHENSION STRATEGIES
Inferential Thinking
Understanding Text Structure

WRITING
News Article

VOCABULARY
Illustrated Mini-Glossary

PHONICS/WORD STUDY
Short *u* and Short *a*

Lesson Vocabulary
sound	piers
engineers	suspension
stranded	bridge

MATERIALS
Motion, pp. 11–16
Student Journal, pp. 11–15
Word Study Manual, p. 37

CHARACTERS

Narrator

Winfield Brown—a 25-year-old college student

Toll Collector

Clark Eldridge—bridge project engineer

Walter Miles—Pacific Bridge Company employee

Driver

Police Officer

Ruby Jacox—Rapid Transfer Company truck passenger

Arthur Hagen—Rapid Transfer Company truck driver

Workman

Leonard Coatsworth—*Tacoma News Tribune* news editor

Bert Farquharson—University of Washington professor of engineering

11

Before Reading
 Use one or more activities.

Make a List
Tell students that they will read about a bridge named the Tacoma Narrows Bridge, built in Washington State. Have students free-associate to make a class list on the topic of bridges. Revisit the list after students read.

Bridges
1. over water, highways, railroad tracks
2. come in different shapes and sizes
3. drawbridges open for boats
4.

Vocabulary Preview
Have students begin the knowledge rating chart on *Student Journal* page 11. Revisit the chart later. (See Differentiated Instruction.)

Preview the Selection
Have students scan the play. Ask:
- What do you notice about a radio play that is different from a stage play?
- What do you predict will happen in the play?

Make Predictions/ Set Purpose
Students should use the information they gathered in previewing the selection to make predictions about what they will learn. If students have trouble generating a purpose for reading, suggest that they read to discover what happened to the Tacoma Narrows Bridge.

Vocabulary Preview

Work with students to read, pronounce, and establish meaning for the word *sound*.

How many syllables are in the word?	one
What other words have the same *ou* vowel sound?	*mound* *round* *found*
What other spelling patterns have that *ou* sound?	*cow* *how* *plow*
What is a synonym for this word?	*noise*
When might you use this word?	I heard a strange *sound*.
Can you think of or locate a meaning for *sound* other than "noise"?	a body of water, like Long Island Sound

Student Journal page 11

Building Vocabulary: Knowledge Rating Chart
Show your knowledge of each word by adding information to the other boxes in the row.

Word	Define or Use in a Sentence	Where Have I Seen or Heard It?	How Is It Used in the Selection?	Looks Like (Words or Sketch)
sound				
engineers				
stranded				
pliers				
suspension bridge				

Motion • Tacoma's Bridge Is Falling Down   11

Narrator: We now take you back to that fateful day of November 7, 1940, in Washington State. In front of us is the Tacoma Narrows Bridge. The bridge is beautiful as it stretches across Puget Sound. It's only been open for four months. People pay a toll to get across Puget Sound and to feel the bridge bounce. Its nickname is "Galloping Gertie." Engineers have been working to solve the bouncing problem. But most drivers, passengers, and walkers don't seem to mind it. They actually like the excitement of a moving bridge.

It's barely 10 a.m., and Winfield Brown is ready for a thrill.

Winfield Brown: How much to walk across?

Toll Collector: A dime each way.

(Change jingles.)

Brown: Gertie has a real gallop today.

Toll Collector: That wind must be blowing forty miles an hour.

Brown: I was hoping to get a little fun out of it.

Toll Collector: I'm sure you won't be disappointed.

Narrator: Brown walks to the other side, enjoying the bridge's galloping movement. Then he decides to walk back. As he does, the wind begins to blow harder. Suddenly, the bridge begins to move wildly. When it does, the phone rings in Clark Eldridge's office. He supervised the building of the bridge. Now he's in charge of fixing its problem.

(Phone rings.)

Clark Eldridge: Hello?

Walter Miles: Clark, it's Walter Miles of the Pacific Bridge Company.

Eldridge: Oh, yes. Hello, Walter.

Miles: You've got to get to the Tacoma Narrows Bridge.

Eldridge: Why?

Miles: It's moving. A lot. I'm looking at it right now.

Eldridge: I just drove across this morning. It wasn't rippling any more than usual.

Miles: Well, it is now. It's starting to swing.

Eldridge: Swing? What do you mean?

Miles: It's twisting up into the air. It's about to go!

> 12

During Reading

Comprehension

INFERENTIAL THINKING

Use these questions to model how to make inferences from the narrator's speech at the top of page 12. Then have students reveal inferences they make as they read another section.

- What does the narrator say?
- What do I already know about bridges?
- What new ideas can I infer?

(See Differentiated Instruction.)

Teacher Think Aloud

The narrator says that the Tacoma Narrows Bridge is new and that it bounces a lot. I've driven across very long, high bridges that didn't seem to move at all. I've heard on the news about bridges that have broken apart. Therefore, I infer that a bridge that moves as much as this bridge does may be dangerous.

Comprehension

UNDERSTANDING TEXT STRUCTURE

Use these questions to model how to identify the rising action of the play, using details on pages 12 and 13. Then have students describe the climax of the play on pages 14 and 15.

- What happens on pages 12 and 13?
- What is the rising action?
- How is the suspense created?

Officer: That's Professor Farquharson (FAR qwar sun). He's one of the bridge engineers. He's been trying to figure out how to fix the bridge for months. He's been up there taking pictures since 9:30 this morning.

Driver: Is anyone else on the bridge?

Officer: I'm afraid so.

Narrator: Two guys are in their delivery truck. Their names are Arthur Hagen and Ruby Jacox.

(A loud wind howls.)

Ruby Jacox: Arthur, what's going on? The truck is moving across the road.

Arthur Hagen: I can't control it. The bridge is rocking. The toll collector warned us it was a little shaky.

Jacox: Well, it's more than a little shaky. Stop the truck! We've got to get out.

(There's the sound of truck doors opening and shutting. Then, a thud as bodies land on pavement.)

Jacox: Owwww!

Hagen: Ooomph!

Jacox: Arthur, I can't walk.

Hagen: Grab the center of the road. There's a ridge. We're going to have to crawl.

Jacox: But there's no way I can make it. . . .

Hagen: Just keep talking. That will make it easier. We'll get there together.

(A horrible groan of twisting steel fills the air.)

Hagen: Oh no! Concrete is breaking off the bridge. It's falling apart.

Eldridge: Oh no! You mean go into the water?

Miles: Yep. It looks like it.

Eldridge: I'll be right there!

(Phone hung up quickly. Door slams.)

Narrator: As the bridge begins to twist more and more, the police close it down. Drivers are stranded at the bridge entrance.

Driver: Officer, what's going on?

Police Officer: Nobody's going across. Too dangerous.

Driver: What about that guy on the tower? The one with the cameras.

Comprehension
INFERENTIAL THINKING

To help students think inferentially, use this activity.

1. Tell students that they can make inferences from what they read or see, as well as from prior knowledge.
2. Have students practice making inferences about these brief scenarios.
   - There was a party next door. Luisa couldn't sleep.
   - Ty lived near a busy street. He heard a crashing noise.
   - A swing in the playground was moving back and forth.

Teacher Think Aloud

On pages 12 and 13, the action rises. Winfield Brown decides to take a walk across the new bridge to feel it bounce. On his way back, the bridge begins to twist and move wildly. A truck on the bridge loses control. Walkers can hardly stand. Parts of the bridge are breaking off. This buildup of suspense is called rising action.

Fix-Up Strategies

Offer these strategies to help students read independently.

If you don't understand what you're reading:

- Reread the difficult section to look for clues to help you comprehend.
- Read ahead to find clues to help you comprehend.
- Retell, or say in your own words, what you've read.
- Visualize, or form mental pictures of, what you've read.

If you don't understand a word:

- Reread the sentence. Look for ideas and words that provide meaning clues.
- Find clues by reading a few sentences before and after the confusing word.
- Look for the base or root word and think about its meaning.
- Think about the topic or plot at this point to see if either offers meaning clues.

Discussion Questions

To help students respond to the second discussion question, discuss the different purposes authors have for writing.

1. Tell students that authors write for three main purposes: to inform (or explain), to persuade, or to entertain.

2. Ask volunteers to provide examples of books or stories they've read that reflect each purpose. Make a list by category on the board.

3. Try out each purpose for this selection. Which one makes the most sense? Could the author have had more than just one purpose for writing?

Student Journal pages 12–13

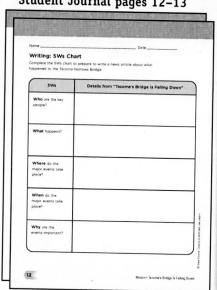

Jacox: The bridge can't break! Government engineers inspected it. Experts planned it.

Hagen: Well, they didn't plan on *this*. We've got to get to the end.

Jacox: I can't go any farther. My knees are bruised. And my hip and ankles are killing me.

(A loud crash. Sound of shattering glass.)

Jacox: Aaaaa! That lamppost just missed my head.

(More crashes and shattering.)

Hagen: They're all coming down. We need to get out of here. I've got you by the shoulder. Just keep crawling. I think the wind is dying down.

Jacox: Look in front of us! That van is backing our way. Does it see us? Are we going to get run over?

(Brakes screech. Van door opens.)

Workman: Get in! We'll get you off the bridge.

Jacox: You saved our lives!

(Van speeds away.)

Narrator: At the same time, Winfield Brown makes it off safely. He stumbles into the toll collector's booth.

Toll Collector: You're pretty beaten up.

Brown: *(gasping)* I've ridden on a roller coaster. Let me tell you, it was nothing compared to this!

Toll Collector: They should have closed the bridge before you got on.

Brown: I think someone else is still on the bridge. I passed him. I couldn't stop. He was on his knees trying to make it to the other side.

Narrator: The man whom Brown passed Leonard Coatsworth. He drove the la car onto the bridge. He is a newspape editor, traveling to his vacation home. The winds forced him out of his car. I makes it off the bridge and heads for the tollbooth.

Toll Collector: Are you all right?

Leonard Coatsworth: My car was slidin across the road. The wind slammed me against the side. I had to crawl out through the window. I left everything in it. Even my daughter's dog, Tubby. I tried to go back for him. I was afraid the bridge was about to break up.

Toll Collector: You're probably right. Lo at the way it's twisting up into the air!

Coatsworth: I should call the newspaper office. Can I use your phone? We need a photographer here, fast.

Toll Collector: Help yourself.

Narrator: Photographers arrive from the newspaper, but Bert Farquharson neve stops taking pictures. Clark Eldridge gets to the bridge, too. He climbs to the top of the tower with Farquharson.

Eldridge: What's going on, Bert? It looks like a corkscrew.

Bert Farquharson: It has never twisted like this before. That wind is lifting it forty-five degrees.

Eldridge: The wind is blowing about forty-two miles per hour. This bridge should be able to stand up to nearly three times that.

Farquharson: It's my job to figure out why it can't.

14

After Reading   Use one or more activities.

Check Purpose

Have students determine whether their purpose was met. Did students discover what happened to the Tacoma Narrows Bridge?

Discussion Questions

Ask the following questions. (See Differentiated Instruction.)

1. How would you have reacted if you were on the Tacoma Narrows Bridge on November 7, 1940? (Making Connections)

2. What do you think is the author's purpose for writing the play? (Inferential Thinking)

3. What can be learned from the fall of the Tacoma Narrows Bridge? (Evaluate)

Revisit: List

Give students an opportunity to add information to the list about bridges that they began before reading.

Revisit: Knowledge Rating Chart

Have students complete their knowledge rating chart on *Student Journal* page 11. Are there any adjustments or changes they would like to make? Students can add new notes, if necessary.

Eldridge: I'll tell you why. They should have used my design. They just wanted to save money. That roadway deck is too light. And those cables aren't spaced right. When the wind stops, we'll have to install more cables. They'll run from the piers to the road.

Narrator: Eldridge leaves Farquharson at the tower. He waits in the tollbooth for the bridge to settle down. It never does. A 600-foot piece of bridge drops into the water. The road drops and rises under Farquharson, bouncing him like a trampoline. He keeps taking photos.

The bridge continues to fall. Farquharson races to safety. Eldridge watches his bridge twist violently in the strong winds and finally collapse into the cold water.

Sadly, Coatsworth sees his car with his dog inside plunge into the water. While the disaster took no human life, it shook the engineering community. It forever changed the way bridges were built around the world. ◆

Facts About Tacoma Narrows Bridge

Opening day: July 1, 1940
Number of cars crossing opening day: 2,000
Length: 5,939 feet, third-longest suspension bridge in the world.
Height of each tower: 443 feet
Weight of each tower: 1,927 tons
Cost: $6,618,138

15

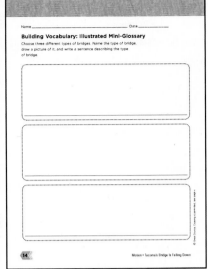

Student Journal page 14

Answers for **Student Journal page 15** are Short *u* Words: *suddenly, stumbles;* Short *a* Words: *fact, cameras.*

Writing News Article

Have students write a newspaper article describing the fall of the Tacoma Narrows Bridge. Model by showing a short newspaper article that has a headline, byline, and city/date. Point out how the article addresses the 5Ws (*who, what, where, when,* and *why*). Then have students prepare to write their article by writing responses to the 5Ws questions on *Student Journal* page 12. Students can refer to those details as they write the news article on *Student Journal* page 13.

Vocabulary
Illustrated Mini-Glossary

Help students prepare for *Student Journal* page 14 by brainstorming a list of different types of bridges. Have students refer to page 16 for ideas. Then have students use *Student Journal* page 14 to create an illustrated mini-glossary for three different types of bridges. Possible bridge types include cantilever, drawbridge, railway, and arch.

Phonics/Word Study
Short *u* and Short *a*

Write the words *blunt* and *splash* on the board and read them aloud. Ask students what short vowel sounds they hear. (*u, a*) Together, brainstorm other words with the same short vowel sounds. Now, work with students to complete the in-depth short vowel activity on TE page 25. For additional support, have students complete *Student Journal* page 15.

BREAKING BRIDGES

Often, more can be learned through failure than through success. The Tacoma Narrows Bridge was designed to be tall and graceful. It *was* beautiful, but it wasn't strong enough. After it fell, scientists learned more. They studied how wind and moving cars affect a bridge. A bridge should be able to move a little.

It just shouldn't move too much. Engineers improved the design of bridges. Now they can be both beautiful and strong.

Unfortunately, some lessons come the hard way. Several bridges fell before "Galloping Gertie" did. They fell before the scientists and engineers had learned enough.

Bridge: Tay Railway Bridge
Type: Railway
Collapsed: 1879
Connected: Dundee and Wormit, Scotland
Body of Water: Firth of Tay

Bridge: Niagara-Clifton Bridge
Type: Suspension
Collapsed: 1889
Connected: Niagara Falls, New York, and Clifton, Ontario, Canada
Body of Water: Niagara River

Bridge: Quebec City Bridge
Type: Cantilever
Collapsed: 1907
Connected: North and south shores of Quebec City, Canada
Body of Water: St. Lawrence River

 16

Phonics/Word Study

Short *u* and Short *a*

▶ Place the following words on the board or on chart paper: *much* and *crash*. Read aloud the words. Ask: *What are the two short vowel sounds that you hear? How are their sounds different?*

▶ Segment each word so that students can find and concentrate on the vowel. First, say the whole word. Then, say the vowel and what comes after it, followed by the vowel alone. This helps students hear the vowel clearly.

much   uch   u
crash   ash   a

▶ Provide students with copies of the Short Vowel Patterns Sort Three: Short *u* and Short *a* sheet and have them begin sorting by the three headings shown. (See *Word Study Manual* page 37.) Model the correct placement for the first few words. Have students work in pairs. One student can read the word aloud while the other determines the placement. When they are finished, have both students read each column to see if all the words have the same sound. Then have students switch roles.

▶ When confronted with a word with two or more syllables, students should identify the syllable with the short *u* or *a* vowel sound and concentrate only on that syllable.

▶ As a group, discuss the sort, students' observations, and why *start* and *harder* ended up in the Oddball column. Both words have an *r* following the vowel, and that always makes the vowel lose its pure sound.

Short Vowel Patterns Sort Three: Short *u* and Short *a*		
Short *u*	**Short *a***	**Oddball**
truck	crash	start
much	stand	harder
stumble	sadly	install
plunge	strand	
number	shatter	
thud	transfer	
shut	passenger	
fun	can't	
up	slam	
plump	camera	

For more information on word sorts and spelling stages, see pages 5–31 in the *Word Study Manual*.

Focus on . . .

Use one or more activities in this section to focus on a particular area of need in your students.

Comprehension   STRATEGY SUPPORT

To help those students who need more practice using the strategies covered in this lesson, work one-on-one or in small groups to apply the strategy prompts below. Apply the prompts to a *Reading Advantage* paperback, a classroom library book, or a new or familiar selection in the magazine. Always model your own thinking first.

Inferential Thinking

• What are the causes or effects of this event?

• What do I learn from the character or person's thoughts, words, or actions?

• What do I know (or infer) from the text that the author hasn't stated directly?

• What conclusions can I draw?

Understanding Text Structure

• What kind of text is this? (book, story, article, guidebook, play, manual)

• How does the author organize the text? (cause-effect, problem-solution, chronological order, description, question-answer, comparison-contrast)

• What details support my thoughts about the text structure?

• What is the cause (effect, problem, solution, order, question, answer)?

• If fiction, who are the characters? What is the setting, plot, conflict, and resolution?

Writing Acrostic Poem

Have students write an acrostic poem using the word *bridge*. Explain to students that an acrostic poem uses the letters in a topic word (*bridge*) to begin each line. All lines of the poem should relate to or describe the topic word. Each line can be a phrase or a complete sentence. On the board or on chart paper, write the following example of an acrostic for the word *sun*.

> **S**hines brightly
> **U**p in the sky
> **N**ice and warm on my skin

Now have students begin their **BRIDGE** poem.

Fluency: Expression

After students have read the selection at least once, have them focus on reading it aloud. First, model reading a section expressively. Then, form small groups for reading aloud. Assign each group a different section. Tell students that the dialogue should flow smoothly, as though they were conversing naturally, not reading. Have students practice the reading in their groups and then present the radio play to the class.

As you listen to groups read, use these prompts to guide them.

▶ Read your lines several times so you are comfortable with them.

▶ Read with expression. Put yourself in the role of the character.

▶ Use the punctuation marks for clues to expression. Raise your voice slightly at the end of a question. Pause when you see a comma or a period.

When students read aloud, do they—

✓ reflect an understanding of the text?

✓ demonstrate appropriate timing, stress, and intonation?

✓ incorporate appropriate speed and phrasing?

English Language Learners

Support students as they preview the selection on TE page 19.

1. Display a K-W-L chart with the headings "What We Know," "What We Want to Know," and "What We Learned."

2. Have students discuss what they know and want to know about bridges. Record their responses.

3. After reading, revisit the chart. Ask students to discuss what they've learned. Clarify any misconceptions. Record information that students learned in the third column.

Independent Activity Options

While you work with individuals or small groups, others can work independently on one or more of the following options.

▶ Foundations paperback books, see TE pages 195–200

▶ Foundations *eZines*

▶ Repeat word sorts for this lesson

▶ *Student Journal* pages for this lesson

Assessment

Strategy Assessment

To help you and your students assess their use of comprehension strategies, ask the following questions. Students can complete a written response or provide verbal answers in a one-on-one reading conference.

1. **Inferential Thinking** Suppose that an old bridge, which has worked well for many years, suddenly collapses. What inference could you make from this? (Answers will vary. Students may infer that parts of the bridge had most likely worn out, or that the bridge had been built for a lighter traffic load than it had later experienced.)

2. **Understanding Text Structure** What are some details of the rising action of the play? (Answers will vary. Students may say that a bridge worker made a frantic call to the man who supervised the building of the bridge, the bridge was moving more than usual, a truck loses control on the bridge, and walkers could hardly stand.)

See *Foundations Assessment* pages 10–13 for formal assessment to go with *Motion*.

Word Study Assessment

Use these steps to help you and your students assess their understanding of short *u* and short *a* vowel sounds.

1. Display the following words: *mud, crash, shatter, luck, mattress, mutt, cram, fumble, duck,* and *sham.*

2. Ask students to say the words aloud and write them in the correct column. The answers are shown.

Short *u*	Short *a*
mud	crash
luck	shatter
mutt	mattress
fumble	cram
duck	sham

When Nothing Can Stop You

Artist **Chuck Close** became paralyzed. He could no longer walk. He could no longer hold a paintbrush. **Christy Brown** was born with cerebral palsy. He could not control his body. But he could control his left foot. Imagine if you couldn't use your hands? Would you let that stop you? It didn't stop Chuck Close or Christy Brown.

17

SUMMARY
Profiles of artists Chuck Close and Christy Brown tell how they achieved their artistic goals despite daunting physical disabilities. A **poem** follows.

COMPREHENSION STRATEGIES
Inferential Thinking
Determining Importance

WRITING
Letter

VOCABULARY
Prefixes *im-, dis-*

PHONICS/WORD STUDY
Sorting across the Short Vowels (*a, e, i, o, u*)

Lesson Vocabulary

coped	impatient
paralyzed	cerebral palsy
photo-realism	

MATERIALS
Motion, pp. 17–23
Student Journal, pp. 16–20
Word Study Manual, p. 38

Before Reading Use one or more activities.

Make an Association Web ▶

Make an association web to help students identify characteristics or traits that they associate with someone who is a role model. Suggest to students that as they read the selection, they consider whether the two men profiled are role models for others, and why. After students have finished reading, return to the association web to record their additional ideas.

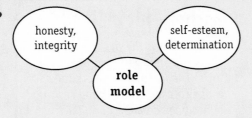

honesty, integrity

self-esteem, determination

role model

Vocabulary Preview

Write the vocabulary words on the board or on chart paper and read them aloud to clarify pronunciations. Ask students to share what they already know about the words. Have students begin the predictions chart on *Student Journal* page 16. Tell students to fill in only the prediction column. They will complete the chart after they have finished reading the selection. (See Differentiated Instruction.)

Vocabulary Preview

Work with students to read, pronounce, and establish meaning for the word *photo-realism*.

What are the word parts?	*photo- realism*
Where have you seen the first word part before?	*photograph* *photocopy* *photogenic*
What do you call the word part?	a root
What does the root mean?	light
What does the word mean?	a kind of painting so realistic that it resembles a photograph, including any flaws a photograph might capture
When might you use this word?	The artist who did a portrait of the president used the technique of *photo-realism*.

Chuck Close

Growing up in Washington State, Chuck Close wasn't good at sports. He wasn't good at math, history, or English. But he was very good at art. It made him feel special.

Close had trouble learning in school. So he painted for his teachers to show he cared about their lessons. For history class, he painted the Lewis and Clark Trail. For English class, he made drawings in a book of poems.

Close's father died when Chuck was only eleven. He coped with his sadness by drawing. As he grew older, Close went to college. He studied art and worked hard. Later, he moved to New York City. He worked even harder. Soon, the art world began to notice Close. Galleries were showing his paintings. His work was selling. People said he had talent. Everything was going great.

This self-portrait of Chuck Close was created before his stroke.

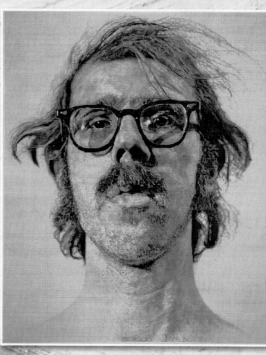

A Terrible Blow

In 1988, Close had a stroke. He was forty-eight. An artery broke inside him. His body went very still. The doctors told him the bad news. He was paralyzed.

Close's limbs would no longer work. He couldn't use his hands. He couldn't hold a paintbrush. He couldn't even walk. He would have to sit in a wheelchair. The art world thought he would never paint again.

But this did not stop Chuck Close. "In life," he said, "you have to deal with fear. A part of you will say, 'I can't do it.' You have to fight that part." That's what Close believed.

18

Preview the Selection

Have students look through the five pages of the selection to examine the title, the introductory note, the headings, and the photographs. Use these or similar prompts to discuss the selection.

- Will you read fiction or nonfiction? How do you know?
- What clues do the headings on pages 18–20 give you? What do you think you'll read about?

Teacher Think Aloud

After looking at the first few pages, I think that this will be a nonfiction article. The introductory note talks about two people who sound real, and the headings describe how Chuck Close fights back from a terrible blow. The introductory note mentions that Close became paralyzed. My guess is that the terrible blow is the incident that caused his paralysis. I'll read to find out.

Make Predictions/ Set Purpose

Students should use the information they gathered in previewing the selection to make predictions about what they will learn. If students have trouble generating a purpose for reading, suggest that they read to discover how each artist coped with his physical challenges.

Fighting Back

The doctors gave Close exercises. They gave him treatments. But none of it helped him paint again. He'd have to figure that out for himself.

Close liked to make very big paintings. But he could not climb a ladder. So he got a forklift. It raised and lowered him. With the lift, he could reach the entire canvas. Later, he found a motorized easel that moved the canvas around for him.

Close could not hold a paintbrush. So he got a special device. It strapped the paintbrush to his wrist. He could not use his hands to move the brush. So he taught his arm muscles to move it. This was very hard. It took him months to finish one painting.

"I was very upset at first," he said, "because I had no strength, and I couldn't hold my arms up for very long."

Chuck Close at work in his studio

Chuck's Big Night

For three years, Close worked. He painted and painted. Finally, he was ready. The art world was going to see his new work.

Close was nervous. Would the critics like his new paintings? Yes! They did. They said that these new paintings were stronger. They were more impressive. Chuck Close's art was better than before.

What does the art world say now? Chuck Close is one of the most important living artists. His paintings are shown in the world's greatest museums. How much are his paintings worth? One recently sold for nearly 5 million dollars!

"It was always my nature to be positive," says Close. "If you are positive . . . you can be dealt a losing hand. And make it a winning hand."

Here is one of Chuck Close's paintings. It was painted after his stroke.

19

DIFFERENTIATED INSTRUCTION
SMALL GROUP

Comprehension
INFERENTIAL THINKING

To help students practice inferential thinking, follow these steps:

1. Ask these questions:
   - What do you infer about someone who complains a lot?
   - What do you infer about a person who stands in a long line for tickets?
   - What do you infer about someone who makes friends with kids who may not fit in?

2. Point out that students will make different inferences on the basis of their own experiences.

Student Journal page 16

Name _____ Date _____

Building Vocabulary: Predictions
How do you predict these words will be used in "When Nothing Can Stop You"? Write your answers in the second column. Next, read the selection. Then, clarify your answers in the third column.

Word	My prediction for how the word will be used	How the word is actually used
coped		
paralyzed		
photo-realism		
impatient		
cerebral palsy		

16 — Motion • When Nothing Can Stop You and Sea Legs

During Reading

Comprehension
INFERENTIAL THINKING
SMALL GROUP

Use these questions to model how to draw conclusions about Chuck Close. Then have students draw their own conclusions about him.

- What does this article tell me about Chuck Close?
- What do I know from my own life that helps me understand him?
- What words describe Close?

(See Differentiated Instruction.)

Teacher Think Aloud

This article tells what happened to Chuck Close and how he overcame his difficulties. I have never experienced anything as bad as he did, but I do know how hard it is to keep going and not be discouraged when bad things happen. I would describe Close as strong, clever, and determined, with a positive outlook.

Comprehension
DETERMINING IMPORTANCE
SMALL GROUP

Use these questions to model how to determine the most important ideas in the section "Chuck Close" on page 18. Then have students determine the importance of ideas in the next section.

- What are the most important ideas in this section?
- How can I support my beliefs?
- What does the author want me to understand?

Making Faces

Chuck Close paints faces. He sees many things in faces. He sees thoughts, feelings, and emotions. Faces are alive to him.

Close's work is called photo-realism. He takes a photo of a face. Then he paints what he sees in that photo. A picture may seem still, but he gives it life. He paints it on a huge canvas. How huge? Nine or more feet tall!

The Grid Method

Close's way of painting is very interesting. He paints thousands of squares. Each square is like a puzzle piece. All together the squares form one big image.

One Square at a Time

Could you spend months painting just one picture? Doesn't Close get impatient? He says no. He says it's like knitting a sweater. If you do a little knitting every day, one day you will be done. And finally you'll have a sweater.

What if you have a big job to do? Do you wonder how you are ever going to finish it? You should focus on one small step at a time. That's what Close does. He paints big paintings. But each one is made up of many small squares.

"Each little square is like a painting," he says. "And it's like a celebration when each one is done."

That's how Close goes through life. He takes one day at a time. He does not brood about the past. Or worry about the future. He's never said, "Why me?"

This is a close-up of just one part of Close's 2000 self-portrait. See how it is made up of small squares? This is Close's grid method. He takes a photo. He makes a grid on it. Each square in the grid is a small painting in itself. It has its own shapes and colors.

"People find this hard to believe," says Close. "[Even] sitting in a wheelchair with hands that don't work, and unable to walk, I would define myself as being lucky. But I feel lucky. . . . The last seventeen years have been the happiest seventeen years of my life."

This is a self-portrait of Chuck Close. He painted it in 2000.

20

Fix-Up Strategies

Offer these strategies to help students read independently.

If you don't understand what you're reading:

- Reread the difficult section to look for clues to help you comprehend.
- Read ahead to find clues to help you comprehend.
- Retell, or say in your own words, what you've read.
- Visualize, or form mental pictures of, what you've read.

If you don't understand a word:

- Reread the sentence. Look for ideas and words that provide meaning clues.
- Find clues by reading a few sentences before and after the confusing word.
- Look for the base or root word and think about its meaning.
- Think about the topic or plot at this point to see if either offers meaning clues.

Christy Brown

Imagine that you cannot walk, and your hands won't work. You cannot feed yourself or bathe yourself. There is only one part of your body that *does* work. You can control your left foot.

What would you do? Could you learn how to do the things you want to do by using just your left foot? Could you learn to paint? To write? To turn on the radio by using your left foot? Impossible? It's not. That's what Christy Brown did.

Brown was born in Ireland. His family was very big and very poor. He had cerebral palsy. He couldn't control his body or his speech. The doctors said there was a problem with his mind. But there wasn't. His mother believed in her son. "It is his body that is shattered, and not his mind," she said. "I'm sure of it."

One day, his sister was playing with chalk and a blackboard. Brown picked up the chalk with his left foot. He made marks on the blackboard. His mother was thrilled. She taught him the alphabet. It was very hard for Brown. But he started to write with his foot. He signed his initials C. B. Then, he wrote his name. Finally, he began to write.

He also began to draw and to paint, always with his left foot. At twelve years old he won a children's painting competition. He went on to become an accomplished painter.

As he grew older, his writing improved. He wrote his life story. His book is called *My Left Foot*. It was made into a famous movie of the same name. Christy Brown also wrote four other novels and a collection of poetry. He died in 1981 at the young age of forty-nine, but he inspired people all over the world.

Christy Brown draws with his left foot.

No Dis

Disability. That's what these men were told they had. But take away the *dis*. And what are you left with? *Ability*. That's what these two men focused on. Their abilities. And that's why nothing could stop them. ◆

21

After Reading
Use one or more activities.

Check Purpose

Have students determine whether their purpose was met. Did they discover how each artist coped with his disabilities and was able to work?

Discussion Questions

Continue the group discussion with the following questions.

1. What did each artist do to overcome his physical challenges? (Details)

2. Why do you think the author chose to write about Chuck Close and Christy Brown? (Draw Conclusions)

3. Do you think the two artists qualify as role models for others? Why? (Making Connections)

Revisit: Association Web

Have students return to the association web they began in Before Reading, to add any additional ideas or thoughts they have about being a role model.

Revisit: Predictions Chart

Have students return to the predictions chart on *Student Journal* page 16 to complete the third column and show how the vocabulary words are actually used in the selection.

Vocabulary

Prefixes *im-, dis-*

To help students respond to the activity on *Student Journal* page 19, use these steps:

1. Explain that a prefix is a word part added to the beginning of a word, changing the meaning of that word.

2. Write the prefixes *im-* and *dis-*. Tell students that these prefixes give base words an opposite or negative meaning. Guide students in identifying the prefixes, base words, and meanings of *imperfect* and *distrust*.

Student Journal page 19

Name_____ Date_____

Building Vocabulary: Prefixes *im-* and *dis-*
The words listed in the first column all have the prefixes *im-* or *dis-*. Write the definition of each word in the second column. Then, with a partner, think of and say several possible sentences for each word.

Both *im-* and *dis-* can mean "not" or "the opposite of."

Word	Definition
improper	
dislike	
impolite	
impractical	
disrespect	
disorder	

Motion • When Nothing Can Stop You and Sea Legs — 19

Sea Legs

22

Writing Letter

Have students write a letter to either Chuck Close or the family of Christy Brown, explaining why they think the artist is an important role model to them or to other young people. To begin, have students review the text, noting details about the artist and his life that they consider admirable. Have students record these details on *Student Journal* page 17. Students can then use their list of details to write a letter on *Student Journal* page 18.

Vocabulary Prefixes *im-, dis-*

Tell students that the word *impatient* has a prefix that changes the meaning of the base word. The prefix *im-* means "not or opposite." (*patient*: able to wait; *impatient*: not able to wait) Tell students that the prefix *dis-*, as in *disability*, can also give a base word the opposite meaning. Work together to identify other words with the prefix *dis-*. (*disbelieve, disregard*) Then have students complete *Student Journal* page 19. (See Differentiated Instruction.)

Phonics/Word Study

Short Vowels (*a, e, i, o, u*)

Display the following words: *chat, egg, hint, flop,* and *cusp*. Ask volunteers to identify the short vowel sound in each word. As each vowel sound is identified, ask students to suggest other words with the same sound. Now, work with students to complete the in-depth short vowels activity on TE page 34. For additional support, have students complete *Student Journal* page 20.

Sun comes up, tide is down,
And my feet touch the ground.
Solid earth holds me up on the bank.

Wet sand's cool, dock is smooth.
It stays put when I move.
But on water, you never stay still.

There's a current that's strong,
Always moves you along.
It's a power you have to get used to.

We've been fishing for years,
But I once had my fears.
Dad would joke about getting my sea legs.

It's a laugh we have now:
I once didn't know how
To get used to the great waves that rocked us.

Our first trip, I was eight.
I looked down and thought, "Great."
Didn't know then "Sea Legs" was a mindset.

I sat still in our boat,
My heart stuck in my throat.
I was too scared to move from the corner.

When the sea became calm,
My dad gave me his palm,
Made me stand next to him at the wheel.

I had heard it was true
That the world was bright blue,
But I needed to see for myself.

There's a strength to the sea,
But it shared it with me.
Standing up, I was part of its greatness.

Now ten years since that May,
Still I think of the day,
When I first learned to walk on the ocean.

>>> 23

Poem: Sea Legs

Read the poem aloud as students follow along. Discuss the poem.

- What is the setting of the poem?
- Who are the characters?
- What does the title of the poem mean or suggest to you?
- How does the speaker in the poem seem to feel about the experience?

Answers for **Student Journal page 20** are Short *a*: *slab, packet, attract*; Short *e*: *Web site, pebbly, fetch*; Short *u*: *donut, chuckle, public*; Short *o*: *shoppers, novels, forgot*; Short *i*: *pickle, window, since.*

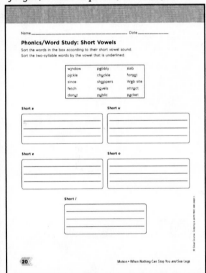

Sorting across the Short Vowels (*a, e, i, o, u*)

This sort is an opportunity to revisit and review all five short vowels.

▶ Provide students with copies of the Sort across the Short Vowels (*a, e, i, o, u*) sheet and have students sort for both speed and accuracy. (See *Word Study Manual* page 38.) Since this is a sound sort, not a pattern sort, it is imperative that students' attention be on the sound of the vowel. You can use picture cards or have students work in pairs. One student can read the word aloud, while the other student listens and places the word in the correct column.

▶ When confronted with a word with two or more syllables, students should identify the syllable with the vowel sound under consideration and concentrate only on that syllable.

▶ When pairs have completed their sorts, have students time themselves to see how fast they can do it. Being able to sort both quickly and accurately means mastery of the short vowel sounds.

▶ Note: You may wish to create an oddball category for *walk, tall,* and *small.* They do not have the same short *a* sound as the other short *a* words.

Sort across the Short Vowels (*a, e, i, o, u*)				
Short *a*	Short *e*	Short *i*	Short *o*	Short *u*
hand	lesson	English	stop	Chuck
class	selling	still	body	paintbrush
ladder	went	himself	prop	muscle
strapped	never	sit	doctor	upset
walk	help	sick	long	focus
tall	upset	forklift	strong	lucky
small	egg	wrist		thud
	himself			months

For more information on word sorts and spelling stages, see pages 5–31 in the *Word Study Manual.*

Focus on . . .

Use one or more activities in this section to focus on a particular area of need in your students.

Comprehension STRATEGY SUPPORT

To help those students who need more practice using the strategies covered in this lesson, work one-on-one or in small groups to apply the strategy prompts below. Apply the prompts to a *Reading Advantage* paperback, a classroom library book, or a new or familiar selection in the magazine. Always model your own thinking first.

Inferential Thinking

- What are the causes or effects of this event?
- What do I learn from the character or person's thoughts, words, or actions?
- What do I know (or infer) from the text that the author hasn't stated directly?
- What conclusions can I draw?

Determining Importance

- What is the most important idea in the paragraph? How can I prove it?
- Which details are unimportant? Why?
- What does the author want me to understand?
- Why is this information important (or not important) to me?

Writing Personal Timeline

Ask students to think about the challenges and successes in their own lives. Have students make personal timelines on which they record events that have been especially important in their lives. Encourage students to use the timeline included in the selection "Crazy Cars" as a model. If students prefer, they can arrange their timeline events horizontally. Display the sample below. Encourage students to illustrate their timelines.

Timeline

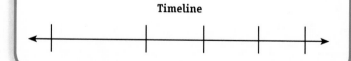

Fluency: Pacing

After students have read the profile of Christy Brown at least once, have them work on fluency by rereading it aloud. For this fluency activity, have students focus on pacing, reading at an appropriate rate and pausing at natural spots. Before pairs begin rereading the profile aloud, model reading aloud with an appropriate pace. Then point out the fundamentals of pacing.

▶ Read at a steady, smooth speed.
▶ Show an understanding of key phrases through changes in tone and inflection.
▶ Use punctuation such as commas, periods, and question marks to guide your pauses.
▶ Adjust your pacing to heighten or stress dramatic content.

When students read aloud, do they—

✓ demonstrate a smooth pace, not too fast or too slow?
✓ incorporate well-timed pauses between words and phrases?
✓ reflect an awareness and understanding of punctuation?

English Language Learners

Support students as they preview the selection on TE page 28 by examining multiple-meaning words.

1. Write these words on the board: *work, broke,* and *stroke.*
2. Discuss the multiple meanings of each word. For example, *work* can be "what someone does for a living" and "something someone creates."
3. Model how to determine the meaning of each word as it is used on page 18 of the selection.

Independent Activity Options

While you work with individuals or small groups, others can work independently on one or more of the following options.

▶ Foundations paperback books, see TE pages 195–200
▶ Foundations *eZines*
▶ Repeat word sorts for this lesson
▶ *Student Journal* pages for this lesson

Assessment

Strategy Assessment

To help you and your students assess their use of comprehension strategies, ask the following questions. Students can complete a written response or provide verbal answers in a one-on-one reading conference.

1. **Inferential Thinking** What conclusions can you draw about Christy Brown? (Answers will vary. Students might conclude that he was very intelligent as well as talented, and that his desire to express himself was strong.)
2. **Determining Importance** If you were telling a friend about Chuck Close, what are the important ideas you would relate? (Answers will vary. Students might tell what happened to him and how he overcame his disability.)

For ongoing informal assessment, use the checklists on pages 61–64 of *Foundations Assessment.*

Word Study Assessment

Use these steps to help you and your students assess their understanding of sorting across the short vowels *a, e, i, o,* and *u.*

1. Display the following words: *let, luck, pass, stick, drop, body, flap, tell, thud,* and *miss.*
2. Have students say each word aloud and then say which short vowel sound they hear. The answers are shown.

Word	Short Vowel
let	*e*
luck	*u*
pass	*a*
stick	*i*
drop	*o*
body	*o*
flap	*a*
tell	*e*
thud	*u*
miss	*i*

Foundations Assessment

LESSON 5
The Other Side of Flying

Motion, pages 24–28

SUMMARY

This **short story** tells about a teenage boy who knows a lot about planes, but only truly begins to understand them when he experiences his first airplane trip.

COMPREHENSION STRATEGIES

Monitor Understanding

WRITING

Character Sketch

VOCABULARY

Antonyms

PHONICS/WORD STUDY

Short and Long *a*

Lesson Vocabulary

offense	mismatched
obsessed	hazy
predictable	

MATERIALS

Motion, pp. 24–28
Student Journal, pp. 21–25
Word Study Manual, p. 39

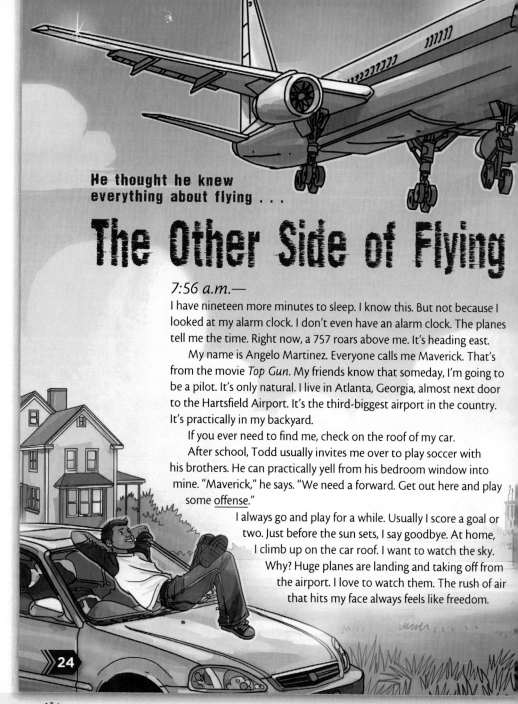

He thought he knew everything about flying . . .

The Other Side of Flying

7:56 a.m.—

I have nineteen more minutes to sleep. I know this. But not because I looked at my alarm clock. I don't even have an alarm clock. The planes tell me the time. Right now, a 757 roars above me. It's heading east.

My name is Angelo Martinez. Everyone calls me Maverick. That's from the movie *Top Gun*. My friends know that someday, I'm going to be a pilot. It's only natural. I live in Atlanta, Georgia, almost next door to the Hartsfield Airport. It's the third-biggest airport in the country. It's practically in my backyard.

If you ever need to find me, check on the roof of my car.

After school, Todd usually invites me over to play soccer with his brothers. He can practically yell from his bedroom window into mine. "Maverick," he says. "We need a forward. Get out here and play some <u>offense</u>."

I always go and play for a while. Usually I score a goal or two. Just before the sun sets, I say goodbye. At home, I climb up on the car roof. I want to watch the sky. Why? Huge planes are landing and taking off from the airport. I love to watch them. The rush of air that hits my face always feels like freedom.

24

Before Reading

 Use one or more activities.

Make a Chart

Create a chart to help students identify the main elements of a story.

Story Elements	
Characters	the people in the story
Setting	where and when the story takes place
Plot	the events or what happens; usually involves a goal or solves a problem
Outcome	how the story ends
Theme	the main message of a story

Vocabulary Preview

Have students fill in the chart on *Student Journal* page 21. Return to the chart later. (See Differentiated Instruction.)

Preview the Selection

As students scan the story, ask:

- What do you learn from reading the title and looking at the illustrations?

- Who is the narrator of the story? (Maverick) What clues let you know? (use of first-person pronouns)

Make Predictions/ Set Purpose

Students should use the information they gathered in previewing the selection to make predictions about what they will learn. If students have trouble generating a purpose for reading, suggest that they read to find out what Maverick discovers about planes.

I don't mind the heat in the summer. The cold in the winter doesn't bother me. I'll even lie there if it's snowing. I catch snowflakes in my mouth. I eat breakfast out there. Weekend afternoons, I bring a snack. Sometimes at night, I fall asleep out there. I dream of what it must be like to be in a plane, really flying. Someday, I'm going to find out.

At school, we had to write a research paper on flight. It was for physics class. It was so easy for me. I almost felt as if I was cheating. Some kids know a lot about baseball. I know a lot about planes and flight. Other kids don't know about lift, thrust, and drag. I do.

I got an A on the paper.

In my room, I have posters of planes. Models of planes sit on my bookcase. The books in the bookcase are all about planes and flying. My friends think I'm obsessed, but I don't care. I think it's cool. When I take them all out in my private jet, they won't make fun of me anymore.

At 11:30 at night, a 747 rushes over our house. It means I should probably get into bed. In the morning, a jumbo jet takes off at 8:15. It's my alarm clock. In bad weather, though, the schedule gets messed up. Then I'm late for school. On sunny, calm days, I know what to expect. The airport runs like clockwork. I can set my watch by it.

It wasn't always this way. Five years ago, we moved here from a farm. I was nine years old. I had never even seen a plane. It's hard to believe that now. At first, I couldn't sleep. It was so loud here all the time. My parents said that I'd get used to it. They said that it would become a part of our life. I didn't believe them. But they were right.

Now, I like the sounds. I know what's coming. I know what's leaving. The airport is like a member of the family. It's as everyday as my mom pouring cereal. It's as predictable as my dad's mismatched socks.

Today, the jumbo jet takes off at exactly 8:15. Five hundred people are being lifted up high into the air. Are they going to Dallas? Los Angeles? I watch the tail end of the plane. Its engines blur in the hazy sky. For a minute, I am sad to see it go. The plane is going to a far away place. I am just going to school. We'll probably have a pop quiz in physics.

Still, I get up and get dressed. It's time for me to go.

25

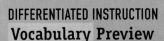

Vocabulary Preview

Work with students to read and establish meaning for the word *mismatched*.

Which word part is a prefix?	*mismatched*
Where have you seen this prefix before?	*mislead* *misread* *misconduct*
What does the prefix mean?	wrong or wrongly
What does the base word *match* mean?	go together; very similar
What does *mismatched* mean?	do not go together; paired wrongly
When might you use this word?	A blue sock and a brown sock are a *mismatched* pair.

Student Journal page 21

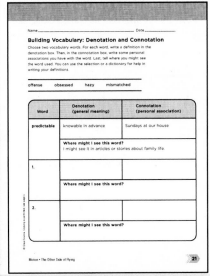

During Reading

Comprehension
MONITORING UNDERSTANDING

Use these questions to model how to visualize what you are reading about. Then have students tell about a part they visualized and which details helped them visualize it.

- What do I picture in my mind?
- Which details help me create this image in my mind?
- How does visualizing help me understand the text?

Teacher Think Aloud
I can picture Maverick lying on the roof of his car and watching the planes. The text says that he sometimes falls asleep out there, so I picture the setting sun and huge planes overhead. I like the detail about Maverick catching snowflakes. I can picture him lying on the car's roof, sticking out his tongue. The details help me "see" what's going on.

Fix-Up Strategies

Offer these strategies to help students read independently.

If you don't understand what you're reading:

- Reread the difficult section to look for clues to help you comprehend.
- Read ahead to find clues to help you comprehend.
- Retell, or say in your own words, what you've read.
- Visualize, or form mental pictures of, what you've read.

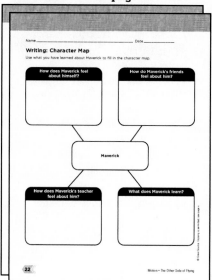

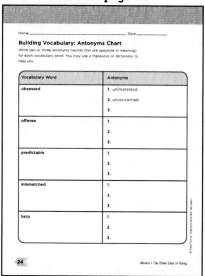

Three months later—

I cannot believe what is happening. Just when you think your life is getting boring, the winds of change come along. I am about to take off in an airplane!

No, I'm not kidding. This is for real.

I'm finding out what it's like to be *inside* one of the silver jets I've been watching.

Let me start at the beginning.

In physics, we were learning about planes. As I said before, I know a lot. Mr. Robinson is my teacher. I think he thinks I'm smart. So one day last month, he tapped me on the shoulder. He asked me to stay after class. Was I in trouble? No. It was just the opposite.

Mr. Robinson told me about a scholarship. It pays for a weeklong trip to Houston, Texas. There's a Spring Break camp there. It's for high-school kids. Why Houston, Texas, you ask? That's where NASA is.

The camp is for kids interested in flying. It's for kids who want to learn more about planes and the work of pilots. The camp is for kids like me.

I didn't tell anyone. My parents and friends had no idea. I didn't want to get my hopes up. I filled out the forms for the scholarship. I wrote the essay. I took a picture of my bookcase to show how much reading I do about planes. And I mailed it all in.

After Reading

Use one or more activities.

Check Purpose

Have students determine whether their purpose was met. Did students find out what Maverick discovered about planes?

Discussion Questions

Continue the group discussion with the following questions.

1. Do you think the title "The Other Side of Flying" is a good one? Why? (Making Connections)

2. What was the effect of Maverick's winning the scholarship? (Cause-Effect)

3. What conclusions can you draw about Maverick's teacher, Mr. Robinson? Why? (Draw Conclusions)

Revisit: Denotation and Connotation

Have students return to *Student Journal* page 21. Would students like to change or adjust their answers? Discuss the different connotations students have.

Two weeks ago, I got a packet in the mail. I had actually won the scholarship! I could go to the camp. I couldn't believe it, but everyone else could.

Todd clapped me on the back and said, "Duh, Maverick. Who else is as crazy about flying as you?" He was making fun of me, but in a way that felt good. Maverick was actually going to fly.

And now, here I am on a 737. A 737 takes off somewhere in the world every 5.3 seconds.

If you want to know the truth, I'm nervous. I didn't think I'd feel this way. I already know so much about the way things work at the airport. But somehow, when you are actually the one doing it, it's different. I didn't know it took thirty minutes to board a plane. I didn't know the buckle on my belt loop would set off the security sensors. I didn't know I'd get to choose between a window and an aisle seat. That, at least, was easy. Who wouldn't want a window seat?

27

Possible answers to **Student Journal page 25** include Short *a* Words: *natural, practically, catch*; Long *a* Words: *take, name, planes, face*. In the second activity, the short *a* words are *happen, answer, black, plant, apple, handy, back,* and *blast*. The long *a* words are *became, trade, space,* and *nickname. Above, waffle, asleep,* and *washroom* are oddballs.

Name _____ Date _____

Phonics/Word Study: Short Vowel *a*, Long Vowel *a*
Finish both lists. Look through "The Other Side of Flying" in *Motion* magazine for ideas. Try to include words with more than one syllable.

Short *a* Words
1. sad
2. ___
3. ___
4. ___
5. ___
6. ___
7. ___
8. ___
9. ___
10. ___

Long *a* Words
1. plane
2. ___
3. ___
4. ___
5. ___
6. ___
7. ___
8. ___
9. ___
10. ___

Pronounce each word. Circle the words that have a short *a* sound. Put a box around the words with a long *a* sound. Put a line through the words with neither a short *a* nor a long *a* sound. Hint: Find four oddball words.

1. happen   5. black   9. waffle   13. blast
2. above   6. plant   10. back   14. space
3. answer   7. apple   11. asleep   15. nickname
4. became   8. handy   12. trade   16. washroom

Motion • The Other Side of Flying   **25**

Writing Character Sketch

Ask students what they now know about Maverick. Jot down their ideas on the board. Then have students use these ideas to help them complete the character map on *Student Journal* page 22. Explain to students that they will next write a character sketch, which is a very short description of what a person in a story is like. Have students refer to their character map to write a character sketch of Maverick on *Student Journal* page 23.

Vocabulary Antonyms

Display the word *obsessed*. Ask students: *What is the meaning of the word* obsessed *as it is used in the story?* (thinking about something all the time) *What word can you think of that's opposite in meaning?* (uninterested, unconcerned) Explain to students that these words are antonyms of *obsessed*. Now have students complete the antonyms chart on *Student Journal* page 24.

Phonics/Word Study

Short and Long *a*

Display the following words: *plane* and *plan*. Ask: *How is the vowel sound in each word different?* (plane: long *a*; plan: short *a*) Then ask students to suggest other words that contain short and long *a* sounds. Now, work with students to complete the in-depth short and long *a* activity on TE page 41. For additional support, have students complete *Student Journal* page 25.

We boarded the plane. I stood in line with a whole bunch of people. A lot of them looked as if they'd done this tons of times before. I tried not to look like a first-timer. I nodded at the pilot when I passed the cockpit.

I'm in a window seat in the twelfth row. I can see the other planes taking off. That, at least, is a familiar sight. But everything else is new—even a little scary.

I try to swallow the lump in my throat. I'm going to be a pilot someday. I remind myself of that. I need to get used to this side of flying. After all, I got used to the noise in my backyard. That used to scare me, too.

Soon, our engine roars. We are rolling down the runway. My stomach is one big knot. I can't help gripping the armrests. The runway feels rougher than I imagined. We are moving fast.

After a minute, I look out the window. I scan the ground. There's something I want to see.

Yes! I see my house below. I smile down at the top of that red car. It's so shiny. It's so small. And it's getting smaller and smaller and smaller. I stare until I can't see it anymore.

Then it hits me. We're floating up like a balloon. I stop looking back. I start looking ahead. The whole rest of the world is before me. So this, I think, is the other side of flying. Cool! ◆

28

Phonics/Word Study

Short and Long *a*

▶ Place the following words on the board: *cap* and *cape*. Have students segment out the words as follows, listening for the sound of the *a* as they do so.

cap	*ap*	*a*
cape	*ape*	*a*

▶ Have partners brainstorm four more words for short *a* and four more words for long *a*. Then have partners share their words. As they do, ask which column each word would go in, and write the words on the board. This lets you know that students are hearing the difference between short *a* and long *a*.

▶ Provide students with copies of the Short *a* versus Long *a* Sort sheet and have students begin sorting by the three headings shown. (See *Word Study Manual* page 39.) Be sure to model the correct placement for the first few words. Have students work in pairs. One student can read the word aloud while the other determines the placement. When they are finished, have both students read each column to see if all the words have the same sound. Then have students switch roles.

▶ When confronted with a word with two or more syllables, students should identify the syllable with the vowel sound under consideration and concentrate only on that syllable.

▶ As a group, discuss the sort, students' observations, and why *great* and *said* ended up in the Oddball column. *Great* has the long *a* sound, but it is an unusual long *a* pattern. *Said* has the long *a* pattern, but it actually sounds like a short *e*. *Watch, calm, small,* and *palm* are in the Oddball column because they do not have the same short *a* sound as the other short *a* words.

Short *a* versus Long *a* Sort		
Short *a*	**Long *a***	**Oddball**
catch	face	great
snack	always	said
camp	baseball	watch
pass	late	calm
sand	change	small
stand	airplane	palm
	essay	
	bookcase	
	crazy	
	waves	

For more information on word sorts and spelling stages, see pages 5–31 in the *Word Study Manual.*

Focus on . . .

Use one or more activities in this section to focus on a particular area of need in your students.

Comprehension STRATEGY SUPPORT

To help those students who need more practice using the strategies covered in this lesson, work one-on-one or in small groups to apply the strategy prompts below. Apply the prompts to a *Reading Advantage* paperback, a classroom library book, or a new or familiar selection in the magazine. Always model your own thinking first.

Monitor Understanding

• Do I understand what I'm reading? If not, what part is confusing to me?

• What fix-up strategies can I use to solve the problem? (See During Reading for fix-up strategies.)

• Why did a character say (do, think, ask) that?

• What images do I visualize from the text? What parts can't I visualize?

• Why did the author include (or not include) those details?

Writing Story Map

Have students make their own story maps to identify the main elements of the story, and then use their completed story maps to help retell the story in their own words.

Story Map: "The Other Side of Flying"	
Characters	Maverick, Mr. Robinson
Setting	in the present; inside and outside a house in Atlanta across from an airport; school; inside an airplane
Plot	A boy who thinks he knows everything about planes encounters his first real plane ride.
Outcome	Maverick learns about the "other side of flying"—the actual experience of flying—and finds it "cool."
Theme	Knowing about how to do something and then doing it are two different things.

Fluency: Expression

Explain that part of reading aloud fluently involves reading with appropriate expression. After students have read "The Other Side of Flying" at least once, use a passage from the story to model reading expressively. Then have students work in pairs to take turns reading aloud the last part of the story, on page 28, beginning with "We boarded the plane." Remind them that the tone of the story is informal and conversational.

As student pairs read, use these prompts to guide them to speak expressively.

▶ Read conversationally, or the way you talk.

▶ Ask yourself what the narrator is feeling.

▶ Match your tone of voice to the feelings of the narrator.

When students read aloud, do they—

✓ reflect an understanding of the text?

✓ demonstrate appropriate timing, stress, and intonation?

✓ incorporate appropriate speed and phrasing?

English Language Learners

Support students as they draw conclusions in the third discussion question on TE page 38.

1. Explain that active readers draw conclusions based on the text and what they know. List some things Mr. Robinson said and did.

2. Model the language of drawing conclusions using this sentence frame: *Based on Mr. Robinson's actions, I conclude that . . .*

3. Have students draw conclusions using the sentence frame.

Independent Activity Options

While you work with individuals or small groups, others can work independently on one or more of the following options.

▶ Foundations paperback books, see TE pages 195–200

▶ Foundations *eZines*

▶ Repeat word sorts for this lesson

▶ *Student Journal* pages for this lesson

Assessment

Strategy Assessment

To help you and your students assess their use of comprehension strategies, ask the following questions. Students can complete a written response or provide verbal answers in a one-on-one reading conference.

- **Monitor Understanding** In the next-to-last paragraph on page 28, Maverick is looking down on his house from the plane. Which details help you picture in your mind what he sees? (Answers will vary.)

For ongoing informal assessment, use the checklists on pages 61–64 of *Foundations Assessment*.

Word Study Assessment

Use these steps to help you and your students assess their understanding of short and long vowel *a*.

1. Display a chart like the one below, but include only the headings and the words in the first column.

2. Have students tell whether each word has a short or long *a* sound. The answers are shown.

Word	Short or Long?
crate	long
latch	short
change	long
play	long
class	short
lack	short
lazy	long
land	short

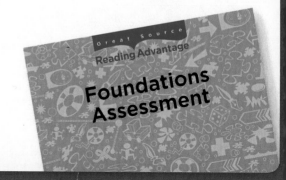

Great Source
Reading Advantage
Foundations Assessment

Got Questions About Motion?

Ask the Science Wizard

The Science Wizard answers all!

Do movies actually move?

Why do some people get carsick?

29

LESSON **6**
Ask the Science Wizard *and* Motion of Myself
Motion, pages 29–end

SUMMARY
In this **question-answer** selection, the Science Wizard answers questions relating to two very different types of motion—motion pictures and motion sickness. A **poem** follows.

COMPREHENSION STRATEGIES
Understanding Text Structure
Making Connections

WRITING
Explanatory Paragraph

VOCABULARY
Word Web

PHONICS/WORD STUDY
Short and Long *e*

Lesson Vocabulary
illusion   canal
sloshes

MATERIALS
Motion, pp. 29–end
Student Journal, pp. 26–30
Word Study Manual, p. 40

Before Reading
WHOLE CLASS Use one or more activities.

Anticipation Guide
Write three or four statements about the selection, such as those listed in the example. (See Differentiated Instruction for an example. See TE page 214 for an anticipation guide BLM.) Copy the guide for each student. Ask students to indicate whether they agree or disagree with each statement. Return to the guide after students have read the selection.

Vocabulary Preview
Review the vocabulary list. Have students begin *Student Journal* page 26. Revisit the page after students read. (See Differentiated Instruction.)

Preview the Selection
Have students look through the selection. Ask:

• What form of writing will you read? How do you know?

• How is the text organized?

Make Predictions/Set Purpose
Students should use the information they gathered in previewing the selection to make predictions about what they will learn. If students have trouble generating a purpose for reading, suggest that they read to learn more about different kinds of motion.

ANTICIPATION GUIDE

Here is an example of an anticipation guide. Use it to help students access prior knowledge and develop questions and interest before they read.

Anticipation Guide

AGREE	DISAGREE	
		1. A movie is many still pictures shown quickly.
		2. Motion sickness has only been around since the invention of the automobile.
		3. Motion sickness is related to your ears and eyes.

Student Journal page 26

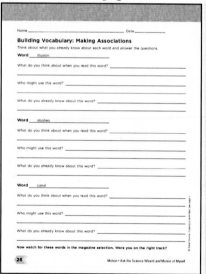

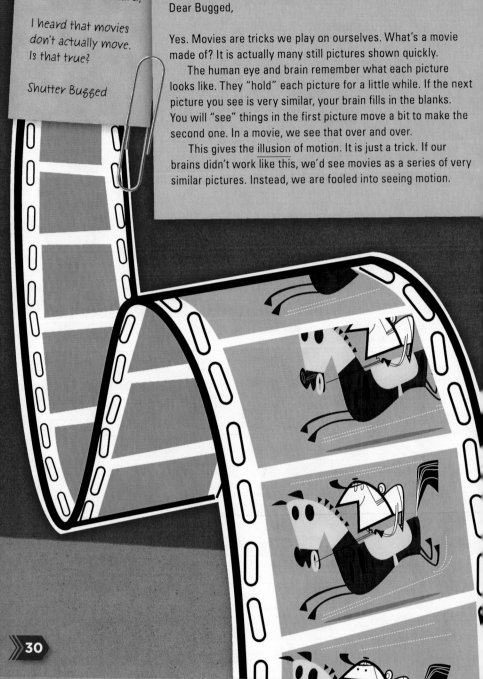

Dear Science Wizard,

I heard that movies don't actually move. Is that true?

Shutter Bugged

Dear Bugged,

Yes. Movies are tricks we play on ourselves. What's a movie made of? It is actually many still pictures shown quickly.

The human eye and brain remember what each picture looks like. They "hold" each picture for a little while. If the next picture you see is very similar, your brain fills in the blanks. You will "see" things in the first picture move a bit to make the second one. In a movie, we see that over and over.

This gives the illusion of motion. It is just a trick. If our brains didn't work like this, we'd see movies as a series of very similar pictures. Instead, we are fooled into seeing motion.

30

During Reading

Comprehension
UNDERSTANDING TEXT STRUCTURE

Use these questions to model how to identify the question-answer text structure of this selection. Then have students retell a question and answer.

- How does the author organize the text?
- What details support my thoughts?

Teacher Think Aloud
In this selection, the Science Wizard is answering questions. Therefore, I would say that the author has organized ideas in a question-answer format. I have seen this text structure used in interviews and in advice columns. I think that this text structure makes the information easy to find.

Comprehension
MAKING CONNECTIONS

Use these questions to model how to make connections with the text. Then have students tell about connections they have made.

- What does this selection remind me of?
- What do I already know about this topic?
- How does my experience help me understand this selection?

Dear Science Wizard,

I love to read, but whenever I read in the car, I feel sick to my stomach. Why does this happen to me?

Staying Home Next Time

Dear Staying Home,

You're not alone. Lots of people get motion sickness, even astronauts on the space shuttle. Motion sickness is related to your ears and eyes. Here's how it works.

When you ride in a car, fluid in your inner ear senses the movement. The fluid <u>sloshes</u> around in a tiny ear canal. The sloshing tells your brain that you're moving. But your eyes are focused on the book. The book is not moving. So your eyes tell your brain that you're sitting still. That's a mixed message. Your brain gets confused. The result? You feel sick.

How can you avoid motion sickness? Face forward. Focus on a distant object. This will help keep your eyes and ears "on the same page." Next time, just leave the books at home, not yourself!

It's Been Around a Long Time

Motion sickness has been around for thousands of years. Historians have even found references to camel sickness. Camel riders would sometimes feel sick from the animal's gentle swaying. Later, when ship travel became more common, the ailment's name changed to seasickness. The word *nausea* comes from Greek, meaning "ship." Now, we have carsickness, airsickness, space motion sickness, simulator sickness, and virtual reality motion sickness.

DIFFERENTIATED INSTRUCTION
Vocabulary Preview

Work with students to read, pronounce, and establish meaning for the word *sloshes*.

What is the base word? What is the ending?	slosh es
What is the final sound in the base word? What letters stand for the final sound?	slo<u>sh</u> es
What's a synonym for this word?	*splashes*
Where have you seen the two ending sounds before?	*push* *pushes* *wi<u>sh</u>* *wi<u>sh</u>es*
When might you use this word?	The girl *sloshes* through the big puddle.

31

Teacher Think Aloud

When I used to go on long car trips with my family, I often tried to read a book or play a game. And it always made me feel sick. But if I just looked out the window, I felt fine. After reading the Science Wizard's answer on page 31, I finally understood why I had had that problem, and learned that lots of people experience it.

Fix-Up Strategies

Offer these strategies to help students read independently.

If you don't understand what you're reading:

- Reread the difficult section to look for clues to help you comprehend.
- Read ahead to find clues to help you comprehend.
- Retell, or say in your own words, what you've read.
- Visualize, or form mental pictures of, what you've read.

If you don't understand a word:

- Reread the sentence. Look for ideas and words that provide meaning clues.
- Find clues by reading a few sentences before and after the confusing word.
- Look for the base or root word and think about its meaning.
- Think about the topic or plot at this point to see if either offers meaning clues.

Student Journal pages 27–28

Student Journal page 29

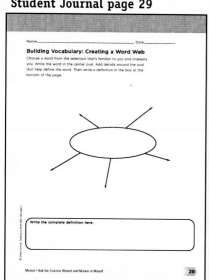

CREDITS

Program Authors
Laura Robb
James F. Baumann
Carol J. Fuhler
Joan Kindig

Editorial Board
Avon Connell-Cowell
R. Craig Roney

Supervising Editor
Ruth S. Rothstein

Project Manager
Alison Blank

Writers
Alice Alfonsi
Karen Baicker
Ari and Joan Epstein
Megan Howard
Anina Robb
Michele Sobel Spirn
Lauren Velevis

Design and Production
Anthology, Inc.

Photography
Cover Gary Doack/Photonica/Getty Images; IFC-01 bkgd © Royalty-Free/Corbis; IFC l, 8t, b, 9cl, br © Motoring Picture Library/Alamy; IFC c © Focus Group/Alamy; IFC r © Onne van der Wal/CORBIS; 20t © Focus Group/Alamy; 22-23 © Onne van der Wal/CORBIS; 7 AP Photo/Michael Stravato; 9tl © National Motor Museum/Topham-HIP/The Image Works; 9tr © Topham/The Image Works; 9cr (Aurora) AP Photo; 9cr Evans/Getty Images; 9bl HARRY MELCHERT/EPA/Landov; 10tc © Transtock Inc./Alamy; 10bc © George D. Lepp/CORBIS; 10b David Taylor/Allsport; 14 Courtesy Sony Entertainment; 16t © Mary Evans Picture Library/The Image Works; 16bl The Only Route via Niagara Falls and the Suspension Bridge, 1876 (colour litho), American School, (19th century)/© New-York Historical Society, New York, USA/Bridgeman Art Library; 16br The Granger Collection, New York; 18 Ben Blackwell/Courtesy of the Estate of William Bass; 19t © Gordon M. Grant/Alamy; 19b The Philadelphia Museum of Art/Art Resource, NY; 20b The Museum of Modern Art/Licensed by SCALA/Art Resource, NY; 21 © POPPERFOTO/Alamy

Illustration
All graphic elements created by Anthology, Inc. unless otherwise indicated; IFC a, 2-6 Brian White; IFC c, 11-15 Bruce Hutchison; 1a, 24-28 Ben Shannon; 1b, 30-31 David Semple; 1c, 32 Tom Foty

Motion of Myself

After Reading
Use one or more activities.

Check Purpose

Have students determine whether their purpose was met. Did they learn about different kinds of motion?

Discussion Questions

Continue the group discussion with the following questions.

1. What causes motion sickness? (Cause-Effect)

2. Why don't still pictures in a slide show blend together to make us see motion like stills in a movie do? (Inferential Thinking)

3. Have you ever felt motion sickness? What were you doing when you felt it? (Making Connections)

Revisit: Anticipation Guide

Have students review the anticipation guide statements. Ask students if they would like to change any of their opinions, now that they have read the selection. Discuss the reasons for any changes.

Revisit: Making Associations

Have students revisit the making associations activity on *Student Journal* page 26. Are there any adjustments or changes they would like to make?

I take pleasure in standing still.
When I wake, I savor the moment:
it's just me peeking over the covers in a dim room.
I can hear the hum of the house alive downstairs,
but for a moment I have calm before the chaos
of breakfast plates, backpacks, and rides to school.

I don't want to play video games all day
until my thumbs swell from action,
and my eyes glaze over watching the lights dart.
Instead, I'd rather sit on the stoop watching
the parked cars, imagining the lives of the people
who left them along the avenue.

I don't enjoy constant company, the clatter
of other people's lives. When I am lucky enough
to be tranquil, at a standstill,
I can finally hear the motion of myself.

At the end of the day, I don't need to run into the wind.
I choose to stand like a tree,
with my limbs reaching out, feeling the wind rush past me.

Poem: Motion of Myself

Direct students' attention to the poem "Motion of Myself." After students have read the poem at least once, use these or similar questions to discuss it.

- What is the topic of the poem?
- What do you think the title means?
- What type of person do you think the narrator is? Why?

Answers for **Student Journal page 30** are 1. *deep*, long *e*; 2. *present*, short *e*; 3. *test*, short *e*; 4. *speech*, long *e*; 5. *screen*, long *e*; 6. *press*, short *e*; 7. *wheel*, long *e*; 8. *check*, short *e*.

Name _____ Date _____

Phonics/Word Study: Short Vowel *e*, Long Vowel *e*
Use the words below to complete the sentences. Then write the words in the correct columns.

check	deep	speech	wheel	test	press	screen	present

1. The _____ end of the pool is not for young children.
2. A diamond bracelet is an expensive _____
3. We must study for the _____ to get a good grade.
4. The mayor's _____ was very long and boring.
5. The movie is shown on the big _____ television.
6. If you _____ your hands on wet sand, you can leave handprints.
7. A unicycle has only one _____
8. The waiter gave Mom the _____ after we finished eating dinner.

Short *e* Words   **Long *e* Words**

Choose three words from the box and use each one in a sentence.

1. _____
2. _____
3. _____

30   Motion • Ask the Science Wizard and Motion of Myself

Writing

Explanatory Paragraph

Have students make a sketch on *Student Journal* page 27 that illustrates one of the Science Wizard's answers. Tell students to use labels or short captions to annotate parts of the sketch. Then have students use the sketch and notes to write an explanatory paragraph on *Student Journal* page 28, explaining, in their own words, the Science Wizard's response to the question.

Vocabulary Word Web

Write the vocabulary word *illusion* on the board. Have students break it into syllables. (*il-lu-sion*) Point out the two syllable breaks. Ask a volunteer to read aloud the sentence on page 30, in which the word appears. Then ask: *What does* illusion *mean? When might you use the word* illusion? Have students use the word *illusion* or another vocabulary word to complete the word web activity on *Student Journal* page 29.

Phonics/Word Study

Short and Long *e*

Display and say aloud the words *pet* and *feet*. Ask: *What vowel sounds do you hear?* (short and long *e*) *How are they different?* Then ask students to suggest other words with short and long *e* sounds. Now, work with students to complete the in-depth short and long *e* activity on TE page 48. For additional support, have students complete *Student Journal* page 30.

Phonics/Word Study

Short and Long *e*

▶ Place the following words on the board or on chart paper: *bed* and *green*. Have students segment out the words as follows, listening for the sound of the *e* as they do so.

bed	*ed*	*e*
green	*een*	*ee*

▶ Provide students with copies of the Short *e* versus Long *e* Sort sheet and have students begin sorting by the three headings shown. (See *Word Study Manual* page 40.) Be sure to model the correct placement for the first few words. Because it's important for students to hear the difference between the two vowels, and not just see the difference, have students work in pairs. One student can read the word aloud while the other determines the placement. When they are finished, have both students read each column to see if all the words have the same sound. Then have students switch roles.

▶ When confronted with a word with two or more syllables, students should identify the syllable with the vowel sound under consideration and concentrate only on that syllable.

▶ As a group, discuss the sort, students' observations, and why *breakfast, instead,* and *said* ended up in the Oddball column. *Breakfast* and *instead* have the short *e* sound (as in *bread*), but it's an unusual short *e* spelling pattern. *Said* looks like a long *a* pattern (as in *paid*), but it actually sounds like a short *e*. Bringing these oddities to students' attention is useful and helps them discover new aspects of their language.

Short *e* versus Long *e* Sort		
Short *e*	**Long *e***	**Oddball**
bed	green	breakfast
gets	beach	instead
them	reason	said
sense	squeeze	
expect	really	
press	peek	
left	reach	
edge	these	
	feel	
	deep	

For more information on word sorts and spelling stages, see pages 5–31 in the *Word Study Manual*.

Focus on . . .

Use one or more activities in this section to focus on a particular area of need in your students.

Comprehension STRATEGY SUPPORT

To help those students who need more practice using the strategies covered in this lesson, work one-on-one or in small groups to apply the strategy prompts below. Apply the prompts to a *Reading Advantage* paperback, a classroom library book, or a new or familiar selection in the magazine. Always model your own thinking first.

Understanding Text Structure

• What kind of text is this? (book, story, article, guidebook, play, manual)

• How does the author organize the text? (cause-effect, problem-solution, chronological order, description, question-answer, comparison-contrast)

• What details support my thoughts about the text structure?

• What is the cause (effect, problem, solution, order, question, answer)?

• If fiction, who are the characters? What is the setting, plot, conflict, and resolution?

Making Connections

• What does this story (article, passage) remind me of?

• What do I already know about this topic?

• Where have I heard about this topic before?

• What do I have in common with the characters, people, or situations in the text?

• What other books, stories, articles, movies, or TV shows does this text make me think about?

Writing Explanation

Have students choose a machine or scientific process that they would like to try to explain. As a group, brainstorm some ideas (in the form of questions), and write them on the board. Examples include *Why do leaves fall off certain trees? How do flea collars work?* Students should write a few paragraphs to explain their processes as clearly as they can. When the pieces are finished, students should read them aloud. Discuss as a group how to discover more information about the topics.

To help students prepare for the writing, have them fill out a planning chart like the one shown.

Question	Why do leaves fall off certain trees?
Details	• colder temperature • sunlight changes • not enough chlorophyll for leaves

Fluency: Expression

Explain to students that part of reading aloud fluently involves reading with appropriate expression. After students have read the selection at least once, use the question and answer on page 30 to model reading expressively. Then have students work in pairs to take turns reading aloud the question and answer on page 31.

Use these prompts to guide pairs as they read.

▶ Suppose that you are the person talking to the Science Wizard. How would you sound?

▶ Use punctuation marks for clues to expression. Raise your voice slightly at the end of a question. Pause when you see a comma or a period.

When students read aloud, do they—

✓ reflect an understanding of the text?

✓ demonstrate appropriate timing, stress, and intonation?

✓ incorporate appropriate speed and phrasing?

English Language Learners

Support students as they examine cause and effect in the first discussion question on TE page 46.

1. Display cause-effect boxes with an arrow between them. In the "Effect" box, write *motion sickness*.

2. Find causes for motion sickness in the selection. Record this information in the "Cause" box.

3. Have partners discuss the causes of motion sickness using this sentence frame: *Motion sickness is caused by . . .*

Independent Activity Options

While you work with individuals or small groups, others can work independently on one or more of the following options.

▶ Foundations paperback books, see TE pages 195–200

▶ Foundations *eZines*

▶ Repeat word sorts for this lesson

▶ *Student Journal* pages for this lesson

Assessment

Strategy Assessment

To help you and your students assess their use of comprehension strategies, ask the following questions. Students can complete a written response or provide verbal answers in a one-on-one reading conference.

1. **Understanding Text Structure** Do you find a question-answer text structure easy to understand? Why or why not? (Answers will vary.)

2. **Making Connections** What was familiar to you from this selection? What did you learn that you didn't know before? (Answers will vary. Students will be familiar with movies, but may be surprised at how they work. Many students will be familiar with motion sickness.)

See *Foundations Assessment* pages 14–21 for formal assessment to go with *Motion*.

Word Study Assessment

Use these steps to help you and your students assess their understanding of short and long vowel *e*.

1. Display the following words: *beach, lens, weep, really, mess, wedge, wheel,* and *hem.*

2. Ask students to tell whether each word has a short or long *e* sound. The answers are shown.

Word	Short or Long?
beach	long
lens	short
weep	long
really	long
mess	short
wedge	short
wheel	long
hem	short

Foundations, Magazine 2

Fun and Games

Magazine Summary

Fun and Games magazine contains stories, articles, poems, and an interview. Students will read about places designed specifically for the business of fun and games—an amusement park, a computer game company, and a chocolate convention. They will also read about the role of science in card shuffling, football, and hot-air ballooning.

Content-Area Connection: social science, science
Lexile measure: 380L

Fun and Games Planner

LESSON	BEFORE READING	DURING READING	AFTER READING
LESSON 7 **Up Above the World So High** (story) page 54	List Vocabulary Preview Preview the Selection Make Predictions/ Set Purpose	Understanding Text Structure	Check Purpose Discussion Questions Writing: summary Vocabulary: context Phonics/Word Study: short and long *i*
LESSON 8 **Ask the Science Wizard** (question-answer) page 61	List Vocabulary Preview Preview the Selection Make Predictions/ Set Purpose	Monitor Understanding Inferential Thinking	Check Purpose Discussion Questions Writing: advice column Vocabulary: antonyms Phonics/Word Study: short and long *a, e, i*
LESSON 9 **Designing for Fun** (interview) page 68	K-W-L Chart Vocabulary Preview Preview the Selection Make Predictions/ Set Purpose	Making Connections	Check Purpose Discussion Questions Writing: interview Vocabulary: suffixes Phonics/Word Study: short and long *u*

Overview

Preview the Magazine

Have students page through the magazine to look at the selection titles, photographs, illustrations, and captions to discover the topics they will read about. Talk briefly about the front and back covers, too. Then, with students' help, create a chart similar to the one shown. Encourage students to share their ideas about ways people can have fun.

How Do We Have Fun?			
Games	Sports	Shows and Attractions	Other
board games	football	water park	travel
computer games	soccer	amusement park	dance
Sardines	tennis	music concert	play instrument
			play with baby sister
			read

PHONICS/ WORD STUDY	FOCUS ON	ASSESSMENT	HIGHER-ORDER THINKING QUESTIONS
Short and Long *i*	Writing: double-entry journal Fluency: phrasing English Language Learners Independent Activity Options	Understanding Text Structure Short and Long *i*	How do you think amusement parks got their name? Use details and information from the story to support your answer. Have you ever been to an amusement park? Compare and contrast your experience with Joey and Harvey's trip to Great Wonder. What happens that changes their plans? Use details and information from the story to support your answer.
Short and Long *a, e, i*	Writing: explanation Fluency: expression English Language Learners Independent Activity Options	Monitor Understanding Inferential Thinking Short and Long *a, e, i*	Describe why it is important to shuffle a deck of cards. Use details and information from the Science Wizard to support your response. Explain how a hot-air balloon moves. Use details and information from the Science Wizard to support your response.
Short and Long *u*	Writing: essay Fluency: punctuation English Language Learners Independent Activity Options	Making Connections Short and Long *u*	In the selection, Sheri did not discuss any disadvantages of being a game designer. What are the disadvantages? Use details and information from the interview to support your response. The typical high school student most likely thinks game designing is all fun and games. What high school classes did Sheri recommend that were essential to designing games? Use details and information from the interview to support your answer.

Fun and Games Planner

LESSON	BEFORE READING	DURING READING	AFTER READING
LESSON 10 **Blackout** (story) page 75	Concept Web Vocabulary Preview Preview the Selection Make Predictions/ Set Purpose	Making Connections Monitor Understanding	Check Purpose Discussion Questions Writing: brief essay Vocabulary: antonyms Phonics/Word Study: short and long *o*
LESSON 11 **Crazy for Chocolate!** *and* **Race Day** (newspaper article and poem) page 82	Anticipation Guide Vocabulary Preview Preview the Selection Make Predictions/ Set Purpose	Determining Importance Monitor Understanding	Check Purpose Discussion Questions Writing: description Vocabulary: homophones Phonics/Word Study: short and long *i, o, u*
LESSON 12 **Stinky Wins by a Nose** *and* **Jump Kid** (article and poem) page 90	List Vocabulary Preview Preview the Selection Make Predictions/ Set Purpose	Inferential Thinking Understanding Text Structure	Check Purpose Discussion Questions Writing: letter Vocabulary: concept ladder Phonics/Word Study: long vowels and final *y*

PHONICS/WORD STUDY	FOCUS ON	ASSESSMENT	HIGHER-ORDER THINKING QUESTIONS
Short and Long *o*	Writing: character sketch Fluency: expression English Language Learners Independent Activity Options	Making Connections Monitor Understanding Short and Long *o*	How does James's mother tolerate his negative attitude and disrespectful tone? Use details and information from the story to support to support your response. What lesson does James learn about his family while visiting his grandmother? Use details and information from the story to support your answer.
Short and Long *i, o, u*	Writing: advertisement Fluency: pacing English Language Learners Independent Activity Options	Determining Importance Monitor Understanding Short and Long *i, o, u*	Jenny Velasquez had a great experience at the International Chocolate Show. Explain which parts of the show you would have enjoyed most, and why. Use details and information from the article to support your response. What is the outcome of the poem, "Race Day"? Use details and information from the poem to support your answer.
Long Vowels and Final *y*	Writing: problem-solution paragraph Fluency: expression English Language Learners Independent Activity Options	Inferential Thinking Understanding Text Structure Long Vowels and Final *y*	What were the key factors that helped Stinky's team win the competition? Use details and information from the article to support your answer. Why is "Jump Kid" a good title for this poem? Use details and information from the poem to support your response.

LESSON 7
Up Above the World So High
Fun and Games, pages 2–6

SUMMARY
This **short story** describes the unexpected adventure Harvey and his younger brother, Joey, have at an amusement park.

COMPREHENSION STRATEGIES
Understanding Text Structure

WRITING
Summary

VOCABULARY
Context

PHONICS/WORD STUDY
Short and Long *i*

Lesson Vocabulary
ravenous	tinker
scrambled	crackling

MATERIALS
Fun and Games, pp. 2–6
Student Journal, pp. 31–35
Word Study Manual, p. 41

Before Reading ⊕ WHOLE CLASS Use one or more activities.

Make a List
Discuss students' experiences with amusement park rides. Ask: *What is the scariest ride you have ever been on? What is the ride that went the highest?* Then ask students to picture themselves on the biggest Ferris wheel or the highest roller coaster, and it stops when they are at the very top. Something is mechanically wrong. How will they remain calm until it's fixed? List their ideas. Revisit the list after students read.

▶
How to Stay Calm
1. Keep your eyes closed.
2. Don't look down.
3.

Vocabulary Preview
Display the vocabulary words and read them aloud to clarify pronunciations. Next, extend the understanding of the vocabulary words by having students complete the synonyms chart on *Student Journal* page 31. Use the vocabulary word *ravenous* to model a response for the page. Students will revisit the activity after reading. (See Differentiated Instruction.)

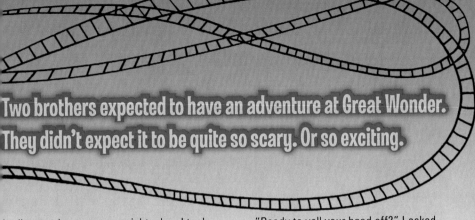

Two brothers expected to have an adventure at Great Wonder. They didn't expect it to be quite so scary. Or so exciting.

It all started one summer night when I took my little brother, Joey, to Great Wonder. You might not know about Great Wonder. It has two roller coasters, the Mega and the Marvel. They are great rides. Then it has the biggest Ferris wheel. I mean, it's the biggest in the world. I know because they've measured it.

Joe is a tough kid, but he's only ten. I wanted to start him off slowly. We walked around the rides.

"What do you think?" I asked.

"Cool, let's go," he said.

"Which one should we do first?" I asked.

"The Mega roller coaster," he said.

"I only have so much money," I warned. "We can't go on everything."

"I'm sure I want to go on that one," he said.

"Okay, time for some real fun," I told him. We walked to the roller coaster. All around us the air had the salty-sweet smell of food. I sniffed hot dogs and cotton candy. We passed a popcorn booth. The rich, buttery smell floated out and blended with the screams of the people on the rides. I was more than hungry. I was <u>ravenous</u>.

"Ready to yell your head off?" I asked. Joey nodded and grinned real wide.

We got on the Mega and blasted off. We went up and down, then around. We strained upward, chugging up a hill. Then we swooped down so fast that my stomach felt as if it was leaving my body. Finally, we slowed to a crawl. Then we stopped and got off.

It was getting darker. I felt a breeze and was a little dizzy.

"You want your jacket?" I asked Joey.

"No, Harvey, let's go on the next ride," he said. We went on the Marvel. Then we shot some balloons. I won a big purple stuffed dog. We tried to fish a prize out of a pond. But all we got was our arms wet.

"Last ride, so pick a good one," I said. I had enough money for one more. It was getting late and very dark. The moon shone above us, looking down on the crowds.

Joey looked around for a moment. Then his gaze fell on the Ferris wheel. It was all lit up. It looked as if it was on fire in the night sky.

"That's the one," he said. "I've got to go on the biggest ride."

DIFFERENTIATED INSTRUCTION

Comprehension
UNDERSTANDING TEXT STRUCTURE

To help students understand the features of realistic fiction, use these questions:

- Do the characters seem like real people? Do they speak and act like people you know?

- Does the story take place in a realistic place?

- Does the problem seem like a problem that can happen in real life? Is the solution realistic?

We walked over to the Ferris wheel. The attendant was putting people into their seats. Joey scrambled into a gold-colored car. I went to join him. Just then, two smaller kids ran in front of me. They hopped into the car with Joey.

"Hey, wait a minute!" I said. I had wanted to ride with Joey on the Ferris wheel.

The man in charge said, "Sorry, son, but that's the last car." He clanged the bar into place.

I tried to smile for Joe. "It's okay, I'll wait here," I yelled. Then I had an idea.

"Call me on the cell phone Mom lent you," I cried. "We can talk while you're going around."

Joe held up the phone and waved it at me. I waved mine back.

The big wheel started turning. I stepped away to look up. I caught a glimpse of Joey. He was wearing a blue shirt. Then he disappeared into the night as the big wheel circled the park.

My cell phone did a little dance in my hand. It was Joey calling.

"How is it up there?" I asked.

"Great, really great!" He said something else. It was hard to hear him. He was breaking up.

"What did you say?" I asked.

"It's fun up here," he said. His voice was clearer now. "You look like a little ant."

"And I can't see you at all," I answered.

"We're at the very top now," he said. "Don't worry." He sounded kind of funny.

"I'm not worried," I said.

"I wasn't talking to you," Joe said. "One of the kids here is a little scared."

"Oh, is he okay?" I asked.

"He's kind of shaking," Joe said.

"Maybe you can talk to him," I said. "I'll call you back in a minute."

Then the phone cut off. I thought the wheel was staying in the same spot for a long time. When was it going to move?

Then I saw men running toward the

During Reading

Comprehension
UNDERSTANDING TEXT STRUCTURE

Use these questions to model how to understand the structure of realistic fiction. Then have students identify and describe the story elements.

- Who are the main characters? What problem or conflict do they face?

- What is the setting of the story?

- How do I know that this is realistic fiction?

(See Differentiated Instruction.)

Teacher Think Aloud
The kids in this story seem like kids I know. The brothers look out for each other, and they like amusement parks. The conflicts are ones that could actually happen in real life, and so is the resolution. The story is moved forward by the central problem: the Ferris wheel gets stuck. The story ends with the resolution: the ride is fixed.

Fix-Up Strategies
Offer these strategies to help students read independently.

If you don't understand what you're reading:

- Reread the difficult section to look for clues to help you comprehend.

- Read ahead to find clues to help you comprehend.

- Retell, or say in your own words, what you've read.

- Visualize, or form mental pictures of, what you've read.

wheel. What was up? At the same time, my cell phone jumped.

"What's going on, Harvey?" Joe asked. "We haven't moved for a while. This kid is freaking out."

"Hold on, Joey," I said. "I'll find out."

People were crowding around the men. I heard one woman say, "Get them down now!"

A man answered her, "We're trying, lady."

"What's going on?" I asked one of the men.

"One of the parts of the wheel is stuck. We can't get it moving," he said.

I watched them tinker with the machinery. I was putting off calling Joey. He would have a lot of questions I simply couldn't answer. I took a deep breath. I'd have to call him. Just then, he called me.

"What's going on, Harvey?" he yelled. "This kid is losing it."

I felt as if I had been punched. "Keep him as calm as you can," I said. "They're having a little trouble with the wheel. It'll be fixed soon."

"Not soon enough," Joey said. "This ride is turning into a nightmare. I've got one kid crying and another one who says he's feeling sick. What am I supposed to do?"

"Hold on, I'm thinking," I said.

"Think fast or get us out of here," Joey said. The phone started crackling again.

I had an idea from something I had seen on TV.

"I've got something you can try," I said. "I think it might help."

"I can't hear you," Joey replied. "You're breaking up."

Then I heard him shout, "No, no, don't do that!"

I switched to text messaging.

HERE'S WHAT TO DO. TELL HIM TO SIT DOWN AND CLOSE HIS EYES.

OKAY, NOW WHAT? Joe messaged back.

TELL HIM TO IMAGINE A SAFE PLACE, I wrote.

OH, RIGHT, THAT WILL BE EASY, Joe wrote back.

JUST TRY IT, I insisted.

I waited a few minutes. Then I wrote Joey again.

DID HE DO IT? I asked. WHERE IS THE SAFE PLACE?

AT THE BEACH, came the answer.

TALK TO HIM ABOUT THE BEACH, I said. ASK HIM QUESTIONS. LET ME KNOW IF HE CALMS DOWN.

A strong breeze sprang up, and I watched the cars swing in the wind. You could hear the screams of the kids in the Ferris wheel cars as they rocked back and forth.

One woman cried, "What if they can't get them down?"

I watched the men trying to fix the machine while I waited to hear from Joe. One kept shaking his head. Then another in black jeans and a white T-shirt began climbing up the steel beams that held the wheel. The crowd watched him climb higher and higher.

DIFFERENTIATED INSTRUCTION

Vocabulary Context

To help students use context clues to find the meanings of words, follow these steps:

1. Tell students that the first place to look for a context clue is in the sentence in which the difficult word appears.

2. Explain that the clue may be a synonym (word with similar meaning), an antonym (word with opposite meaning), a definition, or an example.

3. If the sentence itself does not provide a clue, students should look at the sentences just before and just after the sentence in which the unfamiliar word appears.

Student Journal pages 32–33

Name _____ Date _____
Writing: Somebody Wanted But So Chart
Fill in this chart to help you organize your thoughts for a summary of "Up Above the World So High."

	My Notes
Somebody (an important character)	
Wanted (a key problem with details)	
But (conflict for the character)	
So (an outcome)	

32   Fun and Games • Up Above the World So High

After Reading

Use one or more activities.

Check Purpose

Have students determine whether their purpose was met. Did they learn what was exciting and scary about the brothers' adventure?

Discussion Questions

Ask the following questions.

1. Do you think Joey will ride a Ferris wheel again? (Predict)

2. From this adventure, what do you think Harvey learns about his little brother? (Inferential Thinking)

3. Do the relationships, feelings, or dialogue in the story remind you of similar experiences you've had? (Making Connections)

Revisit: List

Have students revisit the list they made in Before Reading. Do they think that picturing themselves somewhere safe would help them stay calm? Do students have any other ideas they would like to add to the list?

Revisit: Synonyms Chart

Have pairs or groups of students share and compare their synonyms on *Student Journal* page 31.

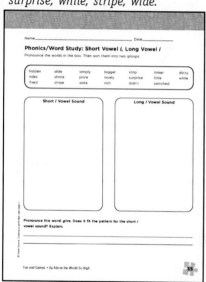

Answers for **Student Journal page 35** are Short *i* Vowel Sound: *hidden, simply, bigger, strip, tinker, dizzy, shrink, little, fixed, rich, didn't, switched;* Long *i* Vowel Sound: *slide, rides, prize, nicely, surprise, while, stripe, wide.*

WHAT'S THAT MAN DOING? Joe asked. I guess he could see him climbing up.

NEVER MIND HIM. HOW'S THE KID? I answered back.

NOT SO GOOD, Joe wrote. WE HAVE TO HOLD HIM DOWN.

The man kept climbing like a spider up the beams. He could really climb fast. But then, somehow, he slipped. The crowd gasped and stared up at him. He was dangling by one hand over the crowd. He tried to grab on to the beams with his other hand, but he kept missing. It looked as if he was going to fall. Finally, he hooked his feet into the opening in the beams. He was able to lean all the way over one car. He gave it a mighty heave. Then he began to move down slowly. Emergency workers stood below in case they were needed.

But the man jumped to the ground safely and pulled a lever. And, all of a sudden, the Ferris wheel started moving again! A shout rose from the crowd.

As each car came toward the ground, the wheel slowed and kids climbed out. Parents grabbed them and hugged them.

I moved closer to the wheel. The top car was coming down now. A woman moved in front of me and grabbed the two kids, squeezing them and crying. I heard one of them say, "Mom, I was so scared. But I thought about the beach, and then I felt better."

Then Joey appeared and I ran up and hugged him. I hugged him until he said, "I'm fine, Harvey. I was never worried at all."

"How come?" I asked.

"I didn't have time," he said. "I was too busy trying to take care of that kid. I never had a chance to think about what was going on."

Joey stopped and looked back at the wheel.

"So can I have another ride?" he asked. ◆

Writing Summary

Explain that summarizing what they have read helps readers identify and remember an author's main ideas. Tell students that they will write a summary of the short story "Up Above the World So High." Have students prepare for writing the summary by completing the Somebody Wanted But So chart on *Student Journal* page 32. Then have them use their notes from this activity to write the summary on *Student Journal* page 33.

Vocabulary Context

Point out the vocabulary word *crackling* on selection page 5. Ask a volunteer to read the sentence in which it appears. Then ask: *What does* crackling *mean?* (making many short, sharp noises) *When might you use the word* crackling? (The fire is *crackling* in the fireplace.) Then have students choose another word to complete the context activity on *Student Journal* page 34. (See Differentiated Instruction.)

Phonics/Word Study
Short and Long *i*

Display and read aloud this sentence: *When Bill flew his kite, he ran up a hill and held tight to the string.* Ask: Which words have a short *i* sound? (*Bill, his, hill, string*) Which words have a long *i* sound? (*kite, tight*) Now, work with students to complete the in-depth short and long *i* activity on TE page 59. For additional support, have students complete *Student Journal* page 35.

Phonics/Word Study

Short and Long *i*

▶ Place the following words on the board: *switch* and *time*. Have students segment out the words as follows, listening for the sound of the *i* as they do so.

switch	*itch*	*i*
time	*ime*	*i*

▶ Have partners brainstorm four more words for each category, short *i* and long *i*. Share the words as a class. As each word is said, ask which column it should go in, and record it.

▶ Provide students with the Short *i* versus Long *i* Sort sheet and have them begin sorting by the three headings shown. (See *Word Study Manual* page 41.) Be sure to model the correct placement for the first few words. Have students work in pairs. One student can read the word aloud while the other determines the placement. When they are finished, have both students read each column to see if all the words have the same sound. Then have students switch roles.

▶ When confronted with a word with two or more syllables, students should identify the syllable with the vowel sound under consideration and concentrate only on that syllable. Note that students should concentrate on the long *i* sound in *trying*, the vowel sound of the base word.

▶ As a whole group, discuss the sort, students' observations, and the oddballs. Both *minute* and *wind* can be pronounced with a short or long *i*. A *minute* (MIN-it) is an increment of time, whereas *minute* (my-NOOT) is something very small. *Wind* (short *i*) is what blows down trees, and *wind* (long *i*) is something we do to a clock. How do we tell which is which as we read? Offer the following two sentences and see if students read them correctly: *In the fall, leaves falling from trees are tossed about by the* wind. *I will help you in a* minute *when my hands are free.* What made students read them correctly? The sentence structure and the context gave clues.

Short *i* versus Long *i* Sort		
Short *i*	**Long *i***	**Oddball**
biggest	mind	minute
did	while	wind
miss	cried	
fix	time	
him	find	
switch	trying	
sit	night	
dizzy	might	
big	eye	
fish	prize	

For more information on word sorts and spelling stages, see pages 5–31 in the *Word Study Manual*.

Focus on . . .

Use one or more activities in this section to focus on a particular area of need in your students.

Comprehension | STRATEGY SUPPORT

To help those students who need more practice using the strategies covered in this lesson, work one-on-one or in small groups to apply the strategy prompts below. Apply the prompts to a *Reading Advantage* paperback, a classroom library book, or a new or familiar selection in the magazine. Always model your own thinking first.

Understanding Text Structure

• What kind of text is this? (book, story, article, guidebook, play, manual)

• How does the author organize the text? (cause-effect, problem-solution, chronological order, description, question-answer, comparison-contrast)

• What details support my thoughts about the text structure?

• What is the cause (effect, problem, solution, order, question, answer)?

• If fiction, who are the characters? What is the setting, plot, conflict, and resolution?

Writing Double-entry Journal

Double-entry journals encourage students to become more engaged with a text by focusing on and making connections to small parts of the text. Tell students to create a double-entry journal by selecting four quotations that they especially liked from the story, and then writing their thoughts about each. (See TE page 206 for a double-entry journal BLM.)

Quotation	My Thoughts
"Joey looked around for a moment. Then his gaze fell on the Ferris wheel. It was all lit up. It looked as if it was on fire in the night sky."	In the summer, when I visit my cousins, there is usually a carnival wheel down the road. I can see the Ferris wheel at night from my bedroom window. This quotation reminds me of the good times I have there.

Focus on . . .

Use one or more activities in this section to focus on a particular area of need in your students.

Fluency: Phrasing

Explain that part of reading aloud fluently involves reading groups of words that naturally go together. After students have read the selection at least once, use a passage from it to model reading aloud with proper phrasing. Then have student pairs choose two paragraphs to alternate reading aloud to each other.

Use these prompts to guide students as they read.

▶ Preview what you will read. Notice the different punctuation marks and what they signal to you. Pause at commas and periods. Put excitement into your voice when you see an exclamation point. Let your voice rise at the end of a sentence with a question mark.

▶ Look for groups of words that go together. Words are often "chunked" together with commas. Reading these words in "chunks" will help you sound natural.

When students read aloud, do they—

✓ demonstrate quick recognition of words and phrases?

✓ exhibit an understanding of phrasal construction?

✓ incorporate appropriate timing, stress, and intonation?

English Language Learners

Support students as they preview vocabulary on TE page 54.

1. Write the word *ravenous* on the board. Have students discuss what they know about the word.

2. Reread the text on the bottom of page 3 of the selection. Model how to use context clues to figure out the meaning of *ravenous*.

3. Have partners describe how a person might act when they are ravenous.

Independent Activity Options

While you work with individuals or small groups, others can work independently on one or more of the following options.

▶ Foundations paperback books, see TE pages 195–200

▶ Foundations *eZines*

▶ Repeat word sorts for this lesson

▶ *Student Journal* pages for this lesson

Assessment

Strategy Assessment

To help you and your students assess their use of comprehension strategies, ask the following questions. Students can complete a written response or provide verbal answers in a one-on-one reading conference.

• **Understanding Text Structure** What is the main problem in this story? (Joe is stuck at the top of the Ferris wheel, next to two kids who are scared.)

For ongoing informal assessment, use the checklists on pages 61–64 of *Foundations Assessment*.

Word Study Assessment

Use these steps to help you and your students assess their understanding of short and long *i* sounds.

1. Display a chart like the one below, but include only the headings and the words in the first column.

2. Have students read the words and sort them into the correct column. The answers are shown.

Word	Short *i*	Long *i*	Oddball (can have either short or long *i* sound)
night	rich	night	wind
rich	hill	ride	minute
ride	big	wide	
wide	pick	final	
hill	fixed	light	
final		try	
big		climb	
pick			
wind			
light			
fixed			
try			
minute			
climb			

Reading Advantage

Foundations Assessment

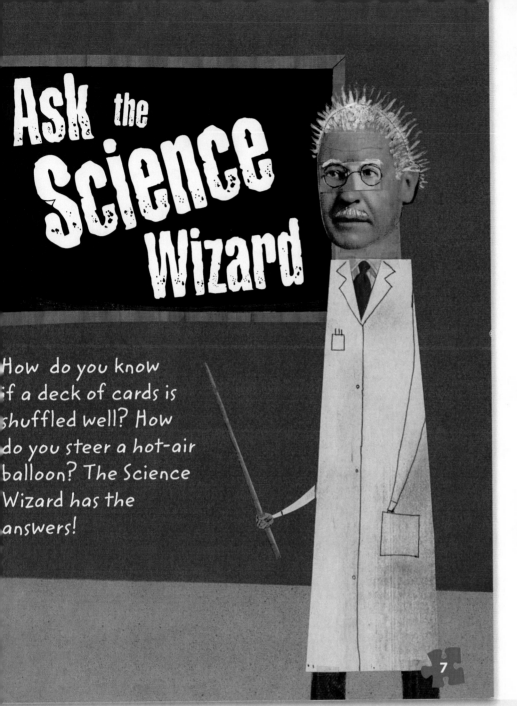

How do you know if a deck of cards is shuffled well? How do you steer a hot-air balloon? The Science Wizard has the answers!

SUMMARY
Through a **question-answer** selection, the Science Wizard explains the science behind shuffling cards, bulky football players, and steering hot-air balloons.

COMPREHENSION STRATEGIES
Monitor Understanding
Inferential Thinking

WRITING
Advice Column

VOCABULARY
Antonyms

PHONICS/WORD STUDY
Short and Long *a, e, i*

Lesson Vocabulary
shuffle	momentum
release	bulk

MATERIALS
Fun and Games, pp. 7–11
Student Journal, pp. 36–40
Word Study Manual, p. 42

Before Reading WHOLE CLASS Use one or more activities.

Make a List
Ask students what they think a scientist might explain that relates to fun and games. List their ideas. Revisit the list later.

What the Science Wizard Might Explain
1. Why kites stay in the air
2. How a boomerang works
3.

Vocabulary Preview
Have students begin the predictions chart on *Student Journal* page 36. They will complete it after reading. (See Differentiated Instruction.)

Preview the Selection
Have students look through the selection. Ask:

- Do you think you will read fiction or nonfiction? Why?

- How is the information in the selection organized?

Make Predictions/ Set Purpose
Students should use the information they gathered in previewing the selection to make predictions about what they will learn. If students have trouble generating a purpose for reading, suggest that they read to learn how science plays a role in fun activities such as playing cards and football.

Vocabulary Preview

Work with students to read, pronounce, and establish meaning for the word *shuffle*.

What letter is at the end of the word? What happens to the letter *e* when -*ing* is added to the base word?	*shuffle* The letter *e* is dropped.
Where have you seen this kind of spelling change before?	*make, making* *write, writing*
What's a synonym for *shuffle*?	*mix (up)*
When might you use *shuffle*?	I'll *shuffle* the cards before we begin the game.

Dear Science Wizard,
   I really like playing cards, but people say I shuffle too much. How much mixing is enough? How much is too much?
                                          —Decked Out

Dear Decked Out,
   That's a good question. It's good to have a well-shuffled deck. But what does that mean? What's a well-shuffled deck? What's a deck that needs more shuffling?
   Cards that have been played with are in some kind of order. Maybe they're grouped in sets. Maybe they're in runs. A five may be near another five. A heart is near other hearts. That's not true in a well-shuffled deck. In that deck any card might be next.
   How much shuffling is enough? Mathematicians have studied that. One of these people is Persi Diaconis. He is a professor of mathematics and statistics at Stanford University. He is also a professional magician.
   Diaconis studied "riffle-shuffles." To riffle-shuffle, split the deck into two piles. Place them next to each other. Use your thumbs to raise the corners of each pile. Release, or let go of, the cards slowly so that the piles overlap each other.
   What did Diaconis find? It takes six or seven riffle-shuffles to mix a deck well. Shuffling more doesn't mix it much better. Shuffling five times leaves some cards in order.
   Don't worry about shuffling too much. Shuffling extra times won't unmix cards, though it might wear them out.

8

Student Journal page 36

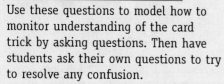

Name_____ Date_____

Building Vocabulary: Predictions
How do you predict these words will be used in "Ask the Science Wizard"? Write your answers in the second column. Next, read the selection. Then, clarify your answers in the third column.

Word	My prediction for how the word will be used	How the word is actually used
shuffle		
release		
momentum		
bulk		

36   Fun and Games • Ask the Science Wizard

During Reading

Comprehension
MONITOR UNDERSTANDING

Use these questions to model how to monitor understanding of the card trick by asking questions. Then have students ask their own questions to try to resolve any confusion.

- How does the card trick work?
- What fix-up strategy can I use to fix my confusion?

(See Differentiated Instruction.)

Teacher Think Aloud
As I read the card trick on page 9, I didn't understand how the helper was supposed to figure out the right card. Then I reread the steps, studied the illustrations, and tried to visualize the trick. I finally figured out that each card on the table represents a diamond on the 10-card.

Comprehension
INFERENTIAL THINKING

Use these questions to model how to make inferences from the Science Wizard's answer about football players on page 10. Then have students reveal inferences they make as they read another of the Science Wizard's answers.

- What does the text tell me?
- Using the text and what I already know, what new ideas can I infer?

Amaze Your Friends—No Shuffling Needed

Here's an easy card trick.

 Choose a helper. Explain the trick privately. Make sure you both know the layout for the spots on a 10 card.

 Shuffle the deck for the audience. Casually (and secretly) find a 10 and slip it to the top of the deck.

 Lay out ten cards in the same layout as the spots on a 10 card. Make sure the 10 is placed at the upper-left corner.

 Ask your helper to leave the room.

 Ask an audience member to point to a card.

 Call your helper back into the room. Start pointing to the cards one by one. For each card, ask the helper, "Is this the card?"

 Here's the secret: When you point to the first card, which is the 10 card, point to the symbol (heart, diamond) whose position on the 10 card corresponds to the position of the card on the table.

8 Variation: Tell your audience member not to pick any card. When your helper returns, point to the space between symbols. Your audience will be amazed!

9

Comprehension
MONITOR UNDERSTANDING

To help students monitor their understanding by asking questions, use these steps:

1. Have students reread the question and answer about hot-air balloons on page 11.
2. Ask: *What questions do you have about this section?*
3. Ask: *How can you find answers to your questions?*
4. Remind students that they can reread, read ahead, make mental pictures, and retell the text to help them clarify the information.

Teacher Think Aloud

The text tells me that large linemen are massive, which makes them harder to stop or be pushed in another direction. I wonder if that's why some people like to buy heavy cars. On the basis of this article, I infer that heavier cars are more stable than lighter cars in strong winds and car crashes.

Fix-Up Strategies

Offer these strategies to help students read independently.

If you don't understand what you're reading:

- Reread the difficult section to look for clues to help you comprehend.
- Read ahead to find clues to help you comprehend.
- Retell, or say in your own words, what you've read.
- Visualize, or form mental pictures of, what you've read.

If you don't understand a word:

- Reread the sentence. Look for ideas and words that provide meaning clues.
- Find clues by reading a few sentences before and after the confusing word.
- Look for the base or root word and think about its meaning.
- Think about the topic or plot at this point to see if either offers meaning clues.

Writing

Advice Column

To help students prepare for writing about their process, have them use a separate sheet of paper and follow these steps:

1. Tell students to visualize themselves doing the process. They might even close their eyes, if it helps. The first step is to list the materials they will need.

2. Then they should picture the steps in the process and jot these down.

3. Have students read over what they've written to reorder items or add anything they've forgotten. Then they can fill in *Student Journal* page 37.

Student Journal pages 37–38

Name_____ Date_____
Writing: Question and Answer Planning Page
List the materials you need to do your project.

Materials:

List the steps for your project.
1. _____
2. _____
3. _____
4. _____
5. _____
6. _____
7. _____
8. _____

Fun and Games • Ask the Science Wizard   37

Dear Science Wizard,
  People say to take care of our bodies. But look at some athletes. Professional football linemen, for example, look out of shape and overweight. How can that be?
—Proud Couch Potato

Dear Proud Couch Potato,
  They do have big bellies. But they are strong and fast. Big bellies help them do their job. When a lineman crouches, his belly hangs down. That means his center of gravity is low. That helps him stay on his feet. It is hard to knock him over.
  Also, large linemen are hard to move out of the way. They are so massive. Mass gives them more momentum when they run. That means it's hard to stop them. It's hard to make them change direction.

  But don't try this at home. Bulk without strength and speed doesn't help. Being very heavy can cause health problems. Some professional linemen have health problems. Often, these problems occur after they retire.

10

After Reading Use one or more activities.

Check Purpose

Have students determine whether their purpose was met. Did they discover how science plays a role in activities related to fun and games?

Discussion Questions

Continue the group discussion with the following questions.

1. In what other sports is the weight of a player important? (Inferential Thinking)

2. How do the questions and answers relate to fun and games? (Draw Conclusions)

3. Which of the questions and answers interested you the most? Why? (Making Connections)

Revisit: List

Revisit the list that was started in Before Reading. What other ideas can students add?

Revisit: Predictions Chart

Have students complete the predictions chart on *Student Journal* page 36. Students can compare and contrast their original predictions with how each vocabulary word is used in the article.

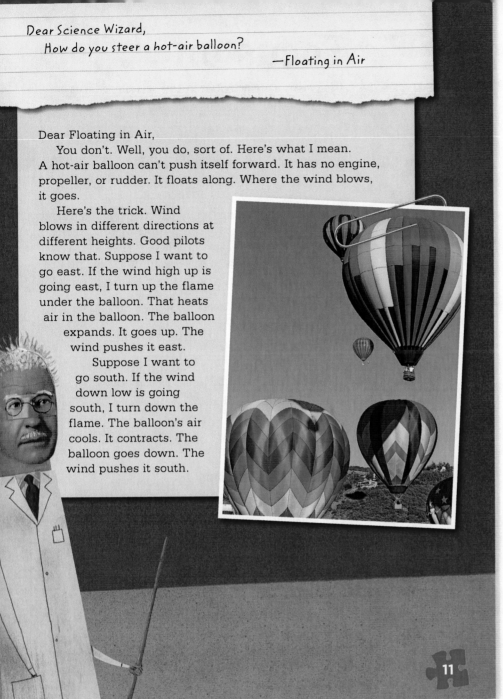

Dear Science Wizard,
How do you steer a hot-air balloon?
—Floating in Air

Dear Floating in Air,
You don't. Well, you do, sort of. Here's what I mean. A hot-air balloon can't push itself forward. It has no engine, propeller, or rudder. It floats along. Where the wind blows, it goes.

Here's the trick. Wind blows in different directions at different heights. Good pilots know that. Suppose I want to go east. If the wind high up is going east, I turn up the flame under the balloon. That heats air in the balloon. The balloon expands. It goes up. The wind pushes it east.

Suppose I want to go south. If the wind down low is going south, I turn down the flame. The balloon's air cools. It contracts. The balloon goes down. The wind pushes it south.

11

Student Journal page 39

Name _____ Date _____

Building Vocabulary: Antonyms Chart

Write two or three antonyms (words or phrases that are opposite or almost opposite in meaning) for each word from the selection. You may use a thesaurus or dictionary to help you.

Word	Antonyms
release	1. keep
	2. retain
	3. hold
split	1.
	2.
	3.
privately	1.
	2.
	3.
massive	1.
	2.
	3.
crouches	1.
	2.
	3.
problems	1.
	2.
	3.

Fun and Games • Ask the Science Wizard   39

Answers for the first part of **Student Journal page 40** are
1. *rest*; 2. *smile*; 3. *race*; 4. *grab*; 5. *slip*; 6. *greet*; 7. *pack*; 8. *pickle*; 9. *tree*; 10. *iced*.

Name _____ Date _____

Phonics/Word Study: Short Vowels a, e, i and Long Vowels a, e, i

Pronounce the word pairs below. Use one word from each pair to complete a sentence. The words in parentheses tell whether to write a word with a short or long vowel sound.

sleep/rest	smile/grin	race/walk	take/pack	tree/fence
grab/take	slide/slip	greet/help	rice/pickle	iced/mint

1. (short) People and most animals need to _____ each day.
2. (long) I always _____ when I see a puppy or kitten.
3. (long) I'll _____ you to the corner.
4. (short) It is not polite to _____ the last piece of pie.
5. (short) If you don't wear boots, you'll _____ on the ice.
6. (long) Please come _____ our guests.
7. (short) Did you _____ the apple in your lunch box?
8. (short) Can I have that _____ on your plate?
9. (long) The cat climbed the _____.
10. (long) I like to drink _____ tea.

Choose three of the words you did not use in the sentences. Write the words in three new sentences of your own.

1. _____
2. _____
3. _____

40   Fun and Games • Ask the Science Wizard

Writing Advice Column

Explain that students are going to tell someone else how to do something, in the same way as the Science Wizard—by answering a question. As a group, brainstorm some basic tasks students know how to do—such as style hair with gel, cook an omelet, or burn pictures onto a DVD. Avoid tasks with numerous steps. Have students complete *Student Journal* page 37. Then, on *Student Journal* page 38, students can write and answer a question. (See Differentiated Instruction.)

Vocabulary Antonyms

Provide these antonyms: *easy/difficult, bored/interested*. Point out the word *release* on selection page 8. Ask a volunteer to read the sentence in which the word appears. Then ask:

- What does the word *release* mean in this context?
- Which clues helped you figure out the meaning?
- What is an antonym of *release*? (*hold*)

Have students complete the antonyms activity on *Student Journal* page 39.

Phonics/Word Study

Short and Long *a, e, i*

Display and read aloud the following word pairs: *sat, ate; beg, team;* and *trip, glide*. Ask volunteers to identify the short and long vowels in each pair. Then have volunteers suggest other short and long *a, e,* and *i* word pairs. Now, work with students to complete the in-depth vowels activity on TE page 66. For additional support, have students complete *Student Journal* page 40.

Short and Long *a, e, i*

▶ Provide students with the Short *a, e, i* versus Long *a, e, i* Sort sheet and have them sort for both speed and accuracy as they practice the vowels they have studied thus far. (See *Word Study Manual* page 42.)

▶ Because it's important for students to hear the difference between the two vowels, and not just see the difference, have students work in pairs. One student can read the word aloud while the other determines the placement. (Or you can make picture cards.) When pairs are finished, have both students read each column to see if all the words have the same sound. Then have students switch roles.

▶ When confronted with a word with two or more syllables, students should choose a syllable to sort.

▶ Note: You may wish to create an oddball column for *want, call,* and *small.* They do not have the same short *a* sound as the other short *a* words.

▶ Once both partners have taken turns reading the words aloud and sorting them, have students time themselves to see how fast they can do the sort. Being able to sort both quickly and accurately means the student has mastered these vowel sounds.

Short *a, e, i* versus Long *a, e, i* Sort					
Short *a*	Long *a*	Short *e*	Long *e*	Short *i*	Long *i*
band	maybe	belly	feel	whiz	wind
mass	flame	help	gear	mix	fly
want	gave	pedal	teeth	riffle	try
call	change	deck	rear	big	linemen
small	stay	next	need	uphill	bike

For more information on word sorts and spelling stages, see pages 5–31 in the *Word Study Manual.*

Focus on . . .

Use one or more activities in this section to focus on a particular area of need in your students.

Comprehension STRATEGY SUPPORT INDEPENDENT

To help those students who need more practice using the strategies covered in this lesson, work one-on-one or in small groups to apply the strategy prompts below. Apply the prompts to a *Reading Advantage* paperback, a classroom library book, or a new or familiar selection in the magazine. Always model your own thinking first.

Monitor Understanding

- Do I understand what I'm reading? If not, what part is confusing to me?
- What fix-up strategies can I use to solve the problem? (See During Reading for fix-up strategies.)
- Why did a character say (do, think, ask) that?
- What images do I visualize from the text? What parts can't I visualize?
- Why did the author include (or not include) those details?

Inferential Thinking

- What are the causes or effects of this event?
- What do I learn from the character or person's thoughts, words, or actions?
- What do I know (or infer) from the text that the author hasn't stated directly?
- What conclusions can I draw?

Writing Explanation

Tell students that many people probably don't know how a hot-air balloon is steered. Have students reread the Science Wizard's explanation on page 11, jot down some notes, and then retell the process of steering a hot-air balloon to a partner. Then have each student write a letter to a friend, explaining in their own words how to steer a hot-air balloon.

Fluency: Expression

Explain that reading aloud fluently involves reading with appropriate expression. After students have the read the selection at least once, use the last question and answer (about hot-air balloons) in the selection to model reading expressively. Then have students work in pairs to take turns reading aloud another question and answer. Have pairs switch roles.

As you listen to pairs read, use these prompts to guide them.

▶ Preview what you will read to get used to the text and to practice hard words.

▶ Put yourself in the role of the person asking the question. How would someone asking a question sound? Then put yourself in the role of the Science Wizard. How would the explanation sound?

▶ Use punctuation marks for clues to expression. Raise your voice slightly at the end of a question. Pause when you see a comma or a period.

When students read aloud, do they—

✓ reflect an understanding of the text?

✓ demonstrate appropriate timing, stress, and intonation?

✓ incorporate appropriate speed and phrasing?

English Language Learners

Support students as they preview the selection on TE page 61 by doing a word sort.

1. Write the word *games* on the board. Have students make a list of words related to the word *games*.

2. Ask partners to sort their words into categories, such as inside games, outside games, or equipment.

3. Have students explain their sorts.

Independent Activity Options

While you work with individuals or small groups, others can work independently on one or more of the following options.

▶ Foundations paperback books, see TE pages 195–200

▶ Foundations *eZines*

▶ Repeat word sorts for this lesson

▶ *Student Journal* pages for this lesson

Assessment

Strategy Assessment

To help you and your students assess their use of comprehension strategies, ask the following questions. Students can complete a written response or provide verbal answers in a one-on-one reading conference.

1. **Monitor Understanding** What questions did you have about this selection? How did you fix your confusion? (Answers will vary. Students should describe a confusing section and then the strategies they used to resolve their confusion.)

2. **Inferential Thinking** What inferences did you make as you read this selection? (Answers will vary but should reflect information in the selection.)

For ongoing informal assessment, use the checklists on pages 61–64 of *Foundations Assessment*.

Word Study Assessment

Use these steps to help you and your students assess their understanding of short and long *a, e,* and *i* sounds.

1. Display a chart like the one shown, but include only the headings and the words in the first column.

2. Have students read aloud the words in the first column.

3. Then have students sort the words into the correct column. The answers are shown.

Word	Short *a*	Short *e*	Short *i*	Long *a*	Long *e*	Long *i*
chat	chat	stretch	tickle	change	feel	fly
change	flat	bell	mix	stay	hear	
fly	mass			main		
tickle						
feel						
stretch						
stay						
mix						
hear						
main						
flat						
bell						
mass						

Designing for Fun

Fun and Games, pages 12–16

SUMMARY

In this **interview**, a computer game designer describes what it's like to design and play games for a living.

COMPREHENSION STRATEGIES

Making Connections

WRITING

Interview

VOCABULARY

Suffixes

PHONICS/WORD STUDY

Short and Long *u*

Lesson Vocabulary

interactive	economics
mechanics	audience
established	

MATERIALS

Fun and Games, pp. 12–16
Student Journal, pp. 41–45
Word Study Manual, p. 43

Designing for FUN

Would you like to play computer games all day? And get paid for it? Sheri Graner Ray does just that. She is a game designer. She has done this job for fifteen years. Sheri told us about her cool job.

Before Reading Use one or more activities.

Make a K-W-L Chart

Create a K-W-L chart on computer games. Return to the chart later.

What We **Know**	What We **Want** to Know	What We **Learned**
Computer games are challenging.	How are computer games made?	

Vocabulary Preview

Display the vocabulary words and read them aloud to clarify pronunciations. Ask students how they think the words will be used in the selection. Then have students begin the predictions chart on *Student Journal* page 41. They will complete it after reading. (See Differentiated Instruction.)

Preview the Selection

Have students survey the selection. Discuss students' observations.

Make Predictions/ Set Purpose

Students should use the information they gathered in previewing the selection to make predictions about what they will learn. If students have trouble generating a purpose for reading, suggest that they read to learn about how computer games are designed and where the designers get their ideas.

When did you decide to be a game designer?

Sheri: I started in 1990. I'd played Dungeons and Dragons for ten years. I remember walking into my first game studio. I knew it was where I wanted to be. Everybody there understood games. They loved games the way I do. It was magic to be there.

Where do you get your ideas?

Sheri: From classic literature and mythology. I read a lot of history. One of our designers knows all about Civil War history. We look at real battles. Then we see how they could apply to our setting.

What is the most difficult part of the design process?

Sheri: Going home in the evening. I love what I do. I go home in the evening and play games.

What do you enjoy most about your job?

Sheri: I come to work and talk about where to put the wreck of a giant space cruiser. What other job lets you do that? That's so cool. The best thing is the people I work with. They are very smart. I really like that. They challenge me daily.

How do you spend your day?

Sheri: I start with a morning meeting. I speak with all the designers. We go over our plans for the day. We discuss which quests everyone is working on. Each of our designers owns a planet in the game.

We decide what stories the players will be involved in. We figure out how they will be involved. Then we go back to our offices. We put those stories into the game. In the afternoon we get reports. These come from the people testing our games. Then we spend time fixing problems. That means playing games even more.

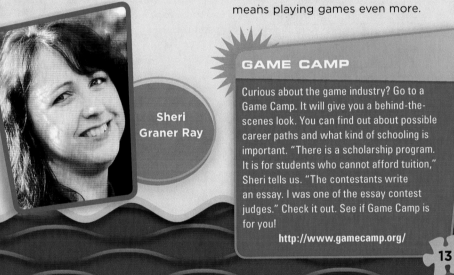

Sheri Graner Ray

GAME CAMP

Curious about the game industry? Go to a Game Camp. It will give you a behind-the-scenes look. You can find out about possible career paths and what kind of schooling is important. "There is a scholarship program. It is for students who cannot afford tuition," Sheri tells us. "The contestants write an essay. I was one of the essay contest judges." Check it out. See if Game Camp is for you!

http://www.gamecamp.org/

13

DIFFERENTIATED INSTRUCTION
Vocabulary Preview

Work with students to read, pronounce, and establish meaning for the word *interactive*.

What are the word parts?	*inter*	*active*
What is the base word?		*active*
What is the prefix?	*inter*	
Where have you seen the prefix before?	*interconnect international*	
What does the prefix mean?	between, among, or within	
What does the word *interactive* mean?	involving the actions or input of a user	
When might you use this word?	The museum has an *interactive* hands-on exhibit.	

Student Journal page 41

Name _____ Date _____

Building Vocabulary: Predictions
How do you predict these words will be used in "Designing for Fun"? Write your answers in the second column. Next, read the interview. Then, clarify your answers in the third column.

Word	My prediction for how the word will be used	How the word is actually used
interactive		
mechanics		
established		
economics		
audience		

Fun and Games • Designing for Fun

41

During Reading

Comprehension

MAKING CONNECTIONS

Use these questions to model how to make connections with the text. Then have students make their own connections as they read the interview.

- Does any of this sound familiar to me?
- Have I ever played any computer games or role-playing games?
- How do my personal experiences help me connect to the information?

Teacher Think Aloud

I once played an online game in which I was a character in Medieval times, and I had to fight a dragon. Along the way to the dragon, I met other online players, who had their own characters in the story. It was really fun—but also addictive! I played all night.

Fix-Up Strategies

Offer these strategies to help students read independently.

If you don't understand what you're reading:

- Reread the difficult section to look for clues to help you comprehend.
- Read ahead to find clues to help you comprehend.
- Retell, or say in your own words, what you've read.
- Visualize, or form mental pictures of, what you've read.

DIFFERENTIATED INSTRUCTION
Writing Interview

Help students choose their questions and conduct their interviews with the following suggestions:

1. To begin, find out what your interviewee's career goal or plan for the future is.

2. Ask questions about that career or plan that you would want answered if you were considering the same path.

3. Avoid asking questions that can be answered with just yes or no. Ask questions that require information in the answers.

4. Keep your questions short to ensure that your interviewee does most of the talking.

Student Journal pages 42–43

Name _____ Date _____

Writing: Interview Planning Page
Ask your partner about his or her future career plans. Jot down notes about what he or she would like to do, why he or she is interested in that field or profession, and what he or she hopes to achieve. Use these notes to write your interview questions.

Career or Future Goal: _____

Notes and Interview Focus Points:

1. _____
2. _____
3. _____
4. _____
5. _____
6. _____
7. _____
8. _____

42   Fun and Games • Designing for Fun

What is a "quest"?

Sheri: Interactive games often involve going on quests. "Interactive" means the game changes with your choices. You log on to the game. You read a bulletin. It says a wealthy prince has been kidnapped. There are clues about who took the prince. There's a trail to follow. You round up friends inside the game. Then you follow the clues to the prince. You overcome many obstacles. There's a reward if you rescue him. That's a quest.

What does a "content designer" do?

Sheri: Those people design the stories. They decide what characters you meet in a game. They write the words a character says. They figure out what the players must do to go forward in a game. They are also called quest designers.

How is that different from a "system designer"?

Sheri: A system designer creates the mechanics of how the game works. That may include how combat is computed mathematically.

Do you ever put yourself or your friends into your games?

Sheri: It depends on the game. There's room to be creative in a small game. I worked on a game with a gallery of haunted portraits. You could talk to them. They would talk back. They were all friends or family members of the team. We rarely do this in an established gaming universe.

What classes helped you become a game designer?

Sheri: English is very important. You have to be able to write a sentence. You have to understand what a story is. That way you can make stories for others. Civics and economics are important. Civics helps me decide how to make a made-up government run. Economics is about what things cost. I have to figure out how to make things happen in this world. Then people can buy and sell things.

WHO DO YOU WANT TO BE?

Have you ever wanted to be someone else? Just for a while? Then an RPG may be for you. That stands for "role-playing game." In RPGs there are no winners or losers. Your character plays for a long time. The character is always there waiting for you when you log in to the game. You can form groups with other players. Together, you solve problems. You fight monsters and search for treasure. The better you get at the game, the more you can do. And the more fun it becomes.

14

After Reading
WHOLE CLASS Use one or more activities.

Check Purpose

Have students determine whether their purpose was met. Did they discover how computer games are designed and where designers get their ideas?

Discussion Questions

Ask the following questions.

1. What do you think is the most challenging part of designing a computer game? (Draw Conclusions)

2. Why do you think knowing about stories and how to tell them is important to designing computer games? (Inferential Thinking)

3. Which computer games do you like the most? Why? Which ones do you like the least? Why? (Making Connections)

Revisit: K-W-L Chart

Have students return to the K-W-L chart that they began before reading. Were all students' questions about computer games answered? What new information can they add to the chart?

Revisit: Predictions Chart

Have students return to the predictions chart on *Student Journal* page 41 and complete the third column.

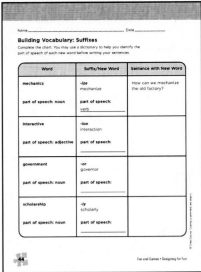

Are you as good a player as you are a designer?

Sheri: I'm good with role-playing games. I'm not good with flight simulations. My office partner once named himself Galandro-Killsheri in a game. That's because I was so easy to shoot down.

Have you ever been surprised by the reactions to your work?

Sheri: I'm sometimes surprised by what players will do. I worked on a game several years ago. A player went into the courtyard of a castle.

He walked backward around a tree lots of times. That made a non-player character turn into a magic sword. The non-player character still talked like a person. We didn't know that would happen!

What are your thoughts about the future of gaming?

Sheri: I see our audience becoming broader all the time. People from all walks of life will be playing online games.

15

Answers for **Student Journal page 45** are 1. short; 2. short; 3. short; 4. oddball; 5. long; 6. oddball; 7. short; 8. long; 9. long; 10. short; 11. long; 12. short.

Writing Interview

On the board, make a quick list of careers or jobs students suggest. List some questions students have about the careers. Have each student choose a career and then pair up. Partners should identify their career choices. Have partners use *Student Journal* page 42 to take notes about each other's career choices. Then, on *Student Journal* page 43, they can use their notes to create interview questions. Partners can "perform" their interviews for the group. (See Differentiated Instruction.)

Vocabulary Suffixes

Display the word *mathematically*. Have students identify the base word. (*mathematics*) Then point out that the base word has two suffixes. Underline *-al* and *-ly*. Explain that the suffix *-al* changes the base word to an adjective, which means "relating to mathematics." The suffix *-ly* changes *mathematical* to an adverb, which means "in a mathematical way." Have students complete *Student Journal* page 44.

Phonics/Word Study

Short and Long *u*

On the board, write *tub* and *use*. Ask students which word has a short *u* sound (*tub*) and which has a long *u* sound (*use*). Have volunteers suggest other short *u* words and list them under *tub*. Then ask for long *u* words and list them under *use*. Now, work with students to complete the in-depth short and long *u* activity on TE page 73. For additional support, have students complete *Student Journal* page 45.

Do you have any advice for young aspiring game designers?

Sheri: Play all kinds of games. And not just computer games. Play board and card games. Play Scrabble with your grandmother. Play jacks or tetherball with your little sister and brother. Play games one-on-one with other people. And have fun! Watch how people play games. Learn what they like. Learn what they don't like. ◆

ONLINE GAMING AROUND THE WORLD

Do you like playing computer games? Have you ever played with other people—people from really far away? The MMOG makes this possible. That stands for Massively Multiplayer Online Game. You use the Internet to play. It connects you to other computers. The other players might live anywhere. They could be across the street or in another country. You can talk to them and plan together what to do in the game. Hundreds of thousands can play at once. That's a lot of players to keep track of.

16

Short and Long *u*

▶ Display *cut* and *cute*. Have students segment out the words as follows, listening for the sound of the *u*.

cut	ut	u
cute	ute	u

▶ Have pairs brainstorm four more words for short *u* and four more for long *u*. Come back together as a class and share the words. As each word is said, ask which column it should go in, and then write it on the board.

▶ Provide students with the Short *u* versus Long *u* Sort sheet and have them begin sorting by the three headings shown. (See *Word Study Manual* page 43.) Be sure to model the correct placement for the first few words. Have students work in pairs. One student can read the word aloud while the other determines the placement. When they are finished, have students switch roles.

▶ When confronted with a word with two or more syllables, students should identify the syllable with the vowel sound under consideration and concentrate only on that syllable.

▶ As a whole group, discuss the sort, students' observations, and why *quest* and the other words ended up in the Oddball column. *Quest* begins with the *qu* blend, in which the *u* isn't short or long. Since it's part of a blend, it's not even heard as a vowel sound. A blend is a sequence of two or more consonant sounds within a syllable. Other words in the Oddball column show words with a long *u* sound, but with an *oo* spelling.

Short *u* versus Long *u* Sort

Short *u*	Long *u*	Oddball
fun	computer	quest
multiplayer	you	shoot
hundred	studio	cool
dungeons	clue	room
difficult	rescue	do
us	include	bulletin
industry	use	
discuss	cruise	
public		
up		
understand		

For more information on word sorts and spelling stages, see pages 5–31 in the *Word Study Manual*.

Focus on . . .

Use one or more activities in this section to focus on a particular area of need in your students.

Comprehension <small>STRATEGY SUPPORT</small>

To help those students who need more practice using the strategies covered in this lesson, work one-on-one or in small groups to apply the strategy prompts below. Apply the prompts to a *Reading Advantage* paperback, a classroom library book, or a new or familiar selection in the magazine. Always model your own thinking first.

Making Connections

• What does this story (article, passage) remind me of?

• What do I already know about this topic?

• Where have I heard about this topic before?

• What do I have in common with the characters, people, or situations in the text?

• What other books, stories, articles, movies, or TV shows does this text make me think about?

Writing Essay

Ask students to each write an essay to persuade a panel of judges that he or she should receive a scholarship for a two-week stay at a game camp. Students can use these questions to help them focus their writing.

• Why am I a worthy candidate for the scholarship?

• What do I hope to learn at the camp?

• How will I use what I learn in the future?

Focus on . . .

Use one or more activities in this section to focus on a particular area of need in your students.

Fluency: Punctuation

Explain that part of reading aloud fluently involves noting punctuation. After students have read "Designing for Fun" at least once, use a section from the interview to model reading aloud. Point out how you raised your voice when you encountered a question mark, and paused for periods. Then have partners take turns reading aloud questions and answers from the interview.

Use these prompts to guide students as they read.

▶ Preview what you will read. Notice the different punctuation marks and what they signal to you. Pause at periods. Let your voice rise at the end of sentences marked with a question mark.

▶ Read with expression. Put yourself in the place of the interviewer asking the questions, or in the place of the interviewee explaining what your job is like.

When students read aloud, do they—

✓ demonstrate appropriate meaning and usage of punctuation marks?

✓ incorporate appropriate timing, stress, and intonation?

✓ exhibit well-timed pauses between words and phrases?

English Language Learners

Support students as they make connections in the third discussion question on TE page 70.

1. Have partners practice asking and answering the question about which computer games they like and don't like.

2. Volunteers can share their answers with the whole class.

3. Invite volunteers to then share the reasons they like and don't like certain games.

Independent Activity Options

While you work with individuals or small groups, others can work independently on one or more of the following options.

▶ Foundations paperback books, see TE pages 195–200

▶ Foundations *eZines*

▶ Repeat word sorts for this lesson

▶ *Student Journal* pages for this lesson

Assessment

Strategy Assessment

To help you and your students assess their use of comprehension strategies, ask the following questions. Students can complete a written response or provide verbal answers in a one-on-one reading conference.

• **Making Connections** What connections did you make with this text? How did those connections help you understand what you were reading? (Answers will vary. Students may say that they really like computer games and would love to have a job like Sheri's.)

See *Foundations Assessment* pages 22–25 for formal assessment to go with *Fun and Games*.

Word Study Assessment

Use these steps to help you and your students assess their understanding of short and long *u* sounds.

1. Display a chart like the one below, but include only the headings and the words in the first column.

2. Have students read the words and sort them into the correct column. The answers are shown.

Word	Short *u*	Long *u*
up	up	use
understand	understand	clue
use	must	cute
must	hundred	juice
clue		salute
cute		
juice		
hundred		
salute		

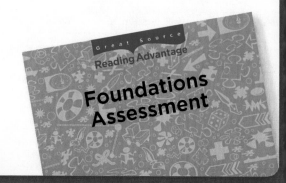

Foundations Assessment

BLACKOUT

SOMETIMES YOU CAN FIND FUN IN THE MOST UNEXPECTED PLACES.

SUMMARY
In the **short story** "Blackout," a reluctant James is visiting his grandmother in a small town and discovers that he actually has fun.

COMPREHENSION STRATEGIES
Making Connections
Monitor Understanding

WRITING
Brief Essay

VOCABULARY
Antonyms

PHONICS/WORD STUDY
Short and Long *o*

Lesson Vocabulary
energized   hover
taunting   sprawled
reclaim

MATERIALS
Fun and Games, pp. 17–21
Student Journal, pp. 46–50
Word Study Manual, p. 44

Before Reading ⊙ Use one or more activities.

Make a Concept Web
Tell students that they will read a story about a blackout in a small town. Ask them what they think of when they hear the word *blackout*. Record responses in a concept web.

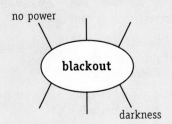

no power

blackout

darkness

Vocabulary Preview
Display the vocabulary words and read them aloud to clarify pronunciations. Have students begin the making associations activity on *Student Journal* page 46. Use the vocabulary word *energized* to model a response for the page. Revisit the page later. (See Differentiated Instruction.)

Preview the Selection
Have students look through the selection. Discuss their observations.

Make Predictions/Set Purpose
Students should use the information they gathered in previewing the selection to make predictions about what the story will be about. If students have trouble generating a purpose for reading, suggest that they read to learn how James changes his attitude about his visit with his grandmother.

DIFFERENTIATED INSTRUCTION
Vocabulary Preview

Work with students to read, pronounce, and establish meaning for the word *reclaim*. Help students understand that the prefix *re-* means "again, back."

What are the word parts?	*re*	*claim*
Which is the prefix?	*re-*	
What does the prefix mean?	again, back	
Where have you seen the prefix before?	redo recapture recopy recycle	
What is a synonym for *reclaim*?	take back	
When might you use this word?	Cindy must *reclaim* her sunglasses at the lost-and-found office.	

Student Journal page 46

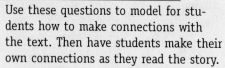

Name _____ Date_____

Building Vocabulary: Making Associations
Pick two words from the vocabulary list below. Think about what you already know about each word and answer the questions.

| energized | taunting | reclaim | hover | sprawled |

Word _____
What do you think about when you read this word? _____
Who might use this word? _____
What do you already know about this word? _____

Word _____
What do you think about when you read this word? _____
Who might use this word? _____
What do you already know about this word? _____

Now watch for these words in the magazine selection. Were you on the right track?

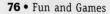

46

Fun and Games • Blackout

"What do you want to do?" My mom holds a board game in one hand and some blank paper in the other. She thinks we might play a game. It's Friday night, and it's not going to happen. Me, playing board games with my family. *Please.*

"Nothing," I say to her.

"We drove four hours to get here. Grandma's excited to see you. You can't say you want to do nothing," says my mom.

"Well, I just did," I say.

My grandma lives in Standardsville, Virginia. Even the name of the town sounds boring: *Standardsville.* Every year we drive down for my grandmother's birthday. There's never anything to do.

My mom sighs and walks into the kitchen. She sighs at me a lot these days. I hear my grandma say, "Does James want to play a game?"

She still calls me James. But I've been Jim to everyone else for years. My mom just says I'm tired.

I am tired, actually. This place makes me tired. It's one big yawn. I wouldn't be tired if I were at home. I'd be in Philadelphia. That's where things actually happen. You feel energized just by walking down the street.

I should be there now. Tonight, there's a party at Tony's. Tomorrow is our baseball team's first game. I hate that I'm missing it. Everyone was mad at me. The Bluejays will be down their best pitcher. I hoped to throw another no-hitter. I did that last year when we played the Pirates.

Instead, I'm in Virginia at my grandma's. Tomorrow, Mom will make a special dinner. There will be a big vanilla birthday cake. Grandma will blow out the candles. It's our only plan for the whole weekend. Ugh! Three days of my life blown away.

I turn on the TV. I might zone out here all weekend. I flip through the channels. The news? No. Cartoons? Maybe. A cooking show? Yeah, right! Pro wrestling will have to do. I put my feet up on the couch.

18

During Reading

Comprehension
MAKING CONNECTIONS

Use these questions to model for students how to make connections with the text. Then have students make their own connections as they read the story.

- Does any of this sound familiar to me?
- Do I know anyone like James?
- How would I feel if I were in the same situation as James?

(See Differentiated Instruction.)

Teacher Think Aloud

I remember one summer when my parents made us go to Boston, Massachusetts, to visit some friends of theirs. I was convinced that the trip would be extremely boring. I can relate to the way James feels about going to Standardsville, Virginia. My trip ended up being really fun, though. I wonder if James will have fun, too.

Comprehension
MONITOR UNDERSTANDING

Use these questions to model for students how to monitor understanding by asking questions. Then have students ask their own questions and try to resolve any confusion.

- What is going on here?
- Why does the character feel that way?
- What fix-up strategy can I use to fix my confusion?

"Are you going to hog the TV all weekend?" That's my cousin, Anna. She's sixteen, too. She lives down the street from Grandma. I bet she comes over here a lot. I bet she likes it here.

Her hair is as short as mine. She's wearing overalls and holding a book. On the drive down, Mom warned, "Say more than two words to Anna this weekend."

"Probably," I say to Anna. Well, that was one word. I'm already halfway there.

"My show is on at eight," says Anna as she reaches for the remote. The clock says 7:52 p.m.

"Too bad for you. The match just started, and it's going to last an hour," I say. I put my hand over the remote so she can't have it. She tries to take it anyway, and I smile. I didn't realize Anna had guts.

"You want this?" I ask. I stand up and hold the remote in the air. She's barely five feet tall. My arms are way longer. Taunting her is a piece of cake.

But Anna's fast. She jumps up on the couch. Before I know it, she whips the remote out of my hands. She changes the channel. Suddenly, wrestling turns into some sappy love story on TV.

"Give it back, Anna." My voice is loud.

"Jim," my mom calls from the kitchen. "Watch it."

That's her warning to me. I know I'm supposed to quiet down and watch Anna's boring show. But I ignore my mom. I try to reclaim the remote, but Anna's got a death grip on it. We pull and glare at each other.

And then, it happens. It doesn't matter who's got the remote. The lights have gone out. There's no more TV. There's just darkness. Everything is black. Anna and I let go of the remote at the same time, and we both fall back.

My grandma and my mom come into the room. They have a flashlight. They point the beam at Anna and me on the ground.

"What happened?" I ask.

"It's another blackout," Grandma says. "It's happened a few times recently. They're working on fixing the lines. It'll come back on in an hour or so."

"An hour!" I say. "What are we supposed to do for an hour?"

"I thought you didn't want to do anything, James." Grandma is teasing me. It's annoying. Even Anna's show would have been better than this. "Come on," Grandma says. "Everybody outside."

"Why?" I ask. I don't feel like going anywhere.

"Anna and I have a solution to your problem," my grandma says. "We've got a game for you. I promise it's better than a board game."

19

DIFFERENTIATED INSTRUCTION SMALL GROUP

Comprehension
MAKING CONNECTIONS

To help students make connections with the text, ask these questions.

- What do you think of James? Would you like to be friends with him? Why or why not?

- What relationships have you experienced that are similar to James's relationship with Anna?

- Were you ever surprised when a trip you thought would be boring turned out to be fun after all? How do your experiences help you relate to this story?

Teacher Think Aloud

As I read page 18, I see that James is not happy about visiting his grandmother. However, I'm not sure why he feels that way. I reread the page. Now I see—he is unhappy about missing a party and his first baseball game of the season. Rereading helped me understand his attitude.

Fix-Up Strategies

Offer these strategies to help students read independently.

If you don't understand what you're reading:

- Reread the difficult section to look for clues to help you comprehend.

- Read ahead to find clues to help you comprehend.

- Retell, or say in your own words, what you've read.

- Visualize, or form mental pictures of, what you've read.

If you don't understand a word:

- Reread the sentence. Look for ideas and words that provide meaning clues.

- Find clues by reading a few sentences before and after the confusing word.

- Look for the base or root word and think about its meaning.

- Think about the topic or plot at this point to see if either offers meaning clues.

Writing Brief Essay

To help students plan and write their brief essay, share these writing tips:

- Include as many details as you can on the *Student Journal* planning page, page 47. Writers always pick and choose from their ideas.

- Try to use strong verbs and specific nouns. They will add energy to your writing. Use varying word choices. For example, try *charged* instead of *ran*, or *shrieked* instead of *yelled*.

- Use the planning page to craft your three paragraphs on *Student Journal* page 48.

Student Journal pages 47–48

Name_____ Date_____

Writing: Brief Essay Planning Page
Fill in this planning page to prepare for writing a brief essay on
Student Journal page 48

Topic Choices: What are three instances in which I ended up having
a better time than I thought I would?

1. _____
2. _____
3. _____

Final Choice from List: _____

Why did I think I'd have a bad time?
_____
_____

What ended up happening?
_____
_____
_____

What did I learn from my experience?
_____
_____
_____

Fun and Games • Blackout   47

I look at Anna. The flashlight is shining on her face, and I can tell she looks embarrassed. I'd be embarrassed, too.

When we go outside, the sun is setting. Here, you can see the horizon all around. You can't see that at home. There are too many buildings blocking the sky. It's been a long time since I've seen a sunset. Maybe it's been since I was a kid. It makes me wonder what I've been doing all these years.

Tonight, the sky looks almost nice. Lots of grayish purple clouds hover over us.

My grandma tells us to sit down on the ground. I start to argue, but then I notice that everyone does it. My mom, my grandma, and Anna are already sitting down. They're sprawled out on the grass as if this is normal. I sigh and sit down, too.

"Do you remember how to play, Jim?" my mom asks. "We used to play this all the time when you were little."

Everyone seems to know what's going on but me. I don't know why, but it makes me feel stupid. I don't say anything.

"Don't worry, James," Grandma says. "You'll catch on quickly. Anna, you can start."

I turn my head to look at Anna. In the dusk, I can see that she is staring up at the sky. "There's an apple," she says. "And someone's hand above it, about to pick it up."

I can't believe it. It's the awful cloud game. We're supposed to lie here for an hour and make pictures out of clouds. I'm about to stand up and go inside. But then I look where Anna's pointing, and I see it. She's right. There's a giant hand in the sky,

20

After Reading
 Use one or more activities.

Check Purpose

Have students determine whether their purpose was met. Did students find out why James changes his attitude during the visit to his grandmother?

Discussion Questions

Continue the group discussion with the following questions.

1. Why are James and his mother visiting his grandmother? (Details)

2. Do you think James had fun in Standardsville during this trip? Why? (Draw Conclusions)

3. What would you have done during a blackout to entertain yourself? (Making Connections)

Revisit: Making Associations

Encourage students to revisit the making associations activity on *Student Journal* page 46. Are there adjustments or changes they would like to make? Students may add new notes, as necessary.

about to pick up an apple. Now I remember playing this game as a kid. I just don't remember ever seeing a shape that looked that real.

Then I see one: a baseball player. He's striking out. I expect this to make me mad. I expect this to remind me of what I'm missing tomorrow. But for some reason, it doesn't. It actually looks kind of cool. It's not my turn, but I call out anyway. I point to it up in the sky. I think there's excitement in my voice.

I look over and see my mom smiling at me. I roll my eyes, but I start smiling, too. I'm remembering now how we used to play. Anna and I used to fight to call out cloud shapes first. She finds a frog. I find a swing set. We go back and forth for a while. Then, at the same time, we point up. Both of us have spotted a giant cloud kite. My grandmother insists she sees a birthday cake. But no one else can find it.

Soon, the lights come back on inside. I can read my watch. It's almost ten o'clock. I can't believe it. We've been playing the cloud game for two hours.

My grandma looks at Anna and me. "I guess you missed your shows," she says. "But the TV's working again. Or . . . we could always keep playing a little longer."

Grandma is eighty years old. She calls me James. But that doesn't seem like such a big deal anymore, sitting on the grass in the dark. By now, the sun has set, and the stars are out. They blink brightly behind the clouds. They begin to fill up the whole sky.

"Okay," I say, smiling, "but only because it's your birthday." ◆

Student Journal page 49

Answers for **Student Journal page 50** are 1. short, long; 2. long, short; 3. short, long; 4. long, short; 5. short, long, short; 6. long, short; 7. long, short; 8. long, short; 9. long, short; 10. short, long.

Writing Brief Essay

Ask students to share some experiences in which they had a better time than they thought they would. Jot down their ideas. Now have students consider their own experiences and choose one to write about in a brief essay. Students can use the planning page on *Student Journal* page 47 to organize their thoughts. Then, on *Student Journal* page 48, they can write their essay. (See Differentiated Instruction.)

Vocabulary Antonyms

Display the word *taunting*. With students' help, list words that are antonyms of *taunting*. Examples include *complimenting, flattering, praising,* and *respecting*. Then have students complete the antonyms activity on *Student Journal* page 49. Student responses may include *energized: dispirited, listless; sprawled: contracted, straightened; reclaim: lose, forfeit;* and *hover: sink, settle.*

Phonics/Word Study

Short and Long *o*

Tell students to listen for and identify the short *o* and long *o* sound as you say *tone* (long *o*) and *rock* (short *o*). Then say *trombone*. Do students hear short or long *o*? (They should hear both.) Now, work with students to complete the in-depth short and long *o* activity on TE page 80. For additional support, have students complete *Student Journal* page 50.

Short and Long *o*

▶ Place the following words on the board or on chart paper: *job* and *ghost*. Have students segment out the words as follows, listening for the sound of the *o*.

job	*ob*	*o*
ghost	*ost*	*o*

▶ Have partners brainstorm four more words for short *o* and four more for long *o*. Come back together as a class and share the words. As each word is said, ask which column it should go in, and then write it on the chart.

▶ Provide students with the Short *o* versus Long *o* Sort sheet. Have them begin sorting by the three headings shown. (See *Word Study Manual* page 44.) Be sure to model the correct placement for the first few words. Because it's important for students to hear the difference between the two vowels, and not just see the difference, have students work in pairs. One student can read the word aloud while the other determines the placement. When they are finished, have students switch roles.

▶ When confronted with a word with two or more syllables, students should identify the syllable with the vowel sound under consideration and concentrate only on that syllable.

▶ As a whole group, discuss the sort, students' observations, and why *won* and *one* ended up in the Oddball column. Both *won* and *one* (homophones) follow the spelling patterns of short and long *o*, but they don't sound like either one.

Short *o* versus Long *o* Sort		
Short *o*	**Long *o***	**Oddball**
mom	most	won
lot	hold	one
on	go	hover
hog	drove	above
clock	Tony	
block	throw	
dodge	blown	
frog	zone	
spot	show	
goggles	home	
	remote	
	both	

For more information on word sorts and spelling stages, see pages 5–31 in the *Word Study Manual*.

Focus on . . .

Use one or more activities in this section to focus on a particular area of need in your students.

Comprehension   STRATEGY SUPPORT

To help those students who need more practice using the strategies covered in this lesson, work one-on-one or in small groups to apply the strategy prompts below. Apply the prompts to a *Reading Advantage* paperback, a classroom library book, or a new or familiar selection in the magazine. Always model your own thinking first.

Making Connections

- What does this story (article, passage) remind me of?
- What do I already know about this topic?
- Where have I heard about this topic before?
- What do I have in common with the characters, people, or situations in the text?
- What other books, stories, articles, movies, or TV shows does this text make me think about?

Monitor Understanding

- Do I understand what I'm reading? If not, what part is confusing to me?
- What fix-up strategies can I use to solve the problem? (See During Reading for fix-up strategies.)
- Why did a character say (do, think, ask) that?
- What images do I visualize from the text? What parts can't I visualize?
- Why did the author include (or not include) those details?

Writing **Character Sketch**

Tell students that they are going to write a character sketch of James. Note that a character sketch is a short description of what a story character is like. Have them reread the story and fill in a character map like the one below before writing. (See TE page 213 for a character map BLM.)

```
  ┌──────────────────┐      ┌──────────────────┐
  │ What character   │      │ What others think│
  │ says and does    │      │ about character  │
  └──────────────────┘      └──────────────────┘
            │                        │
            └────────┐      ┌────────┘
                   ┌─────────┐
                   │  James  │
                   └─────────┘
            ┌────────┘      └────────┐
  ┌──────────────────┐      ┌──────────────────┐
  │ How character    │      │ How I feel       │
  │ looks and feels  │      │ about character  │
  └──────────────────┘      └──────────────────┘
```

Fluency: Expression

Explain that part of reading aloud fluently involves reading with appropriate expression. After students have read "Blackout" at least once, use a passage from the story to model reading expressively. Then have students work in groups of four to practice reading the selection aloud. Each student should focus on a different character: James, Mom, Grandma, or Anna. Before students begin, remind them that the dialogue should be read as if they were speaking naturally.

Use these prompts to help groups read expressively.

▶ Read your lines several times so you are comfortable with them.

▶ Read with expression. Put yourself in the role of the character.

▶ Use the punctuation marks for clues to expression. Raise your voice slightly at the end of a question. Pause when you see a comma or a period.

When students read aloud, do they—

✓ reflect an understanding of the text?

✓ demonstrate appropriate timing, stress, and intonation?

✓ incorporate appropriate speed and phrasing?

English Language Learners

To support students as they preview the selection on TE page 75, examine idioms.

1. Write the following idioms on the board: *piece of cake* and *catch on*.

2. Discuss the meaning of each idiomatic phrase within context on pages 19 and 20 of the selection.

3. Have partners create sentences using these phrases.

Independent Activity Options

While you work with individuals or small groups, others can work independently on one or more of the following options.

▶ Foundations paperback books, see TE pages 195–200

▶ Foundations *eZines*

▶ Repeat word sorts for this lesson

▶ *Student Journal* pages for this lesson

Assessment

Strategy Assessment

To help you and your students assess their use of comprehension strategies, ask the following questions. Students can complete a written response or provide verbal answers in a one-on-one reading conference.

1. **Making Connections** What connections did you make with this story? How did those connections help you understand what you were reading? (Answers will vary.)

2. **Monitor Understanding** What questions did you have as you read this story? How did you find the answers to those questions? (Answers will vary but should include questions that students had.)

For ongoing informal assessment, use the checklists on pages 61–64 of *Foundations Assessment*.

Word Study Assessment

Use these steps to help you and your students assess their understanding of short and long *o* sounds.

1. Display a chart like the one below, but include only the headings and the words in the first column.

2. Have students read the words and sort them into the correct column. The answers are shown.

Word	Short *o*	Long *o*
foggy	foggy	show
show	sock	zone
sock	goggles	both
goggles	frog	troll
zone	stop	moat
both		bold
troll		
frog		
stop		
moat		
bold		

LESSON 11
Crazy for Chocolate! *and* Race Day

Fun and Games, pages 22–27

SUMMARY

This **newspaper article** describes the sights, smells, and tastes that greet visitors to the annual International Chocolate Show. The **poem** "Race Day" is about the excitement of a dirt-bike race.

COMPREHENSION STRATEGIES

Determining Importance
Monitor Understanding

WRITING

Description

VOCABULARY

Homophones

PHONICS/WORD STUDY

Short and Long *i, o, u*

Lesson Vocabulary

mannequins	pods
astrologer	kneading
nibble	

MATERIALS

Fun and Games, pp. 22–27
Student Journal, pp. 51–55
Word Study Manual, p. 45

What would get you out of bed on a cold, rainy Saturday morning? A cup of hot chocolate? How about a fountain of chocolate? Think I'm dreaming? I saw it at the International Chocolate Show.

International Chocolate Show PRESS

CRAZY FOR CHOCOLATE!

22

Before Reading Use one or more activities.

Anticipation Guide

Create an anticipation guide for students. (See TE page 214 for an anticipation guide BLM.) Ask students to place a check in the AGREE or DISAGREE box before each statement. The discussion of anticipation guide statements can be a powerful motivator because once students have reacted to the statements, they have a stake in seeing if they are "right." Have students read the article to check their choices. Revisit the guide later.

Anticipation Guide		
AGREE	DISAGREE	
		1. Artists have used food coloring and white chocolate to make paintings.
		2. The largest chocolate bar ever made weighed over 5,000 pounds.
		3. Cacao beans, from which chocolate is made, grow mostly in the United States.

Vocabulary Preview

Write the vocabulary words on the board or on chart paper and read them aloud to clarify pronunciations. Ask students to share what they know about a particular word or words. Then have students begin the knowledge rating chart on *Student Journal* page 51. Use the vocabulary word *nibble* to model a response for the page. Students will revisit the chart after they have finished reading the selection. (See Differentiated Instruction.)

82 • *Fun and Games*

My Day at the International Chocolate Show

By Jenny Velasquez

Every year thousands of chocolate lovers come to New York City. The International Chocolate Show is the attraction. It is a place to learn new chocolate recipes. There are fantastic items made of chocolate to see. And, of course, there is lots of chocolate to eat. I was there to write this report.

The International Chocolate Show is in a big industrial building. Mannequins wearing chocolate fashions greet you. They look beautiful—and delicious. But no eating the clothes!

The main room has hundreds of tables. Each table has something to do with chocolate. Some are piled high with chocolate candies. Others have chocolate cakes and cookies. You'll find chocolate-making machines. You can see chocolate molds.

You can consult a chocolate expert. You can also buy books about chocolate. An astrologer will even read the swirls in the bottom of your hot-chocolate cup. What is your chocolate fortune today?

You can sample chocolate from all over the world. Each kind is different. You will probably want to try everything.

CHOCOLATE TASTES

I ate white chocolate. I ate dark chocolate. I ate milk chocolate. I ate strawberries dipped in chocolate. I ate things covered with chocolate. There were fortune cookies, peanuts, potato chips. I even tried chocolate-covered hot peppers. Wow! And I ate chocolate dusted with gold.

After all that tasting, I needed a break. Luckily, there was more to do than eat.

CHOCOLATE ART

I walked the Chocolate Art Walk. Music from the Andes Mountains was playing. That's one of the places where cocoa comes from.

I went to the Chocolate Art Gallery. There, I saw chocolate statues and sculptures. There were even paintings created in chocolate.

Artists use food coloring and white chocolate for these paintings.

Comprehension
DETERMINING IMPORTANCE

To help students determine the importance of ideas, use these steps:

1. Have students reread the section called "Where Chocolate Comes From."

2. Then ask these questions:
   - What main idea does the author want you to understand?
   - Which detail is the most interesting to you? Why?

CHOCOLATE FASHION

One of the most amazing sights was the fashion show. Famous designers created chocolate clothes. They made hats. They made dresses and suits. They made gowns and jewelry. They even made boots.

Real models wear the clothes in the fashion show. People buy tickets to go to the show. Money from the show is used for research to help people with AIDS.

COOKING WITH CHOCOLATE

Looking at all that art was fun. Next I went to watch a famous chef. The chefs have special kitchens. You watch them make chocolate dishes. Then you get to taste some. You can learn a lot. Watch closely. Listen carefully. It smells good and tastes even better.

These gowns are pretty. But I wouldn't wear one on a hot day!

FUN FACTS ABOUT CHOCOLATE

- The Aztecs and Mayans discovered how to make chocolate thousands of years ago.
- Cacao seeds were used as money by Aztecs and Mayans.
- When chocolate first came to Europe, only the rich could afford it.
- The Baker Chocolate Company was built in 1780. It was one of the first chocolate factories in the United States.
- In 1875, Daniel Peter and Henri Nestle invented milk chocolate.

- Chocolate makers use more than three million pounds of milk every day.
- The largest chocolate bar ever made weighed 5,026 pounds.
- Chocolate is not popular in China.
- Half of all Americans say chocolate is their favorite flavor.
- The average American eats twelve pounds of chocolate a year.

During Reading

Comprehension
DETERMINING IMPORTANCE

Use these questions to model for students how to determine the importance of ideas in "Chocolate Art." Then have students determine the importance of ideas as they read "Where Chocolate Comes From."

- What are the most important ideas in this section?
- How can I support my beliefs?

(See Differentiated Instruction.)

Teacher Think Aloud
The most important idea that the author wants me to understand is that she saw paintings and sculptures made entirely out of chocolate. Before reading this article, I never imagined that art could be made of chocolate.

Comprehension
MONITOR UNDERSTANDING

Use these questions to model for students how to visualize what they are reading about. Then have students tell about a part they visualized and which details helped them.

- What do I picture in my mind?
- Which details help me create this image in my mind?
- How does seeing this picture help me understand what I am reading?

I learned that chocolate comes from the cacao bean. It grows on a tree. Cacao trees grow where it is warm and rainy. They grow in rainforests. Cacao is big business. Most of the cacao comes from Africa. Some comes from South America. Some is grown in Mexico—closer to home.

I had a great time at the International Chocolate Show. I found a good recipe for hot chocolate. I also found a recipe for chocolate cake. I can't wait to make the cake. Is there such a thing as too much of a good thing? Maybe. I vowed I'd wait a year before I looked at chocolate again. Then I remembered all the chocolate I took home. Maybe just a nibble would be okay. ◆

HOW TO MAKE A CHOCOLATE BAR

1 Chocolate is made from the seeds of the cacao tree. A cacao tree makes seeds after it is about five years old. Cacao seeds grow inside large pods. Each pod is about the size of a football. It holds about fifty seeds. All those seeds make only a few chocolate bars.

2 Workers cut the pods from the trees. They open the pods. They scoop out the seeds. The seeds are white. Workers put the seeds on mats to dry. The seeds turn brown.

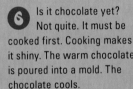

3 The dry seeds are roasted. They have thin shells. Machines remove the shells. Now the seeds are called "cacao nibs." Farmers buy the shells. They feed them to cows.

4 Giant machines grind the cacao nibs into tiny pieces. The machines grind hundreds of pounds of cacao. The nibs turn into thick paste.

5 The paste is mixed with sugar and milk. Then it goes through rolling machines. It goes through a kneading machine. The paste becomes smooth.

6 Is it chocolate yet? Not quite. It must be cooked first. Cooking makes it shiny. The warm chocolate is poured into a mold. The chocolate cools.

7 FINALLY, A CHOCOLATE BAR TO EAT!

25

Teacher Think Aloud

As I read the section about chocolate fashion, I can't picture clothing made out of chocolate. I try to visualize chocolate T-shirts and chocolate jeans, but all I can "see" are messy, melting blobs of chocolate on people. I can't find details in the text to help me. Then I look at the photograph of the woman in a fancy chocolate dress. Now I understand. I wonder how those clothes don't melt, though.

Fix-Up Strategies

Offer these strategies to help students read independently.

If you don't understand what you're reading:

- Reread the difficult section to look for clues to help you comprehend.
- Read ahead to find clues to help you comprehend.
- Retell, or say in your own words, what you've read.
- Visualize, or form mental pictures of, what you've read.

If you don't understand a word:

- Reread the sentence. Look for ideas and words that provide meaning clues.
- Find clues by reading a few sentences before and after the confusing word.
- Look for the base or root word and think about its meaning.
- Think about the topic or plot at this point to see if either offers meaning clues.

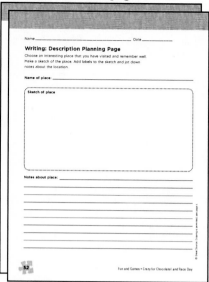

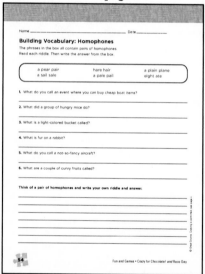

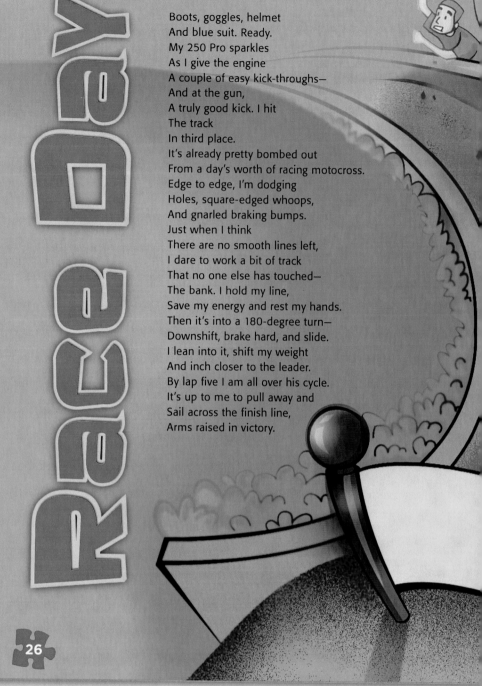

Race Day

Boots, goggles, helmet
And blue suit. Ready.
My 250 Pro sparkles
As I give the engine
A couple of easy kick-throughs—
And at the gun,
A truly good kick. I hit
The track
In third place.
It's already pretty bombed out
From a day's worth of racing motocross.
Edge to edge, I'm dodging
Holes, square-edged whoops,
And gnarled braking bumps.
Just when I think
There are no smooth lines left,
I dare to work a bit of track
That no one else has touched—
The bank. I hold my line,
Save my energy and rest my hands.
Then it's into a 180-degree turn—
Downshift, brake hard, and slide.
I lean into it, shift my weight
And inch closer to the leader.
By lap five I am all over his cycle.
It's up to me to pull away and
Sail across the finish line,
Arms raised in victory.

26

After Reading

Use one or more activities.

Check Purpose

Have students determine whether their purpose was met. Did students discover what happens at the International Chocolate Show?

Discussion Questions

Ask the following questions.

1. Do you think the author of the article enjoyed attending the chocolate show? Why? (Draw Conclusions)

2. What does it mean when the author states that "cacao is big business"? (Inferential Thinking)

3. Which attraction at the International Chocolate Show would you enjoy the most? Why? (Making Connections)

Revisit: Anticipation Guide

Have students revisit the anticipation guide. Were their predictions correct? Are any adjustments needed?

Revisit: Knowledge Rating Chart

Have students revisit the knowledge rating chart on *Student Journal* page 51. Are there changes they would like to make?

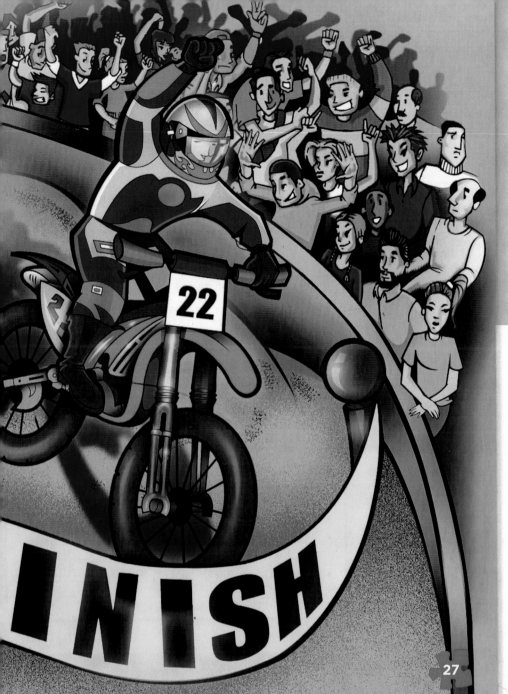

Poem: Race Day

Read the poem aloud as students follow along. Ask:

- How does the poem sound when I read it? Slow and serious? Quick and excited?
- What is happening in the poem? How do you know?
- How do you think the narrator feels about dirt-bike racing? Why?
- What kind of condition is the dirt-bike track in? Which lines tell you this?
- What do you think about the poem?

Answers for **Student Journal page 55** are 1. *stop*, 2. *low*, 3. *hide*, 4. *thick*, 5. *under*, 6. *huge*; Short Vowel Sound: *thin, thick, under, stop*; Long Vowel Sound: *go, high, show, hide, huge, over, tiny, low.*

Name _____ Date _____

Phonics/Word Study: Short Vowels Versus Long Vowels—i, o, u

Each word in the box has the opposite meaning from that of a numbered word. Write the opposite of each numbered word.

| under | stop | huge | low | thick | hide |

1. go _____
2. high _____
3. show _____
4. thin _____
5. over _____
6. tiny _____

Sort the twelve words above into two groups. Add one more word of your own to each group.

Short Vowel Sound _____ **Long Vowel Sound** _____

Fun and Games • *Crazy for Chocolate!* and *Race Day*   55

Writing Description

Tell students that they will write a description of a place they have visited. Have students share ideas about the kinds of places they might write about. List their ideas on the board. Have students use *Student Journal* page 52 to prepare for writing their description. Remind students that vivid descriptions using all the senses will create a powerful piece. Then have students use their notes to write a description on *Student Journal* page 53.

Vocabulary Homophones

Explain that homophones are words that have the same pronunciation but different spellings and meanings. Display *kneading* and identify the base word. (*knead*) Ask students to give a homophone for it. (*need*; "to want or must have") Write *need* alongside *knead*. Note the similar sounds but different spellings. Have students complete *Student Journal* page 54. Answers are 1. a sail sale; 2. eight ate; 3. a pale pail; 4. hare hair; 5. a plain plane; and 6. a pear pair.

Phonics/Word Study

Short and Long *i, o, u*

Tell students to listen carefully for long and short vowel sounds. Say: *kit, cot, cut.* Ask students if they hear long or short vowel sounds. (short) Then say: *kite, coat, cute.* Ask what vowel sounds students hear. (long) Now, work with students to complete the in-depth short and long vowels activity on TE page 88. For additional support, have students complete *Student Journal* page 55.

Review: Short and Long *i, o, u*

▶ Here's an opportunity to revisit and review the three vowels. Provide students with the Short *i, o, u* versus Long *i, o, u* Sort sheet and have them sort for both speed and accuracy as they practice the vowels they have studied thus far. (See *Word Study Manual* page 45.)

▶ Because it's important for students to hear the difference between the two vowels, and not just see the difference, have students work in pairs. One student can read the word aloud while the other determines the placement. When pairs are finished, have both students read each column to see if all the words have the same sound. Then have students switch roles.

▶ When confronted with a word with two or more syllables, students should choose a syllable to sort.

▶ Once both partners have taken turns reading the words aloud and sorting them, have students time themselves to see how fast they can do the sort. Being able to sort both quickly and accurately means the student has mastered these vowel sounds.

Short *i, o, u* versus Long *i, o, u* Sort					
Short *i*	Long *i*	Short *o*	Long *o*	Short *u*	Long *u*
milk	pile	hot	show	cup	suits
will	high	bottom	gold	consult	use
dip	find	chocolate	go	sculpture	shoot
chips	white	lot	close	discuss	cool
tickets	China	not	ago	public	school
discover	five		only	us	room

For more information on word sorts and spelling stages, see pages 5–31 in the *Word Study Manual*.

Focus on . . .

Use one or more activities in this section to focus on a particular area of need in your students.

Comprehension   STRATEGY SUPPORT

To help those students who need more practice using the strategies covered in this lesson, work one-on-one or in small groups to apply the strategy prompts below. Apply the prompts to a *Reading Advantage* paperback, a classroom library book, or a new or familiar selection in the magazine. Always model your own thinking first.

Determining Importance

• What is the most important idea in the paragraph? How can I prove it?

• Which details are unimportant? Why?

• What does the author want me to understand?

• Why is this information important (or not important) to me?

Monitor Understanding

• Do I understand what I'm reading? If not, what part is confusing to me?

• What fix-up strategies can I use to solve the problem? (See During Reading for fix-up strategies.)

• Why did a character say (do, think, ask) that?

• What images do I visualize from the text? What parts can't I visualize?

• Why did the author include (or not include) those details?

Writing Advertisement

Have students write an advertisement for a new kind of chocolate bar. Tell them to create a name for their chocolate bar, list the main ingredients, and write a slogan for it.

Introducing the NEW (name of bar)

It is filled with (list main ingredients)

Slogan

Fluency: Pacing

After students have read the selection at least once, use the "Chocolate Tastes" section on page 23 to model reading smoothly and at an even pace. Then have pairs of students take turns reading aloud "Chocolate Art" and "Chocolate Fashion," on pages 23 and 24.

As you listen to partners read, use these prompts to guide them.

▶ Review the text to avoid starts and stops.

▶ Read at an even, natural pace—not too quickly or too slowly.

▶ Use the punctuation, such as commas and periods, to help guide your pauses and expression.

When students read aloud, do they—

✓ demonstrate a smooth pace, not too fast or too slow?

✓ incorporate well-timed pauses between words and phrases?

✓ reflect an awareness and understanding of punctuation?

English Language Learners

To support students as they visualize, extend the fourth fix-up strategy on TE page 85.

1. Remind students that active readers visualize, or make mental pictures in their minds, as they read.

2. Read and discuss "Chocolate Tastes" on page 23 of the selection. Have students use details from the text to draw a picture of the chocolate treats.

3. Have partners describe their drawings and tell what words from the text helped them, such as *dipped*, *covered*, or *dusted*.

Independent Activity Options

While you work with individuals or small groups, others can work independently on one or more of the following options.

▶ Foundations paperback books, see TE pages 195–200

▶ Foundations *eZines*

▶ Repeat word sorts for this lesson

▶ *Student Journal* pages for this lesson

Assessment

Strategy Assessment

To help you and your students assess their use of comprehension strategies, ask the following questions. Students can complete a written response or provide verbal answers in a one-on-one reading conference.

1. **Determining Importance** Which details are the most important in this selection? How can you support your answer? (Answers will vary. Students may think that the most important details are the descriptions of the chocolate art and clothes. The surprising and interesting information may make students want to go to the Chocolate Show just to see the exhibits.)

2. **Monitor Understanding** What did you have trouble visualizing in this selection? How were you able to "see" these images in your mind? (Answers will vary. Students may say that they couldn't picture what a chocolate painting would look like, just by reading the text, but that the photograph on page 23 helped them.)

For ongoing informal assessment, use the checklists on pages 61–64 of *Foundations Assessment*.

Word Study Assessment

Use these steps to help you and your students assess their understanding of short and long *i*, *o*, and *u* sounds.

1. Display a chart like the one below, but include only the headings and the words in the first column.

2. Have students read the words and sort them into the correct column. The answers are shown.

Word	Short *i*	Short *o*	Short *u*	Long *i*	Long *o*	Long *u*
cup	thicket	hot	cup	flight	slow	suit
suit	milk	bottle	dungeon	white	behold	room
slow						
flight						
thicket						
hot						
behold						
room						
dungeon						
milk						
white						
bottle						

Stinky Wins by a Nose *and* Jump Kid
Fun and Games,
pages 28–end

SUMMARY
This **article** profiles a team of four high-school boys who won a national competition for best underwater robot. A **poem** follows.

COMPREHENSION STRATEGIES
Inferential Thinking
Understanding Text Structure

WRITING
Letter

VOCABULARY
Concept Ladder

PHONICS/WORD STUDY
Long Vowels and Final *y*

Lesson Vocabulary
robotics   absorbent
replica   inventor
competition

MATERIALS
Fun and Games, pp. 28–end
Student Journal, pp. 56–60
Word Study Manual, p. 46

Stinky Wins by a Nose

An **unlikely** group of **robot** builders compete **against** the **big** guys.

They call him Stinky. You can smell him miles off. It's from the glue that holds him together. His body is made of tough plastic pipes. Some are painted red. That means don't touch. Others are blue and gold. Those are the colors of Carl Hayden Community High School. The school is in West Phoenix, Arizona. Stinky was built by the school's Robotics Team. Today is the biggest day of Stinky's life.

28

Before Reading

WHOLE CLASS Use one or more activities.

Make a List
Tell students that they will read about robots. Ask what a robot is. (a mechanical device that is programmed to carry out instructions, often performing human tasks) Ask students if they have ever seen a robot. Discuss their responses. Then tell students to picture having a personal robot. Ask them what kinds of things they would ask their robot to do. List their responses on the board or on chart paper. Return to the list after students read.

Robot Tasks
1. clean my room
2. carry my books
3. make pizza
4.

Vocabulary Preview
Write the vocabulary words on the board or on chart paper and read them aloud to clarify pronunciations. Assess prior knowledge by having students choose one word to start a word map on *Student Journal* page 56. Have them write the word and its definition. Use the word *competition* to model the activity. Students will come back to the page after reading the article. (See Differentiated Instruction.)

It's a sunny day in Santa Barbara, California. Sunlight dances on the water of a swimming pool. But there are no kids in swimsuits here. Instead, there are robots—everywhere!

Dr. Allan Cameron and Fredi Lajvardi are two teachers from Carl Hayden. They watch their student Luis Aranda. Luis lowers Stinky into the pool. Why? Because this is the 2004 MATE National ROV Championships. In other words, it's a robot contest.

MATE stands for Marine Advance Technology Education. ROV stands for Remotely Operated Vehicle. Luis and his friends feel out of place. They are high-school students. But they are competing against college teams. Some of these college teams are the best in the country.

Three other students are on Luis's team. There's Cristian Arcega. He's known as "the

Brain." There's Oscar Vasquez. They call him "the Leader." Cristian and Oscar control Stinky with their joysticks, or control levers. And then there's Lorenzo Santillan. His nickname is "the Mechanic." He watches on a nearby monitor.

It's time for the contest. Stinky explores a replica, or copy, of a sunken submarine. He takes complicated readings. He does it well. At the end, Stinky turns his four makers into national champions. He helps make their dreams of college come true.

The team surprised many people by winning. Here is the story of how it happened.

 How Stinky Came to Be

"I teach computer science," Dr. Cameron explains. "We needed something interesting to do with computers. I thought we could make a mechanical arm. Then we would write a computer program to make the arm move. But the students solved that. It was too easy for them. So we needed to come up with something tougher."

Dr. Cameron found a solution. "Another teacher was building electric racecars with students. He told me about a robotics competition. We tried it the first year. It was rewarding and fun."

There were many challenges. "The students had to raise a lot of money," Dr. Cameron says. "They had to improve their communication skills. It was a lot of hard work. But it was worth it."

"Then we learned about the underwater robot competition. For three years, we had created land robots. We had a bunch of spare parts. So we thought we would do the underwater one."

Imagine you had your own robot. What would you want it to do?

29

DIFFERENTIATED INSTRUCTION
Vocabulary Preview

SMALL GROUP

Work with students to read, pronounce, and establish meaning for the word *inventor*.

What are the parts?	*invent* or
Which word part is a suffix?	*-or*
Where have you seen this suffix before?	*actor* *collector* *supervisor*
What does it mean?	one who
What is the base word? What does it mean?	*invent* to create
What does *inventor* mean?	one who invents
When might you use this word?	She's the *inventor* of a robot that does household tasks.

Student Journal page 56

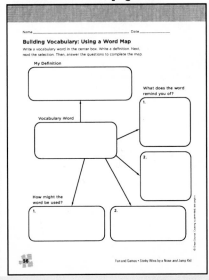

Name _____ Date _____

Building Vocabulary: Using a Word Map
Write a vocabulary word in the center box. Write a definition. Next, read the selection. Then, answer the questions to complete the map.

My Definition

Vocabulary Word

What does the word remind you of?
1.

2.

How might the word be used?
1.   2.

56   Fun and Games • Stinky Wins by a Nose and Jump Kid

Preview the Selection

Have students look through the selection. Use these or similar prompts to discuss the article.

- Do you think the selection is fiction or nonfiction? (nonfiction) How do you know?

- What do the title words "wins by a nose" mean? (wins by a small amount) Where have you heard that expression before?

- What do you find out by reading and looking at the title page?

Teacher Think Aloud

From the title, I think I'm going to read a fictional story about a person or animal called "Stinky." However, when I read the introductory note and subheadings, and look at the photographs, I must reconsider. This selection has to be nonfiction. It's about a group of students who build a robot.

Make Predictions/ Set Purpose

Students should use the information they gathered in previewing the selection to make predictions about what they will learn. If students have trouble generating a purpose for reading, suggest that they read to learn why "today" is the biggest day of Stinky's life.

Comprehension
INFERENTIAL THINKING

To help students think inferentially, ask these questions.

- What does the text tell you about the topic?

- What do you already know about the topic?

- Using the information in the text, and your prior knowledge, what new information can you infer that the author does not state directly?

The teachers chose four students to be the robot makers. Cristian was the school's science whiz. Lorenzo loved to fix cars. Oscar had great leadership skills. Finally, there was the big guy, Luis. He had muscle and drive. Stinky weighs 100 pounds. Luis was strong enough to wrestle the heavy robot into place.

"I wasn't into much before," Cristian explains. "I was getting kind of bored. Now I'm part of a team. I've been getting a lot of calls from colleges. We've been to the governor's office. A lot of people want to hear our story."

How the Competition Was Won

"The teamwork was very important," Dr. Cameron says. "Each team member had his own strengths. But they came up with ideas together. They made decisions together. They solved problems together."

The students also learned to write like scientists. They wrote highly technical reports. The competition was judged only partly on Stinky's performance. It was also judged on written and spoken presentations.

"We placed Stinky's main battery inside the robot. No one did that for underwater robots. It came naturally to us," said Dr. Cameron. "That's how it's done with land robots. It also solved another problem. With the battery inside, we didn't need to attach a power cable to Stinky's back. A cable would have made Stinky harder to move."

The battery did seem like a good idea. But it broke open on the trip to California. The battery was leaking. Stinky's wiring was damaged. It was a tough moment when

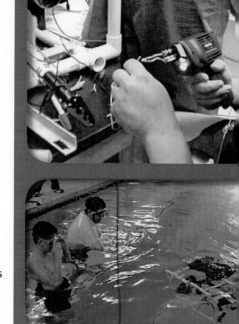

Stinky came out to compete. Other robots were sleek and in perfect condition. When other people saw the shape Stinky was in, they laughed. What could be done?

The team had an idea. Some kind of absorbent material was needed. The material must soak up liquids. Could they stuff paper inside? Should they cut up diapers? Lorenzo recalled a TV commercial. It was for absorbent sanitary products. He found them at a local grocery store. It worked!

A long sleepless night of repairs followed. Then it was time for the competition. The water was hard to see

 30

During Reading

Comprehension
INFERENTIAL THINKING

Use these questions to model how to make inferences from the section called "How Stinky Came to Be." Then have students reveal inferences they make as they read another section.

- What do I know about Cristian?

- What have I already learned about Cristian?

- Using these ideas, what can I infer?

(See Differentiated Instruction.)

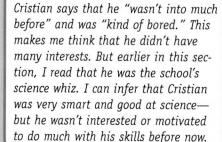
Teacher Think Aloud
Cristian says that he "wasn't into much before" and was "kind of bored." This makes me think that he didn't have many interests. But earlier in this section, I read that he was the school's science whiz. I can infer that Cristian was very smart and good at science—but he wasn't interested or motivated to do much with his skills before now.

Comprehension

UNDERSTANDING TEXT STRUCTURE

Use these questions to model how to identify the problem-solution text structure of "How the Competition Was Won." Then have students identify the question-answer text structure in "A Chat with Cristian" and explain how they know.

- How are the ideas organized?

- What does the author want me to learn?

through. This was going to be tough.

Stinky had to perform certain tasks. Cristian explains, "We had to run tests with Stinky. We had to find the correct submarine. In it was a captain's bell. It had the captain's name on it. We had to find that. We had to bring back a water sample. Finally, we had to measure the temperature of some vents."

The mechanical arm of another robot was very big. At first, the arm blocked Stinky's way. It kept Stinky from reaching the places he needed to. But Stinky could spin back and forth. He could also go up and down and tilt. Would Stinky reach his goal? It was very tense for a few moments. Then Stinky got past the arm. He did it!

Next, it was time to present their work to the judges. Cristian gave the talk. He showed pictures. He explained how they made Stinky. It was good. It was so good that it won the judges over. The students' written report was also perfect.

The team's great hope was to place third. First, they won a special judge's award. And then, they just kept winning. They won the prize for best design. They won a prize for best technical writing. And they won best overall.

Stinky was a winner! ◆

A Chat with Cristian

○ **When did your interest in science begin?**
○ In kindergarten. We were supposed to say what we wanted to be. I wanted to be an inventor. I wanted to build robots. I've always been curious about how things work. How do things fit together in nature?

○ **What would you like to do in the future?**
○ I would like to build a robot that helps people. I would like to create something useful.

○ **Your story should be a movie.**
○ Soon it will be! A movie producer liked our story. He already paid us some money for it. Now they will try to make a movie about us.

○ **Anything else you want to tell us?**
○ We'll be in the competition again. It starts in just a few weeks.

Good luck!

31

Student Journal pages 57–58

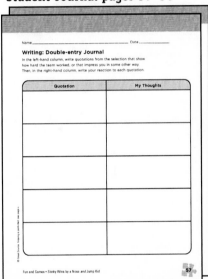

Name _____ Date _____

Writing: Double-entry Journal
In the left-hand column, write quotations from the selection that show how hard the team worked, or that impress you in some other way. Then, in the right-hand column, write your reaction to each quotation.

Quotation	My Thoughts

Fun and Games • Stinky Wins by a Nose and Jump Kid   57

Teacher Think Aloud

Dr. Cameron says that placing the battery inside the robot "solved another problem." The words solved *and* problem *give me clues that this section presents a series of problems and solutions. I read on and see another problem: the battery is leaking. Then I read about the way the team fixes that problem.*

Fix-Up Strategies

Offer these strategies to help students read independently.

If you don't understand what you're reading:

- Reread the difficult section to look for clues to help you comprehend.
- Read ahead to find clues to help you comprehend.
- Retell, or say in your own words, what you've read.
- Visualize, or form mental pictures of, what you've read.

If you don't understand a word:

- Reread the sentence. Look for ideas and words that provide meaning clues.
- Find clues by reading a few sentences before and after the confusing word.
- Look for the base or root word and think about its meaning.
- Think about the topic or plot at this point to see if either offers meaning clues.

DIFFERENTIATED INSTRUCTION
Vocabulary
Concept Ladder

Try these steps:

1. Explain that one way to explore a word is to ask questions related to it.

2. Have students find the word *replica* on page 29 of the article. To help students build a concept for the word, ask the following questions: *What is a replica?* (a copy of something) *What things are similar to a replica?* (models, copies) *What are some examples of replicas?* (a souvenir, a copy of a painting) *How might the word be used?* (The architect collects *replicas* of famous buildings.)

Student Journal page 59

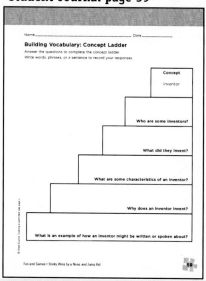

CREDITS

Program Authors
Laura Robb
James F. Baumann
Carol J. Fuhler
Joan Kindig

Editorial Board
Avon Connell-Cowell
R. Craig Roney

Supervising Editor
Ruth S. Rothstein

Project Manager
Alison Blank

Magazine Writers
Scott Ciencin
Ari and Joan Epstein
Anina Robb
Stephanie St. Pierre
Michele Sobel Spirn
Lauren Velevis

Design and Production
Anthology, Inc.

Photography
Cover Daniel Dempster Photography/Alamy; IFC (bkgd), 15, 24b, 25 Royalty-Free/Corbis; IFC, 8l age fotostock/SuperStock; 1l Photodisc Green; 1c, 30 Faridodin "Fredi" Lajvardi; 10t David Bergman/Corbis; 10bl Greg Fiume/NewSport/Corbis; 11r Digital Vision/Getty Images; 13 Courtesy of Sheri Graner Ray/photo: Roger Wong; 14 Courtesy Sony Entertainment; 16bl Lottie Davies/Digital Vision; 16tr DAJ/Getty Images; 16r David Nagle/Getty Images; 22t George Doyle/Getty Images; 22r Digital Vision/Getty Images; 22l Photodisc Green; 23 HARUYOSHI YAMAGUCHI/Reuters/Corbis; 24t AP Photo/Tina Fineberg; 28 ©Livia Corona

Illustration
All maps created by Anthology, Inc. unless otherwise indicated. All graphic elements created by Anthology, Inc. unless otherwise indicated. IFC a George Toomer; IFC c Steve McEntee; IFC d Kim Behm; 1a Juan Alvarez; 1c Dan McGeehan; 2–6 George Toomer; 9 Geoff Smith; 12 Steve McEntee; 17–21 Kim Behm; 25 Geoff Smith; 26–27 Juan Alvarez; 32–33 Dan McGeehan

32

After Reading
WHOLE CLASS Use one or more activities.

Check Purpose

Have students determine whether their purpose was met. Did students discover why "today" is the biggest day of Stinky's life?

Discussion Questions

Continue the group discussion with the following questions.

1. How did the team members support each other? (Draw Conclusions)

2. Would you like to design robots for a living? Why or why not? (Making Connections)

3. To what extent do you think the team's experience with Stinky will help them get into college? (Predict)

Revisit: List

Have students revisit the list about what they would have a personal robot do. Would they like to add or change anything?

Revisit: Word Map

Ask students to look again at their word map on *Student Journal* page 56. Have them adjust their original definitions, as needed. Then have them complete the page.

JUMP KID

Jump KID.
Jumping in the sand pit.
Jumping over fences.
Jumping to get the phone.

Jump KID.
Jumps in HIS house, in HIS yard, in HIS driveway.
Jumps for joy sometimes after a track meet.
Jumps to win every Saturday and Sunday for the past six years.
Jumps when it's cold and rainy, during practice in the spring.
Jumps *everywhere and all the time.*
Jumps even in HIS sleep.

I'm a jump KID on our track team.
Triple jump, high jump, long jump.
I jump them all. I'll jump anything.
Wait, I meant: I'm THE Jump KID.

In my blue and yellow track shorts.
With my hair in braids down my neck.
I'm an East High Eagle.
On a good day, when I jump, I fly.

Jump KID.
Jumping down the hallway before school.
Jumps right into a group of senior GUYS.
They laugh at Jump KID.
Tell HIM to walk like everyone else.

But Jump KID doesn't care.
HE's got to practice if HE wants to jump eighteen feet.
Jumping all the way to the Olympics.
Then they'll see.

Watching from their TVs in the living room.
Eating popcorn, drinking sodas.
Feet up on the sofa.
They'll see me, jumping, soaring, flying.

Like a rabbit who grew up to be an eagle.

Poem: Jump Kid

Have students read the poem silently and then aloud with a partner. Use these or similar questions to discuss students' interpretations of the poem.

- What does the poem mean to you?
- Can you connect or relate to the poem in some way?
- What images did you "see in your mind" when you read the poem?
- Which words or phrases were especially interesting or helped you "see" the poem?

Answers for **Student Journal page 60** are 1. *spicy*; 2. *icy*; 3. *slimy*; 4. *breezy*; 5. *easy*; 6. *pricey*; 7. *weedy*; 8. *gloomy.*

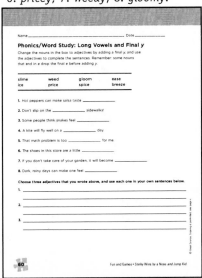

Writing Letter

Tell students that they will write a congratulatory letter to the underwater robotics team at Carl Hayden Community High School. To prepare, students should complete the double-entry journal activity on *Student Journal* page 57. Ask them to look back through the selection to find phrases, passages, and ideas that they would like to comment on or ask questions about. Students should then use these notes to write their letters on *Student Journal* page 58.

Vocabulary Concept Ladder

Have students fill in the concept ladder on *Student Journal* page 59. (Possible answers include Wilbur and Orville Wright—airplane, Mary Anderson—windshield wiper, Ruth Handler—Barbie doll; imagination, persistence, scientific knowledge; to help others, to become rich, to solve a problem; sometimes it takes many years for an inventor to perfect his or her invention.) (See Differentiated Instruction.)

Phonics/Word Study

Long Vowels and Final y

Tell students that they can change some nouns with long vowels into adjectives by adding a final y. For example, *stone* becomes *stony*, and *price* becomes *pricey*. Ask volunteers to suggest other examples. Now, work with students to complete the in-depth long vowels activity on TE page 96. For additional support, have students complete *Student Journal* page 60.

Phonics/Word Study

Long Vowels and Final *y*

▶ Write the following words on the board or on chart paper and read them aloud: *flake, cage,* and *leaf.*

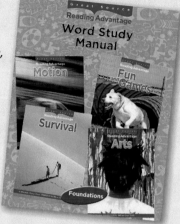

▶ Ask students whether these words with long vowels are all nouns or verbs. (The words are nouns giving the names of objects.) Ask students how they could change each word to a descriptor. They could add a final *y*, and the words would become adjectives: *flaky, cagey,* and *leafy.*

▶ Explain to students that there are three common ways to represent this change phonetically:

1. Drop *e* and add *y.*

2. Keep *e* and add *y.*

3. Add *y.*

▶ With *flake,* we drop the final *e* and add a *y* to make the word *flaky.* The word *cagey* retains its *e.* We simply add a *y* to such words. The third variation is the easiest change of all, from *leaf* to *leafy.* We simply add a *y* to the existing word. Occasionally there will be an oddball like *fire* that changes completely to *fiery.*

▶ Provide students with the Long Vowels and Final *y* Sort sheet and have them begin sorting by the four headings shown. (See *Word Study Manual* page 46.) Be sure to model the correct placement for the first few words. After students finish their sorts, discuss what they noticed and learned.

Long Vowels and Final *y* Sort			
Drop *e* and Add *y*	Keep *e* and Add *y*	Add *y*	Oddball
craze/crazy	poke/pokey	leaf/leafy	fire/fiery
shake/shaky	cage/cagey	weed/weedy	
haze/hazy	price/pricey	dream/dreamy	
paste/pasty	dope/dopey	cream/creamy	

For more information on word sorts and spelling stages, see pages 5–31 in the *Word Study Manual.*

Focus on . . .

Use one or more activities in this section to focus on a particular area of need in your students.

Comprehension STRATEGY SUPPORT

To help those students who need more practice using the strategies covered in this lesson, work one-on-one or in small groups to apply the strategy prompts below. Apply the prompts to a *Reading Advantage* paperback, a classroom library book, or a new or familiar selection in the magazine. Always model your own thinking first.

Inferential Thinking

• What are the causes or effects of this event?

• What do I learn from the character or person's thoughts, words, or actions?

• What do I know (or infer) from the text that the author hasn't stated directly?

• What conclusions can I draw?

Understanding Text Structure

• What kind of text is this? (book, story, article, guidebook, play, manual)

• How does the author organize the text? (cause-effect, problem-solution, chronological order, description, question-answer, comparison-contrast)

• What details support my thoughts about the text structure?

• What is the cause (effect, problem, solution, order, question, answer)?

• If fiction, who are the characters? What is the setting, plot, conflict, and resolution?

Writing Paragraph

Discuss with students the problems that robots could help solve. Jot down a list of students' ideas on the board or on chart paper. Then have students write about one problem for which a robot might provide a solution.

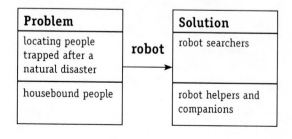

Fluency: Expression

After students have read "Stinky Wins by a Nose" at least once, draw their attention to the "A Chat with Cristian" feature on page 31. Discuss with students how reading dialogue is different from reading plain text. They should read dialogue in the same way that the speakers might speak. Discuss with students the overall tone (informal and conversational) of the chat, or interview. Model by reading the feature aloud. Have students work in pairs to take turns reading aloud the dialogue of the interviewer, and that of Cristian.

Use these prompts to guide them to speak expressively.

▶ Read conversationally, or the way you talk.

▶ Ask yourself what the speaker is feeling.

▶ Match your tone of voice, facial expressions, and gestures to the feelings of the speaker.

▶ Let the punctuation (question marks and exclamation points) guide the expression in your voice.

When students read aloud, do they—

✓ reflect an understanding of the text?

✓ demonstrate appropriate timing, stress, and intonation?

✓ incorporate appropriate speed and phrasing?

English Language Learners

Support students in making inferences on TE page 92.

1. Explain that active readers use what they know and clues in the text to figure out something that is not stated. List some things Cristian says on page 31.

2. Model using the language of making inferences with this sentence frame: *Based on what I know and read, I infer that Cristian . . .*

3. Have partners make inferences using the sentence frame.

Independent Activity Options

While you work with individuals or small groups, others can work independently on one or more of the following options.

▶ Foundations paperback books, see TE pages 195–200

▶ Foundations *eZines*

▶ Repeat word sorts for this lesson

▶ *Student Journal* pages for this lesson

Assessment

Strategy Assessment

To help you and your students assess their use of comprehension strategies, ask the following questions. Students can complete a written response or provide verbal answers in a one-on-one reading conference.

1. **Inferential Thinking** What inferences did you make when reading this selection? (Answers will vary. Students may infer that after Stinky's team won best overall, the pride and excitement that team members felt might encourage them to enter into other kinds of competitions.)

2. **Understanding Text Structure** Choose a section of this article that you enjoyed, and describe its text structure. How does the structure help you understand the text? (Answers will vary. Students may say that they liked the interview with Cristian, because the question-answer format helped them hear the voice of one of Stinky's inventors.)

See *Foundations Assessment* pages 26–33 for formal assessment to go with *Fun and Games*.

Word Study Assessment

Use these steps to help you and your students assess their understanding of adding *y* to words with long vowels.

1. Display a chart like the one below, but include only the headings and the words in the first column.

2. Have students read the words, add *y* to the end of each one, and sort them into the correct column. The answers are shown.

Word	Drop *e* and Add *y*	Keep *e* and Add *y*	Add *y*
spice	spicy		
price		pricey	
dirt			dirty
haze	hazy		
mope		mopey	
craze	crazy		
steam			steamy
leak			leaky
haste	hasty		

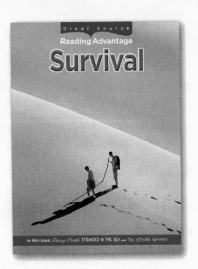

Surviva

Magazine Summary

Survival magazine contains articles, poems, and a play. The topics reflect survival in a number of situations and levels of intensity. Students will also be introduced to the world's ultimate survivor.

Content-Area Connection: science, history
Lexile Measure: 430L

Survival Planner

LESSON	BEFORE READING	DURING READING	AFTER READING
LESSON 13 **Racing Death: The Balto Story** (article) page 102	Concept Web Vocabulary Preview Preview the Selection Make Predictions/ Set Purpose	Making Connections Determining Importance	Check Purpose Discussion Questions Writing: description Vocabulary: suffixes *-er, -or, -ist* Phonics/Word Study: consonant blends and digraphs *th/thr, sh/shr, squ*
LESSON 14 **Alone on a Raft** (article) page 110	Survival Chart Vocabulary Preview Preview the Selection Make Predictions/ Set Purpose	Monitor Understanding Inferential Thinking	Check Purpose Discussion Questions Writing: character sketch Vocabulary: idea completions Phonics/Word Study: complex consonant clusters *sc/scr, st/str, sp/spr*
LESSON 15 **Miner Disaster** (account) page 118	List Vocabulary Preview Preview the Selection Make Predictions/ Set Purpose	Understanding Text Structure	Check Purpose Discussion Questions Writing: journal entry Vocabulary: word root *terra* Phonics/Word Study: long vowel review *a, e, i, o, u*

Overview

Preview the Magazine

Give students time to preview the magazine. Have them look at the front and back covers, selection titles, photographs, illustrations, captions, and sidebars. Explain that the magazine includes literature that focuses on survival situations. Talk with students about survival stories they may know. Ask students how life might be different for survivors after the event or era that was survived. Then work with students to develop a chart that shows some of the possible complexities survivors might face.

Survival	
Positive Results	**Possible Complexities**
lives saved	survivor might want to make major changes, but family and friends might not
now appreciate simple things	might feel guilty if others weren't as lucky
more compassionate toward others	
help others more	

PHONICS/WORD STUDY	FOCUS ON	ASSESSMENT	HIGHER-ORDER THINKING QUESTIONS
Consonant Blends and Digraphs *th/thr, sh/shr, squ*	Writing: inscription Fluency: pacing English Language Learners Independent Activity Options	Making Connections Determining Importance Consonant Blends and Digraphs *th/thr, sh/shr, squ*	Discuss the challenges and adversity that the sled-dog teams encountered while trying to get the serum to Nome, Alaska. Use details and information from the story to support your answer. Compare and contrast the personalities of Sepp and Gunnar. How did these two men view the same dog? Use details and information from the story to support your answer.
Complex Consonant Clusters *sc/scr, st/str, sp/spr*	Writing: interview Fluency: expression English Language Learners Independent Activity Options	Inferential Thinking Monitor Understanding Complex Consonant Clusters *sc/scr, st/str, sp/spr*	Why do you think the British Navy printed booklets that told how Poon survived and placed booklets on every raft on British ships? Use details and information from the story to support your answer. Explain why several countries honored Poon. Use details and information from the story to support your answer.
Long Vowel Review *a, e, i, o, u*	Writing: double-entry journal Fluency: pacing English Language Learners Independent Activity Options	Understanding Text Structure Long Vowel Review *a, e, i, o, u*	Describe the dangers of coal mining. Use details and information from the article to support your answer. What information was missing once the coal miners entered the mine? Use details and information from the article to support your response.

Survival Planner

LESSON	BEFORE READING	DURING READING	AFTER READING
LESSON 16 **Cockroaches: The Ultimate Survivors** (article) page 125	Anticipation Guide Vocabulary Preview Preview the Selection Make Predictions/ Set Purpose	Monitor Understanding Determining Importance	Check Purpose Discussion Questions Writing: short monologue Vocabulary: root *termin* Phonics/Word Study: common long *a* patterns
LESSON 17 **Delayed Belay** (play) page 132	Web Vocabulary Preview Preview the Selection Make Predictions/ Set Purpose	Inferential Thinking Understanding Text Structure	Check Purpose Discussion Questions Writing: summary Vocabulary: synonyms Phonics/Word Study: common long *e* patterns
LESSON 18 **After the Storm** *and* **Final Exam** (poems) page 140	List Vocabulary Preview Preview the Selection Make Predictions/ Set Purpose	Making Connections	Check Purpose Discussion Questions Writing: poem Vocabulary: antonyms Phonics/Word Study: common long *i* patterns

PHONICS/WORD STUDY	FOCUS ON	ASSESSMENT	HIGHER-ORDER THINKING QUESTIONS
Common Long *a* Patterns	Writing: letter Fluency: pacing English Language Learners Independent Activity Options	Monitor Understanding Determining Importance Common Long *a* Patterns	Explain the process of molting. How does molting help in understanding the survival rate of cockroaches? Use details and information from the article to support your answer. Use what you have learned to summarize the main points of this article. Use details and information from the article to support your answer.
Common Long *e* Patterns	Writing: review Fluency: expression English Language Learners Independent Activity Options	Inferential Thinking Understanding Text Structure Common Long *e* Patterns	How does the team work to build relationships? Use details and information from the play to support your answer. Jason was very nervous about the rock climbing. What happened to help Jason build the courage to continue to climb? Did he reach the top of the mountain? Use details and information from the play to support your response.
Common Long *i* Patterns	Writing: easy haiku Fluency: expression English Language Learners Independent Activity Options	Making Connections Common Long *i* Patterns	Use details and information from the poem "After the Storm" to describe how people react to the devastation of a major storm. In the poem "Final Exam" what does the following line mean? "Am I, toothless, doomed to fail the test?" Use details and information from the poem to support your response.

SUMMARY

This **article** describes how Balto and other sled dogs helped save the lives of residents of Nome, Alaska, who were suffering from an outbreak of diphtheria.

COMPREHENSION STRATEGIES

Making Connections
Determining Importance

WRITING

Description

VOCABULARY

Suffixes *-er, -or, -ist*

PHONICS/WORD STUDY

Consonant Blends and Digraphs
th/thr, sh/shr, squ

Lesson Vocabulary

diphtheria	radiotelegraph
serum	musher

MATERIALS

Survival, pp. 2–7
Student Journal, pp. 61–65
Word Study Manual, p. 47

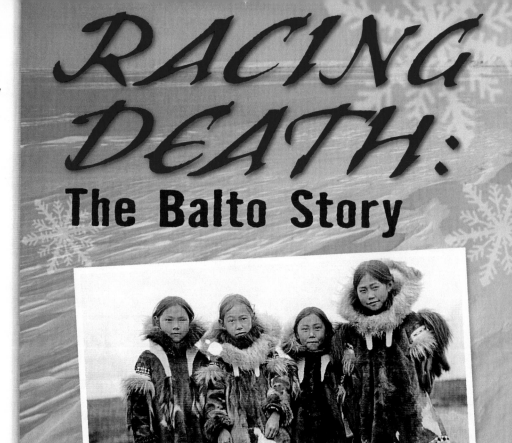

RACING DEATH:
The Balto Story

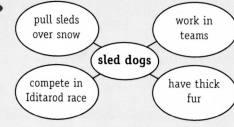

People were sick and dying. They needed help. But 1,000 miles of snow and ice were between them and the medicine they needed.

2

Before Reading

Use one or more activities.

Make a Concept Web

Begin a concept web to help activate students' prior knowledge of sled dogs. Draw an oval and write *sled dogs* in the center. Ask students if they have ever seen pictures of sled dogs, and what they know about them. List their responses in ovals radiating out from the center. Tell students that after they read the selection, they will revisit the concept web to see if their ideas were correct and if there is further information they would like to add.

```
pull sleds          work in
over snow           teams
        sled dogs
compete in          have thick
Iditarod race       fur
```

Vocabulary Preview

Write the vocabulary words on the board or on chart paper and read them aloud to clarify pronunciations. Have students share what they know about a particular word or words. Then have students begin the context activity on *Student Journal* page 61. Use the vocabulary word *serum* to model a response for the page. Students will revisit the chart after they have finished reading the selection. (See Differentiated Instruction.)

JANUARY 21, 1925

A winter wind howled through Nome, Alaska. Deep snow covered the streets. But Dr. Curtis Welch barely noticed the cold. He had more pressing problems on his mind.

Two children were dead. They had died of a terrible disease called diphtheria (dip THEER ee ah). Dr. Welch knew the illness would spread quickly. Unless they got medicine soon, many more people in Nome might die.

But Dr. Welch had no medicine. The serum he needed was in the city of Anchorage. And between Nome and Anchorage lay 1,000 miles of ice, mountains, and snow.

How could he get the serum? It was too windy to fly a plane. No car could travel through the house-deep snow. No train ran to Nome. No ship could dock in the frozen port. In winter, Anchorage felt as far away as the moon.

Besides, Nome needed medicine fast. They called diphtheria "the Black Death." It quickly attacked the throat and made it swell. Soon the patient could not breathe. Without medicine, children rarely survived it.

Dr. Welch was worried. Who could he ask for advice? He could not ask another doctor. He was the only doctor in Nome. In fact, he was the only doctor for hundreds of miles.

A CALL FOR HELP

There was no phone in Nome. But there was a radiotelegraph. Dr. Welch used it to send a plea for help. He said that Nome needed serum.

National newspapers picked up the story. Years before, the gold rush had made Nome famous. Now a different rush made Nome famous again. It was the rush to get serum to the people of Nome.

The people of Alaska wanted to help. But how? The train ran as far as the town of Nenana. That would get the serum 300 miles closer to Nome. But there would still be 700 miles to go. How would they get from Nenana to Nome?

The answer was simple. It was dogs. Sled dogs would carry the serum. It would be like a relay race. Each sled-dog team would wait at a town along the route. When one team of dogs arrived at a town, it would give the serum to the new team.

Dr. Welch was still worried. He thought it would take fifteen days. He wouldn't have the medicine in time. But there was no choice.

3

DIFFERENTIATED INSTRUCTION
Vocabulary Preview

SMALL GROUP

Work with students to read, pronounce, and establish meaning for the word *serum*.

What are the syllables?	*ser*	um
Which syllable is stressed?	*ser*	um
Which letters stand for the vowel sound in the stressed syllable?	*ser*	
What do you call this vowel sound?	*r-controlled*	
What other words have this pattern?	*hero* *cereal*	
What does the word *serum* mean?	a liquid used to cure or prevent a disease	
When might you use this word?	The *serum* would offset the effects of a snakebite.	

Student Journal page 61

Name _____ Date _____

Building Vocabulary: Using Context to Understand a Word
Select a vocabulary word you defined from the context. Complete the statements and answer the questions about your word.

| diphtheria | serum | radiotelegraph | musher |

My Word in Context:

I think this word means _____

because _____

My word is _____

My word is not _____

Where else might I find this word? _____

What makes this an important word to know? _____

Survival • Racing Death: The Balto Story   **61**

Preview the Selection

Have students look through the selection. Use these or similar prompts to discuss the article.

- Do you think the selection is fiction or nonfiction? Why?
- What information do you learn from the introductory note?
- Why do you think the author includes section headings?

Teacher Think Aloud

I think this is a nonfiction article about a dog named Balto. I can tell by the period photographs and by the statue of the dog on page 6. The sub-headings tell me that the event took place in 1925 and involved a call for help. With this information, I predict that this will be an exciting true story about a sled dog that brought help in a dangerous emergency.

Make Predictions/ Set Purpose

Students should use the information they gathered in previewing the selection to make predictions about what they will learn. If students have trouble generating a purpose for reading, suggest that they read to find out how Balto prevented a large number of deaths.

Comprehension

DETERMINING IMPORTANCE

Use these questions to help students determine the important ideas in the section "A Call for Help."

- What does this section tell about?
- How would you state the most important idea or ideas in this section?
- How would you rate these ideas?

  A) Nome was famous again.

  B) Dogs were the only way to get the serum to Nome.

  C) Dr. Welch was worried.

THE RACE IS ON

On January 27, the serum arrived by train in Nenana. William "Wild Bill" Shannon was waiting for it. He was the first musher, or sled-dog driver. It was 40 degrees below zero. That's cold enough to kill a man if he stops moving.

Shannon and his dogs rode fifty-two miles. He passed the serum on to musher Dave Green. Green rode thirty-one miles. Johnny Folger rode the next twenty-eight. And so it went, through blizzards and miles of darkness.

Meanwhile, one dog was sitting at home.

HOME ALONE

Balto lived in Nome. He was a scrub dog. That meant he was a slower working dog. And he was small. His owner was Leonhard "Sepp" Seppala. Sepp thought Balto was too lazy for the serum run.

So when Sepp joined the serum run, he left Balto at home. Instead, he took twelve dogs and put his best dog, Togo, out front. Sepp called Togo "fifty pounds of muscle and fighting heart."

Togo, with his team in the background

After Sepp raced away to meet the team from the Anchorage direction, officials changed the plan. They asked a tall man named Gunnar Kaasen to also join the run. Gunnar always borrowed dogs from Sepp, and he liked Balto. He thought the scruffy dog was a leader waiting to be born. He put Balto and a dog named Fox at the front of his sled-dog team.

Meanwhile, Sepp was in trouble on the Iditarod Trail. The trail was well known. Gold miners used it during the 1800s. But Sepp could not see the trail. It was buried under twelve feet of snow.

During Reading

Comprehension

MAKING CONNECTIONS

Use these questions to model for students how to make connections with the text. Then have students make their own connections with the text.

- Have I ever read about or seen pictures of dogs that pull sleds?
- Have I ever read or heard about people who have faced a medical emergency?

Teacher Think Aloud

I have a friend whose one-year-old once drank some turpentine, which is poisonous. An ambulance raced the child to the hospital just in time. As in many medical emergencies, speed was all-important for the child's survival. Remembering that event helps me understand why the sled drivers were racing night and day to get the serum to Nome!

Comprehension

DETERMINING IMPORTANCE

Use these questions to model how to determine the importance of ideas in "January 21, 1925." Then have students determine the importance of ideas in "A Call for Help."

- What does this section tell about?
- What are the most important ideas?
- How can I be sure these ideas are important?

(See Differentiated Instruction.)

A man driving a dog team, circa 1925

With Togo out front, though, the dogs found the way. In fact, Togo's team ran farther than all the other dogs. They ran 260 miles. Sepp was right. Togo was one strong dog!

TAKING THE LEAD

But would Balto be strong, too? The serum arrived in the town of Bluff, the last stop before Nome. Gunnar and his team took off with it. Now Balto and Fox had an important job to do. They had to guide the other dogs on the team. And they had to stay on the trail. This wasn't easy.

At one point, snow nearly covered the dogs. They were up to their necks. Some of the dogs panicked. But Balto stayed calm. His behavior calmed the others. Then Gunnar dug the dogs out, and they started again.

Balto and Fox pulled the serum toward Nome. Their breath froze on their noses as they ran. Snow clung to their fur. They were the last team on the relay. They had to make it. Then a blast of wind hit them. The sled and the dogs flew into the air. The sled was upside down.

Answers for **Student Journal page 64** are *research*, *foreign*, *conduct*, *profess*, *violin*, *science*.

Gunnar flipped the sled over. The dogs were all fine. Then he felt the sled for the serum. It was gone! All those brave men and dogs carried the serum over six hundred miles and now it was gone!

Gunnar couldn't see in the swirling snow. So he took off his mitts and pushed his frostbitten, bare hands through the snow. He searched for the serum. He hit a hard spot. The serum! He tied it to the sled. Balto and Fox took off. They had twenty miles to go.

THE HOME STRETCH

At the river, Balto stopped. It was frozen, and Gunnar tried to drive the dogs across it. But Balto refused. Gunnar was upset. Had he been wrong about Balto?

Crack!

Gunnar heard a loud popping sound. The ice was breaking. Balto had saved their lives. Balto led them downriver. There, they crossed safely. The blizzard raged on. The dogs pushed on.

Then, there it was. They were in Nome. They had made it! They had run fifty-three miles in only twenty hours. The whole relay had taken just six days. The people of Nome had their serum!

Sadly, five people had already died of diphtheria. But over twenty other people were sick. Dr. Welch quickly gave his patients the serum. No one else died. No one else got sick. Twenty mushers and more than 160 dogs had saved the day.

Balto and his team in Nome

Balto became the most famous dog in the world. His story was in newspapers. Hollywood made a movie about him. New York City even put a statue of him in Central Park.

People all over knew that Balto brought medicine to the people of Nome. He became the symbol for all the dogs that carried the serum. But this hero was headed toward tough times.

Statue of Balto

6

After Reading

Use one or more activities.

Check Purpose

Have students determine whether their purpose was met. Did they find out how Balto prevented a large number of deaths?

Discussion Questions

Ask the following questions.

1. Why did Balto stop at the frozen river instead of crossing it? (Cause-Effect)

2. Which details in the section "The Home Stretch" helped you create a strong mental picture? (Visualizing)

3. Which dog do you think was the real hero—Balto or Togo? Why? (Making Connections)

Revisit: Concept Web

Have students revisit the concept web introduced before reading. Are there any adjustments or changes they would like to make? Is there any additional information about sled dogs they would like to add?

Revisit: Context

Have students take another look at their context activity on *Student Journal* page 61. Are there any changes they would like to make?

A MORE DANGEROUS PATH

Sepp was angry. He thought Togo was the real hero. But the world wanted Balto. Gunnar and the dogs were touring the country like movie stars. Thousands came to see them. Something had to be done.

Finally, Sepp and Togo were invited to New York City. Togo was going to receive a gold medal. When they got there, Gunnar and his team were in New York, too. A supporter of Sepp's went to see Gunnar. He told Gunnar to leave town. He said it was time for Togo to stand in the spotlight.

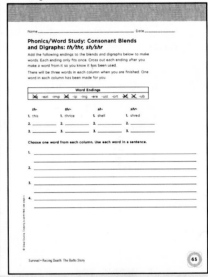

It worked. Gunnar left quickly. He left so fast that he did not take his dogs. Balto and the others were sold. Soon, no one heard about them anymore.

WORKING LIKE A DOG

George Kimble could not believe his eyes. It was 1927, and there in the window of a "dime show" was a picture of Balto.

Balto was being treated like a cheap carnival act. On this dirty street in Cleveland, Ohio, people paid ten cents to go in and look at Balto. George paid his dime. He went in. He was shocked by what he saw.

The dogs were tied up in a filthy room. The air was stale. The dogs were starving. Their water bowls were dry. George knew he had to save them.

RESCUING THE RESCUERS

George needed $2,000 to buy the dogs. He was a businessman, but he did not have the money. Plus, the owners gave George only two weeks to raise the cash.

So George went to the newspapers. He went to radio stations. Suddenly, everyone was interested in Balto again. Children collected nickels. Factory workers donated dimes. A dog club gave the final dollars. The money was raised in just ten days.

The Cleveland Zoo gave the dogs a new home. There, they had their own pen and plenty to eat. They went for walks around the zoo. They went for runs in the park. They seemed happy. They seemed to especially like it when it snowed.

Balto and his team had saved people. Then people saved them. Sometimes survival is about having friends—no matter how many legs they have. ◆

Iditarod Trail

A 1,000-mile path from Anchorage to Nome, Alaska. It began as a Native American trading route. Eventually, coal miners and gold seekers used it. In 1925, the serum run used it. Today, a famous sled-dog race called the Iditarod follows the same trail. The race is held in honor of all sled dogs, especially the dogs of the serum run.

7

DIFFERENTIATED INSTRUCTION
Vocabulary
Suffixes -er, -or, -ist

Try these steps:

1. Explain that a suffix is a word part that is added to the end of a base word and adds meaning to the base word.

2. Write the words *baker, actor,* and *pianist* on the board. Ask students to identify the base word and the suffix. (*bake/er, act/or, piano/ist*)

3. Explain that each suffix adds the meaning "one who" to the base word.

Answers for **Student Journal page 65** are th-: *this, there, thing;* thr-: *thrice, threat, thrust;* sh-: *shell, ship, short;* shr-: *shred, shrimp, shrub.*

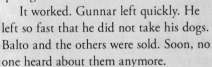

Name _____ Date _____

Phonics/Word Study: Consonant Blends and Digraphs: *th/thr, sh/shr*

Add the following endings to the blends and digraphs below to make words. Each ending only fits once. Cross out each ending after you make a word from it so you know it has been used.

There will be three words in each column when you are finished. One word in each column has been made for you.

Word Endings
-eat -imp -ip -ing -ere -ust -ort -ub

th-	thr-	sh-	shr-
1. this	1. thrice	1. shell	1. shred
2. _____	2. _____	2. _____	2. _____
3. _____	3. _____	3. _____	3. _____

Choose one word from each column. Use each word in a sentence.

1. _____
2. _____
3. _____
4. _____

Survival • Racing Death: The Balto Story   **65**

Writing Description

Ask students which part of the article created the strongest picture in their minds. Have them use *Student Journal* page 62 to make notes about that part, referring back to the text, as necessary. Tell them to also make a sketch of how they visualize the scene. Then have students turn to *Student Journal* page 63 and use their notes and sketch to write a description in their own words of that part of the article.

Vocabulary

Suffixes -er, -or, -ist

Display the vocabulary word *musher.* Have students identify the base word and the suffix. Ask what meaning the suffix -er adds to the verb *mush.* (-er means "one who") Then ask students to explain what the word *musher* means. As needed, let students check how the word is defined on page 4 of the selection. Then have students complete *Student Journal* page 64. (See Differentiated Instruction.)

Phonics/Word Study

Blends and Digraphs

Display *thought* and ask students to identify the beginning sound. Underline the *th* and explain that the two letters combine to make one sound (a digraph). Write *throat,* underlining the *thr.* Explain that these letters blend to create two sounds. Now, work with students to complete the in-depth word study activity on TE page 108. For additional support, have students complete *Student Journal* page 65.

Phonics/Word Study

Consonant Blends and Digraphs
th/thr, sh/shr, squ

To review, a blend contains two letters that combine to form a new sound (_truck_). You can still hear both letter sounds if you listen carefully. A digraph also contains two letters, but they combine to make one sound (_laugh_). A good way for students to remember which is which is to point out that the word *blend* has a blend in it (*bl*), and the word *digraph* has a digraph in it (*ph*).

▶ Write the words *think* and *threw* on the board.

▶ Ask students to identify the beginning element (what comes before the vowel sound) of each word.

▶ Point out the *th* in *think*. Ask: *How many sounds do you hear?* (There's one, but there are two letters involved.) Name it as a digraph and explain that a digraph combines two letters to make one sound.

▶ Point out the *thr* in *threw*. Ask: *How many sounds do you hear?* (Two—/th/ and /r/. Technically, this is still a digraph because of the *th*, but it is often thought of as a blend since the *r* is added.)

▶ It is not important that students know what the terms are called, but rather that students are aware of the patterns and can spell them.

▶ Repeat the same process with the words *shut* and *shrimp*.

▶ Finally, point out the *squ* pattern. There is no two-letter blend for students to compare it to. Have students brainstorm words they can think of that begin with *squ*.

▶ Now have students work in pairs or as a whole group to complete the Consonant Blends and Digraphs Sort: *th/thr, sh/shr, squ* sheet. (See *Word Study Manual* page 47.)

Consonant Blends and Digraphs Sort: *th/thr, sh/shr, squ*				
th	*thr (th + r)*	*sh*	*shr (sh + r)*	*squ (s + k + w)*
though	threw	short	shrill	squiggle
think	thrown	shun	shrift	squat
this	thrice	she	shriek	squirt
that	through	show	shrimp	squall
thought	thrust	shall	shred	squirm
thistle	thrash	shoot	shrank	square
Theo	thrift	shut	shrunk	squeak

For more information on word sorts and spelling stages, see pages 5–31 in the *Word Study Manual*.

Focus on . . .

Use one or more activities in this section to focus on a particular area of need in your students.

Comprehension STRATEGY SUPPORT

To help those students who need more practice using the strategies covered in this lesson, work one-on-one or in small groups to apply the strategy prompts below. Apply the prompts to a *Reading Advantage* paperback, a classroom library book, or a new or familiar selection in the magazine. Always model your own thinking first.

Making Connections

• What does this story (article, passage) remind me of?
• What do I already know about this topic?
• Where have I heard about this topic before?
• What do I have in common with the characters, people, or situations in the text?
• What other books, stories, articles, movies, or TV shows does this text make me think about?

Determining Importance

• What is the most important idea in the paragraph? How can I prove it?
• Which details are unimportant? Why?
• What does the author want me to understand?
• Why is this information important (or not important) to me?

Writing Inscription

Have students suppose that they have been commissioned to write the inscription for Balto's statue, located in Central Park in New York City. Talk briefly about what an inscription is. (words that are written or cut into something) Then brainstorm ideas with students before they write independently. After they have written their own inscriptions, encourage students to read the actual inscription on Balto's statue and compare and contrast their inscriptions with the original. Students can go to the following website to view the inscription: http://www.forgottendelights.com/NYCsculpture/salute/SalutesMarch.htm#Balto.

Fluency: Pacing

After students have read the selection at least once, use the section of text on page 6, titled "The Home Stretch," to model reading aloud smoothly and at an even pace. Then have students work in pairs to practice reading the same or another section of text at a smooth pace, paying attention to punctuation.

As you listen to partners read, use these prompts to guide them.

▶ Review the text to avoid starts and stops.

▶ Read at an even, natural pace—not too quickly or too slowly.

▶ Use the punctuation, such as commas, periods, and exclamation points, to help guide your pauses and expression.

When students read aloud, do they—

✓ demonstrate a smooth pace, not too fast or too slow?

✓ incorporate well-timed pauses between words and phrases?

✓ reflect an awareness and understanding of punctuation?

English Language Learners

Support students as they make connections in the third discussion question on TE page 106.

1. Make a T-chart with the headings "Balto" and "Togo."

2. Have students discuss the qualities of each dog. Then complete the chart together, writing descriptive words in each column about each dog.

3. Ask students to use the information in the chart to determine which dog was the real hero. Then have students support their answers.

Independent Activity Options

While you work with individuals or small groups, others can work independently on one or more of the following options.

▶ Foundations paperback books, see TE pages 195–200

▶ Foundations *eZines*

▶ Repeat word sorts for this lesson

▶ *Student Journal* pages for this lesson

Assessment

Strategy Assessment

To help you and your students assess their use of comprehension strategies, ask the following questions. Students can complete a written response or provide verbal answers in a one-on-one reading conference.

1. **Making Connections** As you read this article, what connections did you make with it? (Answers will vary. Students may say that the article reminded them of information they already knew about dogsleds, epidemics, or the courage of dogs.)

2. **Determining Importance** What are some of the important ideas in this selection? (Answers will vary. Students may say that Balto had never led a dog team before; that the dog relay occurred in weather that was forty degrees below zero; or that at one point, the sled tipped over and the serum was almost lost.)

For ongoing informal assessment, use the checklists on pages 61–64 of *Foundations Assessment*.

Word Study Assessment

Use these steps to help you and your students assess their understanding of consonant blends and digraphs.

1. Display the chart below, but include only the headings.

2. Read the following words aloud, one at a time: *thank, shrink, shoot, thrifty, thought, thickness, thrice, ship, shrill, squabble, squirt, thrust, shrunk, shower,* and *squeak.*

3. Have students write each word in the appropriate column. The answers are shown.

th	thr	sh	shr	squ
thank	thrifty	shoot	shrink	squabble
thought	thrice	ship	shrill	squirt
thickness	thrust	shower	shrunk	squeak

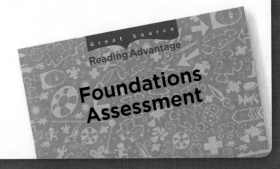

LESSON 14
Alone on a Raft
Survival, pages 8–13

SUMMARY
This **article** tells the true story of a Chinese sailor who survived being lost at sea on a small raft for four months.

COMPREHENSION STRATEGIES
Monitor Understanding
Inferential Thinking

WRITING
Character Sketch

VOCABULARY
Idea Completions

PHONICS/WORD STUDY
Complex Consonant Clusters
sc/scr, st/str, sp/spr

Lesson Vocabulary
tremendous	notch
torpedoed	civilian
desperate	permanent

MATERIALS
Survival, pp. 8–13
Student Journal, pp. 66–70
Word Study Manual, p. 48

ALONE ON

CAN YOU IMAGINE BEING ALONE IN THE MIDDLE OF THE OCEAN FOR FOUR MONTHS? MEET POON LIM, WHO SURVIVED TO TELL THE TALE.

8

Before Reading Use one or more activities.

Make a Survival Chart ▶

Ask students what dangers a person might face if lost at sea on a raft. Draw a two-column chart on the board or on chart paper, like the one shown, and list the dangers in the left-hand column as students mention them. Then ask how a person might survive the dangers, and list students' suggestions in the right-hand column. After students have read the selection, return to the chart to record students' additional ideas and to modify the ones listed.

Dangers	Responses
No food	Fishing
No fresh water	
Large waves	
Not knowing day or time	
Sunburn	

Vocabulary Preview

Write the vocabulary words on the board or on chart paper and read them aloud to clarify pronunciations. Ask students to share what they already know about the words. Have students begin the predictions chart on *Student Journal* page 66. Tell students to fill in only the second column. Use the vocabulary word *tremendous* to model a response for the page. Students will complete the chart after they have finished reading the selection. (See Differentiated Instruction.)

A RAFT

It was wartime. The British were battling the Germans. But no one on the British ship *Ben Lomond* was worried. On that clear November day in 1942, they just sailed peacefully near South Africa. They were not a fighting ship. They were only carrying supplies. The ship was nowhere near any battles. Who would attack the *Ben Lomond*?

Poon Lim, a Chinese sailor, had just finished his duties on the ship. He was happy to work on the *Ben Lomond*. During wartime, it was hard to find ships that were not used in fighting. The twenty-five-year-old was tired, though. He was looking forward to a good rest.

Then, suddenly, he heard a tremendous blast. Boom! A Nazi submarine had torpedoed the ship. The ship started sinking fast.

Poon tied a life jacket around himself. Then he jumped overboard. There were fifty-four other men onboard. They too leaped into the water. They all swam away from the ship as fast as they could. Soon the ship's boilers exploded. The *Ben Lomond* sank below the surface of the Atlantic Ocean.

Meanwhile, Poon was desperate. For two hours, he swam. He tried to keep his head above the waves. He tried to spot a life raft. It was hard. The waves slapped him in the face. He had to gulp the air when he could. Finally, he saw a raft. He swam to it. He managed to get on.

9

DIFFERENTIATED INSTRUCTION
Vocabulary Preview

Work with students to read, pronounce, and establish meaning for the word *permanent*.

How many syllables do you hear in *permanent*?	three *per ma nent*
What does the word mean?	something that will not change; a chemical process that changes hair from straight to curly, or vice versa
What are some examples of things that are *permanent*?	stains, sturdy buildings, hair dye
What is a synonym for *permanent*?	*lasting*
What is an antonym for *permanent*?	*temporary*
What are some words that are related to *permanent*?	*permanence* *permanently* *permanent press* *permafrost*
When might you use the word *permanent* (or a related word)?	I was *permanently* moved to the other team.

Preview the Selection

Have students look through the selection. Ask:

- Is this selection fiction or nonfiction? How can you tell?
- What information does the introductory note on page 8 tell you?
- From looking at the illustrations, what predictions can you make about what will happen?

Teacher Think Aloud

The title, introductory note, and art on pages 8 and 9 tell me what this selection is about: a man named Poon Lim spent four months on a raft on the ocean. I can't wait to read the article to see how he did it. Stories of survival, like this one, inspire me. They show that human beings are capable of enduring and overcoming tremendous hardships.

Make Predictions/ Set Purpose

Students should use the information they gathered in previewing the selection to make predictions about what they will learn. If students have trouble generating a purpose for reading, suggest that they read to discover how Poon Lim survived his ordeal.

Comprehension

INFERENTIAL THINKING

To help students think inferentially, ask these questions:

- What did Poon Lim use for a hook, bait, and a line to catch fish?

- What do you know about catching fish?

- Using this information, what can you infer about Poon Lim?

Student Journal page 66

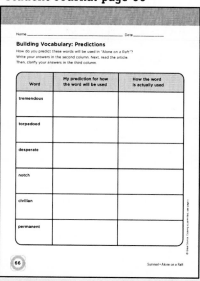

What good luck! The raft was made of wood. It was eight feet by eight feet. Tied to it were some tin boxes of British biscuits. There were also some flares to send up light signals. A flashlight and a large water jug were also onboard.

But what about the others? Poon only saw a few alive. He called to them. He tried to paddle the raft toward them. The water currents were too strong, though. The water carried him farther and farther away. Soon, he was alone.

Poon knew he might spend many days on the raft. Who knew when another ship would sail by? He needed a plan. He figured out he could eat four biscuits and drink a few swallows of water a day. If he did this, he could stay alive for a month. Then the wait began.

One day, a big ship passed near him. Poon shouted and waved. He thought they saw him. But the ship sailed away. Another day, a U.S. Navy airplane spotted him. Then a storm struck, and the navy never found him.

The worst was when a Nazi submarine poked itself up out of the water. He knew the German sailors saw him. The submarine did not attack him. Poon thought they believed he would soon die. Why waste their time killing him? Days passed. Poon realized that no one was coming to save him. He would show the Germans they were wrong. He would save himself.

The first thing he did was keep fit. He had to get some exercise. He wanted

During Reading

Comprehension

MONITOR UNDERSTANDING

Use these questions to model for students how to visualize what they are reading. Then have students tell about a part they visualized and which details helped them visualize it.

- What do I picture in my mind as I read?

- How does this picture in my mind help me understand what I read?

Teacher Think Aloud

I didn't understand the part about Poon's wire fishhook, on page 11. Water bottles are plastic, so how could Poon use it like a hammer to shape a hook? Then I saw the illustration of a steel water bottle, which people used in the 1940s. This helped me understand and visualize.

Comprehension

INFERENTIAL THINKING

Use these questions to model for students how to draw conclusions about Poon Lim. Then have students draw their own conclusions about Poon.

- What does Poon Lim do to show me what he is like?

- What do I know from my own life that helps me understand Poon's actions?

(See Differentiated Instruction.)

to stay strong. So he swam twice a day when the sea was calm. He swam around the raft. He kept his head above water. Poon Lim always looked for sharks when he swam.

His food and water started running low. Nearly one month had passed. Without enough to drink and eat, he would die. Again, he came up with a plan.

He decided to catch rainwater. He used the canvas cover of his life jacket to collect the rain. He also decided to fish. Inside his flashlight, there was a wire. Using his water jug as a hammer, he shaped the wire into a fishhook. A rope would be his fishing line.

Poon used a piece of biscuit as fishing bait. Then he held his breath. Would he be able to catch one? Could he land it without upsetting the raft? He waited patiently. Finally, he caught one. He cut it in half with the edge of the biscuit tin box. Hungrily, he ate half the raw fish. He kept the other half to use as bait.

Another month passed. Poon now had a new plan for food. He saw some sea gulls flying nearby. He shaped seaweed into a nest. He left pieces of leftover fish to rot next to the nest. The smell might attract the birds.

Sure enough, one flew toward the nest. It went for the fish. As the bird did so, Poon grabbed it by its neck. The bird fought desperately. So did Poon. Finally, he killed it. Because he had no water, he

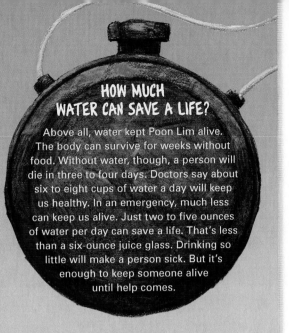

HOW MUCH WATER CAN SAVE A LIFE?

Above all, water kept Poon Lim alive. The body can survive for weeks without food. Without water, though, a person will die in three to four days. Doctors say about six to eight cups of water a day will keep us healthy. In an emergency, much less can keep us alive. Just two to five ounces of water per day can save a life. That's less than a six-ounce juice glass. Drinking so little will make a person sick. But it's enough to keep someone alive until help comes.

drank the bird's blood. He cut some flesh with a knife he had made. Then he stored the rest to eat another day.

Poon grew bold. He decided to fish for a small shark. He used part of a bird as bait. The shark bit. He was caught on Poon's hook. The shark was only a few feet long. But it was strong. It attacked Poon after he pulled it onto the raft. He had to hit it with his water jug to kill it. Again, he was out of water and gulped the shark's blood. He dried the shark fins in the sun for food.

For four months, Poon drifted on the ocean. He worried he was doomed. Would he spend the rest of his life alone

11

Teacher Think Aloud

After being torpedoed, Poon Lim swims for two hours looking for a raft. Once on the raft, he tries to save other sailors. I know how hard it is to tread water for just twenty minutes or so. To do it for two hours shows how strong and determined Poon is. Also, he's compassionate, using what little strength he has left to try to save others.

Fix-Up Strategies

Offer these strategies to help students read independently.

If you don't understand what you're reading:

- Reread the difficult section to look for clues to help you comprehend.
- Read ahead to find clues to help you comprehend.
- Retell, or say in your own words, what you've read.
- Visualize, or form mental pictures of, what you've read.

If you don't understand a word:

- Reread the sentence. Look for ideas and words that provide meaning clues.
- Find clues by reading a few sentences before and after the confusing word.
- Look for the base or root word and think about its meaning.
- Think about the topic or plot at this point to see if either offers meaning clues.

Student Journal pages 67–68

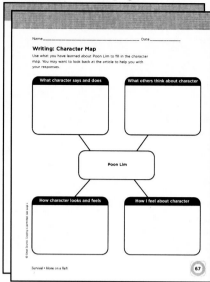

Student Journal page 69

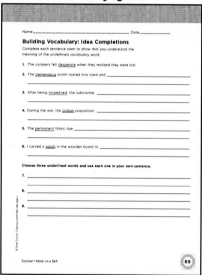

on a raft? Every day, he scratched another notch into the side of the raft. Every night, he made an X.

There were 131 notches and X marks when he began to notice some things. More birds flew overhead. More seaweed floated by. Could land be near?

Poon grew hopeful. Maybe he would reach land. Maybe he would be saved. Maybe he wouldn't die.

It was April 5, 1943. Poon spotted a small sailboat in the distance. He had been on the raft for 133 days. That was more than four months. Poon had no flares left. He waved his shirt. He jumped up and down to signal the sailboat crew.

SURVIVAL STATS

Poon Lim's days on the raft: 133

Daily food ration: 4 biscuits

Food he caught: fish, seagulls, shark

What he drank to survive:
water, seagull's blood, shark's blood

How he kept fit:
swam around the raft twice a day

Size of raft: 8 feet by 8 feet (about the size of a very small room)

Date of attack: November 23, 1942

Date of rescue: April 5, 1943

Would they see him?

The boat changed direction. It headed straight for him. Then three men climbed off the sailboat. They spoke Portuguese. Poon did not. They took him aboard. They gave him water and dried beans. Then they headed west to Brazil. Without knowing it, Poon had crossed the Atlantic Ocean.

It took three days before they saw land. The men who rescued Poon were fishermen. First, they had to catch their fish. Then, they would take Poon ashore. When he finally reached land, Poon could walk by himself. All the swimming around the raft had kept him fit.

But he still needed help. He spent four weeks in a hospital. Poon had lost twenty pounds. He was weak from the weight loss. He was tired from his battle to survive.

Once he was well, Poon went to New York City. He received many honors from the British.

The king of England, George VI, gave him the British Empire Medal. It was the highest honor a civilian could get. The British navy had booklets about Poon printed. The booklets described how Poon had survived. They put these booklets in every life raft on British ships.

Probably Poon's best honor came from the United

After Reading

WHOLE CLASS Use one or more activities.

Check Purpose

Have students determine whether their purpose was met. Did students discover how Poon Lim survived his ordeal?

Discussion Questions

Continue the group discussion with the following questions.

1. Can you relate to any of the emotions expressed in this story? Explain. (Making Connections)

2. How did Poon Lim keep track of days and nights while on the raft? (Details)

3. What do you think was the biggest problem or challenge Poon Lim faced? Why? How did he solve it? (Problem-Solution)

Revisit: Survival Chart

Return to the survival chart students made before reading the selection. Were students correct in guessing the challenges a person would face, and how he or she would respond? Add details from the selection to the chart.

Revisit: Predictions Chart

Have students return to the predictions chart on *Student Journal* page 66 to write how the vocabulary words are actually used in the article.

States. He wanted to live there. Many other people wanted to move to America, too. World War II was still going on. Most of the world was fighting. People were desperate to get to the safety of the United States. But there were limits on how many people could come into the country.

Senator Warren Magnuson came to Poon's rescue. The senator was from the state of Washington. He introduced a bill. The bill asked the United States to allow Poon to enter the country. It said he should become a permanent resident. The U.S. Congress passed the bill into law in 1943. Poon had a new home.

Poon also had a world record. He had survived on a raft longer than any other person. He made only one comment when he learned about his record. He said, "I hope no one will ever have to break it." ◆

13

Name _____ Date _____

Phonics/Word Study: Complex Consonant Clusters: *sc/scr, st/str, sp/spr*

Each word below contains the consonant blend sc, st, or sp. Circle the blend in each word.

| spent | scarf | spill | storm | start | scoop |

Choose two of the words and write a sentence for each one.

1. _____
2. _____

Each word in the box has a three-letter blend. Write one of the words to complete each sentence. Then circle the blend in the word you wrote.

| scratch | sprint | scrap | straight | spread | streak | strong | sprout |

1. The opposite of weak is _____

2. Do you have a _____ of paper I can write on?

3. If a potato sits long enough, it will _____

4. To get rid of an itch, you _____ it.

5. My mother has a gray _____ in her hair.

6. When you run really fast, you _____

7. The line isn't crooked; it's _____

8. When you put peanut butter on bread, you _____ it.

70

Survival • Alone on a Raft

Character Sketch

Have students write a character sketch about Poon Lim. Explain that a character sketch is a brief description of what a person is like. Discuss Poon Lim for a few minutes, asking students to share their reactions to him. Then have students complete the character map on *Student Journal* page 67. Have students use the information from their completed character maps to write their character sketches about Poon Lim, on *Student Journal* page 68.

Idea Completions

Write the following sentence stem on the board or on chart paper: *The campers felt desperate when they realized . . .* Discuss the meaning of the word *desperate*. (suffering extreme anxiety) Have students suggest situations that could logically finish the sentence. List their responses. Have students complete the rest of the sentences on *Student Journal* page 69, showing that they understand the meaning of each vocabulary word.

Complex Consonant Clusters

On the board, write *scream, stream,* and *spring*. Ask students to identify the beginning cluster sound in each word and underline it. Point out that each one of the three-consonant clusters contains three distinct sounds. Now, work with students to complete the in-depth consonant clusters activity on TE page 116. For additional support, have students complete *Student Journal* page 70.

Complex Consonant Clusters
sc/scr, st/str, sp/spr

A complex consonant cluster is a grouping of three consonants within a word. Because they contain more than the usual two-letter pattern that makes up a blend or a digraph, they can be troublesome for spellers.

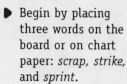

▶ Begin by placing three words on the board or on chart paper: *scrap, strike,* and *sprint.*

▶ Ask students to identify the beginning element of each word. The beginning element is what comes before the vowel sound.

▶ Point out the *scr* in *scrap.* Ask: *How many sounds do you hear? What are they?* (There are three different sounds in this complex blend—/s/, /c/, and /r/.)

▶ Explain that a blend has two or more consonants that combine to make a new sound (as in the word <u>blend</u>). Continue the same process with *str/strike* and *spr/sprint.*

▶ It is not important that students know the term *complex consonant cluster,* but rather that students are aware of the patterns and can spell them.

▶ Now have students work in pairs or as a whole group to complete the Complex Consonant Clusters Sort: *sc/scr, st/str, sp/spr* sheet. (See *Word Study Manual* page 48.) Later, students can sort on their own for any practice they need. Students who are able to sort both quickly and accurately show that they have mastered these patterns.

Complex Consonant Clusters Sort: *sc/scr, st/str, sp/spr*					
sc	**scr**	**st**	**str**	**sp**	**spr**
scout	script	start	strap	speak	spring
scorch	scram	storm	strong	spunky	sprint
scam	scrimp	store	struck	spill	sprout
scum	scratch	still	straight	spotted	spry
scarf	scrounge	stop	stroke	spent	spread
scant	scrap	stone	strike	special	spray

For more information on word sorts and spelling stages, see pages 5–31 in the *Word Study Manual.*

Focus on . . .

Use one or more activities in this section to focus on a particular area of need in your students.

Comprehension STRATEGY SUPPORT

To help those students who need more practice using the strategies covered in this lesson, work one-on-one or in small groups to apply the strategy prompts below. Apply the prompts to a *Reading Advantage* paperback, a classroom library book, or a new or familiar selection in the magazine. Always model your own thinking first.

Monitor Understanding

• Do I understand what I'm reading? If not, what part is confusing to me?

• What fix-up strategies can I use to solve the problem? (See During Reading for fix-up strategies.)

• Why did a character say (do, think, ask) that?

• What images do I visualize from the text? What parts can't I visualize?

• Why did the author include (or not include) those details?

Inferential Thinking

• What are the causes or effects of this event?

• What do I learn from the character or person's thoughts, words, or actions?

• What do I know (or infer) from the text that the author hasn't stated directly?

• What conclusions can I draw?

Writing Interview

Tell students that Poon Lim was probably interviewed many times after his ordeal. Explain that students are going to write interview questions for Poon Lim. They will then ask the questions of a partner, who will answer by taking the role of Poon Lim. Suggest that students begin by going through the article and writing down major events during Poon Lim's time at sea. Then they should turn each event into a question. Draw the following chart on the board or on chart paper as an example. Have partners take turns being the interviewer and interviewee.

Event	Question
A Nazi submarine torpedoed the ship Poon Lim was on.	How did you land in the water in the first place?
Poon Lim swam for two hours before finding a raft.	Did you find the raft right away?

Fluency: Expression

After students have read the article at least once, use the five paragraphs on page 12, beginning with "Poon grew hopeful," to model reading aloud with expression. Then have pairs of students take turns reading the same section aloud.

As you listen to pairs read, use these prompts to guide them.

▶ Read the paragraphs several times so you are comfortable reading them.

▶ Read with expression. Think about how you would be feeling if you were Poon Lim. Use those feelings to bring life to the narrator's voice.

▶ Use punctuation marks for clues to expression.

When students read aloud, do they—

✓ reflect an understanding of the text?

✓ demonstrate appropriate timing, stress, and intonation?

✓ incorporate appropriate speed and phrasing?

English Language Learners

To support students' vocabulary development, extend the vocabulary preview activity on TE page 110.

1. Make a word bank that includes vocabulary from page 9 of the selection, such as *ship, sailor, life jacket, raft,* and *waves.*

2. Discuss the meaning of each word.

3. Have students illustrate each word for a picture dictionary. Volunteers can choose words from the dictionary and create new sentences with them.

Independent Activity Options

While you work with individuals or small groups, others can work independently on one or more of the following options.

▶ Foundations paperback books, see TE pages 195–200

▶ Foundations *eZines*

▶ Repeat word sorts for this lesson

▶ *Student Journal* pages for this lesson

Assessment

Strategy Assessment

To help you and your students assess their use of comprehension strategies, ask the following questions. Students can complete a written response or provide verbal answers in a one-on-one reading conference.

1. **Monitor Understanding** What did you visualize to better understand the selection? (Answers will vary. Students may have visualized Poon Lim's raft, his fishing tackle, or the seaweed nest he fashioned to lure seagulls.)

2. **Inferential Thinking** What are some inferences you made about Poon Lim, using the details in the story, plus your own experience? (Answers will vary. Students might infer that Poon Lim was ingenious, rugged, and determined.)

For ongoing informal assessment, use the checklists on pages 61–64 of *Foundations Assessment.*

Word Study Assessment

Use these steps to help you and your students assess their understanding of complex consonant clusters.

1. Display the chart below, but include only the headings.

2. Read the following words aloud, one at a time: *scam, sprout, strong, storm, spunky, scram, stone, stroke, spotted, spry, scare, scrumptious, stump, scrounge, scant, spread, special,* and *stray.*

3. Have students write each word in the appropriate column. The answers are shown.

sc	scr	st	str	sp	spr
scam	scram	storm	strong	spunky	sprout
scare	scrumptious	stone	stroke	spotted	spry
scant	scrounge	stump	stray	special	spread

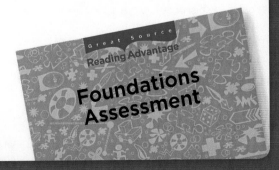

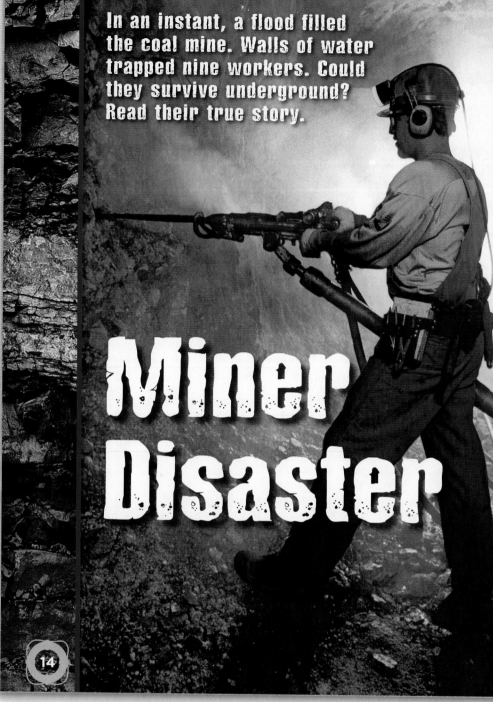

In an instant, a flood filled the coal mine. Walls of water trapped nine workers. Could they survive underground? Read their true story.

Miner Disaster

14

SUMMARY
This **article** describes how nine coal miners were trapped and then rescued from the Quecreek Mine in Pennsylvania.

COMPREHENSION STRATEGIES
Understanding Text Structure

WRITING
Journal Entry

VOCABULARY
Word Root *terra*

PHONICS/WORD STUDY
Long Vowel Review *a, e, i, o, u*

Lesson Vocabulary
abandoned	subterranean
mantrips	bit

MATERIALS
Survival, pp. 14–18
Student Journal, pp. 71–75
Word Study Manual, p. 49

Before Reading Use one or more activities.

Make a List
Tell students that they will read about several coal miners trapped underground. Ask students what they think of right away when they hear the phrase *coal mine dangers*. Display their responses.

Coal Mine Dangers	
floods	fires
explosions	lack of air
cave-ins	

Vocabulary Preview
Display the vocabulary words and read them aloud. Have students share what they know about a particular word or words, and then begin *Student Journal* page 71. Have students fill in the vocabulary word and a definition for it. They will complete the page later. (See Differentiated Instruction.)

Preview the Selection
Have students look through the selection. Discuss their observations.

Make Predictions/Set Purpose
Students should use the information they gathered in previewing the selection to make predictions about what they will learn. If students have trouble generating a purpose for reading, suggest that they read to discover if and how the miners were rescued.

Tap. Tap. Tap.

A coal miner banged on a pipe. Rescue workers listened. Tap. Tap. Tap. Nine miners were trapped underground. Each tap was a code: one tap for each surviving miner. Tap. Tap. Tap. Great news! All nine miners were alive—at least for now.

But the men were still not safe. They were trapped 250 feet underground—with no food or water. They could not escape. They were cold and wet. The floodwater was rising. They were losing oxygen and knew they might die.

Look Out Below

Wednesday, July 24, 2002. Eighteen coal miners were working in the Quecreek Mine. Their shift began at 3 p.m. The coal mine was located in Pennsylvania, a state that has many mines. Some are abandoned and dangerously fill up with water. The Saxman Mine had been closed since the 1950s. Quecreek is located next to Saxman.

Deeper. Deeper. The men rode the mantrips for half an hour. Mantrips are carts that carry miners through the tunnels. The men divided into two groups. The groups rode off in different directions.

The air twenty-five stories below ground was cold and dark. According to their map, Saxman's wall was 300 feet away. They had to leave 200 feet for safety. But that wasn't a problem. They had 100 feet to go.

Randy Fogle led one crew. They worked for six hours. Some cut into the coal wall. Others scooped up the coal. Still others held the ceiling in place with bolts.

Suddenly, disaster struck. The wall burst and water rushed into Quecreek. Mark Popernack saw it first. "Get out now!" he shouted. The men were in danger. They were 8,000 feet from the nearest exit.

Dennis Hall hurried away on a cart. But the water quickly caught up to him. The cart motor stopped.

The others yelled for him to grab the mine phone. The phone allowed workers to talk to one another. Hall wanted to warn the other crew. They were in danger, too. But their machines were making noise. They couldn't hear the phone at all.

The "outside man" picked up. This miner stays outside every mine entrance. He handles emergencies. Hall told him the news.

Finally, someone from the other crew answered. "Get out! You've got major water!" Hall yelled.

The second crew piled into their carts. But the water caught up with them, too. The carts stopped. The men quickly jumped off. Bent over in the four-foot-high tunnel, they raced toward the exit. The water was up to their chests. They slipped and they fell, but they kept moving. Forty-five minutes later, they escaped the mine.

The map was wrong. Saxman Mine was closer than they thought. Millions of gallons of water pushed

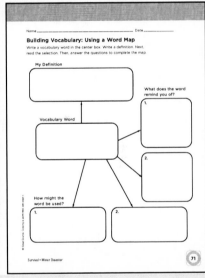

15

DIFFERENTIATED INSTRUCTION
Vocabulary Preview

Use *subterranean* to guide students to recognize that a prefix changes the meaning of a base word.

What are the word parts?	*sub* *terranean*
Which part is a prefix?	*sub*
Where have you seen this prefix before?	*subfreezing* *submarine*
What does the prefix mean?	under or below
What does *subterranean* mean?	situated or operating beneath the earth's surface; underground
When might you use this word?	A *subterranean* train is called a "subway."

Student Journal page 71

Name _____ Date _____

Building Vocabulary: Using a Word Map
Write a vocabulary word in the center box. Write a definition. Next, read the selection. Then, answer the questions to complete the map.

My Definition

What does the word remind you of?
1.

Vocabulary Word

2.

How might the word be used?
1.

2.

Survival • Miner Disaster

71

During Reading

Comprehension   SMALL GROUP
UNDERSTANDING TEXT STRUCTURE

Use these questions to model for students how to determine the chronological text structure of the article. Then have students tell how the text structure helps them understand the information.

- How is the text structured?
- What clues support my beliefs?

Teacher Think Aloud

I see that the third paragraph on page 15 begins with a specific date: Wednesday, July 24, 2002. This tells me that the author is using chronological, or time, order to organize the text. As I read on, I find that events are described in the exact order in which they occur. There's also a timeline. The timing of events will help me understand how the crisis unfolded.

Fix-Up Strategies

Offer these strategies to help students read independently.

If you don't understand what you're reading:

- Reread the difficult section to look for clues to help you comprehend.
- Read ahead to find clues to help you comprehend.
- Retell, or say in your own words, what you've read.
- Visualize, or form mental pictures of, what you've read.

through the thin mine wall. In some parts, the water touched the ceiling. Now Fogle's crew was trapped inside. Outside, the men who escaped had a new job. They were now rescue workers.

To the Rescue

Down below, the miners thought they were forgotten. Above ground, the fight to save them began.

First, rescuers had to find the miners. The mine was 60,000 square feet. They had a good idea where the men had been working. They started in that area.

Meanwhile, water filled the mine. Water was replacing air. The air that was left would run out. The miners sloshed through chin-high water to reach higher ground. Rescuers needed to get fresh air in. They also needed to pump water out.

ROBOT MINERS

Maps of mines are updated often. Each day, miners tunnel and dig underground. There are many maps for one mine. It may be hard to find the latest version.

Sometimes maps don't show enough. Coal robbers steal coal. Because this is a crime, they don't map their work.

So how can miners be sure they're safe? Robots.

After the Quecreek tragedy, scientists went to work. They hope to perfect subterranean robots. They want the robots to go where it is unsafe for humans. The robots send out lasers. The lasers record distance. The data produces accurate 3-D maps. The robots have already mapped some mines. With more of these robots, miners won't have to worry about old maps.

16

Student Journal pages 72–73

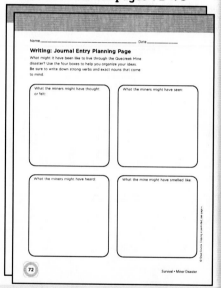

Name _____ Date _____

Writing: Journal Entry Planning Page
What might it have been like to live through the Quecreek Mine disaster? Use the four boxes to help you organize your ideas. Be sure to write down strong verbs and exact nouns that come to mind.

What the miners might have thought or felt:

What the miners might have seen:

What the miners might have heard:

What the mine might have smelled like:

72

Survival • Miner Disaster

After Reading
WHOLE CLASS
Use one or more activities.

Check Purpose

Have students determine whether their purpose was met. Did students discover if and how the miners were rescued?

Discussion Questions

Continue the group discussion with the following questions.

1. What caused the flooding of Quecreek Mine? (Cause-Effect)

2. Do you think the trapped miners worked well as a team? Why or why not? (Evaluate)

3. What do you know now that you didn't know before reading? (Making Connections)

Revisit: Word Map

Have students complete the word map they began on *Student Journal* page 71. Encourage them to share and compare their maps.

Rescuers began drilling. Eight hours had passed since the flood began. Finally, the air pipe reached the miners. Rescue workers tapped on the pipe. The miners tapped back nine times. Thank goodness! All nine men were alive!

The rescue wasn't over, though. The miners were still trapped. No one knew how long it would take. No one knew how long the men could survive.

Rescuers began drilling an escape hole. As they listened to the drilling above them, the miners struggled to stay alive. They climbed higher in the tunnel to escape the water. They built a wall to hold back the water. When someone shivered, the other miners piled on top to warm him. They needed to make sure no one's body temperature got too low. If anyone got too cold, they could die.

Hall's lunchbox floated by. He shared his corned beef sandwich and drink. The men found cans of soda, too.

They kept banging on the pipe. They also planned for their death. They wrote goodbye notes to their families. They sealed them in a plastic bucket. They tied themselves together. They figured that way it would be easier to find their bodies if they died.

Suddenly, the drilling stopped. Some of the crew thought the rescuers had given up. But Fogle kept their spirits up. He said the drill's bit probably broke. He was right. It had fallen into the hole.

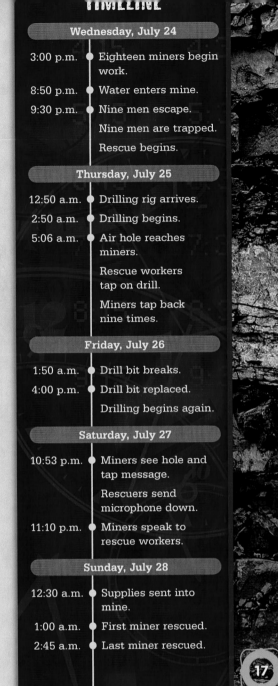

TIMELINE

Wednesday, July 24

3:00 p.m.	Eighteen miners begin work.
8:50 p.m.	Water enters mine.
9:30 p.m.	Nine men escape.
	Nine men are trapped.
	Rescue begins.

Thursday, July 25

12:50 a.m.	Drilling rig arrives.
2:50 a.m.	Drilling begins.
5:06 a.m.	Air hole reaches miners.
	Rescue workers tap on drill.
	Miners tap back nine times.

Friday, July 26

1:50 a.m.	Drill bit breaks.
4:00 p.m.	Drill bit replaced.
	Drilling begins again.

Saturday, July 27

10:53 p.m.	Miners see hole and tap message.
	Rescuers send microphone down.
11:10 p.m.	Miners speak to rescue workers.

Sunday, July 28

12:30 a.m.	Supplies sent into mine.
1:00 a.m.	First miner rescued.
2:45 a.m.	Last miner rescued.

17

DIFFERENTIATED INSTRUCTION

SMALL GROUP

Writing Journal Entry

To help students understand the importance of using exact verbs, use these strategies:

1. Display the following sentences and underline the verbs: *Suddenly, disaster happened. The wall broke, and water ran into Quecreek.*

2. Then have students turn to page 15 of the selection and read the sentences at the beginning of paragraph two in the second column: "Suddenly, disaster struck. The wall burst, and water rushed into Quecreek." Discuss how the verbs in these sentences do a better job of capturing the suddenness and enormity of the disaster.

Student Journal page 74

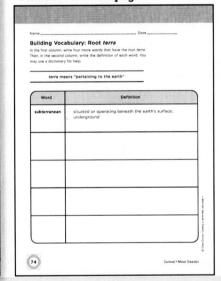

Writing Journal Entry

Discuss with students what this disaster might have been like for the miners. Then tell students that they will write a journal entry from the point of view of one of the miners. Students should make notes on *Student Journal* page 72, and then, on *Student Journal* page 73, use their notes to write a journal entry from the point of view of one of the miners. Encourage students to use strong verbs in their writing. (See Differentiated Instruction.)

Vocabulary Word Root *terra*

Write the vocabulary word *subterranean* on the board or on chart paper. Ask volunteers to tell the meanings of the prefix *sub-* (under or below) and the root *terra* (ground, earth). Combine the two meanings to get "under the ground." Have students think of other words that contain the root *terra*, to complete *Student Journal* page 74. Possible responses may include *terrace, terrain, terracotta, terrestrial, extraterrestrial,* and *territory*.

Phonics/Word Study

Long Vowels *a, e, i, o, u*

Display *stay, treat, hide, lone,* and *tube*. Ask students to identify the long vowel in each word. (*a, e, i, o, u*) Have volunteers suggest other words with a long vowel sound, and write them under the word with the same vowel sound. Now, work with students to complete the in-depth long vowels activity on TE page 123. For additional support, have students complete *Student Journal* page 75.

Possible answers for **Student Journal page 75** include

race (long *a*): *save, escape, day, break, state*

steep (long *e*): *deep, ceiling, replace, reach*

pipe (long *i*): *miner, nine, inside, alive, rise*

ghost (long *o*): *below, coal, phone, rode*

cube (long *u*): *rescue, human, scooped*

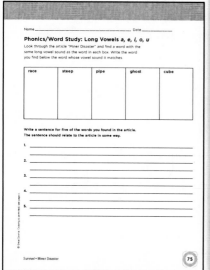

How would the rescuers get the bit out? They would need a special tool to pick it up. They had to make the tool. Rescue workers, miners, and their families waited. Fourteen hours later the drill worked again.

Out of the Mine

At about 10:15 p.m. on Saturday, miner Ron Hileman heard a hiss. "We got a hole!" he shouted. The others got up to look. The rescue hole had reached them.

Rescue workers lowered a microphone into the hole. "Are you the trapped miners?" a voice asked.

"Yes, we are," miner John Phillippi told him.

Rescuers lowered a cage into the hole. It carried food, drinks, and blankets. Now they had to lift the men out of the hole.

After seventy-seven hours underground, the first miner came out. It was Fogle. His chest had been hurting. His crew was worried he might have a heart attack.

Popernack was the last man out. At 2:45 a.m. on Sunday, July 28, the rescue mission was over. Thanks to quick thinking and teamwork, eighteen men were lucky to be alive. ◆

18

Long Vowel Review *a, e, i, o, u*

In previous sorts, students discriminated between short and long vowel sounds. In this sort, students will sort across all the long vowels on the basis of sound alone.

▶ Place the following words on the board or on chart paper: *race, steep, pipe, ghost,* and *cube*. Ask for volunteers to identify the long vowel in each word. Remind students that isolating the vowel is a good way to identify it.

race	ace	*a*
steep	eep	*ee*
pipe	ipe	*i*
ghost	ost	*o*
cube	ube	*u*

▶ Ask pairs to brainstorm at least two more words for each category and then share their additions with the class. As pairs say each word, ask which category it should go in, to indicate that students are hearing the difference between the long vowel sounds. Now have students complete the Long Vowel Review Sort: *a, e, i, o, u* sheet. (See *Word Study Manual* page 49.)

▶ When confronted with a word with two or more syllables, students should identify the syllable under consideration and concentrate only on that syllable.

▶ As a whole group, discuss the sort, students' observations, and why *noise* and *would* ended up in the Oddball column. Both words are examples of ambiguous vowels that aren't long or short.

Long Vowel Review Sort: *a, e, i, o, u*					
Long *a*	**Long *e***	**Long *i***	**Long *o***	**Long *u***	**Oddball**
they	each	miner	close	scoop	noise
state	deep	nine	rode	rescue	would
major	below	rise	below	human	
raced	leave	die	go		
escape	feet	outside	coal		
save	ceiling	piled	phone		
replace	replace	high	show		

For more information on word sorts and spelling stages, see pages 5–31 in the *Word Study Manual.*

Focus on . . .

Use one or more activities in this section to focus on a particular area of need in your students.

Comprehension STRATEGY SUPPORT

To help those students who need more practice using the strategies covered in this lesson, work one-on-one or in small groups to apply the strategy prompts below. Apply the prompts to a *Reading Advantage* paperback, a classroom library book, or a new or familiar selection in the magazine. Always model your own thinking first.

Understanding Text Structure

- What kind of text is this? (book, story, article, guidebook, play, manual)
- How does the author organize the text? (cause-effect, problem-solution, chronological order, description, question-answer, comparison-contrast)
- What details support my thoughts about the text structure?
- What is the cause (effect, problem, solution, order, question, answer)?
- If fiction, who are the characters? What is the setting, plot, conflict, and resolution?

Writing Double-entry Journal

Have students create a double-entry journal. Ask students to select several quotations, phrases, or sentences from the selection that they found meaningful or especially interesting. Encourage students to reread the article carefully, searching for quotations that affected them, and write them in the left-hand column. Then, in the right-hand column, students should write their reactions to each quotation. An example is shown below. (See TE page 206 for a double-entry journal BLM.)

Quotation	My Thoughts
"They wrote goodbye notes to their families."	I thought this was really sad. I was scared for the miners at this point.

Fluency: Pacing

After students have read the selection at least once silently, use the "To the Rescue" section on page 16 to model reading smoothly and at an even pace. Then have pairs of students take turns reading aloud the feature called "Robot Miners" on the same page.

As you listen to partners read, use these prompts to guide them.

▶ Review the text to avoid starts and stops.

▶ Pause after reading section headings. This will let your partner know that you have started a new section.

▶ Read at an even, natural pace—not too quickly or too slowly.

▶ Use the punctuation, such as commas, periods, and question marks, to help guide your pauses and expression.

When students read aloud, do they—

✓ demonstrate a smooth pace, not too fast or too slow?

✓ incorporate well-timed pauses between words and phrases?

✓ reflect an awareness and understanding of punctuation?

English Language Learners

Support students by extending the vocabulary preview activity on TE page 118.

1. Write *abandoned* on the board. Discuss what students know about the word.

2. Define *abandoned* as "something or someone that is left alone or uncared for."

3. Examine the use of *abandoned* on page 15 of the selection. Ask partners to discuss how understanding *abandoned* helps them understand more about the dangers of working in mines.

Independent Activity Options

While you work with individuals or small groups, others can work independently on one or more of the following options.

▶ Foundations paperback books, see TE pages 195–200

▶ Foundations *eZines*

▶ Repeat word sorts for this lesson

▶ *Student Journal* pages for this lesson

Assessment

Strategy Assessment

To help you and your students assess their use of comprehension strategies, ask the following questions. Students can complete a written response or provide verbal answers in a one-on-one reading conference.

- **Understanding Text Structure** In addition to a chronological text structure, this selection uses a problem-solution text structure. Explain. (Students may explain that the main problem in the selection is that the miners are trapped in the flooded mine; the solution is the miners' attempts to stay alive while rescuers worked to reach them.)

See *Foundations Assessment* pages 34–37 for formal assessment to go with *Survival*.

Word Study Assessment

Use these steps to help you and your students assess their understanding of long vowels.

1. Display the chart below, but include only the headings.

2. Read the following words aloud, one at a time: *studio, slide, each, major, nine, scoop, cube, phone, traced, leaves, snowman, facelift, moat, feature,* and *fright.*

3. Have students write each word in the appropriate column. The answers are shown.

Long *a*	Long *e*	Long *i*	Long *o*	Long *u*
major	each	slide	phone	studio
traced	leaves	nine	snowman	scoop
facelift	feature	fright	moat	cube

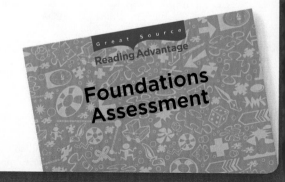

Great Source
Reading Advantage

Foundations
Assessment

COCKROACHES:
the Ultimate Survivors

You may not like them. But you have to admire them. They're true survivors. Cockroaches have been around far longer than humans!

SUMMARY
This **article** tells about the cockroach—an extremely adaptable insect that has survived for over 300 million years.

COMPREHENSION STRATEGIES
Monitor Understanding
Determining Importance

WRITING
Short Monologue

VOCABULARY
Root *termin*

PHONICS/WORD STUDY
Common Long *a* Patterns

Lesson Vocabulary

species	colony
molting	asthma
sole	exterminator

MATERIALS
Survival, pp. 19–23
Student Journal, pp. 76–80
Word Study Manual, p. 50

Before Reading
WHOLE CLASS Use one or more activities.

Anticipation Guide
Create an anticipation guide for students like the one shown. (See TE page 214 for an anticipation guide BLM.) Ask students to place a check in the AGREE or DISAGREE box before each statement. Revisit the guide after students read. (See Differentiated Instruction.)

Vocabulary Preview
Have students begin the knowledge rating chart on *Student Journal* page 76. Revisit the chart later.

Preview the Selection
Have students look through the selection. Ask:

- What do the title and the introductory note tell you about the selection?

- What do the first two pictures tell you about most people's attitude toward cockroaches?

Make Predictions/Set Purpose
Students should use the information they gathered in previewing the selection to make predictions about what they will learn. If students have trouble generating a purpose for reading, suggest that they read to discover why roaches are the "ultimate survivors."

Anticipation Guide		
AGREE	DISAGREE	
		1. There were cockroaches on Earth even before there were dinosaurs.
		2. All cockroaches live indoors.
		3. Some cockroaches make hissing sounds.
		4. Cockroaches can cause asthma.

Student Journal page 76

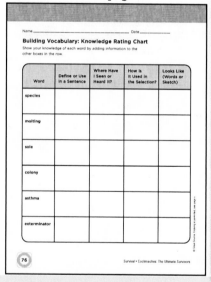

You see a cockroach. What do you want to do? Step on it? Squash it? Don't feel bad. You're not alone. Can you name one person who likes cockroaches?

Most of us don't. But you have to respect them. There are quite a lot of them. In fact, there are over 3,000 species of cockroaches. They've also been on Earth a long time. How long? They've been here about 300 million years. That means they were here about 50 million years before the first dinosaurs! And, during all that time, cockroaches have changed little. They are truly survivors.

Most of us have seen them. At night, you may see cockroaches racing into kitchen corners. They run to hide after you turn on the light. What you may see is the German cockroach. It came to America hundreds of years ago. How? It came by boat from Germany. And it likely came to Germany from Asia.

In Germany, this cockroach is called the Russian roach. In Russia, they call it the Polish roach. It seems no country wants to name a roach after itself.

You may also see American cockroaches here. This cockroach came here from Africa. How did it get here? It also came by boat. Most likely, it came here during the period of the slave trade.

To us, cockroaches are household pests. Indoors, they live all over the planet. They even live on the South Pole. They survive in the warmth of our buildings and homes.

But some roaches live outside. They live in the damp rainforest jungles. They live in cool underground caves. You can even find them in the hot, dry deserts in Africa.

There's no way around it. They're everywhere.

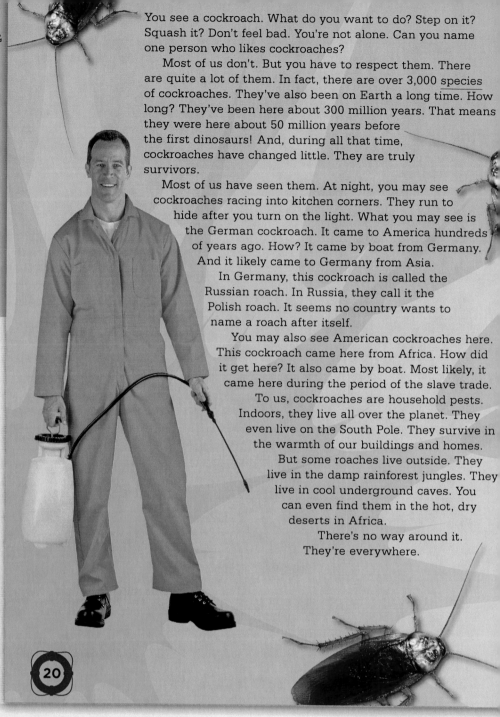

20

During Reading

Comprehension

MONITOR UNDERSTANDING

Use these questions to model for students how to monitor understanding by asking questions. Then have students ask their own questions to try to resolve any confusion.

- What is going on here?
- What did the author mean by that?
- What fix-up strategy can I use to fix my confusion?

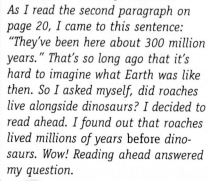

Teacher Think Aloud

As I read the second paragraph on page 20, I came to this sentence: "They've been here about 300 million years." That's so long ago that it's hard to imagine what Earth was like then. So I asked myself, did roaches live alongside dinosaurs? I decided to read ahead. I found out that roaches lived millions of years before dinosaurs. Wow! Reading ahead answered my question.

Comprehension

DETERMINING IMPORTANCE

Use these questions to model for students how to determine the importance of ideas in the first two paragraphs of page 20. Then have students determine the importance of ideas on the rest of page 20.

- What are the most important ideas in the first two paragraphs?
- How can I support my beliefs?

(See Differentiated Instruction.)

What makes cockroaches such survivors? For one thing, cockroaches will eat just about anything. Their food can be dead or alive. If they're hungry enough, they'll even eat each other. They can also go a long time without eating. They can go weeks and weeks!

Are two heads better than one? Ask a cockroach. It has two brains. One is inside its head. The second is near its stomach. A cockroach can live a week without its head. Now that's surviving.

Cockroaches grow by <u>molting</u>. As they grow, they shed the hard cover on the outside of their bodies. A cockroach molts six times. A growing roach can lose a leg or an arm. That's not a problem. It will grow it back the next time it molts.

Roach for Dinner?

Grasshoppers and crickets are eaten all over the world. They are fried. They are sautéed. They are breaded. They are baked. Sometimes they are even dipped in chocolate. Yum! Cockroaches, however, are almost never eaten. Why, you ask? Well, they taste bad. And they smell.

21

DIFFERENTIATED INSTRUCTION

Comprehension
DETERMINING IMPORTANCE

Use these questions to help students find more important ideas on page 20.

- What is the most important idea in paragraph three? (Some of our cockroaches came from Germany and are called German cockroaches.)
- What is the most important idea in paragraph four? (Countries name their roaches after other countries.)
- What is the most important idea in paragraph five? (The American roaches in the United States originally came from Africa.)

Teacher Think Aloud

The first paragraph talks about people's dislike of cockroaches. The second paragraph gives facts. Roaches are 300 million years old; there are 3,000 species; they haven't changed much, either. I could sum up these two ideas in one big idea: even though people don't like cockroaches, they've been around for a very long time.

Fix-Up Strategies

Offer these strategies to help students read independently.

If you don't understand what you're reading:

- Reread the difficult section to look for clues to help you comprehend.
- Read ahead to find clues to help you comprehend.
- Retell, or say in your own words, what you've read.
- Visualize, or form mental pictures of, what you've read.

If you don't understand a word:

- Reread the sentence. Look for ideas and words that provide meaning clues.
- Find clues by reading a few sentences before and after the confusing word.
- Look for the base or root word and think about its meaning.
- Think about the topic or plot at this point to see if either offers meaning clues.

Short Monologue

Have students suggest an ending for the last sentence in each short monologue below.

I was born under the sink in apartment 9C. When I was still young, I was almost stepped on by the FOOT. After that . . . (I made sure I knew all the escape routes).

I used to live in the city, but I kept having to move to escape the exterminator. Finally, I had had enough. I moved to the country. I thought I was in roach heaven. Then I discovered . . . (the CAT).

Student Journal pages 77–78

Name_____ Date_____

Writing: Short Monologue Planning Page
Under each of the headings, list some ideas for your monologue.

Where I live:

My enemies:

Close encounters:

Favorite foods:

Things I do:

Survival • Cockroaches: The Ultimate Survivors 77

Making babies is easy for roaches. Sometimes, a male only has to mate with a female once to make her pregnant for life! The mother carries her eggs in a sac outside her body. A German cockroach can carry up to six sacs during her lifetime. Each sac can hold about forty eggs. That means that one roach can give birth to about 240 new roaches!

Roaches also have speed on their side. They can run about fifty body lengths a second. How fast is that? If we ran that fast, we'd go about 200 miles per hour.

Roaches can even survive a nuclear bomb. It takes about one hundred times more radiation to kill a roach than a human. Now we know why roaches are such survivors. Will they be the sole survivors some day?

Madagascar Hissing Cockroaches

Ever heard of Madagascar hissing cockroaches? They're different from the German cockroach. They're huge. They grow up to three inches long. They can weigh as much as a mouse!

The World's Largest Roaches

Where are some of the planet's largest roaches? In Australia. There, you'll find the giant burrowing cockroach. It can grow to just over three inches long. That means it would fill the palm of your hand! You won't step on one in the kitchen, though. They live in the desert in holes three feet underground.

22

After Reading
WHOLE CLASS
Use one or more activities.

Check Purpose

Have students determine whether their purpose was met. Did students discover why roaches are the "ultimate survivors"?

Discussion Questions

Continue the group discussion with the following questions.

1. What important ideas does the author want you to understand about cockroaches? (Determining Importance)

2. What has enabled the cockroach to survive for about 300 million years? (Details)

3. What was the most interesting fact you learned from the selection? (Making Connections)

Revisit: Anticipation Guide

Have students review the statements. Ask them if they would like to change any of their opinions, now that they have read the selection. Discuss the reasons for any changes.

Revisit: Knowledge Rating Chart

Have students complete the knowledge rating chart on *Student Journal* page 76. Are there any adjustments or changes they would like to make?

They can be loud. Males hiss when they're fighting or mating. Females hiss only when disturbed. Roaches live together in colonies. Sometimes a whole colony will hiss as one—for no reason at all!

Some insects make sound by rubbing body parts. Crickets chirp by rubbing their legs together. But Madagascar roaches hiss through their breathing tubes.

Hissing roaches are not household pests. They prefer the jungles of Madagascar. There, they spend their days under logs. They eat fallen fruit and rotten wood.

Madagascar is an island. It's just off the eastern coast of Africa. But hissing roaches may live in your neighborhood. That's because some people keep hissing roaches as pets. They say they make great pets. They cost very little to care for. They don't need much attention. In fact, they prefer to be left alone. ◆

Student Journal page 79

Name _____ Date _____

Building Vocabulary: Root *termin*

Use one of the words below to complete each sentence. Underline the root *termin* in each word.

terminate	terminal	determine	interminable

1. We drove to the airport _____ to meet my brother, who had been away for a year.
2. The wait for the plane to arrive seemed endless, or _____.
3. I looked at the arrival notices to _____ if the plane would be on time.
4. I wish his company would _____ his overseas contract, so he could work closer to home.

How many words can you find in the word **interminable**? Write them below.

in _____

term _____

rat _____

Survival • Cockroaches: The Ultimate Survivors — 79

Asthma and Roaches

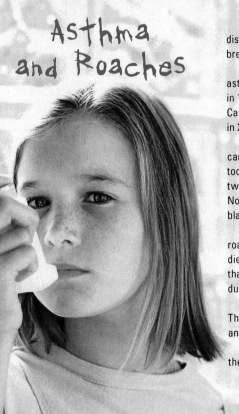

Do you know anyone who has asthma? It's a disease that affects the lungs. It makes it hard to breathe. Sometimes asthma attacks are fatal.

Over 20 million Americans suffer from asthma. That's three times as many people than in 1980. Many of the sufferers are children. Caring for everyone with asthma cost $9.4 billion in 2004.

Cigarette smoke, dust, furry pets, and mold can cause asthma attacks. Air pollution can, too. But pollution levels have dropped in the past twenty years. Asthma cases have risen. Why? No one knows for sure. But some scientists blame cockroaches.

Scientists have known for some time that roaches can cause asthma. How? After roaches die or molt, they become dust. Then we breathe that dust. Many people are allergic to cockroach dust.

Asthma cases have risen the most in cities. That may be partly because apartment buildings and high-rises are favorite roach hideouts.

Do you know someone with asthma? Tell them to get a good exterminator. It may help!

23

Possible answers for **Student Journal page 80** include *ai* pattern: *complain, rainbow, obtain, pain, raid, main*; *ay* pattern: *maybe, gray, hay, stray, fray, way*; *aCe* pattern: *trade, came, mate, rage, flame, hate*.

Name _____ Date _____

Phonics/Word Study: Common Long *a* Patterns

Finish both lists. Try to include words with more than one syllable. Look through "Cockroaches: The Ultimate Survivors" for ideas.

ai pattern	*ay* pattern	*a*-consonant-*e* pattern
1. brain	1. day	1. make
2.	2.	2.
3.	3.	3.
4.	4.	4.
5.	5.	5.

Choose three words from the lists above and write a sentence for each one.

1. _____
2. _____
3. _____

Choose two words from the lists above and illustrate them.

Word _____   Word _____

80   Survival • Cockroaches: The Ultimate Survivors

Writing Short Monologue

Explain to students that a monologue is a speech given by one person. Have students each write a monologue from the viewpoint of a cockroach, telling about its life. On *Student Journal* page 77, students can jot down ideas for their monologue, and then use these ideas to write a short monologue on *Student Journal* page 78. Have students present their monologues to the class, reading with expression. (See Differentiated Instruction for examples of monologues.)

Vocabulary Root *termin*

Remind students that recognizing a word's root may help them better understand an unfamiliar word. Write *exterminator* on the board and read it aloud. Ask students what the word means. (somebody who kills insects, rats, and other pests) Underline *termin*. Identify it as a word root that comes from Latin, meaning "end, last, final, boundary." Then have students complete the sentences on *Student Journal* page 79. (Answers: 1. *terminal*; 2. *interminable*; 3. *determine*; 4. *terminate*)

Phonics/Word Study

Common Long *a* Patterns

Display the words *stain, gray,* and *game.* Have students identify the vowel sound in each word. (long *a*) Ask volunteers to underline the spelling pattern in each word that makes the long *a* sound. (*ai, ay, ame*) Now, work with students to complete the in-depth long *a* patterns activity on TE page 130. For additional support, have students complete *Student Journal* page 80.

Phonics/Word Study

Common Long *a* Patterns

In this lesson, students will begin to look at how the vowel sounds are represented on paper.

▶ Place the following words on the board: *train, play,* and *brake.* Ask students to say the words out loud. Then ask: *What do all of these words have in common?* If students don't say "long *a*" right away, encourage them to think about the vowel sounds. Once students identify long *a* as the common feature, have them segment the words.

train	*ain*	*ai*
play	*ay*	
brake	*ake*	*a*

▶ Then ask: *All of these long a words have the same vowel sound, but what's different about all of them?* (They all have a different spelling.) Point out that these three patterns of long *a* are the most common long *a* patterns in the English language. Ask pairs to brainstorm at least two more words for each category and then share their additions with the class.

▶ Provide students with copies of the Common Long *a* Patterns Sort sheet. (See *Word Study Manual* page 50.) Have students begin sorting by the four headings shown. Be sure to model the correct placement for the first few words.

▶ When confronted with a word with two or more syllables, students should identify the syllable with the long *a* vowel sound and concentrate only on that syllable.

▶ As a group, discuss the sort, students' observations, and why words such as *they, baby,* and *weigh* ended up in the Oddball column. Each of these words represents other long *a* patterns that will be studied later.

Common Long *a* Patterns Sort			
ai as in *train*	*ay* as in *play*	*aCe* as in *brake*	Oddball
brain	may	name	they
complain	way	shake	baby
strain	day	race	weigh
chain	bray	came	
pain	fray	slave	
drain	gray	trade	
stain	hay	make	
taint	lay	mate	
obtain	clay	frame	
maim	stray	crane	

For more information on word sorts and spelling stages, see pages 5–31 in the *Word Study Manual.*

Focus on . . .

Use one or more activities in this section to focus on a particular area of need in your students.

Comprehension STRATEGY SUPPORT

To help those students who need more practice using the strategies covered in this lesson, work one-on-one or in small groups to apply the strategy prompts below. Apply the prompts to a *Reading Advantage* paperback, a classroom library book, or a new or familiar selection in the magazine. Always model your own thinking first.

Monitor Understanding

• Do I understand what I'm reading? If not, what part is confusing to me?

• What fix-up strategies can I use to solve the problem? (See During Reading for fix-up strategies.)

• Why did a character say (do, think, ask) that?

• What images do I visualize from the text? What parts can't I visualize?

• Why did the author include (or not include) those details?

Determining Importance

• What is the most important idea in the paragraph? How can I prove it?

• Which details are unimportant? Why?

• What does the author want me to understand?

• Why is this information important (or not important) to me?

Writing Letter

Madagascar hissing roaches have long been used for educational purposes in zoos and schools. Have students write a letter to the administrator of the school, or to the science department, explaining why they would like a hissing roach in their school. The letter should use information from the article to tell why the roach is interesting and why it is easy to take care of, pointing out that some people keep them as pets. Encourage students to talk over their ideas as a group or with a partner before they begin to write. Next, have each student jot down a list of ideas to include in the letter. Remind students about the five parts of a friendly letter: heading, greeting, body, closing, and signature.

Fluency: Pacing

SMALL GROUP

After students have read the selection at least once, use the section of text beginning on page 22, titled "Madagascar Hissing Cockroaches," to model reading aloud smoothly and at an even pace. Then have students work in pairs to practice reading the same or another section of text at a smooth pace, paying attention to punctuation.

As you listen to partners read, use these prompts to guide them.

▶ Review the text to avoid starts and stops.

▶ Read at an even, natural pace—not too quickly or too slowly.

▶ Use punctuation, such as commas, periods, and question marks, to help guide your pauses and expression.

When students read aloud, do they—

✓ demonstrate a smooth pace, not too fast or too slow?

✓ incorporate well-timed pauses between words and phrases?

✓ reflect an awareness and understanding of punctuation?

English Language Learners

SMALL GROUP

To support students' understanding of the selection, explore a word family.

1. Remind students that word families consist of words that contain the same root.

2. Write *survivor* on the board. Define *survivor* as "a person or animal that lives longer than expected." Discuss words related to *survivor*, such as *survivors*, *survive*, and *surviving*.

3. Have students examine the use of these words on pages 20–22 of the selection.

Independent Activity Options

INDEPENDENT

While you work with individuals or small groups, others can work independently on one or more of the following options.

▶ Foundations paperback books, see TE pages 195–200

▶ Foundations *eZines*

▶ Repeat word sorts for this lesson

▶ *Student Journal* pages for this lesson

Assessment

Strategy Assessment

To help you and your students assess their use of comprehension strategies, ask the following questions. Students can complete a written response or provide verbal answers in a one-on-one reading conference.

1. **Monitor Understanding** To monitor your understanding of this selection, what questions did you ask yourself? (Answers will vary. Students may have asked themselves why cockroaches have survived for so long, how they have traveled to all parts of the world, or why they haven't evolved very much over millions of years.)

2. **Determining Importance** What important ideas did you find in this selection? (Answers will vary. Students may say that cockroaches survive in all environments, that cockroaches will eat just about anything, that cockroaches have two brains, or that cockroaches produce many offspring.)

For ongoing informal assessment, use the checklists on pages 61–64 of *Foundations Assessment*.

Word Study Assessment

Use these steps to help you and your students assess their understanding of common long *a* patterns.

1. Display a three-column chart as shown, but include only the headings.

2. Read the following words aloud: *gray, brave, drain, paint, stray, frame, domain, maybe, namesake, payday, bakeoff,* and *explain*.

3. Have students write each word in the appropriate column. The answers are shown.

ai as in *train*	*ay* as in *play*	*aCe* as in *brake*
drain	gray	brave
paint	stray	frame
domain	maybe	namesake
explain	payday	bakeoff

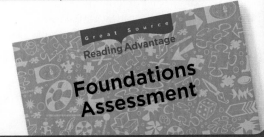

Great Source
Reading Advantage
Foundations Assessment

Characters:

Marco: junior class representative, a star forward on the soccer team

Jason: president of the student council

Sarah: Marco's friend, the school's fastest runner

Kim: Jason's friend

Mr. Martinez: a social studies teacher and adviser to the student council

LESSON 17
Delayed Belay
Survival, pages 24–29

SUMMARY
This **play** tells about how a school rock-climbing trip affects two boys and their relationship with each other.

COMPREHENSION STRATEGIES
Inferential Thinking
Understanding Text Structure

WRITING
Summary

VOCABULARY
Synonyms

PHONICS/WORD STUDY
Common Long *e* Patterns

Lesson Vocabulary
mediating	ascent
belay	protrusion
flustered	

MATERIALS
Survival, pp. 24–29
Student Journal, pp. 81–85
Word Study Manual, p. 51

Background:
Marco, Jason, Sarah, and Kim are all officers on the student council. Jason and Marco have lived next door to each other since elementary school.

But Marco and Jason do not get along. Jason is the president of the student council. Marco is the junior class representative. They can never agree on anything. Sarah and Kim usually end up mediating at student council meetings.

Setting:
A group of students are at an indoor rock-climbing gym. They are preparing for an overnight camping trip. Marco and Jason are working together on a climb. Marco is strapped into a harness and is about to begin his climb. Jason is standing behind and holding the rope. He will stay on the ground and spot Marco.

LORD OF THE CLIMBING RINGS

A belay is a small metal ring that a climber fastens her rope around.

The word *belay* is used in mountain climbing. It is a way of keeping in check with your partner. A climber will use it when she needs to make sure her spotter has her covered. She will call out, "Belay on." The spotter will respond, "On belay" if she has the ropes under control. Then it's up you go.

(24)

Before Reading   Use one or more activities.

Make a Web ▶

Ask students if they know the difference between rock climbing and mountain climbing. (Mountain climbing is walking, hiking, and climbing up high mountains, such as Mount Everest. Rock climbing involves using one's hands and feet to climb up steep, rocky surfaces that may or may not be part of mountains.) Start a word web about rock climbing. Write anything students know about it in the outer ovals. Revisit the web later.

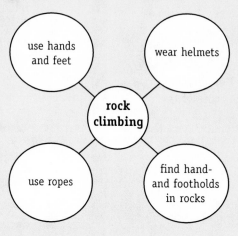

Vocabulary Preview

Have students discuss what they already know about any of the vocabulary words. Discuss any associations they might have with the words. Where have they seen or heard them used before? Then have students complete *Student Journal* page 81. Use the vocabulary word *ascent* to model a response for the page. Tell students that they will revisit the page after they have finished reading the play. (See Differentiated Instruction.)

Marco: *(calling behind him)* Belay on.

Jason: *(looking flustered)* Yeah.

Marco: I said, "Belay on."

Jason: Right. I've got it.

Marco: You're supposed to answer "On belay." That's how it happens every time. The climber calls out, "Belay on," once he's ready to climb. Then the spotter calls back, "On belay." It's a simple way to stay safe. All you have to say is, "On belay."

Jason: On belay.

Marco: That's right. See, it's easy. Now just say it at the right time.

Jason: *(adjusting the ropes in his hands)* Sorry, there's just a lot to remember.

Mr. Martinez: How's it going over here? Anyone need a soda pop?

Marco: We haven't even done one ascent.

Jason: It took a long time to get changed and hooked up to the ropes. We just started—

Marco: Twenty minutes ago.

Mr. Martinez: What's the rush, Marco? Everyone will get to practice today. Just climb at your own pace. The real mountain climb isn't for another week.

Jason: *(gulping)* It's only a week away?

25

Preview the Selection

Have students look through the play, paying special attention to the genre and the illustrations. Use these or similar prompts to discuss the selection.

- What kind of a selection is this? How do you know?
- Who are the main characters?
- From the illustrations, what predictions can you make about the play? (Kids are rock climbing; someone seems to be in trouble.)

Teacher Think Aloud

As I preview this play, the "Background" text on page 24 alerts me that the two main characters, Marco and Jason, never agree and don't get along. That might be the conflict that moves events along. I also think that the rock-climbing setting shown in the illustrations could provide action, danger, and excitement.

Make Predictions/Set Purpose

Students should use the information they gathered in previewing the selection to make predictions about what they will learn. If students have trouble generating a purpose for reading, suggest that they read to discover how belaying can save a climber's life.

Comprehension

UNDERSTANDING TEXT STRUCTURE

Use these questions to help students recognize the resolution of Jason's conflict.

- What event happens at the high point, or climax, of the play? (Marco loses his footing, and Jason saves his life by having his belay on.)

- What does Jason do after this event? (Jason climbs up the rock face without difficulty.)

- Why do you think Jason overcame his fear? (Possible responses include that saving Marco's life gave Jason more confidence.)

Setting:

A week later. It's 9 a.m. A school bus is parked at the foot of Black Bear Mountain. Mr. Martinez's students climb down from the bus. They stand around talking and looking at the mountain. Marco and Sarah are talking near a path to the mountain.

Sarah: *(looking up at the mountain)* Awesome. This thing is huge.

Marco: Yeah, it's so cool. I've never seen it up close.

Sarah: It's even bigger than it looked in the pictures. I can't believe we're going to climb it.

Marco: I wish we were allowed to pick our own climbing partners. You and I could tear up this mountain so fast. It would make everybody's head spin.

Sarah: Yeah, but either way, we'll all be up there eating s'mores by tonight.

Marco: *(under his breath)* Let's hope.

(Cut to the other side of the bus where Jason and Kim are sitting down on their backpacks. Jason squirts water from his bottle into his mouth. Then he glances around nervously.)

Kim: You okay?

Jason: Fine. Don't I look fine? I'm fine.

Kim: You look a little pale.

Jason: My stomach feels a little sick. Maybe I ate too many breakfast burritos on the bus or something.

Kim: You're not nervous about this, are you?

Jason: *(looking terrified)* No, of course not. I'm excited. It's going to be fun!

Mr. Martinez: Okay, everyone. Can I have your attention, please? We're going to get started with the climb.

Sarah and Kim: *(together)* Awesome!

Mr. Martinez: This whole trip should take about six hours from start to finish. Some of the time, we'll just be hiking. But we will also be doing some partnered rock climbing. You've all done a great job practicing for this. It's going to be a lot of fun. Just remember what we've learned about the belay system, and we'll all have a good, safe trip up.

(The students gather at the foot of the trail. Then they begin their hike up the mountain. Jason is the only one who holds back.)

26

During Reading

Comprehension

INFERENTIAL THINKING

Use these question to model for students how to make inferences about Jason at the beginning of the play. Then have students reveal inferences they make as they continue to read.

- When practicing climbing, what does Jason do and say on page 25?

- What does my own experience tell me about his behavior?

- What can I infer about Jason?

Teacher Think Aloud

The text tells me that Jason looks flustered during practice. He makes up excuses, and he gulps when he hears that the real climb is just a week away. I know people—myself included—who get flustered and gulp when they're nervous, and making excuses is a way to put off an unpleasant task. So I infer that Jason is afraid to make the climb.

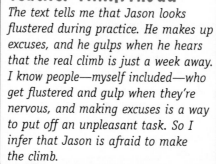

Comprehension

UNDERSTANDING TEXT STRUCTURE

Use these questions to model for students how to identify the structure of the play. Then have students identify and describe the elements of the play.

- Who is the main character in the play?

- What problem or conflict does the main character face?

- What is the setting of the play?

(See Differentiated Instruction.)

Jason: *(to himself)* You're the president of the student council. You're the only one who's afraid of heights. You need to get yourself together. You just have to climb it. It can't be that bad.

(He falls in line behind Kim.)

Kim: Are you feeling better?

Jason: Yeah, I'm great.

(While they hike, they each stick with friends. Marco and Sarah walk ahead of the group, while Jason and Kim go more slowly, pulling up the rear. At 2 p.m., they reach the toughest part of the climb. Just above it is the mountaintop.)

Mr. Martinez: Almost there, everybody. This is the last stretch up the mountain. How does everyone feel? *(laughing)* No one needs to turn back, I hope? *(He points down the mountain.)*

(Jason makes the mistake of following Mr. Martinez's hand with his eyes. He gasps. When he looks down, he sees the school bus far below. It's so small that it looks like a toy. They are about 3,000 feet high.)

Jason: *(to himself)* You can do this. You can do this.

Marco: *(clapping Jason on the back)* So you decided to join us up here. You ready for this?

Jason: Yeah, it should be fun.

Marco: Are you ready to holler back at me when I climb?

Jason: On belay.

Marco: *(squinting at him)* All right, let's do it.

Jason: Sure, I just want to watch a few go up first. I want to make sure people get the hang of it. Because I'm the

president, I should make sure things are going okay for everyone else.

Marco: Are you scared or something?

Jason: No! You know, I'm the president. I should make sure things are going okay for everyone else.

Marco: Okay, sure.

(They watch the first pairs climb. Other teachers on the trip stand at the top of the rock wall and coach the students up. Mr. Martinez makes the rounds. He checks that each student has a partner. He makes sure their harnesses are secure. He inspects their belays to make sure the rope is safely in its metal ring.)

A chorus of other students at various times: Belay on.

Their partners' responses: On belay.

Marco: *(looking at Jason)* See, it's a piece of cake.

27

Teacher Think Aloud

It's clear from the beginning that Jason isn't excited to make the climb, and when the scene changes to the mountainside, it is finally clear why. Jason is afraid of heights! This is a serious conflict. Jason is a class leader, and everyone expects him to climb. Knowing the nature of the conflict, I'm curious to read on to see whether it is resolved.

Fix-Up Strategies

Offer these strategies to help students read independently.

If you don't understand what you're reading:

• Reread the difficult section to look for clues to help you comprehend.

• Read ahead to find clues to help you comprehend.

• Retell, or say in your own words, what you've read.

• Visualize, or form mental pictures of, what you've read.

If you don't understand a word:

• Reread the sentence. Look for ideas and words that provide meaning clues.

• Find clues by reading a few sentences before and after the confusing word.

• Look for the base or root word and think about its meaning.

• Think about the topic or plot at this point to see if either offers meaning clues.

Student Journal pages 82–83

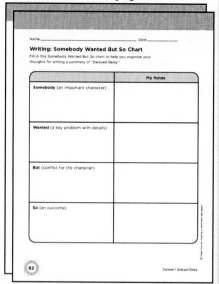

Student Journal page 84

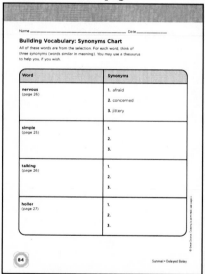

(After about an hour, almost all of the other students have made it up the climb. As each minute passes, Marco looks more and more anxious. Jason looks more and more nervous. Finally, they are the only two students left.)

Mr. Martinez: Ah, here's my class president and my junior rep. They saved the best for last. Are you guys ready for an awesome climb?

Marco: Of course.

(Jason nods his head. They hook their ropes into the pulley and take their places before the cliff.)

Marco: Belay on.

Jason: (nodding his head) On belay!

Marco: Alright! You got it!

(Marco begins his ascent. He moves quickly up the steep cliff. Jason is watching him, awed. He knows that he will have to do the same thing next.)

Jason: (calling up to him) You're doing great!

(But then, something goes wrong. As Marco moves his foot to the next foothold, he slips. He falls ten feet before the rope that Jason is holding catches him. He is dangling in midair about forty feet above Jason. The rock wall is several feet away.)

Marco: (gasping, sounding desperate) I can't reach the rocks.

Mr. Martinez: You're doing fine, Marco. You've got a good partner who's not going to let you slip. Check in with him.

Marco: (his voice shaking) What do I do?

Mr. Martinez: You know what to do.

(There is a moment of tense silence.)

28

After Reading Use one or more activities.

Check Purpose

Have students determine whether their purpose was met. Did students discover how belaying can save a climber's life?

Discussion Questions

Ask the following questions.

1. How and why did Marco and Jason's relationship change? (Cause-Effect)

2. What role does cooperation play in dangerous activities such as rock climbing? (Draw Conclusions)

3. Think about a problem or challenge you solved with the help of others. How might the outcome have been different if you hadn't cooperated with others? (Making Connections)

Revisit: Web

Have students revisit the web they made about rock climbing. What can they add, now that they have read the selection? Would they like to change anything?

Revisit: Making Associations

Have students return to *Student Journal* page 81. Would they like to change or add anything? Discuss their responses.

Jason: *(from the ground, calling up to Marco)* Remember, "Belay on?"

Marco: Oh yeah. Belay on.

Jason: *(instantly)* On belay. The ropes are tight. You should be fine to start climbing again.

(After a minute, Marco reaches out again for the rock. This time he is calmer. He manages to grab on to a protrusion in the rock. He pulls himself back onto the wall and takes a deep breath. Then he climbs. When he gets to the top, he collapses with relief. He looks down below and sees Jason preparing for the climb. Mr. Martinez will be his partner.)

Marco: Hey, Jason?

Jason: Yeah.

Marco: I think you just saved my life. Thanks. I guess you were paying attention during training after all.

Jason: You're welcome, partner. Now, it's my turn.

Marco: Don't worry, Jason. I think you have what it takes. Why don't you show me how it's done.

(Quickly, Jason begins to climb. His fear from a moment ago is gone. Somehow, catching Marco made him feel better. He felt in control. But Marco's words gave him even more courage. Finally, he pulls himself up the last few feet and steps onto the mountaintop. Marco slaps him on the back.)

Marco: *(grinning)* Belay on, buddy.

Jason: On belay. ◆

29

DIFFERENTIATED INSTRUCTION
Vocabulary
Synonyms

To help students, try these steps:

1. Display *flustered, ascent,* and *protrusion.*

2. Have students explain the meaning of each word. They may use context clues.

3. Ask: *What are synonyms?* (words with similar meanings)

4. Next, display the synonyms *rise, overhang,* and *upset.*

5. Have students match the vocabulary word with the correct synonym. (*flustered/upset; ascent/rise; protrusion/overhang*)

Answers to **Student Journal page 85** are 1. *feet;* 2. *heat;* 3. *baby;* 4. *thief;* 5. *we.*

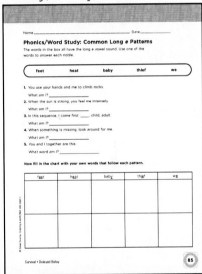

Writing Summary

Remind students that a summary is a shorter version of a text and contains only the main points of the longer text. Have students begin their summaries of "Delayed Belay" by completing the Somebody Wanted But So chart on *Student Journal* page 82. Then, on *Student Journal* page 83, students should use their completed charts to write a summary of the play.

Vocabulary Synonyms

Explain that many words have synonyms, or other words with similar meanings. Point out this sentence on page 26: *"You're not nervous about this, are you?"* Tell students that *worried* is a synonym for *nervous.* Ask for other synonyms for *nervous.* (*afraid, concerned, jittery*) Have students complete *Student Journal* page 84. (Possible responses include *simple/easy, elementary, basic; talking/conversing, chatting, discussing; holler/yell, scream, shout.*) (See Differentiated Instruction.)

Phonics/Word Study
Common Long *e* Patterns

Ask volunteers to suggest words that contain the long *e* sound, and write them on the board. Underline in each word the spelling pattern that makes the long *e* sound. Be sure that words listed include the patterns *ee, ie,* and *ea.* Now, work with students to complete the in-depth long *e* patterns activity on TE page 138. For additional support, have students complete *Student Journal* page 85.

Phonics/Word Study

Common Long *e* Patterns

▶ To introduce the most common long *e* patterns, write the following words on the board: *keep*, *chief*, and *beak*. Ask students to say the words out loud. Then ask: *What do all of these words have in common?* If students don't say "long *e*" right away, encourage them to think about the vowel sounds. Once students identify long *e* as the common feature, have them segment the words.

keep	eep	ee
chief	ief	ie
beak	eak	ea

▶ Then ask: *All of these long e words have the same vowel sound, but what's different about all of them?* (They all have a different spelling.) Point out that these three patterns of long *e* are the most common long *e* patterns in the English language.

▶ Ask pairs to brainstorm at least two more words for each category and then share their additions with the class. As pairs say each word, ask which category it goes in.

▶ Provide students with copies of the Common Long *e* Patterns Sort sheet. (See *Word Study Manual* page 51.) Have students begin sorting by the four headings shown. Be sure to model the correct placement for the first few words.

▶ When confronted with a word with two or more syllables, students should identify the syllable with the long *e* vowel sound and concentrate only on that syllable.

▶ As a group, discuss the sort, students' observations, and why words such as *we*, *he*, *great*, and *breath* ended up in the Oddball column. Each of these words represents other vowel patterns that will be studied later.

Common Long *e* Patterns Sort			
ee as in *keep*	*ie* as in *chief*	*ea* as in *beak*	Oddball
agree	chief	each	we
keep	believe	team	he
need	piece	teacher	great
week	relief	easy	breath
seen		real	
feel		weak	
feet		near	
teem		fear	
reel		knead	
steep		feat	
deep		peace	

For more information on word sorts and spelling stages, see pages 5–31 in the *Word Study Manual*.

Focus on . . .

Use one or more activities in this section to focus on a particular area of need in your students.

Comprehension STRATEGY SUPPORT

To help those students who need more practice using the strategies covered in this lesson, work one-on-one or in small groups to apply the strategy prompts below. Apply the prompts to a *Reading Advantage* paperback, a classroom library book, or a new or familiar selection in the magazine. Always model your own thinking first.

Inferential Thinking

• What are the causes or effects of this event?

• What do I learn from the character or person's thoughts, words, or actions?

• What do I know (or infer) from the text that the author hasn't stated directly?

• What conclusions can I draw?

Understanding Text Structure

• What kind of text is this? (book, story, article, guidebook, play, manual)

• How does the author organize the text? (cause-effect, problem-solution, chronological order, description, question-answer, comparison-contrast)

• What details support my thoughts about the text structure?

• What is the cause (effect, problem, solution, order, question, answer)?

• If fiction, who are the characters? What is the setting, plot, conflict, and resolution?

Writing Review

Have students write a brief review of the play. Explain that a review is a piece of critical writing in which the reviewer, or critic, first makes a short statement about the content of the play, and then gives the reader his or her opinion of the play. If possible, have some reviews onhand for students to look at, or read one or two aloud. To organize their thoughts before writing, students should create a chart such as the one shown.

Review of "Delayed Belay"

Good Points	Bad Points

My overall opinion:

Fluency: Expression

After students have read the selection at least once silently, have them focus on reading it aloud. Model reading aloud expressively. Remind students that dialogue should flow smoothly, as though spoken naturally instead of read. Have students form groups to practice reading before presenting sections of the play.

As you listen to the groups practice, use these prompts to help students read expressively.

▶ Read your lines several times so you are comfortable with them.

▶ Read with expression. Put yourself in the role of the character.

▶ Use the punctuation marks for clues to expression. Raise your voice slightly at the end of a question. Pause when you see a comma or a period.

When students read aloud, do they—

✓ reflect an understanding of the text?

✓ demonstrate appropriate timing, stress, and intonation?

✓ incorporate appropriate speed and phrasing?

English Language Learners

Use the following sentence frames to support students as they make connections in the third discussion question on TE page 136.

I needed a friend when . . .

I helped someone by . . .

If I hadn't asked for help, I might have . . .

After students make connections, have them discuss how their experiences helped them understand the play.

Independent Activity Options

While you work with individuals or small groups, others can work independently on one or more of the following options.

▶ Foundations paperback books, see TE pages 195–200

▶ Foundations *eZines*

▶ Repeat word sorts for this lesson

▶ *Student Journal* pages for this lesson

Assessment

Strategy Assessment

To help you and your students assess their use of comprehension strategies, ask the following questions. Students can complete a written response or provide verbal answers in a one-on-one reading conference.

1. **Inferential Thinking** What inferences did you make while reading this play? (Answers will vary. Students may have made inferences about the characters in the play; the process of facing and overcoming fears; or the importance of being able to depend on one another in dangerous sports, such as rock climbing.)

2. **Understanding Text Structure** How did Jason's unwillingness to reveal his fears add to the suspense in the play? (Answers will vary. Students may say that with Jason putting off his climb to the very end, readers' interest in the outcome increased.)

For ongoing informal assessment, use the checklists on pages 61–64 of *Foundations Assessment*.

Word Study Assessment

Use these steps to help you and your students assess their understanding of common long *e* patterns.

1. Display the chart below, but include only the headings.

2. Read the following words aloud, one at a time: *speak, believe, weekday, knead, wreath, teeming, piece, sleep, relief, thief, deep,* and *weakness.*

3. Have students sort each word into the appropriate column. The answers are shown.

ee as in *keep*	*ie* as in *chief*	*ea* as in *beak*
weekday	believe	speak
teeming	piece	knead
sleep	relief	wreath
deep	thief	weakness

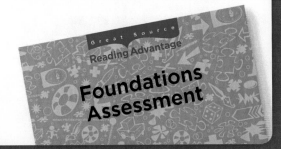

Great Source

Reading Advantage

Foundations Assessment

LESSON 18
After the Storm *and* Final Exam
Survival, pages 30–end

SUMMARY
In the **poem** "After the Storm," a teenager speaks of her resolve to start over after the devastation to her home and town by a hurricane. In the **poem** "Final Exam," a student tells how she's mobilizing herself to study for a test.

COMPREHENSION STRATEGIES
Making Connections

WRITING
Poem

VOCABULARY
Antonyms

PHONICS/WORD STUDY
Common Long *i* Patterns

Lesson Vocabulary
timidly	cram
bashful	doomed
howled	

MATERIALS
Survival, pp. 30–end
Student Journal, pp. 86–90
Word Study Manual, p. 52

Before Reading Use one or more activities.

Make a List
Have students free-associate about poetry. Record and display all responses. Return to the list later.

Poetry
1. rhymes
2. about feelings
3. hard to understand
4. haiku
5.

Vocabulary Preview
Display the vocabulary words. Tell students that words have denotations (general meanings) and connotations (personal associations). Have students fill in *Student Journal* page 86. Use the word *howled* to model the activity. (See Differentiated Instruction.)

Preview the Selection
Have students look at the poems and their illustrations. Discuss students' observations.

Make Predictions/Set Purpose
Students should use the information they gathered in previewing the selection to make predictions about what they will learn. If students have trouble generating a purpose for reading, suggest that they read to find out what each poem is about.

Storm

We peek outside
Timidly,
Like bashful children hiding behind
    mothers' legs.

The sky howled last night,
Endlessly,
As an angry giant tossed aside our cars
    and homes,
Thinking they were only toys.

This hurricane did not play favorites.

The world watched our nightmare.
Televisions showed reporters
Swaying in the winds like palm trees,
Enormous waves crashing madly,
Flooded streets flowing like rivers,
Piles of splintered wood where homes
    once stood.

Our town's library lost its roof.
My school has become a shelter
For those with nothing left.
A boat,
Its smooth, rounded bottom reflecting
    today's bright sun,
Sits on my neighbor's smashed garage.

Our house is gone.
The wooden box Grandpa made for me
    and I've had
Since I was five—
Gone.

But we are here.

Tomorrow, the reporters will wander off,
Looking for the next storm.
The world will click off their televisions
And forget.

And our work will begin,
One nail at a time.
Our town will grow back.

31

DIFFERENTIATED INSTRUCTION
Vocabulary Preview
Work with students to read, pronounce, and establish meaning for the word *bashful*.

What are the word parts?	*bash* *ful*
What is the base word?	*bash*
What letter or letters stand for the final consonant sound in *bash*?	*sh*
In what other words do you find the blend *sh*?	*dish, wash, ship*
What does *bashful* mean? Where might you use it?	*Bashful* means "shy." My *bashful* little sister hid behind a chair.

Student Journal page 86

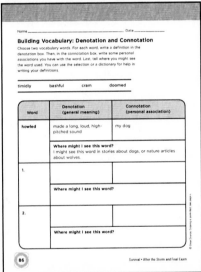

During Reading

Comprehension

MAKING CONNECTIONS

Use these questions to model how to make connections with "After the Storm." Then have students make connections with "Final Exam."

- What does "After the Storm" remind me of?
- Have I ever lived through a hurricane, blizzard, or other storm?
- Have I ever seen or experienced damage from a storm?

Teacher Think Aloud

This poem reminds me of the time when a powerful thunderstorm hit my hometown. The wind blew over an old maple tree, and the falling tree tore down power lines, plunging our neighborhood into darkness. The tree also crushed a neighbor's minivan. No one was hurt, but I'll never forget the havoc a storm can cause.

Fix-Up Strategies
Offer these strategies to help students read independently.

If you don't understand what you're reading:

- Reread the difficult section to look for clues to help you comprehend.
- Read ahead to find clues to help you comprehend.
- Retell, or say in your own words, what you've read.
- Visualize, or form mental pictures of, what you've read.

DIFFERENTIATED INSTRUCTION
Writing Poem

SMALL GROUP

To help students write their free-verse poems, try the following:

1. Discuss the characteristics of a free-verse poem: there's no requirement for rhyme or a specific rhythm; the first word in each line does not have to be capitalized; the poem does not have to contain any punctuation marks, but if included, punctuation marks should be used as they would be in other writing.

2. Discuss how to create images for the audience, using strong verbs and specific nouns. Brainstorm some phrases and write them on the board.

Student Journal pages 87–88

Name_____ Date_____

Writing: Poem Planning Page

Write notes about a topic that interests you. Try to visualize what is happening. Think about strong descriptive nouns and verbs that will help someone else "see" the event.

Topic: _____

Specific nouns you might like to use: _____

Strong verbs you might like to use: _____

Sights, smells, sounds you might like to use: _____

Other notes: _____

Survival • After the Storm and Final Exam

87

CREDITS

Program Authors
Laura Robb
James F. Baumann
Carol J. Fuhler
Joan Kindig

Editorial Board
Avon Connell-Cowell
R. Craig Roney

Supervising Editor
Ruth S. Rothstein

Project Manager
Alison Blank

Magazine Writers
Catherine Chiarello
Erin Fry
Megan Howard
Anina Robb
Michele Sobel Spirn
Lisa Trusiani
Lauren Velevis

Design and Production
Anthology, Inc.

Photography
Cover Lester Lefkowitz/Corbis; IFC bkgd © Otto Rogge/CORBIS; IFC c Craig Aurness/CORBIS; IFC r © Anthony Bannister; Gallo Images/CORBIS; IFC l © Lee Snider/Photo Images/CORBIS; pp. 6b, 17l © Lee Snider/Photo Images/CORBIS; pp. 1l, 30 Burton McNeely/Getty Images; pp. 1r, 32 David McGlynn/Getty Images; pp. 2, 3 © Museum of History and Industry/CORBIS; pp. 2–3 bkgd Eastcott Momatiuk/Getty Images; pp. 4b, 6t © 2006 Carrie McLain Museum/AlaskaStock.com; pp. 4–5t © Bettmann/CORBIS; pp. 4–5 bkgd, 20l, 21b, 23b © Royalty-Free/Corbis; p. 7 © 2006 Bill Devine/AlaskaStock.com; pp. 14l, 15r, 16l, 18l Phillip Spears/Getty Images; p. 16t REUTERS/Guy Wathen/POOL/Landov; p. 16b Credit: Sebastian Thrun and Carnegie Mellon; p. 18t AP Photo/Gene J. Puskar/POOL; p. 19t Jason Reed/Getty Images; pp. 19b, 20t, b, r, 22t, cl, 23t © Anthony Bannister; Gallo Images/CORBIS; p. 21t © David Aubrey/CORBIS; p. 21b inset © Angelo Cavalli/Getty Images; p. 22b Siede Preis/Getty Images; p. 22cr © Reuters/CORBIS

Illustration
All maps created by Anthology, Inc. unless otherwise indicated. All graphic elements created by Anthology, Inc. unless otherwise indicated. IFCb, pp. 8–13 James Bentley; 1a, pp. 24–28 Bruce MacPherson

32

After Reading

WHOLE CLASS Use one or more activities.

Check Purpose

Have students determine whether their purpose was met. What did they find out about in each poem?

Discussion Questions

Continue the group discussion with the following questions.

1. What was some of the damage done by the storm in "After the Storm"? (Details)

2. How can you relate to the girl's methods of studying for a test in "Final Exam"? (Making Connections)

3. What can you infer about the reporters in "After the Storm"? (Inferential Thinking)

Revisit: List

Return to the poetry list that was started before reading. Would students like to add or change anything?

FINAL EXAM

How can I cram a year of knowledge
out of my head, through my arm, down
into the salmon pink eraser of my number 2 pencil
and out into an oval on a scan sheet?

I'm in survival mode:
drinking coffee
and splashing cold water
on my face. My books
are open, and I'm scanning
the pages, reading captions,
bar graphs, and chapter titles.
I'm highlighting notes,
sticking stickies here
and there. I've even called
Max and asked him to copy
all the handouts I missed last Thursday
when I had to go to the dentist
to get my wisdom teeth pulled.

Was that a bad sign?
Am I, toothless, doomed to fail this test?
There are only eight more hours till morning.
I'd better get some rest.

Student Journal page 89

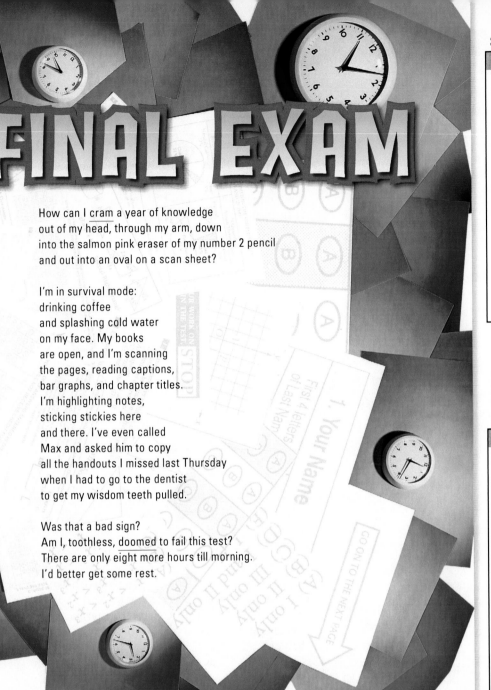

Answers for **Student Journal page 90** are *i: I, find, mind; ie: tried; igh: night, bright; y: sky, cry, my, try; i-e: hide, like.*

Writing Poem

Tell students that they will write a free-verse poem, without rhyme or a specific rhythm, like the poems they just read. You may want to brainstorm possible topics as a class. Have students choose their topic and write ideas about it on *Student Journal* page 87. Then have students complete *Student Journal* page 88. (See Differentiated Instruction.)

Vocabulary Antonyms

Display the word *timidly*. Ask students:
- What does *timidly* mean? (fearfully, without confidence)
- What word can you think of that has the opposite meaning of *timidly*? Make a list of words that students suggest. (Possible responses include *boldly, courageously,* and *confidently*.) Explain that words that are opposite in meaning are called *antonyms*. Then have students fill in *Student Journal* page 89.

Phonics/Word Study

Common Long *i* Patterns

Display the following sentence: *Tonight the moon is hard to find as it hides behind clouds in the sky.* As students identify the long *i* words, underline the long *i* spelling patterns. (*tonight, find, hides, behind, sky*) Now, work with students to complete the in-depth long *i* patterns activity on TE page 144. For additional support, have students complete *Student Journal* page 90.

Common Long *i* Patterns

▶ To introduce the most common long *i* patterns, write the following words on the board or on chart paper: *night, hide, mind,* and *sky.* Ask students to say the words out loud. Then ask: *What do all of these words have in common?* If students don't say "long *i*" right away, encourage them to think about the vowel sounds. Once students identify long *i* as the common feature, have them segment the words.

night	*ight*	*i*
hide	*ide*	*i*
mind	*ind*	*i*
sky		*y*

▶ Then ask: *All of these long i words have the same vowel sound, but what's different about all of them?* (They all have a different spelling.) Point out that these three patterns of long *i* are the most common long *i* patterns in the English language.

▶ Ask pairs to brainstorm at least two more words for each category and then share their additions with the class. As pairs say each word, ask which category it goes in.

▶ Provide students with copies of the Common Long *i* Patterns Sort sheet. (See *Word Study Manual* page 52.) Have students begin sorting by the five headings shown. Be sure to model the correct placement for the first few words to show students what is expected of them.

▶ When confronted with a word with two or more syllables, students should identify the syllable with the long *i* vowel sound and concentrate only on that syllable.

▶ As a group, discuss the sort, students' observations, and why words such as *height, dye, rye,* and *lye* ended up in the Oddball column. Each of these words represents other long *i* patterns that will be studied later. *Wind* with a short *i* sound may also be an oddball.

Common Long *i* Patterns Sort				
igh as in **night**	*iCe* as in **hide**	*ind* as in **mind**	*y* as in **sky**	**Oddball**
night	hide	mind	sky	height
bright	like	behind	why	dye
right	aside	kind	try	rye
light	rite	rind	fly	lye
sight	outside	wind	cry	
might	mite	find	dry	
	site	grind	fry	

For more information on word sorts and spelling stages, see pages 5–31 in the *Word Study Manual.*

Focus on . . .

Use one or more activities in this section to focus on a particular area of need in your students.

Comprehension STRATEGY SUPPORT

To help those students who need more practice using the strategies covered in this lesson, work one-on-one or in small groups to apply the strategy prompts below. Apply the prompts to a *Reading Advantage* paperback, a classroom library book, or a new or familiar selection in the magazine. Always model your own thinking first.

Making Connections

• What does this story (article, passage) remind me of?
• What do I already know about this topic?
• Where have I heard about this topic before?
• What do I have in common with the characters, people, or situations in the text?
• What other books, stories, articles, movies, or TV shows does this text make me think about?

Writing **Easy Haiku**

Have students write a haiku poem. Note that the syllabication of haiku is not discussed in this activity. The essence of haiku is that it creates an image in very few words, like a snapshot. Tell students that haiku is a form of Japanese poetry that describes something in three lines. The lines don't have rhyme or rhythm. Display and read aloud the following haiku. Discuss the simple picture the poet describes.

An old pond!
A frog jumps in—
The sound of water.
　　　—Basho

Then tell students that they can create a haiku by writing two or three sentences about something they see or hear. Students can then reread their sentences and underline key words and phrases. Have students use the underlined text to create a poem, using a graphic like the example shown below.

> There is a <u>sudden rainstorm</u>, and <u>people are getting soaked</u>. It is so hot out, though, that they seem to find it <u>a relief</u>.
>
> Sudden rainstorm.
> People getting soaked.
> Relief from the heat!

Fluency: Expression

After students have read the poems at least once silently, model reading "After the Storm" aloud. Explain that when you read, you try to capture the way the speaker might be feeling. You also pay more attention to punctuation, rather than the ends of lines, to know when to pause. However, the ends of lines sometimes call for a brief dramatic pause. Read the poem aloud once more as students follow along. Then have partners practice reading "Final Exam" aloud to each other.

As you listen to partners read, use these prompts to guide them.

▶ Put yourself in the place of a student cramming for a test.

▶ Use punctuation marks and line breaks to help you read expressively.

▶ Think about what the words are saying as you read.

When students read aloud, do they—

✓ reflect an understanding of the text?

✓ demonstrate appropriate timing, stress, and intonation?

✓ incorporate appropriate speed and phrasing?

English Language Learners

Examine multiple-meaning words in the poem on page 31 of the selection.

1. Write these words on the board: *storm, nail,* and *back*.

2. Discuss the multiple meanings of each word. For example, *storm* can mean "heavy rain with wind, thunder, and lightning" and "rush loudly and quickly into a room or building."

3. Reread the poem together. Have partners determine the meaning of each word in context.

Independent Activity Options

While you work with individuals or small groups, others can work independently on one or more of the following options.

▶ Foundations paperback books, see TE pages 195–200

▶ Foundations *eZines*

▶ Repeat word sorts for this lesson

▶ *Student Journal* pages for this lesson

Assessment

Strategy Assessment

To help you and your students assess their use of comprehension strategies, ask the following questions. Students can complete a written response or provide verbal answers in a one-on-one reading conference.

- **Making Connections** As you read the poems, what connections did you make? (Answers will vary. Students may mention that the poems reminded them of situations they had seen or heard about, or that the poems raised questions.)

See *Foundations Assessment* pages 38–45 for formal assessment to go with *Survival*.

Word Study Assessment

Use these steps to help you and your students assess their understanding of common long *i* patterns.

1. Display the chart below, but include only the headings.

2. Read the following words aloud, one at a time: *remind, fly, confide, fright, aside, by, why, grind, like, bright, sunlight,* and *blind*.

3. Have students sort each word into the appropriate column. The answers are shown.

igh as in *night*	*iCe* as in *hide*	*ind* as in *mind*	*y* as in *sky*
fright	confide	remind	fly
bright	aside	grind	by
sunlight	like	blind	why

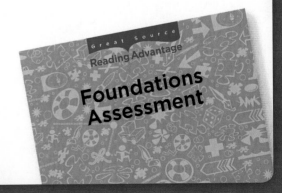

Foundations, Magazine 4

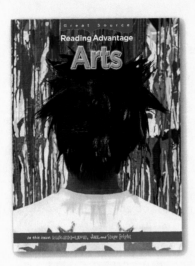

Arts

Magazine Summary

Arts magazine contains poems, articles, a story, a debate, and an interview—all related to the arts. Students will read selections on the visual arts, music, and literature.

Content-Area Connection: social science, science
Lexile measure: 470L

Arts Planner

LESSON	BEFORE READING	DURING READING	AFTER READING
LESSON 19 **Mix and Mash** *and* **Untitled #4** (article and poem) page 150	Anticipation Guide Vocabulary Preview Preview the Selection Make Predictions/ Set Purpose	Monitor Understanding Making Connections	Check Purpose Discussion Questions Writing: opinion paragraph Vocabulary: using the right word Phonics/Word Study: common long *o* patterns
LESSON 20 **But Is It Art?** (debate) page 158	Concept Web Vocabulary Preview Preview the Selection Make Predictions/ Set Purpose	Understanding Text Structure	Check Purpose Discussion Questions Writing: persuasive paragraph Vocabulary: compound words Phonics/Word Study: common long *u* patterns
LESSON 21 **All That Jazz** (article) page 164	K-W-L Chart Vocabulary Preview Preview the Selection Make Predictions/ Set Purpose	Determining Importance	Check Purpose Discussion Questions Writing: summary Vocabulary: multiple meanings Phonics/Word Study: common long vowel patterns review

Overview

Preview the Magazine

Allow time for students to do a thorough preview of the magazine. Have them read the selection titles and look at the photographs and illustrations. Also have students read the front and back covers. Explain that the magazine includes different forms of writing and that it addresses the arts from many angles. Begin a web similar to the one shown by gathering students' ideas about the different kinds of arts they know about. Define the word *arts* as "different forms of creative activity."

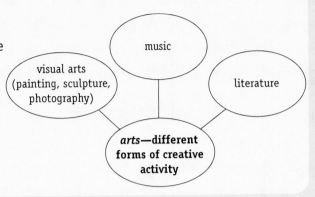

PHONICS/ WORD STUDY	FOCUS ON	ASSESSMENT	HIGHER-ORDER THINKING QUESTIONS
Common Long *o* Patterns	Writing: survey Fluency: expression English Language Learners Independent Activity Options	Monitor Understanding Making Connections Common Long *o* Patterns	Define *mash-ups*. Why are they considered illegal? Use details and information from the article to support your answer. How does the speaker feel about her first experience at an art museum? Why would she stick to the back of the line? What would she prefer to be doing? Use details and information from the poem to support your answer.
Common Long *u* Patterns	Writing: point/counterpoint Fluency: expression English Language Learners Independent Activity Options	Understanding Text Structure Common Long *u* Patterns	According to the article, what has happened to art since the 1700s? Use details and information from the article to support your answer. What do you consider true art? Use details and information from the debate to support your response.
Common Long Vowel Patterns Review	Writing: timeline Fluency: pacing English Language Learners Independent Activity Options	Determining Importance Common Long Vowel Patterns Review	What does Alex believe helped him and his brother to become successful jazz musicians? Use details and information from the article to support your response. How did jazz get its beginning, middle, and end? Use details and information from the article to support your answer.

Arts Planner

LESSON	BEFORE READING	DURING READING	AFTER READING
LESSON 22 **Ask the Science Wizard** (question-answer) page 171	Chart Vocabulary Preview Preview the Selection Make Predictions/ Set Purpose	Making Connections Determining Importance	Check Purpose Discussion Questions Writing: advertisement Vocabulary: synonyms and antonyms Phonics/Word Study: plurals *-s, -es*
LESSON 23 **Picture This** (story) page 178	Plot Organizer Vocabulary Preview Preview the Selection Make Predictions/ Set Purpose	Understanding Text Structure Monitor Understanding	Check Purpose Discussion Questions Writing: summary Vocabulary: denotation and connotation Phonics/Word Study: endings to words that end in *y*
LESSON 24 **Meet the Author: An Interview with Jacqueline Woodson** *and* **Opening Night** (interview and poem) page 186	Concept Web Vocabulary Preview Preview the Selection Make Predictions/ Set Purpose	Inferential Thinking Making Connections	Check Purpose Discussion Questions Writing: journal entry Vocabulary: context Phonics/Word Study: sounds of the past tense /d/, /t/, /ed/

PHONICS/ WORD STUDY	FOCUS ON	ASSESSMENT	HIGHER-ORDER THINKING QUESTIONS
Plurals -s, -es	Writing: personal experience Fluency: pacing English Language Learners Independent Activity Options	Making Connections Determining Importance Plurals -s, -es	What job does a scientist have at an art museum? Use details and information from the article to support your response. How do animals create art, and why? Use details and information from the article to support your answer.
Endings to Words That End in y	Writing: self-portrait Fluency: pacing English Language Learners Independent Activity Options	Understanding Text Structure Monitor Understanding Endings to Words That End in y	Why does Ronnie peep into Miss Miro's art class every day? What does he like about her class? Use details and information from the story to support your answer. When Miss Miro assigns Ronnie a detention in her classroom, what does he think he's in trouble for? Use details and information from the story to support your answer.
Sounds of the Past Tense /d/, /t/, /ed/	Writing: interview Fluency: expression English Language Learners Independent Activity Options	Inferential Thinking Making Connections Sounds of the Past Tense /d/, /t/, /ed/	Jacqueline Woodson says, "I loved watching words flower into sentences. I loved watching sentences blossom into stories." What does she mean? Use details and information from the interview to support your answer. The author of the poem, "Opening Night," has mixed feelings about opening night in a play. What is she really suffering from? Use details and information from the poem to support your answer.

Mix and Mash
and Untitled #4
Arts, pages 2–7

SUMMARY
This **article** describes the controversial music technique of mixing and matching pieces of different songs. The **poem** that follows describes one student's view of a field trip to an art museum.

COMPREHENSION STRATEGIES
Monitor Understanding
Making Connections

WRITING
Opinion Paragraph

VOCABULARY
Using the Right Word

PHONICS/WORD STUDY
Common Long *o* Patterns

Lesson Vocabulary
vocals   architect
compliment   personalize

MATERIALS
Arts, pp. 2–7
Student Journal, pp. 91–95
Word Study Manual, p. 53

What if you could make the sweetest pop star sing with a grungy punk band, or make the toughest rapper perform with a top country music star? Sound horrible? Sound impossible? Well, it's all just part of a day for a mash-up DJ.

2

Before Reading Use one or more activities.

Anticipation Guide

Create an anticipation guide like the one shown. (See TE page 214 for an anticipation guide BLM.) Ask students to read the statements and place a check in the AGREE or DISAGREE box before each statement. The discussion of anticipation guide statements can be a powerful motivator because once students have reacted to the statements, they have a stake in seeing if they are "right." Revisit the guide later.

Anticipation Guide		
AGREE	DISAGREE	
		1. Mash-up artists write their own music and lyrics.
		2. Published songs are raw material for others to use.
		3. Computers are changing the music world.
		4. Record companies love mash-up songs.

Vocabulary Preview

Read the vocabulary words aloud and write them for students to view. Clarify pronunciations. Before students read the article, assess their prior knowledge by having them begin the predictions chart on *Student Journal* page 91. Model the process, using the word *vocals.* Revisit the chart after students read. (See Differentiated Instruction.)

London, October 2002

Roy Kerr was about to break the law. No one would see him. He was safe inside. In fact, he was just sitting. He was hunched over in the blue light that glowed from his computer.

Nonetheless, he was also about to become famous. Soon he would be a big name in music. He was about to create a hit song. But that song would be entirely illegal.

You see, Kerr was a mash-up artist. That meant he liked to take apart popular songs. He had computer software to do this. Taking songs apart was not the problem, though. The law-breaking was in how he put them back together.

Kerr liked to mix and match the pieces of different songs. On his computer, Kelly Clarkson could sing with Metallica. Or Usher could do a single with Green Day. Anything was possible. The stranger the mix, the more Kerr liked it.

How did it work? Think about how you write on a computer. Sometimes you edit your work. You copy and paste sentences. Using music software, Kerr could do something similar. He could copy just the vocals out of a song. Then he could paste that singer's voice over the music of another song.

The result was a whole new song. Mash-ups are not like the samples you hear in rap music. Those samples borrow just a few seconds from another song. But mash-ups merge two whole songs from beginning to end. And this was what Kerr was about to do.

The Cool New Thing

Kerr was not the only one remixing music. Mash-up artists were big in London. They made their mix-and-match songs and gave them to club DJs. A few radio stations played mash-ups, too. Mash-ups were the cool new thing.

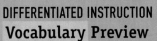

Student Journal page 91

Name _____ Date _____

Building Vocabulary: Predictions
How do you predict these words will be used in "Mix and Mash"?
Write your answers in the second column. Next, read the article.
Then, clarify your answers in the third column.

Word	My prediction for how the word will be used	How the word is actually used
vocals		
personalize		
compliment		
architect		

Arts • Mix and Mash *and* Untitled #4   91

Preview the Selection

Have students look through the selection, paying special attention to the title of the article, the introductory note, and the section headings. Use these or similar prompts to discuss the selection.

- What do you think is the purpose of the introductory note?
- What form of writing is this selection? How can you tell?
- What is the purpose of the section headings?

Teacher Think Aloud

By looking at the pictures in this selection, I can tell that it has to do with popular music. I also see a DJ sitting at his controls. That and the title give me a clue that the article is about DJs mixing music. The headings tell what each section is about. Roy Kerr seems to be a real person, and the selection gives facts, so I think that it is nonfiction.

Make Predictions/ Set Purpose

Students should use the information they gathered in previewing the selection to make predictions about what they will learn. If students have trouble generating a purpose for reading, suggest that they read to discover the differences of opinions about mash-up recordings.

Comprehension
MAKING CONNECTIONS

To help students make connections with the selection, discuss music rights. Ask these questions:

- Do you think people should be able to share music over the Internet? Why or why not?

- Do you think it is OK to share mash-ups but not a performer's original songs? Why or why not?

- Do you think people still buy enough music to support the artists? Explain.

But it was music made up of stolen pieces. Kerr felt that it was okay. After all, his crime was in pursuit of art. Plus, he only let a small group of people hear his songs. What difference could a few clubs make?

But that was about to change. Kerr's next song would be too good to contain. People all over the world would want to hear it. At the same time, others would start calling him a thief.

The Song That Changed Everything

It was so simple. First, Kerr found the right pop star. It was Christina Aguilera. He took her vocals from her song "Genie in a Bottle." Her voice sounded clear and clean. The song was slick. It was as polished as pop music gets.

Then he found the perfect band. The group was the Strokes. They had a messy punk-rock sound. Their guitar playing was fast and furious. They were Aguilera's true opposite.

But somehow, together, they worked. Aguilera sounded great over the Strokes' song "Hard to Explain." Kerr made a CD of song. He titled it "A Stroke of Genius." Then he took it to a radio DJ.

It was a hit. Music critics raved about his song. They called it one of the best of th year. They said popular music had become boring. But they said mash-ups offered surprise.

Kerr became famous. Aguilera hired him to remix some of her songs. Paul McCartne liked Kerr's work, too. That was a huge compliment. McCartney had been a membe of the Beatles, one of the most popular band in history.

Kerr started to DJ at McCartney's concerts, where he made live mash-ups. Then he made a whole album of mash-ups McCartney's songs.

Word spread. Mash-ups went global. From Mexico to Belgium new mash-up artists sprouted up everywhere. They mashed lot of songs. They put the songs on the Internet f all to hear. Then things got out of hand.

During Reading

Comprehension
MONITOR UNDERSTANDING

Use these questions to model how to monitor understanding by asking questions. Then have students ask their own questions and try to resolve any confusion.

- What is going on here?
- How does this work?
- What fix-up strategy can I use to resolve my confusion?

Teacher Think Aloud
On page 3, the author says that Roy Kerr could paste a singer's voice over music from another song. This confused me. If one song is pasted over another, wouldn't there just be noise? I decided to reread that part. Then I understood. "Music" meant the instrumental part of a song. The singer would now have different background music.

Comprehension
MAKING CONNECTIONS

Use these questions to model how to make connections with the text. Then have students tell about connections they have made.

- What does this selection remind me of?

- How does my experience help me understand this selection?

(See Differentiated Instruction.)

The Record Companies Step In

The *Grey Album* is what really made the music industry mad. A mash-up artist from California made it. He took the music from the Beatles' *White Album.* Then he added vocals from rapper Jay-Z's *Black Album.* What did he call it? The *Grey Album.* Did he have permission? No.

He only gave the CD to friends. But they put it on the Internet. Suddenly, thousands of people were downloading the CD. The record companies told them to stop. They felt robbed. They went to the courts. They complained to the press. It didn't work.

The more the record companies said no, the more mash-up fans said yes. About one hundred thousand people downloaded the album. Some did so as a protest. They felt as though they were fighting for freedom of expression.

Hands Off!

To others, mash-ups were nothing more than stolen goods. They had a point.

Imagine that you are an architect. You studied long and hard to become one. You build yourself a beautiful house. The house is amazing. It's very original. You become famous for it. But then something odd happens.

Strangers show up. They paint the house pink. They remove the door. They build a moat of water around your home! Then they call it their own. They invite people to tour the house. They let people admire "their" work.

That's how some musicians feel about mash-ups. They spent years studying music. They played countless, lousy shows for little pay. It was hard work. But it was their dream. Then it finally happened. They got a record deal. At last, they had a hit song.

So why should others get to take that song? Why should others use it however they please? You wouldn't repaint a stranger's house. So why should a stranger get to change your song? ◆

Teacher Think Aloud

I know that one way music companies have tried to control the copying of music is by DRM, or Digital Rights Management. DRM technology prevents people from sharing the music they buy. Yet buyers feel that they own the music and don't like technology that limits their use of it. This has led to a big debate on the Internet.

Fix-Up Strategies

Offer these strategies to help students read independently.

If you don't understand what you're reading:

- Reread the difficult section to look for clues to help you comprehend.
- Read ahead to find clues to help you comprehend.
- Retell, or say in your own words, what you've read.
- Visualize, or form mental pictures of, what you've read.

If you don't understand a word:

- Reread the sentence. Look for ideas and words that provide meaning clues.
- Find clues by reading a few sentences before and after the confusing word.
- Look for the base or root word and think about its meaning.
- Think about the topic or plot at this point to see if either offers meaning clues.

Answers for **Student Journal page 94** are 1. *breath*; 2. *breathe*; 3. *dessert*; 4. *desert*; 5. *brake*; 6. *break*; 7. *picture*; 8. *pitcher*; 9. *piece*; 10. *peace*.

WHAT'S AT STAKE?

Two things are at stake in the mash-up debate: money and art.

MONEY

The record companies are worried. Over the past decade, record sales have fallen. In 2004 alone, CD sales dropped 7 percent. That means music lovers bought 48 million fewer albums.

Why? Because computers are changing the music world. In 2004, 150 percent more songs were downloaded from the Internet. That means people bought 140 million more songs from Web sites.

A music star makes about fourteen cents per song sold. If they have a hit, they might sell one million singles. That means they would make $140,000. But they make more selling the whole album. They make about ten times more. That's over a million dollars.

The problem is this: Internet users don't tend to buy whole albums. They also sometimes find ways to take music for free. Most record companies thus fear the shift to Internet sales.

And mash-ups may make sales drop even more. If a mash-up is free, why buy the original?

ART

Mash-up fans say art should come before money. To them, published songs are raw materials. Everyone should be free to use them. That way, if a mash-up genius like Kerr comes along, others get to enjoy what he can create.

They say it's not as if they stole a line from a poem. It's as if they took the best line from that poem and gave it new meaning. And new meaning is what art is all about.

Besides, they argue mash-ups are the future. This is the age of computers. Everyone can personalize what they like. You can alter your photographs. You can load your mp3 player with only songs you like. It's as if you were your own DJ.

So if you think Beyoncé sounds better with the Rolling Stones, why shouldn't you make it happen? And why shouldn't you share it?

Some musicians agree that art is what matters. But they say it's *their* art that is important. They ask mash-up artists to show some respect. They ask them to leave their songs alone.

After Reading
Use one or more activities.

Check Purpose
Have students determine whether their purpose was met. Did students discover the differences of opinions about mash-up recordings?

Discussion Questions
Continue the group discussion with the following questions.
1. What happened as a result of Roy Kerr making the CD "A Stroke of Genius"? (Cause-Effect)
2. Why are the creations of Roy Kerr called mash-ups? (Inferential Thinking)
3. Would you like to be a mash-up artist? Why or why not? (Making Connections)

Revisit: Anticipation Guide
Have students revisit the anticipation guide to see if their responses are correct.

Revisit: Predictions Chart
Have students return to the predictions chart on *Student Journal* page 91 to complete the third column. How are the words actually used? Have partners briefly discuss their observations.

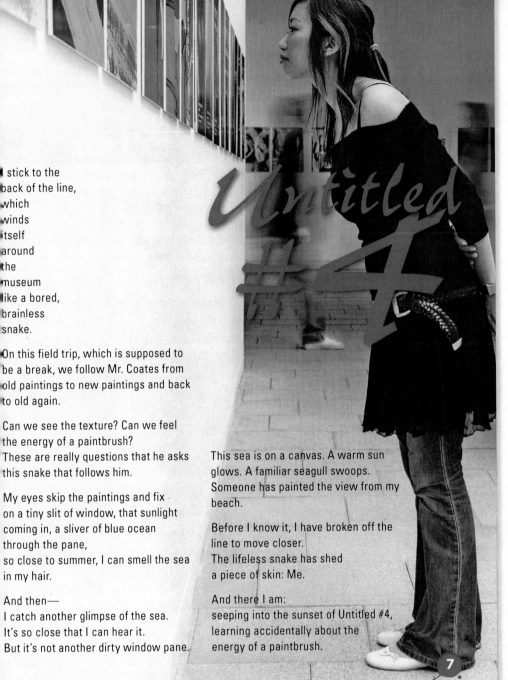

stick to the back of the line, which winds itself around the museum like a bored, brainless snake.

On this field trip, which is supposed to be a break, we follow Mr. Coates from old paintings to new paintings and back to old again.

Can we see the texture? Can we feel the energy of a paintbrush? These are really questions that he asks this snake that follows him.

My eyes skip the paintings and fix on a tiny slit of window, that sunlight coming in, a sliver of blue ocean through the pane, so close to summer, I can smell the sea in my hair.

And then— I catch another glimpse of the sea. It's so close that I can hear it. But it's not another dirty window pane.

This sea is on a canvas. A warm sun glows. A familiar seagull swoops. Someone has painted the view from my beach.

Before I know it, I have broken off the line to move closer. The lifeless snake has shed a piece of skin: Me.

And there I am: seeping into the sunset of Untitled #4, learning accidentally about the energy of a paintbrush.

Answers for **Student Journal page 95** are 1. *most (o)*; 2. *notes (oCe)*; 3. *know (ow)*; 4. *goal (oa)*; 5. *rode (oCe)*; 6. *low (ow)*; 7. *goes (o)*; 8. *moaning (oa)*; 9. *crows, known (ow)*; 10. *woke (oCe)*.

Writing Opinion Paragraph

Remind students that mash-ups are a controversial topic. Write this question on the board or on chart paper: *Are mash-ups good or bad?* Ask students to use *Student Journal* page 92 to jot down notes concerning their opinions. Students may refer to the selection, especially the "Hands Off!" section and the "What's at Stake?" feature, if needed. Then have students use their notes to write an opinion paragraph on *Student Journal* page 93.

Vocabulary

Using the Right Word

Explain that certain pairs of words sound the same. Point out *compliment* on page 4: "*That was a huge compliment.*" Explain that *compliment* means "something said to give praise." Display *complement*. Explain that it means "that which completes." Say: *That hat complements his outfit.* Then have students complete *Student Journal* page 94.

Phonics/Word Study

Common Long *o* Patterns

Display *boat, phone,* and *bold.* Ask students if these words contain the short or long *o* sound. (long) Underline the spelling patterns (*boat, phone, bold*) and write the vowel pattern under each word. (*boat: oa; phone: oCe; bold: oCC*) Now, work with students to complete the in-depth long *o* patterns activity on TE page 156. For additional support, have students complete *Student Journal* page 95.

Phonics/Word Study

Common Long *o* Patterns

▶ Write the following words on the board or on chart paper: *boast, alone, cold,* and *ghost.* Ask students to say the words out loud. Then ask: *What do all of these words have in common?* If students don't say "the long *o* sound" right away, encourage them to think about the vowel sounds. Once students identify the long *o* sound as the common feature, have them segment the words.

boast	oast	oa
alone	one	o
cold	old	o
ghost	ost	o

▶ Then ask: *All of these long o words have the same vowel sound, but what's different about all of them?* (They all have a different spelling.) Point out that these three patterns of long *o* are the most common long *o* patterns in the English language.

▶ Ask pairs to brainstorm at least two more words for each category and then share their additions with the class. As pairs say each word, ask which category it goes in.

▶ Provide students with copies of the Common Long *o* Patterns Sort sheet. (See *Word Study Manual* page 53.) Have students begin sorting by the four headings shown. Be sure to model the correct placement for the first few words.

▶ When confronted with a word that has two or more syllables, students should identify the syllable with the long *o* vowel sound and concentrate only on that syllable.

▶ As a group, discuss the sort, students' observations, and why words such as *sewn, though,* and *no* ended up in the Oddball column. Each of these words represents other long *o* patterns that will be studied later. Briefly discussing these other patterns will help raise students' word awareness.

Common Long *o* Patterns Sort				
oa as in boast	**oCe as in alone**	**oCC as in cold and ghost**	**Oddball**
moat	stolen	own	over
load	whole	old	sewn
coat	stroke	told	okay
toast	phone	known	though
roast	stones	blown	vocal
coast	suppose	host	global
float	mope	most	so
loaf	poke	grown	no
	bone	thrown	

For more information on word sorts and spelling stages, see pages 5–31 in the *Word Study Manual.*

Focus on . . .

Use one or more activities in this section to focus on a particular area of need in your students.

Comprehension STRATEGY SUPPORT

To help those students who need more practice using the strategies covered in this lesson, work one-on-one or in small groups to apply the strategy prompts below. Apply the prompts to a *Reading Advantage* paperback, a classroom library book, or a new or familiar selection in the magazine. Always model your own thinking first.

Monitor Understanding

• Do I understand what I'm reading? If not, what part is confusing to me?

• What fix-up strategies can I use to solve the problem? (See During Reading for fix-up strategies.)

• Why did a character say (do, think, ask) that?

• What images do I visualize from the text? What parts can't I visualize?

• Why did the author include (or not include) those details?

Making Connections

• What does this story (article, passage) remind me of?

• What do I already know about this topic?

• Where have I heard about this topic before?

• What do I have in common with the characters, people, or situations in the text?

• What other books, stories, articles, movies, or TV shows does this text make me think about?

Writing Survey

Explain to students that a survey is a poll to determine people's opinions. Have small groups of students each create and conduct a survey regarding their classmates' feelings about mash-ups. Suggest that groups include in their surveys five questions related to mash-ups and use the following categories after each question: Strongly Agree, Agree, Disagree, Strongly Disagree. Have groups present the results of their surveys to the class.

1. I have heard mash-ups and enjoy them.			
☐ Strongly Agree	☐ Agree	☐ Disagree	☐ Strongly Disagree

2. If professional singers hired Kerr, then mash-ups must be OK.			
☐ Strongly Agree	☐ Agree	☐ Disagree	☐ Strongly Disagree

Fluency: Expression

After students have read the poem "Untitled #4" at least once silently, model reading the poem aloud with expression. Then have partners practice reading it aloud. Explain to students that to read this poem expressively, they must first think about the speaker's tone, which seems annoyed, bored, and trapped at first, but then absorbed. Ask them to tell if and when the speaker's tone changes.

As you listen to partners read, use these prompts to guide them.

▶ Since this is a free-verse poem, you don't need to pause at the end of each line. Instead, use punctuation marks as guides for when to pause and when to change your voice.

▶ Make sure to vary your voice inflection.

▶ Put yourself in the place of the student who's discovering the beauty of a painting for the first time.

When students read aloud, do they—

✓ reflect an understanding of the text?

✓ demonstrate appropriate timing, stress, and intonation?

✓ incorporate appropriate speed and phrasing?

English Language Learners

Support students as they make connections in the third discussion question on TE page 154.

1. Have partners ask and answer the question about whether they would like to be mash-up artists.

2. Volunteers can share their answers with the whole class.

3. Then have students connect their feelings about being a mash-up artist with what they learned in the selection.

Independent Activity Options

While you work with individuals or small groups, others can work independently on one or more of the following options.

▶ Foundations paperback books, see TE pages 195–200

▶ Foundations eZines

▶ Repeat word sorts for this lesson

▶ Student Journal pages for this lesson

Assessment

Strategy Assessment

To help you and your students assess their use of comprehension strategies, ask the following questions. Students can complete a written response or provide verbal answers in a one-on-one reading conference.

1. **Monitor Understanding** What question did you have as you were reading the article? What fix-up strategy did you use to resolve your confusion? (Answers will vary. You might ask students if the strategy they tried was successful. If it wasn't, suggest other strategies they could have used.)

2. **Making Connections** What do you like about the music that DJs create by mixing different songs? (Answers will vary. Most students will have heard DJs' mixes at parties or on the Internet. If students aren't familiar with mash-ups, you might play examples in class.)

For ongoing informal assessment, use the checklists on pages 61–64 of Foundations Assessment.

Word Study Assessment

Use these steps to help you and your students assess their understanding of common long o patterns.

1. Display the chart below, but include only the headings and the words in the first column.

2. Have students identify the long o vowel pattern in each word. The answers are shown.

Word	Pattern
broke	oCe
boast	oa
bowl	oCC
boat	oa
cold	oCC
moat	oa
hope	oCe
awoke	oCe
loan	oa

LESSON 20
But Is It Art?
Arts, pages 8–11

SUMMARY
In this **debate**, two students discuss what should be considered "art." Can art be almost anything, or is it something special?

COMPREHENSION STRATEGIES
Understanding Text Structure

WRITING
Persuasive Paragraph

VOCABULARY
Compound Words

PHONICS/WORD STUDY
Common Long *u* Patterns

Lesson Vocabulary

masterpiece	beholder
eccentric	uniquely
astronomy	conceptual art

MATERIALS
Arts, pp. 8–11
Student Journal, pp. 96–100
Word Study Manual, p. 54

Many artists today say anything can be art. Well, I disagree. Long ago, great artists trained for many, many years. They worked hard to develop their craft. They carefully chose what to create. They produced artwork so good that people still enjoy it today.

People still admire paintings like Leonardo da Vinci's *Mona Lisa*. They are still trying to figure out why she is smiling. Michelangelo's mural on the Sistine Chapel ceiling is another masterpiece. It took him four years to paint it. These are works of art. They are lasting objects of beauty.

Mona Lisa by Leonardo da Vinci

8

Before Reading
WHOLE CLASS Use one or more activities.

Make a Concept Web
Create a concept web on visual art and record students' responses. Revisit the web later.

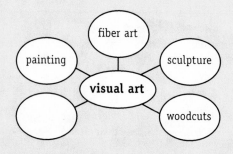

Vocabulary Preview
Display the vocabulary words and read them aloud. Have students share what they know about a particular word or words. Then have students begin a word map on *Student Journal* page 96. Revisit the word map later. (See Differentiated Instruction.)

Preview the Selection
Have students look through the selection. Discuss their observations.

Make Predictions/ Set Purpose
Students should use the information they gathered in previewing the selection to make predictions about what they will learn. If students have trouble generating a purpose for reading, suggest that they read to discover two students' differing ideas about what art is.

Today, it seems anything goes. Last year, I went to New York to visit my cousins. We went to Central Park to see *The Gates, Central Park, New York City, 1979–2005*. Perhaps you saw pictures of *The Gates*. It made magazines and newspapers all over the country.

The Gates were created by Christo and Jeanne-Claude. (They don't use last names.) They spent twenty-five years planning it. They hung 7,503 orange curtains over twenty-three miles of sidewalks.

Some people called it art, but I didn't. It looked like an endless series of shower curtains. I could see no message in it. It communicated nothing to me.

After all that effort, *The Gates* lasted just two weeks. Christo and Jeanne-Claude said they spent $21 million on *The Gates*. Then it was taken down. How can something be art if it only lasts two weeks?

Andy Warhol was an <u>eccentric</u> artist who made huge paintings of soup cans and soap boxes. People thought this was very cool because it was different. Nobody had done this before. But it doesn't seem that difficult to do. I mean, all he did was make an exact copy of what he saw. Perhaps the joke was on those who called it brilliant?

I think art should be inspiring. It should be beautiful. Too many modern artists are just seeking fame and attention.

Art is something special. You know it when you see it.

—Julio Martinez

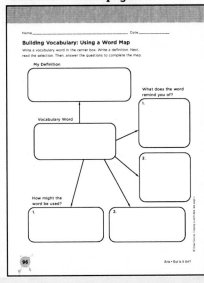

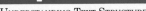
Campbell's Soup I: Beef by Andy Warhol

9

DIFFERENTIATED INSTRUCTION
Vocabulary Preview

Work with students to read, pronounce, and establish meaning for the word *masterpiece*.

What are the two words that make up *masterpiece*?	*master* *piece*
What kind of word is *masterpiece*?	a compound word
What does each word part mean?	*master*: a person of high accomplishment *piece*: an artistic composition or work
What does *masterpiece* mean?	the work of a highly skilled artist
When might you use this word?	Art critics consider the portrait a *masterpiece*.

Student Journal page 96

Name _____ Date _____

Building Vocabulary: Using a Word Map
Write a vocabulary word in the center box. Write a definition. Next, read the selection. Then, answer the questions to complete the map.

My Definition

Vocabulary Word

What does the word remind you of?
1.
2.

How might the word be used?
1.
2.

96   Arts • But Is It Art?

During Reading

Comprehension
UNDERSTANDING TEXT STRUCTURE

Use these questions to model how to identify the compare-contrast text structure of the selection. Then have students tell how the text structure helped them understand the text.

- What kind of text is this?

- How does the author organize ideas in the text?

- Which details support my thoughts about the text structure?

Teacher Think Aloud

This debate has a compare-contrast text structure. The opponents give contrasting views about an issue, and the points they make can be compared. For example, Julio doesn't think that Andy Warhol has created art, because Warhol just copied common objects. Kim thinks that Warhol's work is art because it shows familiar objects in new ways.

Fix-Up Strategies

Offer these strategies to help students read independently.

If you don't understand what you're reading:

- Reread the difficult section to look for clues to help you comprehend.

- Read ahead to find clues to help you comprehend.

- Retell, or say in your own words, what you've read.

- Visualize, or form mental pictures of, what you've read.

YES

Art is a lot more than pretty pictures. Art can be almost anything.

Art is one of the oldest human activities. The earliest people made cave paintings. We don't know why, but it was important to them to create pictures. Art exists in every culture, at every time. It serves many purposes and takes many forms.

In ancient Rome, art simply meant "skill." The word described all human learning. In the Middle Ages, grammar and arithmetic were arts. Medicine and astronomy were called arts, too. Around 1700, art came to mean painting, drawing, or sculpture. By 1800, art meant anything that came from the imagination.

Art affects how we think about things. It can change minds. Art can be personal or political. It can also be made for no reason outside itself.

People are entitled to their own opinions. They are entitled to their own tastes. I might not understand your art. Maybe I like it. Maybe I don't. That doesn't mean you are not an artist. And it doesn't mean that what you made isn't art.

Some people don't like modern art. They say it's not art. What they mean is they don't like it. But no one forced them to look at it. No one elected them to decide what art is. It's all in the eye of the beholder.

Art can be beautiful. Sometimes it makes us feel strong emotions. But it doesn't have to. Sometimes it isn't pretty. What matters is its effect on people.

Pablo Picasso did a painting about Guernica, a town in Spain. Maybe you've seen it. It is a response to the bombings during the Spanish Civil War in the late 1930s. This painting is not pleasant to look at. It is shocking. It shows the horrors of war. But it is still a masterpiece.

10

Student Journal pages 97–98

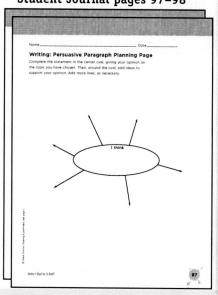

Name_____ Date_____

Writing: Persuasive Paragraph Planning Page

Complete the statement in the center oval, giving your opinion on the topic you have chosen. Then, around the oval, add ideas to support your opinion. Add more lines, as necessary.

I think

Arts • But Is It Art?   97

After Reading

WHOLE CLASS Use one or more activities.

Check Purpose

Have students determine whether their purpose was met. Did they discover two differing ideas about what art is?

Discussion Questions

Continue the group discussion with the following questions.

1. Who do you think would be more likely to enjoy going to a museum of modern art, Julio or Kim? Why? (Inferential Thinking)

2. What didn't Julio like about the art exhibit titled *The Gates*? (Details)

3. What kind of art museum would you most like to visit? (Making Connections)

Revisit: Web

Return to the web that was started before reading. Would students like to add anything?

Revisit: Word Map

Ask students to complete the word map they began on *Student Journal* page 96. Encourage students to share and compare their maps.

Julio talked about the *The Gates.* I thought it looked cool. The artists wanted it to last only two weeks. For those two weeks, it changed the way Central Park looked. It was like a dream: briefly here, then gone forever. Millions of people experienced it.

To many, this artwork was uniquely beautiful. It made the viewers see their world differently. Some people disliked it. But their dislike doesn't make my beliefs wrong.

Andy Warhol was inspired to paint giant soup cans and soap boxes. He wanted us to look at familiar things in new, unexpected ways. That idea was more important than beauty. This was "conceptual art." Its goal is to force us to think differently.

The Gates by Christo and Jeanne-Claude

Art can be made from anything. It can even be made from garbage. I read about a German artist named Kurt Schwitters. He expressed himself with garbage instead of paint. He said, "It is possible to cry out using bits of old rubbish, and that's what I did." He picked up interesting pieces of trash whenever he took a walk. Then he glued and nailed them together.

I think Schwitters's pictures are exquisite. You may think they are strange. That's okay. But he got you thinking.

The job of art is to challenge us to think for ourselves.

—Kim Youn ◆

...struction fuer edle Frauen (Construction for Noble Women) by ...t Schwitters

11

Student Journal page 99

Name _____ Date _____

Building Vocabulary: Compound Words

The words in the first column are closed compound words from the selection. Draw a line between the two words that make up each compound. In the second column, write a definition for the compound word. Then, in the third column, write a sentence that uses the word. You may refer to a dictionary, as necessary.

Compound Word	Definition	Sentence
master/piece	an outstanding work of art	My mom painted a mural on my bedroom wall that is a masterpiece.
artwork		
sidewalk		
newspaper		
something		
soapbox		

Arts • But Is It Art?   99

Possible answers for **Student Journal page 100** include *uCe: rude, cute, protrude; ew: stew, threw, grew; ue: blue, venue, due; oo: drool, pool, broom.*

Name _____ Date _____

Phonics/Word Study: Long *u* Vowel Patterns

Each column shows a different pattern for the long *u* vowel sound. Add words to complete each list.

uCe	ew	ue	oo
huge	few	argue	cool
produce	new	value	tools

Choose five words from the chart above. Write each word in a sentence about art.

1. _____
2. _____
3. _____
4. _____
5. _____

100   Arts • But Is It Art?

Persuasive Paragraph

Tell students that they will each write a persuasive paragraph to try to persuade others to agree with his or her view about a topic. Discuss and list possible topics. Topics might include issues such as always wearing seatbelts, motorcyclists wearing helmets, or cell phone use in movie theaters. Students should complete *Student Journal* page 97, before writing on *Student Journal* page 98.

Display the following words: *watercolor, oil paint,* and *know-how.* Explain that these words are compound words, or words formed by joining two whole words. Explain that compound words may be closed (*watercolor*), open (*oil paint*), or hyphenated (*know-how*). Ask students if they can think of more examples. Ask what words make up each compound and what the meaning of the compound word is. Now have students complete *Student Journal* page 99.

Common Long *u* Patterns

Display this sentence: *He crooned a few blues tunes.* Have students identify the words that contain the long *u* sound and its spelling pattern. (*crooned: oo; few: ew; blues: ue; tunes: uCe*) Have students suggest other words with these patterns. Now, work with students to complete the in-depth long *u* patterns activity on TE page 162. For additional support, have students complete *Student Journal* page 100.

Common Long *u* Patterns

▶ To introduce the most common long *u* patterns, write the following words on the board: *dew, true, rude,* and *brood.* Ask students to say the words out loud. Then ask: *What do all of these have in common?* If students don't say "the long *u* sound" right away, encourage them to think about the vowel sounds. Once students identify the long *u* sound as the common feature, have them segment the words.

dew	ew
true	ue
rude	ude	u
brood	ood	oo

▶ Then ask: *All of these long* u *words have the same vowel sound, but what's different about all of them?* (They all have a different spelling.) Point out that these four patterns of long *u* are the most common long *u* patterns in the English language.

▶ Ask pairs to brainstorm at least two more words for each category and then share their additions with the class. As pairs say each word, ask which category it goes in.

▶ Provide students with copies of the Common Long *u* Patterns Sort sheet. (See *Word Study Manual* page 54.) Have students begin sorting by the five headings shown. Be sure to model the correct placement for the first few words to show students what is expected of them.

▶ When confronted with a word that has two or more syllables, students should identify the syllable with the long *u* vowel sound and concentrate only on that syllable.

▶ As a group, discuss the sort, students' observations, and why words such as *fruit, soup, human, mural,* and *two* ended up in the Oddball column. Each of these words represents other long *u* patterns that will be studied later. Briefly discussing these other patterns will help raise students' word awareness.

Common Long *u* Patterns Sort				
ew as in **dew**	**ue** as in **true**	**uCe** as in **rude**	**oo** as in **brood**	**Oddball**
few	glue	use	cool	fruit
threw	hue	huge	droop	soup
new	blue	ruse	mood	human
drew	flue	delude	food	mural
grew	clue	tune	zoo	two
flew		attitude	croon	

For more information on word sorts and spelling stages, see pages 5–31 in the *Word Study Manual.*

Focus on . . .

Use one or more activities in this section to focus on a particular area of need in your students.

Comprehension   STRATEGY SUPPORT

To help those students who need more practice using the strategies covered in this lesson, work one-on-one or in small groups to apply the strategy prompts below. Apply the prompts to a *Reading Advantage* paperback, a classroom library book, or a new or familiar selection in the magazine. Always model your own thinking first.

Understanding Text Structure

- What kind of text is this? (book, story, article, guidebook, play, manual)
- How does the author organize the text? (cause-effect, problem-solution, chronological order, description, question-answer, comparison-contrast)
- What details support my thoughts about the text structure?
- What is the cause (effect, problem, solution, order, question, answer)?
- If fiction, who are the characters? What is the setting, plot, conflict, and resolution?

Writing Point/Counterpoint

Tell students that the debate is in a "point/counterpoint" format, which means that Julio first expresses his position, and then Kim expresses hers while also responding to Julio's arguments. She counters his points. For example, Julio says that *The Gates* looked like an endless series of shower curtains. Kim says that *The Gates* were beautiful, partly because the artwork made viewers see their world differently. Have students find other points that Julio makes, and discover how Kim counters them. Have partners record and display these findings in a two-column chart with the headings "Point" and "Counterpoint." Then discuss how well students think Kim did in countering Julio's points.

Fluency: Expression

After students have read the selection at least once, model reading a section of it aloud with expression. Then have students work in pairs to read aloud the "No" and "Yes" arguments expressively.

As you listen to partners read, use these prompts to guide them.

▶ Preview what you will read. Put yourself in the situation of Julio or Kim. Read with expression and conviction.

▶ Look for punctuation clues to help guide your expression.

▶ Think about how the pace of your reading will affect your audience. Alter your pace according to the context.

When students read aloud, do they—

✓ reflect an understanding of the text?

✓ demonstrate appropriate timing, stress, and intonation?

✓ incorporate appropriate speed and phrasing?

English Language Learners

To support students as they visualize, extend the fourth fix-up strategy on TE page 159.

1. Remind students that active readers visualize, or create pictures in their minds, as they read.

2. Discuss the section about making art from garbage in the last three paragraphs on page 11 of the selection. Ask students to use details from the text to draw something containing items found in a garbage can.

3. Have partners describe their drawings.

Independent Activity Options

While you work with individuals or small groups, others can work independently on one or more of the following options.

▶ Foundations paperback books, see TE pages 195–200

▶ Foundations eZines

▶ Repeat word sorts for this lesson

▶ Student Journal pages for this lesson

Assessment

Strategy Assessment

To help you and your students assess their use of comprehension strategies, ask the following questions. Students can complete a written response or provide verbal answers in a one-on-one reading conference.

- **Understanding Text Structure** After comparing and contrasting the points that Julio and Kim make, whose opinions do you most agree with? Why? (Answers will vary. Students should cite the arguments they found convincing.)

For ongoing informal assessment, use the checklists on pages 61–64 of *Foundations Assessment*.

Word Study Assessment

Use these steps to help you and your students assess their understanding of common long *u* patterns.

1. Read aloud the following words to the class, one at a time: *fool, true, amuse, stoop, altitude, crew, argue, loon, grew, brute,* and *value*.

2. Have students identify the long *u* vowel pattern in each word. The answers are shown.

Word	Pattern
fool	oo
true	ue
amuse	uCe
stoop	oo
altitude	uCe
crew	ew
argue	ue
loon	oo
grew	ew
brute	uCe
value	ue

All That Jazz
Arts, pages 12–16

SUMMARY
This **article** tells about the Stein brothers, whose early exposure to jazz music led them to a career as professional jazz musicians.

COMPREHENSION STRATEGIES
Determining Importance

WRITING
Summary

VOCABULARY
Multiple Meanings

PHONICS/WORD STUDY
Common Long Vowel Patterns Review

Lesson Vocabulary
octave	Creole
capacity	score
improvisation	

MATERIALS
Arts, pp. 12–16
Student Journal, pp. 101–105
Word Study Manual, p. 55

All That

Before Reading
 WHOLE CLASS Use one or more activities.

Make a K-W-L Chart
Begin a K-W-L chart on jazz music. Revisit the chart later.

What We **Know**	What We **Want** to Know	What We **Learned**
Piano is a jazz instrument.	How do you become a jazz musician?	
New Orleans has jazz music.	What are other jazz instruments?	

Vocabulary Preview
Display the vocabulary words and read them aloud. Have students share what they know about the words. Then have students begin the knowledge rating chart on *Student Journal* page 101. Use the vocabulary word *score* to model a response for the page. Revisit the chart later.

Preview the Selection
Have students look through the selection. Discuss their observations.

Make Predictions/ Set Purpose
Students should use the information they gathered in previewing the selection to make predictions about what they will learn. If students have trouble generating a purpose for reading, suggest that they read to discover how and why the Stein brothers became jazz musicians.

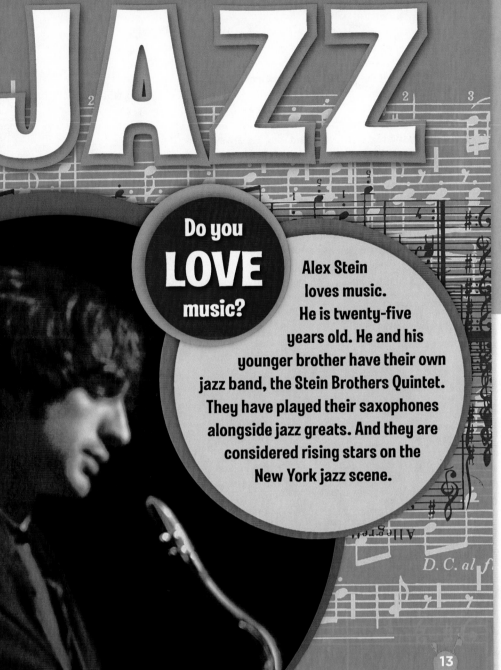

JAZZ

Do you LOVE music?

Alex Stein loves music. He is twenty-five years old. He and his younger brother have their own jazz band, the Stein Brothers Quintet. They have played their saxophones alongside jazz greats. And they are considered rising stars on the New York jazz scene.

13

DIFFERENTIATED INSTRUCTION
Comprehension
DETERMINING IMPORTANCE

To help students determine the importance of ideas, have them reread "Where Did Jazz Begin?" on page 16, and tell what they think are the most important ideas and why. (Important ideas: New Orleans is the home of jazz; jazz mixed three kinds of music together; jazz musicians improvised rather than read music. These ideas are important because they are the main ideas of the first three paragraphs.)

Student Journal page 101

Name _____ Date _____

Building Vocabulary: Knowledge Rating Chart
Show your knowledge of each word by adding information to the other boxes in the row.

Word	Define or Use in a Sentence	Where Have I Seen or Heard It?	How is It Used in the Selection?	Looks Like (Words or Sketch)
score				
octave				
capacity				
improvisation				
Creole				

Arts • All That Jazz

101

During Reading

Comprehension
DETERMINING IMPORTANCE

Use these questions to model how to determine the most important ideas in "The Right Instrument." Then have students determine the importance of ideas in the next section.

- What are the most important ideas?
- How can I support my beliefs?
- What does the author want me to understand?

(See Differentiated Instruction.)

Teacher Think Aloud

To me, this section has one most important idea—that young musicians should try another instrument if they don't like the one they are playing. The details tell how both Alex and his brother switched instruments and were much happier. I think that the author is encouraging young players not to give up.

Fix-Up Strategies

Offer these strategies to help students read independently.

If you don't understand what you're reading:

- Reread the difficult section to look for clues to help you comprehend.
- Read ahead to find clues to help you comprehend.
- Retell, or say in your own words, what you've read.
- Visualize, or form mental pictures of, what you've read.

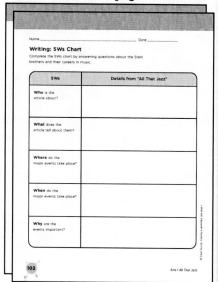

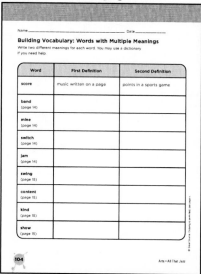

Play It Again, Dad!

Alex Stein's dad had a big record collection. When Alex thinks back to his childhood, he remembers those records. His dad always played them. He played Count Basie, Duke Ellington, and Charlie Parker. Who were they? They were some of the greatest jazz musicians of all time.

It's no surprise that Alex ended up playing jazz. His younger brother Asher did, too. "I play tenor saxophone," said Alex. "Asher plays alto saxophone. Mine is a half octave lower than his."

Why the sax? "It's cool," said Alex. He always loved the sax. Now people love to hear him play one. He plays his sax in clubs in New Jersey and New York. But he was almost talked out of playing it.

The Right Instrument

Alex's school band needed clarinet players. So he was pressured into taking up the clarinet. But he hated it. "I played it for two years. And I almost quit. Then I took up the sax, and I loved it."

His advice to young musicians is simple. He said, "Your first instrument may not be the right one for you, but it will get you started. You can always switch to another instrument later on." That's how it worked for Asher, too.

Asher started piano lessons when he was five. But he really wanted to play the saxophone. So he switched, and both brothers began studying together.

Jammin'

"We started with jazz immediately," said Alex. They took private sax lessons. Later, they went to the Jazz Institute of New Jersey. There, they studied with other students.

They got an early start as performers. They started playing at clubs when Asher was in the fifth grade. Alex was a teenager. But they were joining jam sessions with adults.

"We were playing with professionals," said Alex. "The first time I played, I was nervous. But after that, it was just what we did."

Alex believes a few simple things helped them succeed so young. "We showed an ability, a capacity to play music. And we had a positive attitude. We were willing to learn," he said.

14

After Reading

Use one or more activities.

Check Purpose

Have students determine whether their purpose was met. Did students discover how and why the Stein brothers became jazz musicians?

Discussion Questions

Ask the following questions.

1. Which part of the Stein brothers' experiences did you find the most interesting? Why? (Making Connections)

2. Why do you think the Steins make good role models? How might you apply what you read about them to your own life? (Making Connections)

3. From what you know about Alex and Asher, where do you think they'll be in twenty years? (Predict)

Revisit: K-W-L Chart

Have students return to the K-W-L chart. Were all students' questions about jazz answered? What new information can they add to the chart?

Revisit: Knowledge Rating Chart

Have students complete the knowledge rating chart on *Student Journal* page 101. Are there any adjustments or changes they would like to make?

A Player's Voice

The learning started with reading music. Alex was about ten when he started, and Asher was five. They learned the basics first. Then they learned how to improvise. That meant they learned to make up their own music while they played.

All great jazz musicians can improvise. Rock 'n' roll needs great guitar solos. Hip-hop needs emcees that can rap on the spot. Jazz needs great improvisation on every instrument.

What makes a piece of music jazz? "It has to swing," said Alex. "And it has to involve improvisation. Everybody gets their turn to speak on stage."

For a musician, playing is speaking. "Everyone's involved," said Alex. "If a horn player is soloing, the drummer and bass player are interacting, too."

Thelonious Monk III is a famous jazz musician. His father was a legendary jazz artist. Mr. Monk says jazz is about "storytelling." But what does that mean exactly? For one thing, it's more than just playing notes.

"You're going from one place to another," Alex explained. "It's like going on a journey. You're communicating emotional content through your soloing. And you're bringing the audience with you as you play."

Playing for Life

It's one thing to enjoy playing music. It's another to make it your job. It takes a lot of practice and learning. And you take a risk. Work can be hard to find.

"It's hard to make a living," Alex admitted. But a professional can do a lot of things to pay the bills. Alex plays gigs close to home. He also tours. He records CDs. And he teaches. "All of these things together are part of the professional life," he said.

Jazz is popular around the world. Jazz fans live in Japan. They live in Italy. They live in Russia. And that's just a few examples! "We would love to travel the world with our band," said Alex.

The Stein Brothers Quintet has already recorded its first CD. Alex and Asher both wrote songs for it. So did their pianist Mferghu.

"What's most important is to love what you are playing," said Alex. That's the advice he has for young musicians.

"You can play any kind of music," he continued. "But love the music that you are playing. That's going to come across to the audience. As long as you love what you're doing, that'll show." ◆

15

DIFFERENTIATED INSTRUCTION
Vocabulary
Multiple Meanings

Review the concept of words with multiple meanings by following these steps:

1. Tell students that many English words have more than one meaning, or multiple meanings.

2. Give examples by using *right* and *fly* in sentences. Right: *That is the* right *answer. The driver made a* right *turn.* Fly: *The* fly *was hovering over the food. Some airplanes can* fly *with only one engine.*

3. Have students think of other words they are familiar with that have more than one meaning.

Writing Summary

Tell students that they are going to write a summary of the main article. Remind them that a summary includes only the main points of a text. To begin, have students organize their thoughts by completing the 5Ws chart on *Student Journal* page 102. Then have students use the information from their charts to write their summaries on *Student Journal* page 103.

Vocabulary Multiple Meanings

Read aloud the following sentence from the selection: *"Then the musicians played exactly what was in the score."* Explain that *score* is a word with multiple meanings. Ask students what the word means in the context of the sentence. Have them discuss other meanings for the word. Then have students complete the multiple-meanings chart on *Student Journal* page 104. (See Differentiated Instruction.)

Phonics/Word Study

Common Long Vowel Patterns

On the board, write *play, steep, dive, boast,* and *spruce.* Have volunteers identify the long vowel sound in each word, and underline the spelling pattern that makes that sound. (*a: play; e: steep; i: dive; o: boast; u: spruce*) Now, work with students to complete the in-depth long vowel patterns review activity on TE page 169. For additional support, have students complete *Student Journal* page 105.

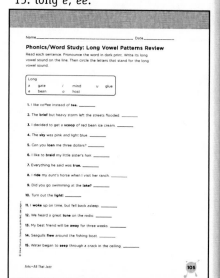

Where Did Jazz Begin?

New Orleans, Louisiana, is considered the home of jazz.
Around 1895, many African American and Creole musicians
lived in New Orleans. They played marching band music
and the blues. They also played lively ragtime music.

Eventually, they started playing a mix of all three.
This new music was jazz. People flocked to the clubs
to hear it. They could barely keep still in their seats. Jazz
got everyone's feet tapping. It made everyone want to
dance. Jazz was the rock 'n' roll of its day.

Jazz broke the rules for how to write music. Until jazz,
a composer wrote out notes on paper. Then the musicians
played exactly what was in the score. In jazz, the song is just
a starting point. The musicians then improvise around the
melody. Usually, everyone in the band takes a turn improvising. Jazz set the musicians free.

Some of the early jazz artists could not read music. Yet their playing thrilled audiences.
The songs they started with were usually popular tunes. They would play around with these
simple songs. They would improvise. By the end of the performance, they would create a
whole new song.

Their music was fresh. It was new. There was a sense of adventure about it. What
would they play next? Audiences loved the suspense.

Jazz Evolution

As time passed, more people began to play jazz. The
musicians began to make it more complex. More styles
of jazz were invented. There was hot jazz, and boogie-
woogie.

Stars emerged like the trumpet player Louis
Armstrong. In the 1920s, he helped invent "Chicago-
style" jazz. Swing emerged in the 1930s and 1940s. Duke
Ellington, Count Basie, and others led big bands. They
played swing-style jazz music.

"Birdland"

Charlie Parker changed the jazz world in the 1940s. This sax player's
nickname was "Bird." He became the leader of a new style called
bebop. This jazz style was radical. Bebop was fast. It was complex.
It had an almost nervous sound.

Parker could play anything on his sax. He could play in any
tempo. He could play in any key. He influenced many of today's
musicians. Some call him one of the greatest geniuses music has
ever seen.

16

Common Long Vowel Patterns Review

The following sort is a review of common long vowel patterns that may help students build automaticity. For the review, use the same word cards that you used with the earlier sorts. New headings for this sort are provided. (See *Word Study Manual* page 55.)

▶ Students should work with a partner. Begin by asking the sorters to sort first by sound (long *a*, long *e*, long *i*, long *o*, long *u*). Once they have sorted the word cards by sound, partners should read over the cards to see if the cards are sorted correctly. If errors appear, the sorter should place the cards where they belong. Partners should then switch roles.

▶ Now, sorters should sort the word cards by their visual spelling patterns. Headings are provided for each vowel. Once sorters have sorted the word cards, partners should read over the cards to see if the cards are sorted correctly. If errors appear, the sorter should place the cards where they belong. Partners should then switch roles.

Common Long Vowel Patterns Review Sort				
Long *a* Sound	Long *e* Sound	Long *i* Sound	Long *o* Sound	Long *u* Sound

Long *a*			
aCe	*ai*	*ay*	Oddball
race	paint	stray	eight

Long *e*			
ee	*ie*	*ea*	Oddball
creep	chief	beak	we

Long *i*				
igh	*iCe*	*ind*	*y*	Oddball
night	pride	blind	try	height

Long *o*			
oa	*oCe*	*oCC*	Oddball
toast	choke	gold	sew

Long *u*				
ew	*ue*	*uCe*	*oo*	Oddball
blew	true	truce	scoop	soup

For more information on word sorts and spelling stages, see pages 5–31 in the *Word Study Manual*.

Focus on . . .

Use one or more activities in this section to focus on a particular area of need in your students.

Comprehension | STRATEGY SUPPORT

To help those students who need more practice using the strategies covered in this lesson, work one-on-one or in small groups to apply the strategy prompts below. Apply the prompts to a *Reading Advantage* paperback, a classroom library book, or a new or familiar selection in the magazine. Always model your own thinking first.

Determining Importance

- What is the most important idea in the paragraph? How can I prove it?
- Which details are unimportant? Why?
- What does the author want me to understand?
- Why is this information important (or not important) to me?

Writing Timeline

On the board or on chart paper, draw a simple timeline like the one shown below. Point out that timelines organize and show events in the order in which they occurred. Explain that timelines can include specific dates, months, years, or longer spans of time such as decades. Have students reread the sections on page 16 and use a timeline to organize the events described. Tell students to include both dates and text in their timelines.

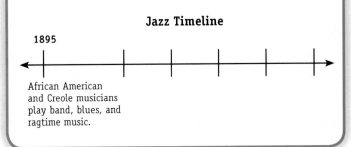

Jazz Timeline

1895

African American and Creole musicians play band, blues, and ragtime music.

Focus on . . .

Use one or more activities in this section to focus on a particular area of need in your students.

Fluency: Pacing

After students have read the article at least once, have them read sections aloud with a focus on pacing. First, model reading aloud to demonstrate a reading rate with changes in inflection and stress that sound natural. Then have students in small groups read paragraphs from the selection.

Before students begin, explain these fundamentals of good pacing.

▶ Indicate an understanding and recognition of key phrases by showing changes in tone and inflection.

▶ Incorporate punctuation, such as commas, periods, question marks, and quotation marks, by changing reading speed and inflection.

▶ Adjust pacing to heighten or stress dramatic content.

When students read aloud, do they—

✓ demonstrate a smooth pace, not too fast or too slow?

✓ incorporate well-timed pauses between words and phrases?

✓ reflect an awareness and understanding of punctuation?

English Language Learners

To support students as they preview the selection on TE page 164, do a word sort.

1. Write the word *music* on the board. Have students write down words related to the word *music*.

2. Have students sort their words into categories. Categories might include instruments or types of music.

3. Have partners explain their sorts.

Independent Activity Options

While you work with individuals or small groups, others can work independently on one or more of the following options.

▶ Foundations paperback books, see TE pages 195–200

▶ Foundations *eZines*

▶ Repeat word sorts for this lesson

▶ *Student Journal* pages for this lesson

Assessment

Strategy Assessment

To help you and your students assess their use of comprehension strategies, ask the following questions. Students can complete a written response or provide verbal answers in a one-on-one reading conference.

- **Determining Importance** After reading this article, what would you say are three important things that may inspire a person to become a professional musician? (Answers will vary. Students may say that one thing is having talent; another, playing an instrument you enjoy; and third, playing the kind of music you love.)

See *Foundations Assessment* pages 46–49 for formal assessment to go with *Arts*.

Word Study Assessment

Use these steps to help you and your students assess their understanding of common long vowel patterns.

1. Read aloud the following words to the class, one at a time: *peep, loop, faint, fight, coast, mold, fray, leak, few,* and *kind*.

2. Have students tell whether the vowel sound in each word is long *a*, long *e*, long *i*, long *o*, or long *u*. Then have them identify the vowel pattern. The answers are shown.

Word	Long Vowel	Pattern
peep	*e*	*ee*
loop	*u*	*oo*
faint	*a*	*ai*
fight	*i*	*igh*
coast	*o*	*oa*
mold	*o*	*oCC*
fray	*a*	*ay*
leak	*e*	*ea*
few	*u*	*ew*
kind	*i*	*ind*

Great Source
Reading Advantage
Foundations Assessment

SUMMARY
In this **question-answer** selection, the Science Wizard answers questions about art and science.

COMPREHENSION STRATEGIES
Making Connections
Determining Importance

WRITING
Advertisement

VOCABULARY
Synonyms and Antonyms

PHONICS/WORD STUDY
Plurals *-s, -es*

Lesson Vocabulary
deteriorate	bowers
varnish	sanctuaries

MATERIALS
Arts, pp. 17–21
Student Journal, pp. 106–110
Word Study Manual, p. 56

Ask the Science Wizard — *Why would a scientist work at a museum? Can animals really create art? Why does your heart race when you're nervous?*

17

Before Reading Use one or more activities.

Make a Chart
Ask students if they've experienced stage fright. Together, make a chart like the one shown. Return to the chart after students read.

When	Symptoms	Ways to Prevent It
performing in a recital	feeling nervous	be well prepared
speaking in front of a group	shaky hands and legs	try to relax

Vocabulary Preview
Display the vocabulary words and read them aloud. Before students read the article, assess their prior knowledge by having them begin the predictions chart on *Student Journal* page 106. Revisit the chart later. (See Differentiated Instruction.)

Preview the Selection
Have students look through the selection. Discuss their observations.

Make Predictions/ Set Purpose
Students should use the information they gathered in previewing the selection to make predictions about what they will learn. If students have trouble generating a purpose for reading, suggest that they read to discover connections between art and science.

Vocabulary Preview

Work with students to read, pronounce, and establish meaning for the word *bowers*.

What other words have the same vowel pattern as the first syllable in <u>bowers</u>?	cow how plow
What other spelling pattern has the same vowel sound?	ou
What are some words that have this spelling pattern?	loud couch shout
What does *bowers* mean?	shady places in the woods or in gardens
When might you use this word?	They sat in the cool *bowers* within the garden.

Student Journal page 106

Name _____ Date _____

Building Vocabulary: Predictions

How do you predict these words will be used in "Ask the Science Wizard"? Write your answers in the second column. Next, read the article. Then, clarify your answers in the third column.

Word	My prediction for how the word will be used	How the word is actually used
deteriorate		
varnish		
sanctuaries		
bower		

106   Arts • Ask the Science Wizard

Dear Science Wizard,
A newspaper article I read talked about a scientist who works at an art museum. Why would an art museum hire scientists?
—Curious Curator

Dear Curious,

It seems surprising that scientists work at art museums. But scientists hold some very important jobs in the world of art.

One job is to preserve art. Art is made out of many different materials. Each material can <u>deteriorate</u>. Paper gets brown and cracks, paint fades, and the canvases that pictures are painted on can mold. Art must be stored well. Otherwise it breaks down quickly. Heat and damp air are especially harmful. Scientists think up ways to store art carefully.

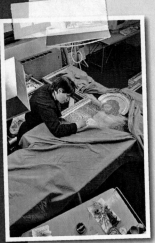
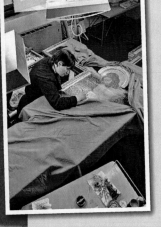

Another job is to restore art. Scientists brighten faded paint. They clean off mold. They peel off yellowed <u>varnish</u>. They do it without harming the art in any other way.

They also check art to be sure it's not fake. They can find out when a piece of art was made. One way is to check the paint. Some kinds of paint have new ingredients. So do some kinds of paper. If new ingredients are found, then the painting cannot be old.

Scientists can also find hidden paintings. Sometimes painters reuse canvases. Scientists can x-ray pictures. X-rays show if there is a painting beneath the painting we see.

These are all interesting jobs. They are also important. If no one did them, many great artworks would never be seen.

18

During Reading

Comprehension

MAKING CONNECTIONS

Use these questions to model how to make connections with the text. Then have students share their connections.

- What does this selection remind me of?
- What do I already know about this topic?
- How does my experience help me understand this selection?

(See Differentiated Instruction.)

Teacher Think Aloud

On page 19, the question is about whether animals make art. One morning, I saw a very complex spider web with dew sparkling on it. It was really beautiful. But, to me, part of making art is thinking creatively. The animals are only doing what comes instinctively. They aren't thinking creatively.

Comprehension

DETERMINING IMPORTANCE

Use these questions to model how to determine the most important ideas in the answer on page 18. Then have students determine the importance of ideas in the answer on page 20.

- What are the most important ideas in this section?
- How can I support my beliefs?

Dear Zoey,

What do you mean by art? Is a spider web art? Is a beaver dam art?

Here's one way to think of art. Art is something that one being creates to get a response from others. If that's what you mean, then yes. Animals do create art.

One example is the bower bird. It lives in Australia and New Guinea. Male bower birds build nests called bowers. They build them to attract females. But these are not your average nests!

Bowers are built out of twigs, leaves, and plants. Some are like tunnels. Some are like platforms. Some are like towers. All, however, are decorated. Bowers stick stones, berries, feathers, and flowers onto their nests.

Some even use trash. They add bottle or pen caps. They use bits of clothing. Birds with duller feathers do the most decorating. Fancier nests draw more females. Some birds spend all day fixing up their bowers.

A trunk full of pictures?

Animals in zoos can get bored. Keepers give them things to do. In the wild, some elephants draw with sticks. They hold the sticks in their trunks. Some keepers give elephants sticks to draw with. Some give them paintbrushes, paint, and canvas.

The elephants learn to paint. Many of them seem to enjoy it. Some paint quickly. Some study the canvas for a long time first.

Elephants can even go to art school. Two artists in Thailand opened several art schools for elephants. The elephants take classes. They learn to hold brushes. They learn basic strokes.

After that, the elephants decide what to paint. They choose the colors. They direct the brush. Other elephants benefit from their work. The paintings are sold. The money goes to support elephant sanctuaries, where elephants live in a protected setting.

19

Comprehension
MAKING CONNECTIONS

To help students make connections with the text, ask these questions about the sidebar on page 19.

- Were you surprised to discover that elephants paint? Why or why not?

- Would you like to own a painting done by an elephant? Why or why not?

- Do you think the elephants are creating art? Explain.

Teacher Think Aloud

This answer tells about what scientists do in art museums. I think the most important ideas are stated at the beginning of each paragraph. Scientists preserve art, restore art, check to be sure art isn't fake, and sometimes look for hidden paintings. The rest of the text gives details to further explain these ideas.

Fix-Up Strategies

Offer these strategies to help students read independently.

If you don't understand what you're reading:

- Reread the difficult section to look for clues to help you comprehend.

- Read ahead to find clues to help you comprehend.

- Retell, or say in your own words, what you've read.

- Visualize, or form mental pictures of, what you've read.

If you don't understand a word:

- Reread the sentence. Look for ideas and words that provide meaning clues.

- Find clues by reading a few sentences before and after the confusing word.

- Look for the base or root word and think about its meaning.

- Think about the topic or plot at this point to see if either offers meaning clues.

Writing Advertisement

Read aloud and discuss this sample ad before students begin writing their own.

Assistant Store Manager. Local computer software store seeks individual to help store manager with day-to-day operations. Responsibilities: customer service, ordering, and shelving. Requirements: college degree; two years retail experience; familiarity with popular computer software, including games; and excellent organizational and communication skills.

Student Journal pages 107–108

Name_____ Date_____

Writing: Help-Wanted Ad Planning Page
Write notes for a help-wanted ad that seeks a scientist to work at a museum. Create the real ad on the next page.

Possible duties: _____

Past experience needed: _____

Skills needed: _____

Education needed: _____

Arts • Ask the Science Wizard   107

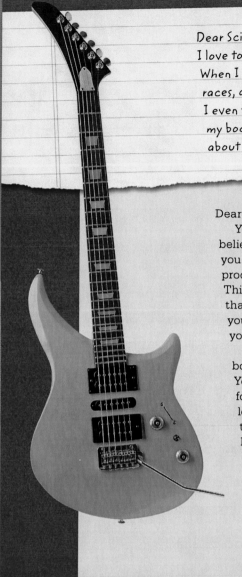

Dear Science Wizard,
I love to play the guitar, but I hate to perform. When I play in public, my legs shake, my heart races, and my hands get ice cold. Sometimes I even feel sick to my stomach. Why does my body do this? Is there anything I can do about it?

—Shaking in My Shoes

Dear Shaking,
You have a case of stage fright. And believe it or not, your body is trying to help you. When you get nervous, your body produces a chemical called adrenaline. This chemical causes your body to think that it might be under attack. Of course, you're only about to play the guitar. But your body doesn't know that.

All of your symptoms come from your body's preparation for "fight or flight." Your muscles contract to prepare you for running. That's what makes your legs shake. Your blood pressure rises to send more oxygen throughout your body. That's what makes your heart race. The tiny blood vessels near your fingers close up to send blood to more important places. That's what makes your hands cold. And your digestive system shuts down. Food is not a priority when you're under attack. So you feel sick. And you still have to play the guitar!

20

After Reading

  Use one or more activities.

Check Purpose

Have students determine whether their purpose was met. Did students discover connections between art and science?

Discussion Questions

Continue the group discussion with the following questions.

1. In what way are the three letters sent to the Science Wizard related? (Compare-Contrast)

2. Why do male bower birds build such fancy nests? (Cause-Effect)

3. When have you suffered from stage fright? (Making Connections)

Revisit: Chart

Have students revisit the stage fright chart. Would they like to add any new information?

Revisit: Predictions Chart

Have students return to the predictions chart on *Student Journal* page 106 to complete the third column. How are the words actually used?

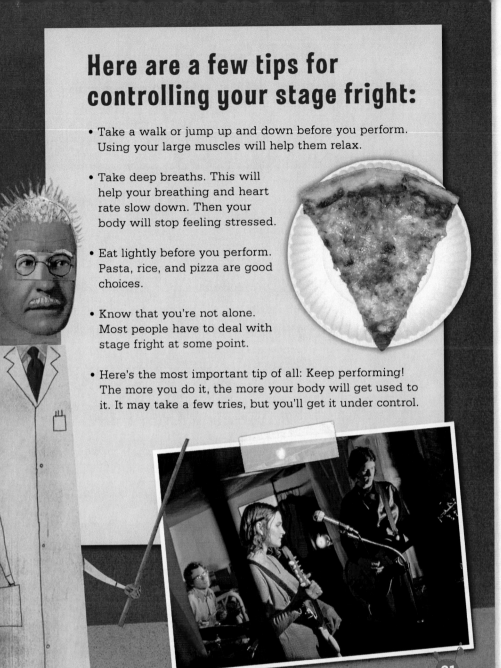

Here are a few tips for controlling your stage fright:

- Take a walk or jump up and down before you perform. Using your large muscles will help them relax.

- Take deep breaths. This will help your breathing and heart rate slow down. Then your body will stop feeling stressed.

- Eat lightly before you perform. Pasta, rice, and pizza are good choices.

- Know that you're not alone. Most people have to deal with stage fright at some point.

- Here's the most important tip of all: Keep performing! The more you do it, the more your body will get used to it. It may take a few tries, but you'll get it under control.

21

Possible answers for **Student Journal page 109** include *benefit*: *help, harm*; *store*: *save, discard.*

Name_____ Date_____

Building Vocabulary: Synonyms and Antonyms

For each selection word, write a word that is a synonym (similar in meaning) and a word that is an antonym (opposite in meaning). Use a thesaurus to help you, if you wish. Then answer the questions in a complete sentence.

Selection Word	Synonym	Antonym
deteriorate	worsen	improve
benefit		
store (verb)		

1. How do you think you might benefit from exercising every day? _____

2. What's a benefit of being a student? _____

3. Where might a family store its winter clothes? _____

4. What kinds of things do you store in your school locker? _____

Arts • Ask the Science Wizard   109

Answers for **Student Journal page 110** are 1. *lunches*; 2. *floors*; 3. *taxes*; 4. *bosses*; 5. *maps*; 6. *drills*; 7. *dishes*; 8. *benches*; 9. *bats*; 10. *inches*; 11. *books*; 12. *rashes.*

Name_____ Date_____

Phonics/Word Study: Plurals with -s and -es

Every noun, or naming word, has a plural form. Look at each noun. Think about how you would pronounce the plural. If you hear one syllable in the plural, just add -s to the noun. If you hear two syllables in the plural, you must add -es to the noun.

Examples:
hat   hats (one syllable)
box   boxes (two syllables)

Add -s or -es to form the plural.

1. lunch _____
2. floor _____
3. tax _____
4. boss _____
5. map _____

Use the plural form of the underlined word to complete each sentence.

6. One fire drill in a week makes sense, but three fire _____ are too much.

7. His younger brother broke another dish, so he bought his mom a new set of _____.

8. This bench is the most comfortable of all the _____.

9. I didn't see just one bat flying near me. I saw five _____!

10. My worm moved one inch, but Joe's worm moved four _____.

11. I returned one book to the library, but checked out three more _____.

12. When I eat carrots, I get a rash. When my brother eats them, he gets many _____.

110   Arts • Ask the Science Wizard

Writing Advertisement

Read aloud the sample ad. (See Differentiated Instruction.) Point out the important elements of the ad (the job title, and a description of the duties and the requirements needed in three areas—experience, skills, education). Then discuss what information might be included in an ad that seeks a scientist to work at a museum. Ask students to fill in *Student Journal* page 107. Then have them use their notes to write the ad on *Student Journal* page 108.

Vocabulary

Synonyms and Antonyms

Display this sentence from the selection: "*Each material can deteriorate.*" Underline *deteriorate* and ask students to think of a synonym, or word with a similar meaning, such as *decline, weaken,* or *fall apart.* Then have students think of an antonym, or opposite, of *deteriorate,* such as *improve* or *recover.* Finally, have students complete *Student Journal* page 109.

Phonics/Word Study

Plurals -s, -es

Display the words *pen, chair, wish,* and *batch.* Ask volunteers to add -s or -es to each word to make it plural. (*pens, chairs, wishes, batches*) What patterns do students notice? (When the plural adds a syllable, -es is used.) Now, work with students to complete the in-depth plurals activity on TE page 176. For additional support, have students complete *Student Journal* page 110.

Plurals *-s*, *-es*

This sort will help students learn when to use *-s* and *-es* to create plurals.

▶ Begin by placing the words *creeps, likes,* and *bunches* as the headings for the first three columns. Say the words out loud. Ask students what these three words have in common. While students are thinking, add another word to each column. Someone may notice that each word is in its plural form. (See *Word Study Manual* page 56.)

▶ Ask students: *The words are all plural, but do they all have the same ending? Look at the columns, one by one.*

▶ Examine the word *creeps* and ask what the word is in its singular form (*creep*). Students should be able to see that adding an *-s* makes it plural.

▶ Examine the word *likes* and ask what the word is in its singular form (*like*). Again, students should be able to see that adding an *-s* makes it plural.

▶ Examine the word *bunches*. This pattern is different. It requires an *-es* to make it plural.

▶ Have students say *creep, creeps; like, likes;* and *bunch, bunches.* What do they notice about the syllables in each pair? *Creeps* and *likes* are one syllable in both the singular and plural forms. *Bunches,* however, becomes two syllables when the plural is added, because wherever there's a syllable, there will also be a vowel. Because *bunches* has two syllables, an *-es* must be added.

▶ If students don't notice, point out that most of the words in the *bunches* column end in /ch/ or /sh/. If you try adding just an *-s* to these words, you'll find that the way you articulate it forces the word into two syllables. Discuss the words in the Oddball column. *Cage, ridge, bulge,* and *force* all end in *e,* just as *like* does, but their plural forms have two syllables.

▶ Now, have students work in pairs to complete the sort on their own. When students have finished and the sorts have been checked for accuracy, discuss students' observations.

Plurals *-s* and *-es* Sort

creeps	*likes*	*bunches*	**Oddballs**
paints	strokes	pitches	cages
winds	leaves	porches	ridges
cartoons	stones	finishes	bulges
travels	waves	dishes	forces
signals	planes	peaches	carries
hears	moves	pushes	berries
breaks	makes	canvases	
factors	lures		

For more information on word sorts and spelling stages, see pages 5–31 in the *Word Study Manual.*

Focus on . . .

Use one or more activities in this section to focus on a particular area of need in your students.

Comprehension   STRATEGY SUPPORT

To help those students who need more practice using the strategies covered in this lesson, work one-on-one or in small groups to apply the strategy prompts below. Apply the prompts to a *Reading Advantage* paperback, a classroom library book, or a new or familiar selection in the magazine. Always model your own thinking first.

Making Connections

- What does this story (article, passage) remind me of?
- What do I already know about this topic?
- Where have I heard about this topic before?
- What do I have in common with the characters, people, or situations in the text?
- What other books, stories, articles, movies, or TV shows does this text make me think about?

Determining Importance

- What is the most important idea in the paragraph? How can I prove it?
- Which details are unimportant? Why?
- What does the author want me to understand?
- Why is this information important (or not important) to me?

Writing Personal Experience

Have students write a short piece about a time when they had stage fright or were very nervous about performing in front of a group. Suggest that they follow a writing guide like this one:

Opening Paragraph: Tell what the event was.
Second Paragraph: Use details to describe how you felt.
Third Paragraph: Describe what happened.
Fourth Paragraph: Tell about what you learned from the experience, or what you might do differently in the future.

Encourage students to read their finished pieces aloud.

Fluency: Pacing

After students have read "Ask the Science Wizard" at least once, model reading one of the letters and responses aloud. Then have students work in pairs to practice reading the same section or another one.

As you listen to partners read, use these prompts to guide them.

▶ Read at an even, natural pace—not too quickly or too slowly. Preview the text, as needed, to avoid stops and starts.

▶ Let punctuation such as commas and periods guide your pauses. Let question marks guide the expression in your voice.

When students read aloud, do they—

✓ demonstrate a smooth pace, not too fast or too slow?

✓ incorporate well-timed pauses between words and phrases?

✓ reflect an awareness and understanding of punctuation?

English Language Learners

Support students as they compare and contrast in the first discussion question on TE page 174.

1. Explain that active readers compare and contrast as they read. List some of the main points about each letter.

2. Model using the language of comparing and contrasting with this sentence frame: *The letters are similar because they all . . .*

3. Have students use the sentence frame to compare the letters.

Independent Activity Options

While you work with individuals or small groups, others can work independently on one or more of the following options.

▶ Foundations paperback books, see TE pages 195–200

▶ Foundations *eZines*

▶ Repeat word sorts for this lesson

▶ *Student Journal* pages for this lesson

Assessment

Strategy Assessment

To help you and your students assess their use of comprehension strategies, ask the following questions. Students can complete a written response or provide verbal answers in a one-on-one reading conference.

1. **Making Connections** What answer did you find most interesting or surprising? Why? (Answers will vary.)

2. **Determining Importance** What information in the selection is important to you personally? Explain. (Answers will vary. Students will probably relate to the information about stage fright, since most will have experienced it.)

For ongoing informal assessment, use the checklists on pages 61–64 of *Foundations Assessment*.

Word Study Assessment

Use these steps to help you and your students assess their understanding of plurals *-s* and *-es*.

1. Display a chart like the one below, but include only the headings and the words in the first column.

2. Have students provide the correct plural ending for each word. The answers are shown.

Word	Plural
catch	catches
faint	faints
hope	hopes
wish	wishes
cave	caves
unravel	unravels
accomplish	accomplishes
bear	bears
canvas	canvases
bake	bakes

Foundations Assessment

LESSON 23
Picture This
Arts, pages 22–27

SUMMARY
This **short story** describes how Ronnie Bajeaux, a timid day-dreamer, becomes more confident with a push of a button—a camera button, that is!

Understanding Text Structure
Monitor Understanding

WRITING
Summary

VOCABULARY
Denotation and Connotation

PHONICS/WORD STUDY
Endings to Words That End in *y*

Lesson Vocabulary
dreaded	bizarre
symbolize	furiously
sculptor	

MATERIALS
Arts, pp. 22–27
Student Journal, pp. 111–115
Word Study Manual, p. 57

Picture This

It was the same every day. The bell for third period would ring. The students would take their seats. Then Miss Miro would look up and see Ronnie Bajeaux peeking into her classroom.

22

Before Reading

Use one or more activities.

Make a Plot Organizer ▶

Introduce the term *short story* to students. To introduce the structure of a short story, create a plot organizer. (See TE page 212 for a plot organizer BLM.) Explain the five main parts of a story plot: *Exposition* (introduction of characters, setting, and conflict), *Rising Action* (main character tries to solve a problem), *Climax* (most exciting or important part), *Falling Action* (events after the climax), and *Resolution* (ending). Revisit the plot organizer later.

3. Climax

2. Rising Action

4. Falling Action

1. Exposition

5. Resolution

Vocabulary Preview

Display the vocabulary words and read them aloud to clarify pronunciations. Extend understanding of the vocabulary words by having students complete the synonyms chart on *Student Journal* page 111. Use the vocabulary word *bizarre* to model a response for the page. (See Differentiated Instruction.)

Miss Miro was the art teacher at Springville High School. Most of the students liked her. So it was normal for some to stop by. But the funny thing was that Miss Miro had never taught Ronnie. So why was he there?

Twice, she tried to invite him in. But he just mumbled, "No, thank you," and left. So, Miss Miro began to pretend he wasn't there. If she said nothing, the tall, thin boy would stay.

Ronnie stood where the other students couldn't see him. He would listen to her lesson for five or ten minutes. In the meantime, he would shift his laptop from hand to hand. He always carried that laptop computer. Then he would go.

Miss Miro wondered what class Ronnie was supposed to be in. But he seemed so interested, and he wasn't bothering anyone. In fact, he paid better attention than some students in her class.

Lost in Study Hall

More than anything, Ronnie dreaded third period. That's when he had study hall. Doing homework during study hall wasn't the problem. Ronnie liked school. The problem was Jana Whitley.

Jana sat next to him. They had assigned seats. Everyone loved Jana. Her friends were always passing her notes, and they were always giggling.

Worse, though, was Freddie Marker. To talk to Jana, Freddie was always pulling up a chair right between Ronnie and Jana. That meant Ronnie had to squeeze way over to make room for him. Who could study like that?

Ronnie would have liked to talk to Jana, too. She was the only girl he knew that could jump six steps on her skateboard. But Ronnie could never think of what to say. All in all, sitting next to Jana made it pretty hard to focus on homework.

The Long Way There

So, Ronnie always took as long as he could to walk to study hall. One day, he stopped to look at the art hanging outside Miss Miro's room. He was just trying to waste time, but some of the pictures were kind of cool.

They were self-portraits. The students took pictures of themselves, and then they cut out pictures from magazines to paste onto them.

23

DIFFERENTIATED INSTRUCTION
Vocabulary Preview

Work with students to read, pronounce, and establish meaning for the word *dreaded*.

What does *dreaded* mean?	causing fear
What is the vowel sound in the first syllable? How is that sound spelled? What other vowel sound is it like?	/eh/ *ea* short *e*
What other words have a short *e* vowel sound spelled with *ea*?	*bread* *spread* *head*
When might you use this word?	Sam *dreaded* telling his mother that he'd dented the car.

Student Journal page 111

Name _____ Date _____

Building Vocabulary: Synonyms Chart

Add two synonyms for *bizarre*. Then write two synonyms for each of the other words from the selection. You can use words or phrases. Use a thesaurus or dictionary to help you.

Vocabulary Word	Synonyms
bizarre	1. strange 2. 3.
dreaded	1. feared 2. 3.
sculptor	1. craftsperson 2. 3.
furiously	1. quickly 2. 3.

Arts • Picture This   111

Preview the Selection

Have students look through the selection. Ask:

- Will you read fiction or nonfiction? How do you know?

- What do you learn from reading the introductory note on page 22? What is the purpose of the note?

- How do the illustrations help you predict what may happen in the story?

Teacher Think Aloud

I can tell by looking at the pictures that this selection takes place in a school. The pictures also make me think that it is a story. After reading the introductory note, I'm curious about why Ronnie peers into Miss Miro's classroom. I also wonder why there is a picture of Ronnie with robotic arms. I look forward to finding out what is going on.

Make Predictions/ Set Purpose

Students should use the information they gathered in previewing the selection to make predictions about what they will learn. If students have trouble generating a purpose for reading, suggest that they read to find out how Ronnie gains a new interest and more confidence in himself.

Comprehension
UNDERSTANDING TEXT STRUCTURE

To help students understand the elements of realistic fiction, have them consider these questions.

- How do you know that Ronnie is the main character in the story?

- Who is the next most important character?

- What makes the setting believable? What might be an unbelievable setting?

- How does Ronnie's problem get resolved?

One guy pasted a few extra heads onto his portrait. A note said that it showed he was "a different person at different times." Another girl glued extra eyes on hers. She wrote, "The eyes symbolize that, one day, I'm going to see the whole world."

Ronnie imagined his own self-portrait. He would use sky for his eyes, and he would glue robot arms onto his body. The sky would show he was a dreamer. His head was always in the clouds. The arms would be his biggest dream: to have arms that could do anything.

Then Ronnie got lost in his thoughts. He thought about the car accident. He was just five when it happened. Another car ran a red light. He knew he was lucky. He could have died, but only his arms were hurt.

Still, there were things he couldn't do. He couldn't hold a pencil for one thing. He had to type with one finger, instead. That's why he had the laptop. Some kids thought the laptop was cool. Others thought it was weird. Only Ronnie knew he couldn't do his schoolwork without it.

"Ronnie, would you like to join us?"

Ronnie looked up startled. It was Miss Miro.

"No, thank you," he mumbled and left.

What a Joke

The next day, Ronnie stopped at the self-portraits again. Sometimes, he wished he could be a painter or a sculptor. He had so many ideas that he could scream, he thought.

That gave him another idea. He wished he could sculpt a giant, metal head that looked as if it was yelling. Its mouth would

be so big that you could walk through it and stand inside the head. He would call it *Welcome to the Party.*

Who was he kidding? He would never be an artist, just as he would never talk to Jana.

"Ronnie, would you like to join us?" It was Miss Miro again, and the kids in her class were laughing.

"No, thank you," he said quietly, and then he left quickly.

During Reading

Comprehension
UNDERSTANDING TEXT STRUCTURE

Use these questions to model how to understand the structure of realistic fiction. Then have students identify and describe the story elements.

- Who is the main character in the story? What is the conflict?

- What is the setting of the story?

- How do I know that this is realistic fiction?

(See Differentiated Instruction.)

Teacher Think Aloud

Ronnie is the main character in this story. The problem he faces is that he has a real interest in art, but he doesn't have the full use of his arms and can't paint or draw. He just thinks about things he would make if he could. The setting is Ronnie's school. I know that this is realistic fiction because the characters talk and act like real people.

Comprehension
MONITOR UNDERSTANDING

Use these questions to model how to visualize what you are reading about. Then have students tell about a part they visualized and which details helped them visualize it.

- What do I picture in my mind as I read?

- Which details help me create this image in my mind?

Caught Again

Every day, Ronnie returned to Miss Miro's door. He liked her class. She didn't just talk about paint, she talked about ideas. One day, she showed the class slides of fast-food restaurants.

"What do you notice?" she asked the class.

"That I'm getting hungry," cracked a kid from the back.

She laughed. "Did anyone notice that all the colors in the restaurants are red, yellow, and orange?"

"These bright colors make you feel happy and move fast," she continued. "That's why these restaurants use them. Artists use colors to make you feel a certain way, too. Now, I want each of you to pick a color and write how it makes you feel."

Then the unthinkable happened. Miss Miro walked to the door.

"Ronnie, I want to talk to you."

"I have to get to study hall," said Ronnie, walking away.

"Ronnie Bajeaux, you stop right there."

Oh no! Ronnie was sure he was in trouble.

"So, you have study hall third period?"

"Yes, Miss Miro," said Ronnie to his feet.

"Why don't you join my class instead?"

Ronnie looked up surprised and nearly dropped his laptop.

"Um, I can't, Miss Miro."

"Of course you can, Ronnie. Plenty of students take a class instead of study hall."

"No, I mean I *can't* can't."

"I'm not sure I understand, Ronnie."

"I can't do art, Miss Miro." And now he whispered. Never had he told anyone at school about his arms.

"I hurt my arms when I was little. It was a car accident, and now I can't paint or anything like that. I can't even hold a paintbrush."

Miss Miro smiled, which really confused Ronnie. What kind of person would smile about that?

"Can you use that laptop?" she asked.

"Well, yeah, of course I can."

25

Teacher Think Aloud

On page 24, Ronnie envisions his own self-portrait, using the sky for his eyes and adding robotic arms to his body. In my mind I saw big eyes colored blue with clouds. And I pictured purple robotic arms with grippers on the ends. Then I remembered the illustration on page 23. I looked at it, but I think I like my image better.

Fix-Up Strategies

Offer these strategies to help students read independently.

If you don't understand what you're reading:

- Reread the difficult section to look for clues to help you comprehend.
- Read ahead to find clues to help you comprehend.
- Retell, or say in your own words, what you've read.
- Visualize, or form mental pictures of, what you've read.

If you don't understand a word:

- Reread the sentence. Look for ideas and words that provide meaning clues.
- Find clues by reading a few sentences before and after the confusing word.
- Look for the base or root word and think about its meaning.
- Think about the topic or plot at this point to see if either offers meaning clues.

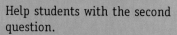

DIFFERENTIATED INSTRUCTION
Discussion Questions

Help students with the second question.

1. Point out that authors do not always directly state what they want a reader to know. Readers must draw conclusions.

2. Make a chart like the one below. Have students identify phrases or sentences in the text that tell about Ronnie, and list these. Then discuss what conclusion students might draw from that information.

Story Information	Possible Conclusion
p. 23; doesn't know what to say to Jana	He is shy.

Student Journal pages 112–113

Name _____ Date _____
Writing: Somebody Wanted But So Chart
Fill in this chart to help you organize your thoughts for a summary of "Picture This."

	My Notes
Somebody (an important character)	
Wanted (a key problem with details)	
But (conflict for the character)	
So (an outcome)	

112   Arts • Picture This

"So, Ronnie, can you type? Can you push a button?"

This was really getting annoying, thought Ronnie.

"Yes, I can push a button," he said.

"Well, then come here after school today at three o'clock sharp. You have detention with me. Now get to study hall. You're late!"

Seeing Red

Great. Now he had detention. His mom would love that. And what were all those questions about buttons? What kind of bizarre punishment did she have planned for him?

Ronnie got to study hall and slapped his laptop down.

"Late again, huh?"

It was the first time Jana had ever spoken

I give up.
I give up.
I give up.

26

---

to him. But Ronnie was too upset to care.

"Yup," he said and turned away. Then he started typing furiously.

He wasn't doing his homework. He was writing what he was thinking.

He wrote, "I give up."

He wrote it over and over again. He couldn't do art. He couldn't fit in. He couldn't talk to Jana. And now he had detention.

"I give up, I give up, I give up, and I don't feel bright orange or yellow. No happy colors for me. I feel like the color of mud," he typed.

This Is Detention?

At three o'clock, Ronnie was at Miss Miro's door. It looked as though a lot of kids had detention. Ronnie counted eight. And guess what? One was Jana. As he sat down next to her, Ronnie wondered what she did to get in trouble.

"What a great turnout," said Miss Miro. "It looks as if the photography club is off to a good start."

"Photography club?" Ronnie blurted out.

"Yes, Ronnie," said Miss Miro.

"But . . ."

"Hold on, Ronnie. Now everyone listen up. We have a digital camera for each of you. As you can see, all you have to do to take a picture is push a button." She winked at Ronnie.

Miss Miro had tricked him. This wasn't detention.

"I have always thought of photography as the art form that has a big welcome mat out for everyone," said Miss Miro. "Not everyone thinks they can draw a picture, but everyone knows they can take a picture. And here,

---

After Reading
Use one or more activities.

Check Purpose

Have students determine whether their purpose was met. Did they find out how Ronnie gains a new interest and more confidence in himself?

Discussion Questions

Ask the following questions.
(See Differentiated Instruction.)

1. What is Miss Miro's solution to Ronnie's problem about not being able to use his hands? Do you think this is a good solution? (Problem-Solution)

2. What conclusions can you draw about Ronnie's character? (Draw Conclusions)

3. What in this story can you connect with? (Making Connections)

Revisit: Plot Organizer

Use story details to complete the organizer. *Exposition*: Ronnie always peeks into Miss Miro's class. *Rising Action*: Miss Miro invites Ronnie in, but he leaves. *Climax*: Miss Miro tells Ronnie that he has detention. *Falling Action*: Ronnie goes to detention but realizes that it is the photography club. *Resolution*: Ronnie is excited to take pictures and even takes one of Jana.

you'll learn to take artful pictures."

All through the meeting, Ronnie thought of all the pictures he could take. He could take photos of shadows or clouds or stuff you never see—like the underside of a car.

"Hey, Ronnie, are you in there?"

Jana had caught him daydreaming.

"Time to go," she said. "Oh, and I'm editor of the yearbook this year, you know? We need photographers. So, if you keep coming to photography club, maybe you could help out with the yearbook, too."

"Yeah, sure, okay," said Ronnie.

Miss Miro was listening. "So you'll be joining us, Ronnie?"

"Yes, I think I will."

"Good. Glad to hear you say yes for once, Ronnie," she smiled. "Now take that camera home and let's see what you can do."

Jana was leaving. "See you in study hall tomorrow, Ronnie. Don't be late!"

"Wait!" Ronnie caught up to Jana in the hall. He put down his laptop and pointed his camera at her.

"I have to start somewhere," he said. "So, smile!" ◆

27

Answers for **Student Journal page 115** are *replies, flies, denies, worries, scurries; berries, trophies, pennies, surveys, monkeys.*

Writing Summary

Remind students that a summary is a short paragraph that tells the topic and the main points of a longer piece. To help students prepare for writing a summary of "Picture This," have them complete the Somebody Wanted But So chart on *Student Journal* page 112. Then, on *Student Journal* page 113, students should use their notes from the chart to write the summary.

Vocabulary

Denotation and Connotation

Point out the word *furiously* at the top of page 26 and tell students that here it means "to do something in a fast, agitated way." Explain that this definition is the denotation, or general meaning. Someone's connotation, or personal association, for the word *furiously* might be "the way my parents react when I come home late." Now have students complete *Student Journal* page 114.

Phonics/Word Study

Words That End in y

On the board, write: *I try to hold one baby.* Have a student write: *She tries to hold two babies.* Point out that in the verb *try* and the noun *baby*, the y is dropped before adding -ies. Now, work with students to complete the in-depth words that end in y activity on TE page 184. For additional support, have students complete *Student Journal* page 115.

Endings to Words That End in *y*

This sort will help students figure out how to add -*s* and -*ies* endings to words that end in *y*.

▶ Write these phrases on the board or on chart paper:

One lady.
Two ladies.

One monkey.
Two monkeys.

▶ Ask students to describe how the endings of the nouns change. If necessary, point out how the *y* gets dropped from *lady* before the ending -*ies* is added. Then point out how a single *s* is added to the end of *monkey* to create *monkeys*.

▶ Ask students: *What spelling patterns do you notice?* If students don't notice, point out that *monkey* ends in -*ey*. Nouns that end in -*ey* simply add an -*s* to create a plural. Nouns (and verbs) that end in a consonant + *y* drop the *y* and take an -*ies* ending.

▶ Ask students to brainstorm some other nouns that end in *y*. Work together to figure out the plural forms. Here are some examples:

fly, flies   *turkey, turkeys*
baby, babies   *key, keys*

▶ When you think students are ready to try the spelling changes on their own, hand out copies of the Endings to Words That End in *y* Sort sheet. (See *Word Study Manual* page 57.) Students should work in pairs.

▶ Check the final sorts for accuracy.

Endings to Words That End in *y* Sort

Base Word	Plural Noun -*ies* as in *ladies*	Plural Noun -*s* as in *monkeys*	Verb Ending -*ies* as in *cries*
baby	babies		
donkey		donkeys	
study	studies		studies
monkey		monkeys	
duty	duties		
carry			carries
chimney		chimneys	
try	tries		tries
deny			denies
turkey		turkeys	
fry			fries
ally	allies		
comply			complies
defy			defies

For more information on word sorts and spelling stages, see pages 5–31 in the *Word Study Manual*.

Focus on . . .

Use one or more activities in this section to focus on a particular area of need in your students.

Comprehension   STRATEGY SUPPORT

To help those students who need more practice using the strategies covered in this lesson, work one-on-one or in small groups to apply the strategy prompts below. Apply the prompts to a *Reading Advantage* paperback, a classroom library book, or a new or familiar selection in the magazine. Always model your own thinking first.

Understanding Text Structure

• What kind of text is this? (book, story, article, guidebook, play, manual)

• How does the author organize the text? (cause-effect, problem-solution, chronological order, description, question-answer, comparison-contrast)

• What details support my thoughts about the text structure?

• What is the cause (effect, problem, solution, order, question, answer)?

• If fiction, who are the characters? What is the setting, plot, conflict, and resolution?

Monitor Understanding

• Do I understand what I'm reading? If not, what part is confusing to me?

• What fix-up strategies can I use to solve the problem? (See During Reading for fix-up strategies.)

• Why did a character say (do, think, ask) that?

• What images do I visualize from the text? What parts can't I visualize?

• Why did the author include (or not include) those details?

Writing Self-Portrait

Have students create a self-portrait similar to the ones hanging outside Miss Miro's classroom. Encourage students to cut out pictures from magazines and/or newspapers to paste onto their self-portraits. Then have students annotate their portraits with labels or captions. Students should then use their annotations to write a short paragraph that explains what each part of their self-portrait symbolizes.

Fluency: Pacing

After students have read the selection at least once silently, model reading a section aloud, using proper pacing. Then have pairs of students take turns reading aloud the sections "What a Joke" and "Caught Again," on pages 24 and 25.

As you listen to partners read, use these prompts to guide them.

▶ Review the text to avoid starts and stops.

▶ Pause after reading section headings. This will let your partner know that you have started a new section.

▶ Read at an even, natural pace—not too quickly or too slowly.

▶ Use punctuation, such as commas, periods, and question marks, to help guide your pauses and your expression.

When students read aloud, do they—

✓ demonstrate a smooth pace, not too fast or too slow?

✓ incorporate well-timed pauses between words and phrases?

✓ reflect an awareness and understanding of punctuation?

English Language Learners

To support students as they monitor their understanding, extend the comprehension activity on TE page 180.

1. Remind students that active readers use details in the text to help them visualize.

2. Have students reread the second paragraph on page 24 of the selection. Then ask them to use the details provided to help them draw Ronnie's portrait.

3. Have students describe their drawings.

Independent Activity Options

While you work with individuals or small groups, others can work independently on one or more of the following options.

▶ Foundations paperback books, see TE pages 195–200

▶ Foundations *eZines*

▶ Repeat word sorts for this lesson

▶ *Student Journal* pages for this lesson

Assessment

Strategy Assessment

To help you and your students assess their use of comprehension strategies, ask the following questions. Students can complete a written response or provide verbal answers in a one-on-one reading conference.

1. **Understanding Text Structure** From what you've learned about the main character, Ronnie, do you think that he will become a good photographer? Why or why not? (Answers will vary.)

2. **Monitor Understanding** What are some strong images that you remember from the story? Why do you think you remember them? (Answers will vary.)

For ongoing informal assessment, use the checklists on pages 61–64 of *Foundations Assessment*.

Word Study Assessment

Use these steps to help you and your students assess their understanding of adding *-s* and *-ies* endings to words that end in *y*.

1. Display a chart like the one below, but include only the headings and the words in the first column.

2. Have students provide the correct plural ending for each word and tell whether the word is a noun or a verb. The answers are shown.

Word	Plural and Part of Speech
try	tries (verb or noun)
story	stories (noun)
jockey	jockeys (noun)
assembly	assemblies (noun)
rely	relies (verb)
boundary	boundaries (noun)
kidney	kidneys (noun)
rely	relies (verb)
battery	batteries (noun)
medley	medleys (noun)

LESSON 24
An Interview . . . *and* Opening Night
Arts, pages 28—end

SUMMARY
In this **interview**, Jacqueline Woodson talks about both her childhood and her career as a children's author. The **poem** "Opening Night" follows.

COMPREHENSION STRATEGIES
Inferential Thinking
Making Connections

WRITING
Journal Entry

VOCABULARY
Context

PHONICS/WORD STUDY
Sounds of the Past Tense /d/, /t/, /ed/

Lesson Vocabulary
graffiti	surly
outright	complex
penned	

MATERIALS
Arts, pp. 28–end
Student Journal, pp. 116–120
Word Study Manual, p. 58

An Interview with Jacqueline Woodson

When Jackie Woodson was a student, she used to sit in the back of the class. She liked to talk a lot. She didn't pay attention, and she missed homework assignments. Jackie also had a habit of telling lies. She later grew up to be an award-winning author. We asked Jackie how she got her start. She also told us some of her tricks of the trade.

Did you always want to be a writer?
People used to ask me what I wanted to be when I grew up. I'd say I'd be a teacher or a lawyer or a hairdresser. But even as I said these things, I knew what made me happiest. It was writing.

What kind of writing did you do as a child?
I wrote on everything and everywhere. I remember my uncle catching me writing my name in graffiti on the side of a building. (It was not pretty for me when my mother found out.) I wrote on paper bags. I wrote on my shoes. I wrote on my denim binders. I chalked stories across sidewalks. I penciled tiny tales in notebook margins. I loved watching words flower into sentences. I loved watching sentences blossom into stories. And I still do.

Did you like to tell stories when you were a child?
Yes, I told a lot of stories! Not "Once upon a time" stories but, basically, outright lies. I loved lying, and I loved getting away with it! There was something about telling the lie-story. You could see your friends' eyes grow wide with wonder. Of course, I got in trouble for lying, but I didn't stop lying until fifth grade.

28

Before Reading
WHOLE CLASS Use one or more activities.

Make a Concept Web ▶
On the board or on chart paper, draw a concept web to help students discuss what they know about writers. Encourage students to think about different written works they have read, authors they are familiar with, and their own writing experiences. After reading the selection, students will return to the concept web to record additional thoughts they may have.

writers
where ideas come from
what they write
what skills are needed
imagination, real life
stories, plays, articles
good vocabulary, creative minds

Vocabulary Preview
Display the vocabulary words and read them aloud to clarify pronunciations. Discuss any associations students have with the words. What do they already know about them? Where have they seen them used? Then have students begin the making associations chart on *Student Journal* page 116. Use the vocabulary word *graffiti* to model a response for the page. Revisit the chart later. (See Differentiated Instruction.)

What happened then?

I wrote a story, and my teacher said, "This is really good." This teacher usually had turned-down lips.

Before that, I had written a poem about Martin Luther King. It was good. It was so good that no one believed I wrote it. There was a lot of fuss. Finally, people believed I had indeed penned the poem that went on to win me a Scrabble game and local fame. So then the story rolled around, and the teacher said, "This is really good."

Then I realized that a lie on the page was a whole different animal. It won you prizes and got surly teachers to smile. A lie on the page meant lots of independent time. Time to create your stories. It meant the freedom to sit hunched over the pages of your notebook. And without people thinking you were strange!

What was your favorite subject in school?

I loved English. I loved anything where we got to do writing. I was terrible at math and science. I loved gym and Spanish. I liked anything that allowed us to dance or jump around. I wasn't a big fan of sitting still for too long. I loved quiet time and reading, though I read the same books over and over.

Do you have a writing routine?

I have to make a quiet space for myself. I just sit down with a notebook and pen. At first, I usually jot down my ideas on paper. Then when my thoughts are flowing quickly, I switch to a computer.

Where do you write?

I have a writing desk. Sometimes I sit there. Sometimes I sit on the stoop. If the ideas start coming, I just write wherever I am. I use whatever I have to write on.

Where do you get your ideas?

I have a three-year-old daughter. She's named Toshi, after her Godmom. Hanging out with Toshi gives me ideas for picture books. For my older books, I tap into my own memories. I think back to what it was like to be that age.

Was it hard to get your first book published?

Well, the hardest part was finishing it. Once I finished my book, I sent it to the publishers whose books I liked to read. The first book I published was called *Martin Luther King and His Birthday*. It's a picture book. My first book for young adults was called *Last Summer with Maizon*.

29

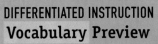

Comprehension
MAKING CONNECTIONS

To help students make connections, follow these steps:

1. Ask and discuss the following questions:
   - What book have you read that you really liked?
   - What did you like about it?
   - If you had the chance, what questions would you ask the author?

2. If students have read a book by Jacqueline Woodson, have them tell the class about it.

What advice would you give to young writers?

Write every day. Write for at least a half-hour every day. Read a lot. It doesn't need to be complex. Study the author's craft. And turn off the television!

Reading lots of books will help you become a better writer. One cool thing about books is that you don't need to buy them. You can borrow them from libraries. If your library doesn't have one of my books, ask the librarian. They can often order it from another library. It usually takes a day or two, but they will get it to you.

What inspires you?

I am still thrilled when I walk into a bookstore and see my name on a book's spine.

Sometimes, I'm sitting at my desk for long hours, and nothing's coming to me. Then I remember my fifth-grade teacher. I remember the way her eyes lit up when she said, "This is really good." I—the skinny girl in the back of the classroom who was always getting into trouble—sat up a little straighter. I folded my hands on the desk, smiled, and began to believe in me. Thinking about that moment inspires me.

What are some of your favorite books?

I have a lot of favorite books. This week I love *Bud, Not Buddy* by Christopher Paul Curtis. I love anything by Chris Lynch. Also, anything by Chris Raschka or Christopher Myers. Not only because they all share the same name, either! I love Karen Hesse's writing. Those are just a few of my favorites. The list is constantly changing. Still, most of these people remain constant.

Where have you traveled?

I've been to all fifty states. I've been to England and France and Virgin Gorda. I've been to Mexico. Next year, I'm going to Greece and Africa!

What languages do you speak?

Mostly English. I also know Spanish. I know a good bit of American Sign Language. If I am desperate, I can find a bathroom, in French.

Do you ever get "writer's block"?

No, I don't. I don't believe there is any such thing as writer's block. I think it's just your mind telling you that the thing you're writing isn't the thing you really want to be writing. If this happens to me, I start writing something else.

30

During Reading

Comprehension
INFERENTIAL THINKING

Use these questions to model how to draw conclusions about Jacqueline Woodson. Then have students draw their own conclusions about her.

- What does this article tell me about Jacqueline Woodson?
- What do I know from my own life that helps me understand her?
- What words would I use to describe Woodson?

Teacher Think Aloud

Woodson says that she used to tell stories to her friends and watch their eyes grow wide with wonder. She talks about when her writing was praised. I know that when I am praised, I feel more confident. I would describe Woodson as a confident writer, who is proud of her ability to tell a good story.

Comprehension
MAKING CONNECTIONS

Use these questions to model how to make connections with the text. Then have students share their connections.

- What does this selection remind me of?
- What do I already know about this topic?
- How does my experience help me understand this selection?

(See Differentiated Instruction.)

How many books do you work on at one time?
I'm usually working on a few books at once. If I get bored or stuck on one, I go on to another.

What's your favorite book that you've written?
I like each of them for different reasons. Sometimes, long after I've finished a book, I'm still thinking about the people in them.

Are any of the characters based on people you know?
Sometimes I use bits and pieces from real life. None of the stories I've written yet are completely autobiographical. And none of the characters are people about whom I could say, "That's so-and-so from this book." I start with a little bit of what I know. Then all the rest is fiction.

If you couldn't write, what would you do?
Be the next Michael Jordan in the NBA.

Do you think you'll ever stop writing?
Probably not even when I die. I love writing that much. ◆

Meet Some of Jacqueline's Friends . . .

You've met Jacqueline Woodson. Now meet some of the people she's brought to life.

Miracle's Boys
Lafayette, Charlie, and Ty'ree are three brothers whose mother dies. Now orphans, trying to get by, they face pain and anger. They also find humor and caring, together.

Locomotion
Lonnie C. Motion, a fifth grader, has had some tough breaks. But he finds poetry and a way to express himself.

Last Summer with Maizon
Maizon and Margaret are best friends. Margaret's father dies, and Maizon gets accepted to boarding school. Margaret wonders if life will ever be the same.

The House You Pass on the Way
Evangeline, nicknamed Staggerlee, and her adopted cousin Trout meet for the first time when they are thirteen. They form a strong friendship and learn what it means to be the children of heroes.

31

Teacher Think Aloud

I read a book by Jacqueline Woodson called Hush. It tells about a girl whose family has to go into the Witness Protection Program. Everything about the girl's life changes, even her name. It was a great story. I kept thinking about this book as I read the interview. It made me really interested in learning about the author.

Fix-Up Strategies
Offer these strategies to help students read independently.

If you don't understand what you're reading:

- Reread the difficult section to look for clues to help you comprehend.
- Read ahead to find clues to help you comprehend.
- Retell, or say in your own words, what you've read.
- Visualize, or form mental pictures of, what you've read.

If you don't understand a word:

- Reread the sentence. Look for ideas and words that provide meaning clues.
- Find clues by reading a few sentences before and after the confusing word.
- Look for the base or root word and think about its meaning.
- Think about the topic or plot at this point to see if either offers meaning clues.

Student Journal pages 117–118

Name _____ **Date** _____

Writing: Notes for Journal Entry

Think about something that happened that made you feel especially good about yourself, and maybe even increased your self-confidence. It might have been when someone praised you, when you won an award, or when you achieved something you didn't think you could. Write some notes about what happened.

What happened? _____

_____

_____

What did you do to prepare for it, or what happened before it? _____

_____

_____

How did you feel afterward? _____

_____

_____

What else can you remember about it? _____

_____

_____

What were some sights, smells, or sounds you remember about it? _____

_____

_____

_____

Arts • An Interview with Jacqueline Woodson and Opening Night   **117**

Student Journal page 119

Name _____ **Date** _____

Building Vocabulary: Using Context to Understand a Word

Select a vocabulary word you defined from the context. Complete the statements and answer the questions about your word.

graffiti	outright	penned	surly

My Word in Context:

I think this word means _____

because _____

_____

My word is _____

My word is not _____

Where else might I find this word? _____

What makes this an important word to know? _____

_____

Arts • An Interview with Jacqueline Woodson and Opening Night   **119**

32

Opening Night

After Reading
 *(WHOLE CLASS)* Use one or more activities.

Check Purpose

Have students determine whether their purpose was met. Did they discover how Jacqueline Woodson became an author?

Discussion Questions

Continue the group discussion with the following questions.

1. What solution does Woodson offer to writers who experience writers' block? (Problem-Solution)

2. What makes a good interview question? (Inferential Thinking)

3. Do you think you would have liked having Woodson as a friend if you and she were the same age? Why or why not? (Making Connections)

Revisit: Concept Web

Have students return to the concept web. Would they like to add any ideas they learned about writers and their work?

Revisit: Making Associations

Have students return to *Student Journal* page 116 and review the associations they made to the different vocabulary words. Encourage students to make adjustments or additions to their entries, as needed.

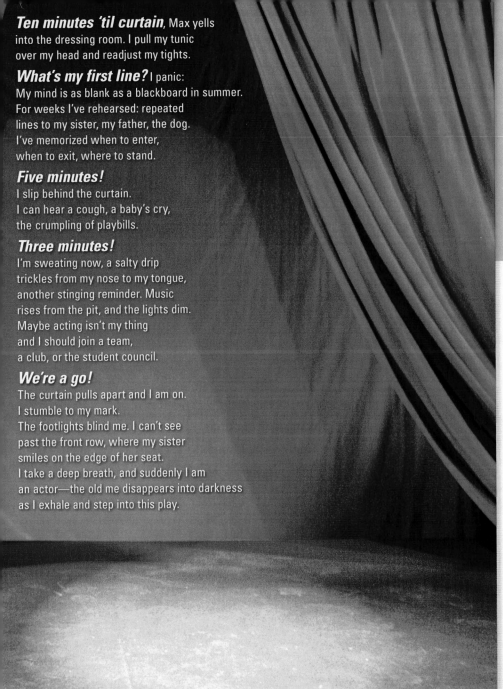

Ten minutes 'til curtain, Max yells
into the dressing room. I pull my tunic
over my head and readjust my tights.

What's my first line? I panic:
My mind is as blank as a blackboard in summer.
For weeks I've rehearsed: repeated
lines to my sister, my father, the dog.
I've memorized when to enter,
when to exit, where to stand.

Five minutes!
I slip behind the curtain.
I can hear a cough, a baby's cry,
the crumpling of playbills.

Three minutes!
I'm sweating now, a salty drip
trickles from my nose to my tongue,
another stinging reminder. Music
rises from the pit, and the lights dim.
Maybe acting isn't my thing
and I should join a team,
a club, or the student council.

We're a go!
The curtain pulls apart and I am on.
I stumble to my mark.
The footlights blind me. I can't see
past the front row, where my sister
smiles on the edge of her seat.
I take a deep breath, and suddenly I am
an actor—the old me disappears into darkness
as I exhale and step into this play.

Poem: Opening Night

Read the poem aloud as students
follow along. Discuss the poem,
using these and similar questions:

- Have you ever been nervous or
  fearful before a performance or
  an important event?
- Could you relate to the person
  in the poem?
- Were there any lines or words
  in the poem that made you
  think or feel a certain way?

Answers for **Student Journal
page 120** are /d/: *burned,
learned, aimed, pleased, played,
stored, hauled, cleaned, amazed,
remained;* /t/: *finished, shocked,
scraped, flapped, unzipped, joked,
chipped, biked, talked, slipped;*
/ed/: *completed, weeded, floated,
shouted, started, created, ended,
disregarded, molded, retreated.*

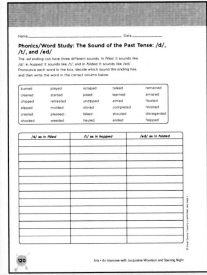

Writing Journal Entry

Have students write a journal entry
about some praise they received, an
award they won, or another achievement
that made them feel good about themselves. Explain that it can be something
small, as long as it gave them a burst
of confidence. On *Student Journal* page
117, students should jot down notes
about the event, and then use their
notes to write their journal entry on
Student Journal page 118.

Vocabulary Context

Have students locate *complex* at the top
of page 30. Explain that reading the
sentences before and after the word
might provide the context needed to
figure out what *complex* means. What
do students think the word means?
(difficult or complicated) Have students
relate *complex* to specific kinds of
tasks. For example, they might identify
organizing a party as a complex task,
and making a sandwich as a simple
task. Have students complete *Student
Journal* page 119.

Phonics/Word Study

Past Tense /d/, /t/, /ed/

Write *grilled, ticked,* and *lasted* on the
board. Say each word, emphasizing the
ending sound. (*grilled,* /d/; *ticked,* /t/;
lasted, /ed/) Point out that although
these past-tense endings sound different,
they are spelled the same. Now, work
with students to complete the in-depth
past-tense activity on TE page 192.
For additional support, have students
complete *Student Journal* page 120.

Phonics/Word Study

Sounds of the Past Tense /d/, /t/, /ed/

The -ed ending has three different sounds. This ending can be tricky because many students try to spell using sound alone.

▶ Write the words *called*, *stopped*, and *wasted* on the board or on chart paper. Ask students: *Are the words present tense or past tense? Are they all the same tense?* (past; yes) *Are all the endings the same?* (This is a trick question because the answer is both yes and no. They look the same, but they all sound different.)

▶ Use the following chart for common misspellings of *called* and *stopped*.

Word	Sound of the -ed Ending	Common Misspelling
called	/d/	cald
stopped	/t/	stopt
wasted	/ed/	

▶ Now, write the words *used* (as in *used* car), *liked*, and *accepted*. Ask students to analyze the endings and determine the category in which each word goes.

▶ When students are familiar with the three different ending sounds, have them work in pairs to complete The Sounds of the Past Tense Sort: /d/, /t/, and /ed/ sheet. (See *Word Study Manual* page 58.)

▶ Check the final sorts for accuracy.

The Sounds of the Past Tense Sort: /d/, /t/, and /ed/

/d/ as in *called*	/t/ as in *stopped*	/ed/ as in *wasted*
used	liked	accepted
loved	guessed	adopted
turned	asked	repeated
believed	chalked	wanted
realized	hunched	counted
allowed	published	acted
opened	rehearsed	folded
thrilled	cracked	parted
nicknamed	winked	boasted
memorized	bumped	

For more information on word sorts and spelling stages, see pages 5–31 in the *Word Study Manual*.

Focus on . . .

Use one or more activities in this section to focus on a particular area of need in your students.

Comprehension [STRATEGY SUPPORT]

To help those students who need more practice using the strategies covered in this lesson, work one-on-one or in small groups to apply the strategy prompts below. Apply the prompts to a *Reading Advantage* paperback, a classroom library book, or a new or familiar selection in the magazine. Always model your own thinking first.

Inferential Thinking

- What are the causes or effects of this event?
- What do I learn from the character or person's thoughts, words, or actions?
- What do I know (or infer) from the text that the author hasn't stated directly?
- What conclusions can I draw?

Making Connections

- What does this story (article, passage) remind me of?
- What do I already know about this topic?
- Where have I heard about this topic before?
- What do I have in common with the characters, people, or situations in the text?
- What other books, stories, articles, movies, or TV shows does this text make me think about?

Writing Interview

Have students write an "inside-out" interview. To begin, tell students to think about some of the things they might want someone to know about them, for example, their favorite sport, their best school subject, their favorite leisure activities, and the music they like. Have students turn these ideas into written questions. Then have students write the answers to their own questions to complete their "inside-out" interviews.

Inside-Out Interview

Question: What is your best school subject?
Answer: I love math. It is interesting and not hard for me. It is logical.

Fluency: Expression

After students have listened to you read the poem "Opening Night," and have read it themselves at least once, read it aloud again and have them listen for your expression. Then have pairs of students take turns reading sections of the poem aloud expressively.

As you listen to pairs read, use these prompts to guide them.

▶ Preview what you will read.

▶ Put yourself both in the place of the poem's narrator and in the situation. How would someone who was nervous about an opening night sound? Would he or she talk quickly or slowly?

▶ Notice which lines of the poem have end punctuation, and which do not. The punctuation will help you adjust your reading rate and the way you group words.

When students read aloud, do they—

✓ reflect an understanding of the text?

✓ demonstrate appropriate timing, stress, and intonation?

✓ incorporate appropriate speed and phrasing?

English Language Learners

Support students as they explore problem and solution in the first discussion question on TE page 190.

1. Make a T-chart with the headings "Problem" and "Solution."

2. Have students discuss the problem of writers' block and the solution from the text, and record their responses in the chart.

3. Ask students to brainstorm other solutions to this problem and add these to the chart. Invite volunteers to choose their favorite solution to this problem.

Independent Activity Options

While you work with individuals or small groups, others can work independently on one or more of the following options.

▶ Foundations paperback books, see TE pages 195–200

▶ Foundations *eZines*

▶ Repeat word sorts for this lesson

▶ *Student Journal* pages for this lesson

Assessment

Strategy Assessment

To help you and your students assess their use of comprehension strategies, ask the following questions. Students can complete a written response or provide verbal answers in a one-on-one reading conference.

1. **Inferential Thinking** After reading the interview, why do you infer that Woodson writes fiction instead of nonfiction? (Answers will vary. Students should note that, from the time she was a child, she loved telling stories. Students can infer that she has always had a vivid imagination and that she might find facts less interesting to relate.)

2. **Making Connections** In what ways did Jacqueline Woodson's experiences remind you of some of your own? (Answers will vary. Students might relate to her not paying attention in class, making up stories, liking to write, and so on.)

See *Foundations Assessment* pages 50–58 for formal assessment to go with *Arts*.

Word Study Assessment

Use these steps to help you and your students assess their understanding of the sounds of the past tense /d/, /t/, and /ed/.

1. Display the chart below, but include only the headings and the words in the first column.

2. Have students identify the sound of each ending: /d/ as in *called*, /t/ as in *stopped*, or /ed/ as in *wasted*. The answers are shown.

Word	Ending Sound
filled	/d/
lacked	/t/
tasted	/ed/
relieved	/d/
loaded	/ed/
dumped	/t/
boasted	/ed/
followed	/d/
munched	/t/
seized	/d/

Great Source Reading Advantage

Appendix

Lessons for READING ADVANTAGE Paperbacks

The purpose of the paperbacks is to encourage independent reading. Minimal guidance is offered here and is optional. Additional sets of books can be ordered from Great Source.

Graphic Organizers (BLMs)

Make photocopies or transparencies of the graphic organizers to use in your classroom instruction.

Double O Junior

Synopsis In this graphic novel, freshman Oscar Obregon Jr. fulfills a dream by making the high-school baseball team. His joy, however, is dampened when he learns that Coach May doesn't play freshman. Instead, Oscar fills in when needed and waits for a chance to make Coach take notice. Oscar does get noticed—when he breaks Coach's number one rule, "Always do what I tell you." Oscar swings when he shouldn't, and, although his three-run triple leads the Falcons to a win, Coach May benches him. Oscar redeems himself in the semifinals. Called in to sub for an injured player, Oscar follows Coach's signals, including one to run home when Oscar feels he should remain on third. He runs, crashes into the catcher, tumbles over him, and scores. When Oscar confesses that he almost stopped at third, Coach May admits his call was a mistake. It was following that call, however, that showed Coach May that Oscar was a team player. *32 pages, Lexile measure 300L*

Strategy Making Connections

Procedure Provide students with four self-stick notes or a sheet of paper, folded in fourths, for them to use as they respond to their reading.

- Ask students to write their names, the date, and the book title on each of the four self-stick notes or at the top of the folded paper.

- Ask students to place a self-stick note at the end of page 9, page 17, page 25, and page 32. Students using folded paper should label each of the four sections with one of the following headings: "After page 9," "After page 17," "After page 25," and "After page 32."

- At the first stopping point (after page 9), have students ask themselves if anything they have read reminds them of a personal experience they or someone they know has had, or of something they have seen on television or in the movies. Ask students to write a sentence about this experience. Have students repeat this process at the second through fourth stopping points.

- After students have finished reading the book, have them share with their fellow students the ways in which they connected with the text.

Activity (Optional) Invite students to extend the story, telling what happens when the Falcons play in the finals. Students may tell an ending orally, presenting it as a play-by-play commentary, or they may want to illustrate the ending as in the graphic novel.

Amazing Animal Senses

Synopsis Humans have five senses—sight, hearing, smell, taste, and touch—through which they experience, explore, and survive in their world. Animals have senses, too. This book takes a look at some of the unusual and amazing ways in which animals use their senses to experience, explore, and survive in their worlds. Learn how fish have goggle eyes and how chameleons have eyes that move independently. Read how spiders "hear" through hairs and how snakes "hear" through their skin. Find out how insects smell with antennae and how dogs can sniff out cancer. Learn that a catfish has taste buds all over its body and that a butterfly has taste receptors on its feet. These and many more amazing facts are presented in the book. *32 pages, Lexile measure 390L*

Strategy Inferential Thinking

Procedure Provide students with three self-stick notes or a sheet of paper, folded in thirds, for them to use as they respond to their reading.

- Ask students to write their names, the date, and the book title on each of the three self-stick notes or at the top of the folded paper. Have students write the words fact, fact, and conclusion on each self-stick note or on each section of the paper, leaving space below each word to write.

- Have students place a self-stick note at the end of Chapter 1, Chapter 3, and Chapter 5. Students using folded paper should label each of the three sections with one of the following headings: "After Chapter 1," "After Chapter 3," and "After Chapter 5."

- At the first stopping point (after Chapter 1), ask students to draw one conclusion and two facts that support it from their reading. Have them write the facts and the conclusion on the self-stick note or on the appropriate section of the folded paper. Ask students to repeat this process at the second and third stopping points.

- After students have finished reading the book, encourage them to compare conclusions and supporting facts with their classmates.

Activity (Optional) Invite students to give a book talk about this book. Encourage students to tell whether they recommend the book, and why.

SS Republic: The Search for Yankee Gold

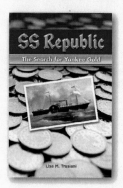

Synopsis In October of 1865, the *SS Republic*, a steamship traveling from New York to New Orleans, lost its battle against a hurricane. For over a hundred years, the *Republic* and its cargo of gold and silver coins lay on the ocean floor. Then in 1990, Greg Stemm and John Morris of Odyssey Marine Exploration assembled a team to find the *Republic*. The team read old newspapers, survivor stories, and reports about the hurricane. They searched 1,500 squares of miles of ocean floor. Finally, in 2003, they found the *Republic*. As scientists and treasure hunters, however, they wanted information as well as objects. They photographed and mapped the site before excavating. Patience, hard work, and an ROV named *Zeus* enabled the team to retrieve the gold coins and many other artifacts from the ship. Their efforts made it possible for scientists and collectors to share in the Republic's past. *32 pages, Lexile measure 400L*

Strategy Understanding Text Structure

Procedure Provide students with three self-stick notes or a sheet of paper, folded in thirds, for them to use as they respond to their reading.

- Ask students to write their names, the date, and the book title on each of the three self-stick notes or at the top of the folded paper. Have students write the words *cause* and *effect* on each self-stick note or on each section of the paper, leaving space below each word to write.

- Have students place a self-stick note at the end of Chapter 2, Chapter 4, and Chapter 6. Students using folded paper should label each of the three sections with one of the following headings: "After Chapter 2," "After Chapter 4," and "After Chapter 6."

- At the first stopping point (after Chapter 2), ask students to recall one cause-effect relationship from their reading. Have them write the cause and the effect on their self-stick note or on the appropriate section of the folded paper. Ask students to repeat this process at the second and third stopping points.

- After students have finished reading the book, encourage groups to compile a list of all the cause-effect relationships they noted and to discuss what these relationships tell us about searching for and excavating shipwrecks.

Activity (Optional) Invite students to take turns role-playing a member of the Odyssey team. Students should prepare monologues to express their feelings about the discovery and excavation of the *Republic*.

Night Watcher: The Life of Astronomer Maria Mitchell

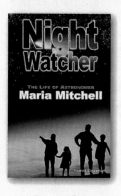

Synopsis This biography tells the story of Maria Mitchell, America's first woman astronomer. Mitchell was born on August 1, 1818, the third of ten children. Mitchell's interest in astronomy began at an early age. Every night, she would climb to the roof of the house with her father to observe the night sky. It was there that she learned to chart the positions of the stars and the planets. And it was there, on October 1, 1847, that she discovered a new comet. With Mitchell's discovery came instant fame. She was invited to join the American Academy of Arts and Sciences and received an offer to work as an astronomer on an almanac of the stars and planets. At a time when many women were discouraged from working or attaining an education, Mitchell led a rich and accomplished life. She was a teacher, a librarian, an astronomer, a college professor, and an advocate for women's rights. *32 pages, Lexile measure 390L*

Strategy Determining Importance

Procedure Provide students with three self-stick notes or a sheet of paper, folded in thirds, for them to use as they respond to their reading.

- Ask students to write their names, the date, and the book title on each of the three self-stick notes or at the top of the folded paper.

- Ask students to place a self-stick note at the end of Chapter 1, Chapter 3, and Chapter 5. Students using folded paper should label each of the three sections with one of the following headings: "After Chapter 1," "After Chapter 3," and "After Chapter 5."

- At the first stopping point (after Chapter 1), ask students to recall two or three details from their reading and write these on the self-stick note or on the appropriate section of the paper. Then ask students to write the main idea that these details support. Have students repeat this process at the second and third stopping points.

- After students have finished reading the book, have them select one section to summarize. Ask them to use the details and the main idea for that section to write a one-paragraph summary of the section.

Activity (Optional) Ask students to discuss what Mr. Mitchell's letter to Harvard professor William Bond may have said about Maria and her discovery of a comet. Invite them to role-play Mr. Mitchell and write a letter to Professor Bond.

Spies and Pies

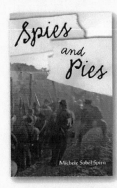

Synopsis In 1863, a civil war between the Union and the Confederacy was raging in the United States. Two Southern teenagers, Charles, fourteen, and Rebecca, thirteen, support the North, despite living with their Aunt Bessie who is a staunch Confederate. In addition to being Union supporters, the youngsters are spies. Rebecca sells pies and Charles sells newspapers in Confederate camps and pick up information as they do so. They write the information down and put it in a hollow tree for their father to pick up and pass on. One night, their father fails to pick up the information, and the teens decide that the information is too important not to pass on immediately. Each sets out via a different route to get to the Union camp. Charles gets detained by Confederate troops. Rebecca, however, finds the Union camp but has trouble getting in. When she does get through, she finds her father and passes on the information, which she had copied and hidden in a pie. Brother and sister are reunited the next morning, exhausted but happy to have contributed to their cause. *32 pages, Lexile measure 330L*

Strategy Monitor Understanding (visualize)

Procedure Provide students with three self-stick notes or a sheet of paper, folded in thirds, for them to use as they respond to their reading.

- Ask students to write their names, the date, and the book title on each of the three self-stick notes or at the top of the folded paper.

- Have students place a self-stick note at the end of Chapter 2, Chapter 4, and Chapter 6. Students using folded paper should label each of the three sections with one of the following headings: "After Chapter 2," "After Chapter 4," and "After Chapter 6."

- At the first stopping point (after Chapter 2), ask students to think back to a setting or an event in their reading that "grabbed" their attention and to picture it in their minds. Then have students list a few words or phrases or sketch a small drawing to remind them of what they visualized. Ask students to repeat this process at the end of the second and third stopping points.

- After students have finished reading the book, have them compile a list of the settings and the events they visualized. Then ask them to put the list in sequential order.

Activity (Optional) Have groups of students design memorials to all the brave youngsters who contributed to the war efforts. Interested students may want to make models of their memorials and write speeches for the dedication ceremonies.

Space Castaways

Synopsis In the year 2156, Hank Anderson misses the shuttle to space camp where he is supposed to work as a junior counselor. He hitches a ride with a really cool space surfer, Ray Medina, who is also the camp cook. Ray's spaceship, however, breaks down, forcing the travelers to crash land on an unknown planet. Ray tries to fix the spacecraft but can't because the lanium magnet is shot. After consuming a couple of old food capsules, the boys explore the uninhabited planet and settle in for the night. Hank awakes to find Ray missing and a silver alien in the pilot's seat of the spaceship. Hank befriends the alien, who has been stranded on the planet for five hundred years and wants to return to his home. When Ray returns, he offers the alien a ride to the space camp in exchange for one of his buttons. It turns out that the alien's buttons are lanium, which Ray uses to fix the ship. Hank, Ray, and the alien blast into hyperspace, looking forward to getting to space camp. *32 pages, Lexile measure 330L*

Strategy Making Connections

Procedure Provide students with three self-stick notes or a sheet of paper, folded in thirds, for them to use as they respond to their reading.

- Ask students to write their names, the date, and the book title on each of the three self-stick notes or at the top of the folded paper.

- Have students place a self-stick note at the end of Chapter 2, Chapter 4, and Chapter 6. Students using folded paper should label each of the three sections with one of the following headings: "After Chapter 2," "After Chapter 4," and "After Chapter 6."

- At the first stopping point (after Chapter 2), ask students to predict one thing they think will happen in the story. Have them write their predictions on their self-stick notes or on the appropriate section of the folded paper. Ask students to repeat this process at the second and third stopping points.

- Have students keep their predictions in mind as they continue reading. If their predictions prove true, have them put a check mark next to the prediction. If their predictions do not prove true, ask them to change their predictions to something that did occur in the story.

Activity (Optional) Invite groups of students to create their own planets with different alien inhabitants. Students can make up their own adventures for the settings and the characters they create.

A Light in the Darkness

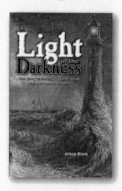

Synopsis A light in the darkness has long been a sign of a safe haven. For thousands of years, this has been especially true for sailors at sea who depend on lights to find home or a safe harbor. This book follows that light from bonfires to lighthouses. It provides a brief history of early lighthouses from Egypt, the Roman Empire, and China, before outlining the history of lighthouses in North America. Anecdotes about lighthouses and their keepers help to illustrate the hardship, loneliness, and risk endured by keepers and their families, while the story of Ida Lewis, one of America's most famous keepers, exemplifies their dedication to the job. The book culminates with a few ghost stories and the current state or landmark status of lighthouses today. *48 pages, Lexile measure 390L*

Strategy Making Connections

Procedure Provide students with three self-stick notes or a sheet of paper, folded in thirds, for them to use as they respond to their reading.

- Ask students to write their names, the date, and the book title on each of the three self-stick notes or at the top of the folded paper.

- Ask students to place a self-stick note at the end of Chapter 2, Chapter 4, and Chapter 7. Students using folded paper should label each of the three sections with one of the following headings: "After Chapter 2," "After Chapter 4," and "After Chapter 7."

- At the first stopping point (after Chapter 2), have students ask themselves if anything they have read reminds them of a personal experience they or someone they know has had, or of something they have seen on television or in the movies. Ask students to write a sentence about this experience. Have students repeat this process at the second and third stopping points.

- After students have finished reading the book, have them share with their fellow students the ways in which they connected with the text.

Activity (Optional) Have students picture their town as a busy harbor. Invite them to work with partners to design a daymark (pages 46–47) for a lighthouse that would best represent their town. Encourage them to write a brief explanation for the patterns and colors they chose.

The Great Dogsled Race

Synopsis In 1925, a diphtheria epidemic hit Nome, Alaska, which was already cut off from the rest of the world by winter snow. The town doctor had only an old supply of serum, which was too weak to prevent the disease from killing people. The only serum available was a thousand miles away in Anchorage, and the only way to get it to Nome was the old-fashioned way—by dogsled. An intricate system of relay teams was devised to get the serum to Nome in a week. The race began in Nenana with "Wild" Bill Shannon and ended with Gunnar Kaasen, who with his lead dog Balto, took the serum the last fifty-three miles of its trek. This book details the exploits of the mushers and their dogsled teams who braved frigid temperatures, high winds, and blizzard conditions to get the serum to Nome in time to save many lives. The brave participants were honored, and today's Iditarod is still run to commemorate that 1925 serum run. *48 pages, Lexile measure 380L*

Strategy Monitor Understanding (ask questions)

Procedure Provide students with three self-stick notes or a sheet of paper, folded in thirds, for them to use as they respond to their reading. (Provide additional self-stick notes for the question strategy.)

- Ask students to write their names, the date, and the book title on each of the three self-stick notes or at the top of the folded paper.

- Have students place a self-stick note at the end of Chapter 1, Chapter 4, and Chapter 6. Students using folded paper should label each of the sections with one of the following headings: "After Chapter 1," "After Chapter 4," and "After Chapter 6."

- At the first stopping point (after Chapter 1), ask students to write two or three questions they would like answered about the race. If students later discover the answers to these questions as they read, have them write each answer on another self-stick note and place it on the page where they found the answer. Have students repeat this process at the second and third stopping points.

- Students may research the answers to questions that remain unanswered after they have finished reading the book. Have students use library materials or the Internet to locate the answers. Ask them to discuss their findings with classmates.

Activity (Optional) Invite students to create headlines and write news stories about the successful race to get diphtheria serum to Nome. Encourage students to lay out their stories using word-processing programs and to incorporate visuals.

What's in a Name?

Synopsis This book explains the origins of names, beginning with the use of last names, which didn't start in Europe until about two hundred years ago. It explores the way in which last names such as *Forest*, *Hill*, and *Rivers* derive from locations, and names that end in son, such as *Jackson*, mean "son of." Last names such as *Weaver*, *Smith*, and *Hunter* stem from occupations. Words such as *boycott*, *samaritan*, and *lynch* derive from the people who first performed the related actions. Inventions such as the Ferris wheel, the sandwich, and graham crackers are named for the people who created them. Some of our calendar months are named after Roman gods, or from their position on the calendar. Roman gods are also the inspiration for the names of the planets in our solar system. The book also explains state names and the origins of some odd names. *48 pages, Lexile measure 390L*

Strategy Inferential Thinking

Procedure Provide students with three self-stick notes or a sheet of paper, folded in thirds, for them to use as they respond to their reading.

- Ask students to write their names, the date, and the book title on each of the self-stick notes or at the top of the folded paper. Have students write the words fact, fact, and conclusion on each self-stick note or on each section of the paper, leaving space to write below each word.

- Have students place a self-stick note at the end of Chapter 2, Chapter 4, and Chapter 7. Students using folded paper should label each of the three sections with one of the following headings: "After Chapter 2," "After Chapter 4," and "After Chapter 7."

- At the first stopping point (after Chapter 2), ask students to draw one conclusion and two facts that support it from their reading. Have them write the facts and the conclusion on the self-stick note or on the appropriate section of the folded paper. Ask students to repeat this process at the end of the second and third stopping points.

- After students have finished reading the book, encourage them to compare conclusions and supporting facts with their classmates.

Activity (Optional) Encourage students to engage in onomastics, or the study of the origins of proper names, to research their own names as well as any other proper names they find interesting.

Into the Wild

Synopsis Sixteen-year-old Jorge is known as "the elephant man" to the workers at the Cleveland Zoo in Ohio because of his fascination with the huge creatures. Jan, a zookeeper there, introduces Jorge to Trent and June, friends of hers who work at Chobe National Park in Botswana, Africa. Impressed with Jorge's love of elephants, Trent invites Jorge to visit him and June in Africa. Jorge can't imagine anything better, but the airfare is far too expensive for him. With help from Jan and his friends, Jorge establishes a flea market, selling everything he can find to raise money. When it's still not enough, a zoo supporter donates frequent-flyer miles for the airfare. In Africa, the number and variety of wild animals fascinates Jorge. He also learns that nature can be cruel when Trent refuses to help an impala injured in the wild, but does help one that was hit by an SUV. At the end of his trip, Jorge returns home much wiser and more knowledgeable. *48 pages, Lexile measure 320L*

Strategy Making Connections

Procedure Ask students to write their names, the date, and the book title on each of the four self-stick notes or at the top of the folded paper.

- Ask students to place a self-stick note at the end of Chapter 2, Chapter 4, Chapter 6, and Chapter 8. Students using folded paper should label each of the four sections with one of the following headings: "After Chapter 2," "After Chapter 4," "After Chapter 6," and "After Chapter 8."

- At the first stopping point (after Chapter 2), have students ask themselves if anything they have read reminds them of a personal experience they or someone they know has had, or something they have seen on television or in the movies. Ask students to write a sentence about this experience. Have students repeat this process at the second through fourth stopping points.

- After students have finished reading the book, have them share with their fellow students the ways they connected with the text.

Activity (Optional) Ask groups of students to choose different scenes from the story. Invite each group to act out the scene, using their own words.

PAPERBACKS

Hoaxes

Synopsis This book explores the art of deception, defining a hoax as a "playful trick," which people fall for because they want to believe it. The first chapter explores art forgeries perpetrated by talented artists who could make more money imitating famous artists than by promoting their own work. A marathoner who didn't actually race and a nonexistent baseball player are exposed in the chapter on sports hoaxes. Fraudulent scientific and anthropological discoveries, including a faked space walk, clones, and a fossil giant, are discussed. Crop circles, Roswell aliens, and fairies are discussed in the chapter on alien hoaxes. Totally made-up creatures such as the jackalope and Bigfoot are presented. And, of course, what book about hoaxes would be complete without noting some "hoaxes" that turned out to be real, such as the duckbill platypus. *64 pages, Lexile measure 380L*

Strategy Determining Importance

Procedure Provide students with three self-stick notes or a sheet of paper, folded in thirds, for them to use as they respond to their reading.

- Ask students to write their names, the date, and the book title on each of the three self-stick notes or at the top of the folded paper.

- Ask students to place a self-stick note at the end of Chapter 2, Chapter 4, and Chapter 7. Students using folded paper should label each of the three sections with one of the following headings: "After Chapter 2," "After Chapter 4," and "After Chapter 7."

- At the first stopping point (after Chapter 2), ask students to recall two or three details from their reading and write these on the self-stick note or on the appropriate section of the paper. Then ask students to write the main idea that these details support. Have students repeat this process at the second and third stopping points.

- After students have finished reading the book, have them select one section to summarize. Ask them to use the details and the main idea for that section to write a one-paragraph summary of the section.

Activity (Optional) Assign students to groups according to their interests: art, sports, science, anthropology, etc. Have groups research and report on other hoaxes perpetrated in their fields.

The Healing Horse

Synopsis Geraldo Blanco is sentenced to three weeks at a special ranch in lieu of going to jail for stealing video games. Aptly named "Second Chance," the ranch is run by an ex-rodeo star named Shirley. A former boxer named Ben runs the kitchen. At the ranch, each boy is assigned a horse to care for and learn to ride during his three-week stay. The task seems easy, but Geraldo gets kicked hard the first time he approaches his horse, which is named Heartbreak. To make matters worse, Geraldo's bunkmate Pete is antagonistic, and Geraldo can't find anything in common with the others. With much encouragement from Shirley and Ben, Geraldo finally rides Heartbreak. And after a physical altercation, Geraldo and two of the boys disclose secrets about themselves and become friends. On the final day, the boys demonstrate what they learned, and Geraldo is invited to return as a counselor. *64 pages, Lexile measure 370L*

Strategy Making Connections

Procedure Provide students with three self-stick notes or a sheet of paper, folded in thirds, for them to use as they respond to their reading.

- Ask students to write their names, the date, and the book title on each of the three self-stick notes or at the top of the folded paper.

- Have students place a self-stick note at the end of Chapter 1, Chapter 4, and Chapter 8. Students using folded paper should label each of the three sections with one of the following headings: "After Chapter 1," "After Chapter 4," and "After Chapter 8."

- At the first stopping point (after Chapter 1), ask students to predict one thing they think will happen in the story. Have them write their predictions on their self-stick notes or on the appropriate section of the folded paper. Ask students to repeat this process at the second and third stopping points.

- Have students keep their predictions in mind as they continue reading. If their predictions prove true, have them put a check mark next to the prediction. If their predictions do not prove true, ask them to change their predictions to something that did occur in the story.

Activity (Optional) Invite students to dramatize a broadcast about Second Chance Ranch. One student can be the reporter; others can be the owner, the staff, and the kids who are being interviewed about the ranch.

Making Associations

Answer the questions for each word you write.

Word _____

What do you think about when you read this word? _____

_____

Who might use this word?_____

_____

What do you already know about this word? _____

_____

_____

Word _____

What do you think about when you read this word? _____

_____

Who might use this word? _____

_____

What do you already know about this word? _____

_____

_____

Word _____

What do you think about when you read this word? _____

_____

Who might use this word? _____

_____

What do you already know about this word? _____

_____

_____

Word Map

My Definition

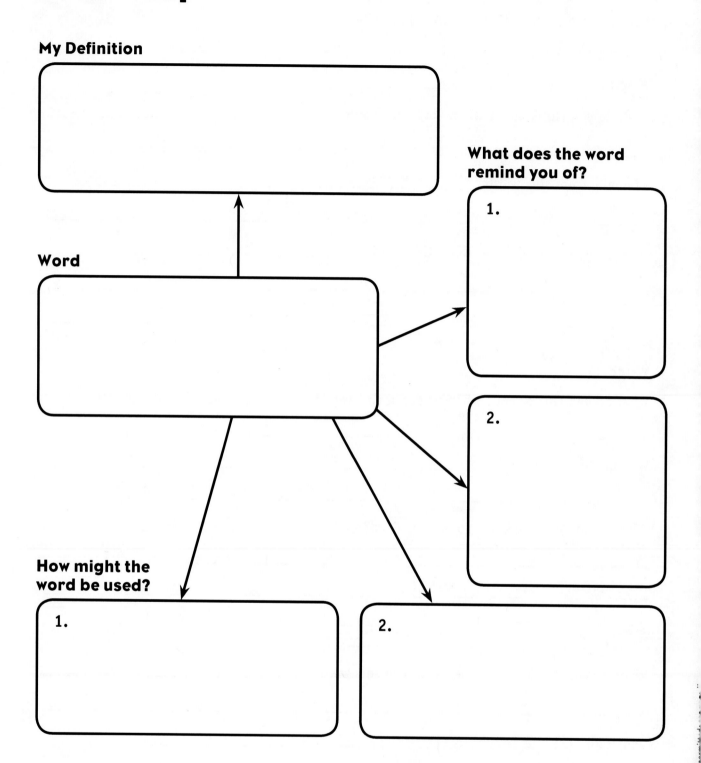

**What does the word
remind you of?**

1.

2.

Word

**How might the
word be used?**

1.

2.

Synonym and Antonym Chart

Think of two or three other words that are synonyms (similar in meaning) for each word. Then think of two or three words that are antonyms (opposite in meaning) for each word. Use a thesaurus to help you in your work.

Word	Synonyms	Antonyms
	1. 2. 3.	1. 2. 3.
	1. 2. 3.	1. 2. 3.
	1. 2. 3.	1. 2. 3.
	1. 2. 3.	1. 2. 3.

Word Web

Write a word in the center oval. Add details around the oval that help to define the word. Then write the complete definition in the box at the bottom of the page.

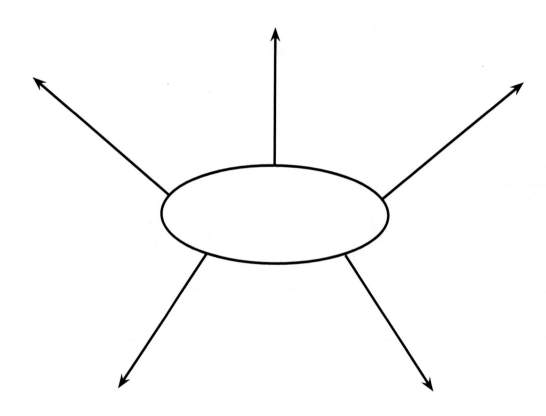

Write the complete definition here:

Concept Ladder

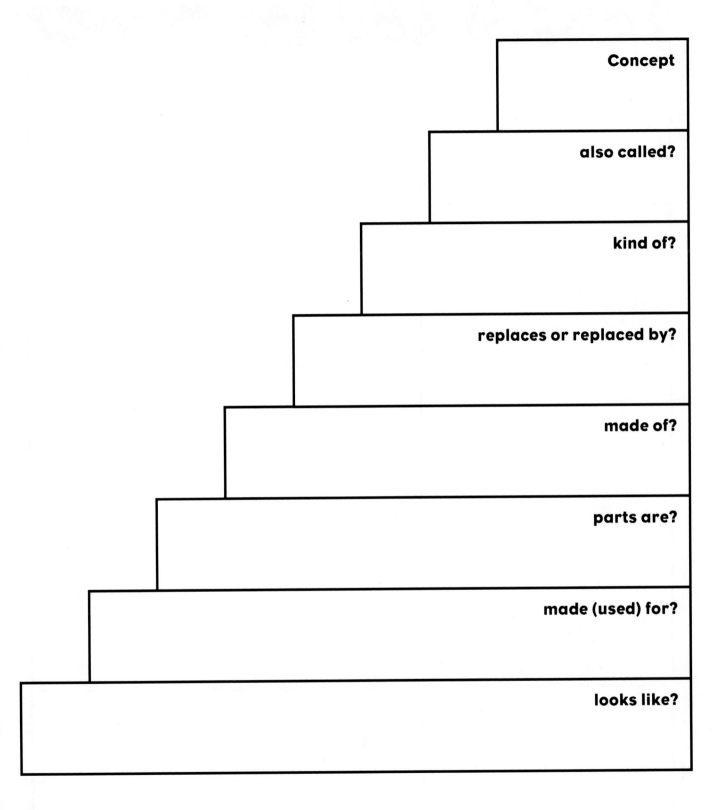

Concept

also called?

kind of?

replaces or replaced by?

made of?

parts are?

made (used) for?

looks like?

Double-entry Journal

Quotation	My Thoughts

Words with Multiple Meanings

Word	First Definition	Second Definition

Somebody Wanted But So

Use this chart to help you organize your thoughts for a summary.

	My Notes
Somebody (an important character)	
Wanted (a key problem with details)	
But (conflict for the character)	
So (an outcome)	

Now write your summary.

_____

_____

_____

_____

_____

_____

_____

_____

_____

_____

5Ws Chart

The 5Ws—*who, what, where, when,* and *why*—give readers the basic information about what happens in a news story or informational article.

5Ws	Details from the Selection
Who is the article about?	
What happens in the article?	
Where does the major event of the article take place?	
When does the major event of the article take place?	
Why is this event important?	

Main Idea Organizer for _____

First, write the details. They will help you figure out the main idea and conclusion.

Main idea:

Detail:	**Detail:**	**Detail:**

Conclusion:

Story String

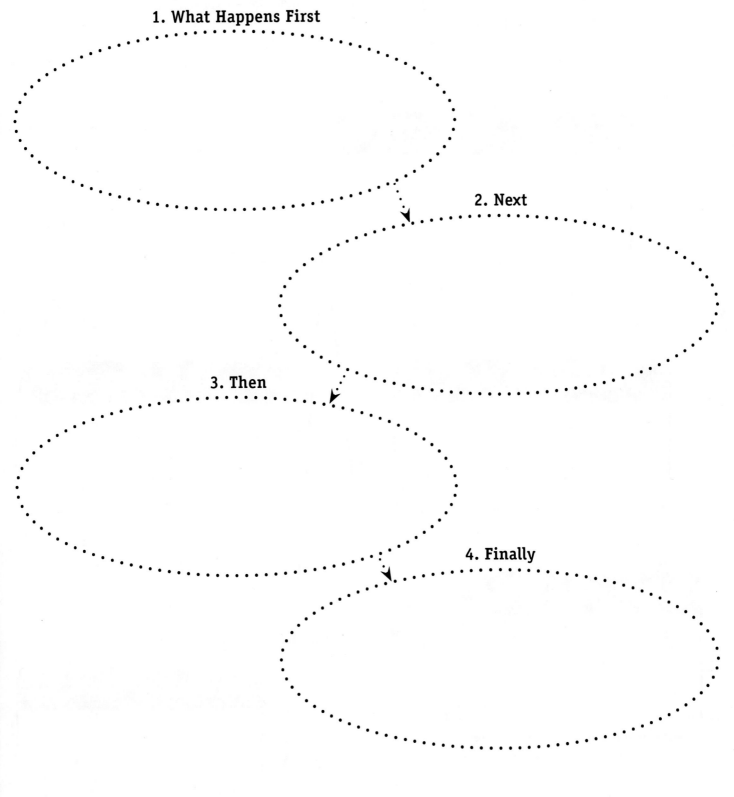

1. What Happens First

2. Next

3. Then

4. Finally

Plot Organizer

A plot organizer helps you to see the main plot stages of a folktale, story, novel, or play. It highlights the five main parts of a fictional plot—exposition, rising action, climax, falling action, and resolution.

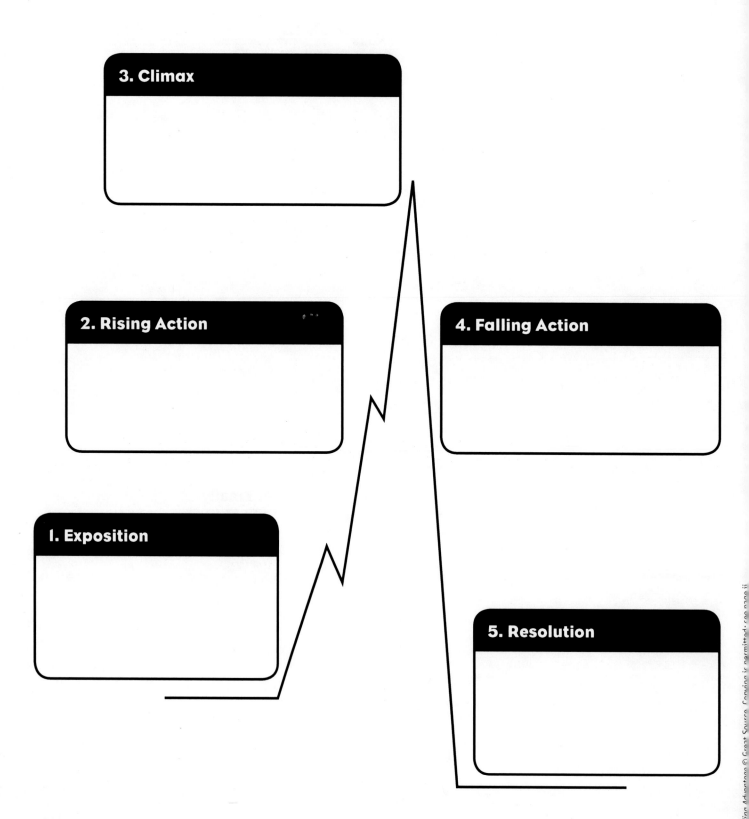

3. Climax

2. Rising Action

4. Falling Action

I. Exposition

5. Resolution

Character Map

A character map helps you understand and analyze a character in a story, play, or novel. This tool helps you see how you—and other characters—feel about the character.

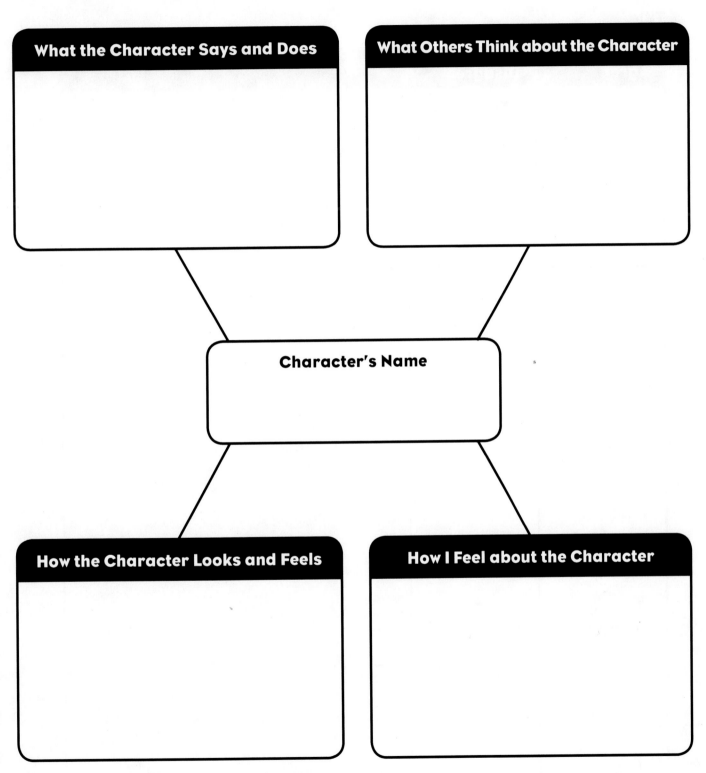

What the Character Says and Does

What Others Think about the Character

Character's Name

How the Character Looks and Feels

How I Feel about the Character

Anticipation Guide

Do you agree or disagree with each statement? Check the appropriate box. Revisit your answers after you read the selection. Do you still feel the same way?

Title _____

Agree	Disagree	
		1.
		2.
		3.
		4.